RONALD MANZER

Public Schools and Political Ideas: Canadian Educational Policy in Historical Perspective

UNIVERSITY OF TORONTO PRESS
Toronto Buffalo London

Toronto Buffalo London
Printed in Canada

ISBN 0-8020-0604-3 (cloth)
ISBN 0-8020-7209-7 (paper)

Printed on acid-free paper

Canadian Cataloguing in Publication Data

Manzer, Ronald A., 1937–
Public schools and political ideas : Canadian educational policy in historical perspective

Includes bibliographical references and index.
ISBN 0-8020-0604-3 (bound) ISBN 0-8020-7209-7 (pbk.)

1. Education – Canada – History. 2. Education and state – Canada. I. Title.

LA411.M35 1994 370′.971 C94-930759-9

University of Toronto Press acknowledges the financial assistance to its publishing program of the Canada Council and the Ontario Arts Council.

This book has been published with the help of a grant from the Social Science Federation of Canada, using funds provided by the Social Sciences and Humanities Research Council of Canada.

PUBLIC SCHOOLS AND POLITICAL IDEAS: CANADIAN EDUCATIONAL POLICY IN HISTORICAL PERSPECTIVE

Education in Canada has become the scene of ongoing conflict, with various factions vying for representation of their political, economic, and cultural interests. Schools have become objects of domination and products of compromise. In this book, Ronald Manzer interprets the political ideas and beliefs that underlie educational policies and give them meaning. His analysis begins with the foundation of state education in the mid-nineteenth century and brings us up to date with the prospective reforms of the early 1990s.

Manzer argues that, from its foundation, elementary and secondary education in Canada has been dominated by liberal conceptions and principles, with each successive liberal ideology taking its place as a public philosophy for state education. He brings a wealth of information to his analysis, examining curricula, district organization, laws, finance, and personnel for each Canadian province. The result is a splendidly detailed national picture and a clear, historical view of each province's values, ideas, and practices.

This interface of public policy with political philosophy is original in its depth and scope. No other book offers such a comprehensive view of the past and potential of Canadian education policy.

RONALD MANZER is Professor, Department of Political Science, Scarborough College, University of Toronto.

Contents

Tables

Acknowledgments

Public Schools and Political Ideas: Canadian Educational Policy in Historical Perspective is not a book I had planned to write. In April 1991 I gave a paper, entitled 'Public Philosophy and Public Policy: The Case of Religion in Canadian State Education,' at the annual meeting of the British Association of Canadian Studies. That was followed in June 1991 by a second paper, entitled 'State Education in Canada: Public Policy and Public Philosophy,' at the third Conference on Comparative Canadian and Japanese Law and Politics at Niigata University. The writing of these two papers, and the response to them, convinced me that in my current research and writing on Anglo-American educational policy there was not only a comparative study, but also a separate book on Canadian educational policy.

Because my paper for the Niigata conference served as the prototype for this book, I am especially grateful to Yasuhiro Kojima, dean of the Faculty of Law at Niigata University; Masahiro Kuwahara, director of the Comparative Canadian and Japanese Law and Politics Program; and Toshimitsu Shinkawa, who initiated the visit to Niigata by the Toronto group. Along with their colleagues and students in the Faculty of Law, their generous hospitality during our week in Niigata, and their kind reception of my work on Canadian educational policy, not only precipitated the writing of this book but also opened my eyes to future possibilities for comparative studies of educational policy in technological society. I also thank Annis May Timpson of the Department of American and Canadian Studies, University of Nottingham, who as conference director provided me with the opportunity to present my paper at the BACS conference.

James Driscoll, of the Department of Political Studies, Trent University, was the discussant for my paper 'In Pursuit of Educational Excellence: Technological Liberalism and Canadian State Education in the 1990s' at the 1993 annual meeting of the Canadian Political Science Association, and his comments on my approach to interpretive analysis were especially helpful as I revised the introductory chapter. The final version of the manuscript, particularly rewriting the introduction and reorganizing chapters, was also improved as a result of critical comments by three anonymous reviewers for the University of Toronto Press and the Social Science Federation of Canada.

Virgil Duff, executive editor at the University of Toronto Press, encouraged me when I first approached him with the proposal for this book and subsequently steered the manuscript through the editorial process with exceptional skill and good humour. Kate Troemel's interventions as copy-editor were unerringly directed and consistently graceful.

Professor E.C. Relph, chair of the Division of Social Sciences at Scarborough College, University of Toronto, has been a continuing source of support and encouragement for my work. Much of the manuscript was written during my research leave in 1992–3. I am grateful to the Humanities and Social Sciences Committee of the University of Toronto Research Advisory Board for the grant that enabled me to attend the BACS conference in 1991.

My greatest debt is owed to members of my family. My daughters, Patricia and Jennifer, now themselves writers, have respected my work while also reminding me not to neglect other important activities such as running and home-brewing. Larthia kept me company through long hours at the computer and insisted that I take a head-clearing walk or run three times a day. Kathryn first told me I had the material and should write a book on Canada, as well as the one on comparative educational policy, then continuously supported and patiently advised me while I was doing it. Kathryn also has influenced this book, and my interpretation of Canadian educational policy and politics, through her involvement as a volunteer activist in public education, especially her crucial part in the development and operation of the immersion summer program Le Camp at Glendon College and her active role in Canadian Parents for French, which included two terms as national president. I admire the skill and intelligence with which she has engaged the process of educational policy-making in Canada and have learned much from watching her at work. Above all I am inspired by her example as a citizen dedicated to the cause of public education in Canada.

PUBLIC SCHOOLS AND POLITICAL IDEAS: CANADIAN EDUCATIONAL POLICY IN HISTORICAL PERSPECTIVE

Introduction: Political Ideas, Educational Policy, and Policy Analysis

Public schools are human communities and public instruments; they are also political symbols. Public schools are places where children and teachers live and learn together. They are means by which people in a political democracy collectively strive for civic virtue, economic wealth, social integration, and cultural survival. In how they are organized and what they teach public schools also express conceptions of human needs, make statements of moral principles, and convey visions of individual and collective development.

Sometimes public schools are built and maintained entirely on the basis of community consensus. More often, however, schools are stakes in struggles for political power. Educational politics and policy-making are rent by conflicting political, economic, and cultural interests that seek to organize schools to fit particular conceptions of a good community and a good life and to teach knowledge and skills serving particular interests, or at least particular conceptions of the public interest.

As stakes in power struggles public schools are not only objects of domination and products of compromise, they are also potentially agencies for creating political consensus. Their organization and curricula may be imposed by a dominant social group or result from accommodation among conflicting interests. They may also result from rethinking and redefining conflicting particular interests into a common public interest or reconstructing competing ideological doctrines into a shared public philosophy.

My purpose in this study of educational policies and public philosophy in Canada is, first, to describe the substantive issues of educational politics, forms of educational governance, and content of educational policies as they have developed over time. Then I shall try to interpret the political ideas that underlie educational institutions and policies and give them meaning, both for those who fought the battles, made the policies, and lived with the consequences (not necessarily the same people) and for those of us who look backwards trying to understand the implications of these legacies from our past and forwards wondering what to do now.

PUBLIC POLICIES, POLITICAL IDEAS, AND INTERPRETIVE ANALYSIS

Public policies are courses of action that deal with public problems. They may be rational choices based on comprehensive, prospective analysis by public-regarding expert planners. They may be outcomes of successive political bargains struck by various self-regarding individuals and groups. They may be constructed by retrospective interpretation of the principles that link a chain of disjointed decisions in specific cases. They may be power strategies selected to defeat political opponents and establish or preserve elite domination of a political community.[1] Whatever the pattern of policy-making, the existence of public policies implies some degree of collective consciousness and choice, either prospectively in selecting among perceived optional courses of collective action or retrospectively in rationalizing outcomes of disjointed incrementalism as officially ordained collective action.[2]

From this concept of public policy as either prospective choice and collective action or collective action and retrospective ordination derives my central concern with political ideas and educational policies. I assume that human beings in society act for reasons. In giving reasons for their actions people draw, whether consciously and directly or implicitly and indirectly, on some conceptualization of the world within which they and their actions are situated. Hence, public policies are made within frameworks of political ideas that structure individual and collective thinking about what constitutes a public problem, what means are properly and practically available to deal with it, what collective action offers an apparently optimal resolution of the problem, and what evaluations are made subsequently about the results of policies.

In studying public policies and political ideas there are two distinct approaches that can be taken. Political ideas can be studied as causal determinants of public policies, or they can be studied as constitutive meanings of public policies. My argument will use both approaches, but my priority is the second.

Political Ideas as Causal Determinants of Public Policies

One approach to studying political ideas and public policies examines the importance of political ideas as causal determinants of public policies. Policies here are seen as results or outcomes of political actions. They can be explained by a range of causal factors, which include the distribution of power among participants in policy-making, organization of political interests, structure of institutional constraints, and influences of socio-economic environment. To explain public policy the effect of political ideas must be weighed against the effect of these other causal factors in the policy-making process.

Public policy-making is an exercise in political power. Political ideas are important as determinants of public policies because policy-makers can use ideas strategically to mobilize, persuade, or manipulate others to support their interests. Political rivals wield ideas as symbols that arouse emotional support, generate communal solidarity, and justify coercive action against political enemies. Policy-makers use ideas to create self-serving perceptions of public problems, generate self-serving beliefs about causes of problems and options for collective action, and produce self-serving assessments of the consequences of public policies. From this perspective political ideas are instruments of political power. The task of policy analysis involves describing and weighing the use of ideas as an instrument of power in comparison with other power resources.

Public policy-making is also an exercise in political thinking. Political ideas are important as determinants of public policies because participants in politics and policy-making depend on ideas in order to know what are public problems, understand potential courses of action, decide which policy is best for them in the circumstances, and later evaluate the overall results. Describing and analysing the political ideas of participants in policy-making will reveal the state of their knowledge about public problems and policy options and hence facilitate explanation of why they acted as they did.

Political ideas are thus used to advance political interests and inform intelligent action. At the same time they possess a logic of their own. Commitment to certain political ideas requires interest groups to explain and defend those ideas, but interest groups also have to adapt and adjust their actions to fit their principles.[3] Explaining the history of public policies requires understanding the effects that derive from the logic of political ideas.

Political ideas interact with political interests; both are influenced by political experience. Political opponents may focus on the logic of political principles, forcing their advocates to recognize previously disguised premises and undeveloped implications. Political opponents may also mobilize powerful societal interests in order to force compromises on principles that in due course become institutionalized and legitimated as public philosophy. Political experience also reveals the results of public policies, at least what people perceive to be the results of policies; rarely in public policy-making do policy outcomes correspond exactly to original policy objectives, let alone currently perceived needs or preferences. Unexpected outcomes in turn lead to reassessments of policy choices and potentially to reformation of political principles.

Political Ideas as Constitutive Meanings of Public Policies

An alternative approach to studying political ideas and public policies examines political ideas as constitutive meanings of public policies. Political ideas constitute meanings of politics and policies because they form the language through which people understand their place in the political world, and thence articulate their interests, conceive modes of association with others in their political community, and devise courses of collective action. Political thinking is the condition for political action; political language is the precondition for political thinking; political ideas are the elements of political language. If the existence of public policies implies collective awareness or consciousness of choice, either prospectively or retrospectively, collective consciousness of the meanings of political institutions and public policies depends on being able to describe them by means of the ideas that comprise the community's political language.

From the standpoint of trying to explain the different results of public policies by their causes, this view of political ideas as inseparable from political thought and action is perhaps not very interesting. After all, if a language of political ideas is the precondition for all public policy-making, then it lacks the explanatory power to differentiate one result from another. If our concern is the meaning of political institutions and public policies, however, then ideas assume crucial importance. From this perspective analysing the political ideas inherent in political institutions and public policies is a way to learn the language of politics and policy-making. Words are used in public life – such as justice, legitimacy, equality, liberty, feasibility, and efficiency – but their substantive meanings are not always transparent. These meanings can be learned from careful study of what people living together in a political community say and do in their public life. What people say and do in public life is incorporated in their political institutions and public policies, and the substantive meanings of the political ideas that form a community's political language can be found embedded in them.

Thus, to follow the Hegelian argument as interpreted by Charles Taylor, the ideas that are incorporated in political institutions and public policies, and that make them what they are, may not be articulated in formal philosophical and theoretical language by participants in politics and public policy-making, but political institutions and policies are expressions of ideas that potentially can be translated into formal philosophical and theoretical language.[4] Such a translation requires, first, the construction of a set of relevant definitions of what political ideas might mean. This involves constructing typologies of the various political theories, beliefs, doctrines, or principles that might provide the substantive meanings of political ideas to be found in institutions and policies. Next, careful study of specific institutional arrangements and policy designs is needed in order to determine which of the relevant sets of meanings of political ideas fit best. In political communities, such as Canada, that have a highly developed language of politics, consideration must be given to what participants say about their intentions. Equally, however, evidence of what they do must be weighed, along with the implications of unexpected outcomes. Then, as political institutions and public policies are studied over time, observations can be made about the changing meanings of political ideas, and, hence, judgments formed about changing political morality or public philosophy.

In a study of political ideas and educational policies in Canada, why should one give priority to studying political ideas as constitutive meanings of institutions and policies? There are two reasons. One is that the goodness of public schools as human communities and public instruments is judged by how well they meet community standards of justice, legitimacy, effectiveness, and efficiency. To assess the authenticity of public schools as expressions of Canadian political community, the constitutive meanings of educational institutions and policies must be analysed in terms of these standards. The other reason is that public schools form an essential part of the Canadian political community. Exploring the changing meanings of the political ideas that are inherent in educational governance and policies is a way of gaining better understanding of public life in Canada. In their changing conceptions of schools as human communities and as public instruments, Canadians can see their common commitments to satisfying basic human needs through public education. They can also see, often starkly and cruelly, their political differences. Such understanding in turn is the starting point for political criticism, which is the condition for moral progress.

HUMAN NEEDS, PUBLIC PROBLEMS, AND POLITICAL THINKING

Public problems derive from human needs. Human needs comprise physiological needs for clean air to breathe and adequate food, drink, sleep, and shelter; safety needs for order, predictability, and dependability of the natural and human environment; needs for love, affection, and a sense of belonging; needs for esteem and respect from other people and for self-esteem and self-respect;

and needs for personal freedom, creativity, and self-development.[5] Both knowledge of human needs and ways of satisfying needs are contingent and historical. They depend on the prevailing language and theory of human needs, which vary among human groups and change over time.

Because humans are social beings who live together in communities, the consciousness, expression, and satisfaction of human needs is both collective and individual. Public educational problems may be formulated as needs of the community, for example, promoting national economic wealth and efficiency, improving community health and welfare, protecting public order and safety, reproducing social integration, strengthening communal identity, and facilitating cultural creativity and development. Public educational problems may also be expressed as needs of individuals, for example, learning economically productive knowledge and skills, knowing the rudiments of healthy living, taking precautions to protect personal and family safety, learning to create and maintain satisfying social relationships, acquiring knowledge and skills necessary for achieving respect and self-respect out of economic and social opportunity, and discovering and developing the unique capacities which constitute a personal foundation for self-determining freedom and creative living.

As a substantive result public education enables individuals and communities to possess and perpetuate the knowledge and skills required to meet basic human needs. As an intersubjective process public education also can be a means to satisfy needs. People find a social order in the structure of classrooms and schools. They form emotional attachments to classmates and teachers. Critical features of personal identities are constructed during school days, for better or worse, and become enduring elements of individual personalities. Some persons in school enjoy respect and self-respect, while others suffer searing discrimination and self-doubt. Schools can provide cumulative creative experiences by which students not only open ways to future personal development but also realize now the satisfaction of discovering and using their talents to the fullest extent possible. Schools can also restrict, stultify, and destroy individual creativity.

Educational policies are made within frameworks of political ideas that structure individual and collective thinking about educational problems, public instruments, policy choices, and political evaluations. At least three types of political thinking can be distinguished in this process of making educational policies: 'justifying' in terms of public philosophy, 'explaining' by reference to policy theory, and 'economizing' by means of program analysis.[6] For each type of political thinking there are distinctive categories of political evaluation, but in each case substantive meanings of evaluative concepts are derived from their being situated in some sort of ideological world-view. In judging public policies there are no criteria without ideological contexts.

Public Philosophy and the Criteria of Legitimacy and Justice

The elements of public philosophy are concepts of human need and political good. A public philosophy explicitly or implicitly expresses some conception of basic human needs and establishes the priority for their satisfaction by collective action. It also deals with such fundamental political questions as which needs can and should be satisfied by governmental action, what is the proper distribution of political goods among constituent segments of the community, and what is the best arrangement of governmental institutions.

For political thinking about public policy in terms of public philosophy, the criteria of evaluation are legitimacy and justice. Some concept of legitimacy and some concept of justice are logically required for undertaking any evaluation of public policy.[7] Legitimacy may be conceded as submission or acquiescence on the part of citizens to agents of the state. Legitimacy can also mean identification and commitment – recognition of collective action through the state as being expressive and constitutive of individual and collective identity. Justice is equity or fairness in the distribution of public benefits and burdens.

Both legitimacy and justice can be substantive or procedural, that is, applied either to the results of policies or to the process of making policies. Legitimacy refers to perceived consistency or harmony with established law or principle. In political evaluation of public policies, legitimacy is the test of purpose and process. Are these ends legitimate areas of state activity? Are these processes consistent with communal traditions and individual rights? Justice is the test of results and process. Is the distribution of benefits and burdens of state activity fair or equitable? Are the institutions and procedures that determine the distribution of public benefits and burdens constructed in such a way as to treat all persons fairly and equitably?

Legitimacy and justice are given meaning by reference to communal tradition, custom, basic individual and collective needs, individual and collective rights, wants, or merit. Which of these criteria should be applied and what they mean are questions that are politically contested. Conservative communitarians will give priority to communal tradition and custom. Radical communitarians will define legitimacy and justice in terms of basic individual and collective needs and collective rights. Political and economic liberals rely on individual wants, individual rights, merit, and majority preferences to define legitimacy and justice. Ethical liberals will stress the standard of basic individual needs rather than wants, and without letting go of individual rights as their ultimate standard they may also be receptive to moderate claims of collective rights. Thus, the substantive meanings of legitimacy and justice are expressions of political ideologies that are politically contested and compromised, imposed as hegemonic doctrines, or consensually agreed as public philosophy.

Policy Theory and the Criteria of Validity and Relevance

Policy theories organize knowledge of the technical and social conditions relevant to a given policy area, the direction of relationships among the main policy variables, and the effects governmental actions will have in achieving policy goals within constraints imposed by community values. Educational policy-making depends on theories of learning that organize social scientific knowledge (and assumptions) about the growth of human capacities and the contribution specific learning experiences make to educated behaviour. Theories of learning also provide the basis for making predictions about the effects of potential state interventions in education – for example, optional methods for teaching reading, alternative forms of classroom organization, sequencing of subject matter in the curriculum, or requirements for formal testing.

Policy theories interact with the prevailing public philosophy. Changes in public philosophy with respect to what are political goods obviously can influence basic assumptions and accepted goals in policy analysis, but innovations in policy theory also can lead to changes in public philosophy, especially with respect to what is the proper scope or role of governmental instruments in achieving shared values. Modern theories of child development emanating from the theoretical and clinical research of Jean Piaget, for example, produced a paradigm shift that had a revolutionary impact on thinking about school organization and curricula, particularly for early childhood and primary education, and inspired a corresponding shift in political ideas about educational justice as equal educational opportunity.[8]

The criteria for judging policy theories are the tests applied to all theorizing in the natural and social sciences: validity and relevance. Are the assumptions on which the theory has been constructed sound? Are propositions derived from the assumptions logically consistent and coherent? Have such propositions been subjected to empirical verification and survived? Are the environmental assumptions of the theory at least approximately reproduced in the empirical conditions which confront policy-makers? Are propositions derived from the theory relevant for explaining a given public problem and predicting the results of theoretically informed policy interventions?

In principle, the criteria of policy theorizing are subject to scientific judgments made within the boundaries of appropriate disciplines of the natural and social sciences. In the practice of policy evaluation, however, the criteria for policy theorizing are usually politically contested. Empirical evidence is unreliable, inconsistent, or missing. In the absence of scientific consensus policy-makers may have to choose between rival theories. Policy theories may also rest on assumptions or result in propositions that are contested as public philosophy. Moreover, in applying scientific theories to public problems social-scientific theories do not have the same status as natural-scientific theories. Social-scientific theories, including theories of human learning in making educational policies, can only work as policy theories when they are constructed on the same ontological premises, the same assumptions about human nature, as prevailing concepts of educational purpose and principles of legitimacy and justice. Social-scientific theorizing about human learning is interpretive theorizing from the premises of a philosophical anthropology, and, as such, it is necessarily embedded in a political theory of education. As Plato taught, a theory of education is a critical element in every political theory; the converse of Plato's dictum is also true: every theory of learning is a theory of politics.

Program Operations and the Criteria of Effectiveness and Efficiency

The overwhelming amount of political thought about public policies occurs at the level of program operations. Policy analysis of program operations, whether prospective or retrospective, focuses on the details of specific problems and particular policies. The historical or potential development of a particular policy is described in terms of its programmatic and organizational instruments. A decision to adopt or revise it is prescribed on the basis of the comparative benefits and costs of alternative designs in achieving stated political goals.

The details of design and implementation of particular programs, the benefits and costs that are projected from continuing current programs compared with incremental (or decremental) changes – these are questions that preoccupy public policy communities, those collectivities of politicians, public administrators, interest-group leaders, academic analysts, and attentive public who are concerned about particular sectors of public policy. Here policy thinking takes as given both community values and theoretical relationships and seeks to determine what impacts are produced by the implementation of existing designs and what changes, if any, in existing designs might produce better results. Although the ideological framework may be routinely taken for granted, analysis of program operations is nonetheless structured by principles that derive from a combination or mixture of prevailing political ideologies and received policy theories. As criteria of policy evaluation, concepts of effectiveness and efficiency are embedded in politically contested concepts of public purpose, norms of legitimacy and justice, and theories of policy intervention.

The questions for program analysis are effectiveness and efficiency: 'Will this program have the desired results?' or 'Will it work?' and 'Does this program achieve the same results as other programs but at less cost?' or 'Does it produce more benefits for the same resource requirements?' What effectiveness and efficiency mean, however, is determined by standards of educational purpose constrained by prevailing standards of legitimacy and justice. Liberals and communitarians differ both between and among themselves in their understanding of the human condition. Hence, they will pursue different educational objectives while subscribing to different principles of legitimacy and justice and adhering to different theories of human behaviour. The answers to questions about the effectiveness and efficiency of policy cannot escape the ideological context within which they are asked and analysed.

IDEOLOGICAL TRADITIONS IN CANADIAN PUBLIC POLICY

Educational policies depend on collective perceptions of basic human needs as public educational problems. People differ in their understanding of what contribution education makes to the satisfaction of human needs, which educational problems should be met through the provision of public education as opposed to collective voluntary or private individual provision, and where the proper balance is between collective and individual needs in setting educational aims and objectives. Hence, institutions of educational governance and designs of educational policies are subject to political contestation and require political determination.

Canadian concepts of educational purpose, models of educational governance, principles of educational policy design, and criteria of political evaluation are drawn from opposing ideological traditions of liberalism and communitarianism. Liberalism has been the hegemonic ideology in Canadian educational politics and policy, but liberalism historically has been divided among distinctive 'political,' 'economic,' and 'ethical' branches. Communitarianism is also divided between opposing versions. Because of the central issues of religion and language, educational politics and policies in Canada have been deeply and continuously influenced by doctrines of conservative communitarianism. The historical importance of social democratic and democratic socialist ideology in Canadian political development means that the ideas of radical communitarianism also merit consideration, even though in educational politics and policy-making they usually have been indistinguishable in practice from those advocated by ethical liberals.

Liberalism: Political, Economic, and Ethical

Liberalism starts with the basic principles that the wants or preferences of each individual are equally valid – that each individual ought to be free both to join cooperatively with others and to compete with others to satisfy his or her wants and preferences, and that all individuals in the political community should have an equal opportunity to compete for material prosperity and individual self-realization. The role of the state should be a limited one, an instrument for facilitating cooperation and ensuring fairness in competition. More specifically, this fundamental value attributed to individualism and liberty is assumed to justify reliance on private enterprise, private exchange in markets, and private property. Liberals will reluctantly endorse state regulation of private markets, however, where economic efficiency and individual liberty may be threatened by monopolies or maladjustments. Liberals also endorse a stratified, unequal society. Individualism means that each person is responsible for earning a living for himself or herself and any dependents. Some individuals succeed better than others; economic stratification is simply the inevitable result of unequal outcomes to competition. As long as competition is fair there is no reason not to accept unequal outcomes. Equal opportunity does not entail equal results.

For political liberalism the focus of politics and public policy is the constitution and preservation of political association, a framework of public institutions freely chosen by individuals within which they are enabled to pursue their private interests. The basic liberal principles of political association are held to protect the political equality of each individual: the existence of free elections to determine who will hold offices of public authority, the right of each citizen to run for public office, the right of each citizen to vote, freedom of thought and expression, freedom of assembly and association, and collective action based on the will of the majority. Political liberalism also defends basic legal rights of each individual to life, liberty, security of person, enjoyment of property, due process, and equal protection of the law. Political liberalism thus protects both individual freedom of participation and individual freedom of independence against interference by others. The liberal principles of freedom of participation protect each citizen's share in public decision-making; the liberal principles of freedom of independence protect each person's sphere of private decision-making.

From the perspective of economic liberalism the crucial focus of politics and public policy is the capitalist market economy comprising free, impersonal private markets in which work and rewards are allocated in response to individual choices. Individuals are rational, they pursue their own wants, and they should be left as free as possible from collective interference consistent with their not infringing unfairly on the freedom of other individuals. Hence, politics and public policies should protect, support, and facilitate exchanges in the market economy but not replace it, except where there are blatant cases of market failure – and even here only if it is obvious that governmental intervention will be effective and that gains will clearly outweigh losses. The basic elements of economic liberalism thus emphasize the rationality of each individual, the freedom of each person to pursue wants consistent with the rights of every other person to do the same, and the central proposition of the market economy as the most efficient and effective social institution for satisfying wants while maximizing individual freedom.

For ethical liberals the crucial focus of political life is the self-development of each individual. In Anglo-American political thought John Stuart Mill first stated this ideal of creating a political community based on a moral vision of the potential for self-determining freedom and authenticity. In Mill's theory 'the good society is one which permits and encourages everyone to act as exerter, developer and enjoyer of the exertion and development, of his or her own capacities.'[9] The human needs for belonging, respect, and opportunities for self-development are strongly emphasized as political ends. The case for a democratic political system and capitalist market economy is that they facilitate this human advancement better than any other political economy, but equally, since material progress or mere satisfaction of material wants is not at all an end in itself, governmental intervention could well be justified by an ethical argument based on the potential contribution of public policies to individual development. Economic liberals, if they consider it at all, believe individual development is a matter of individual choice, inevitably and properly made privately, to which governments can make little or no contribution. Ethical liberals take seriously the potential of governmental intervention and public policies to support, encourage, and even create the conditions for individual growth and development.

Both economic and ethical liberals subscribe to the principles of political liberalism. In contrast with traditional conservatives, both economic and ethical liberals prize individual liberty as the priority among political goods. Both economic and ethical liberals, in contrast with modern socialists, believe in the ultimate efficiency of capitalist market economies and accept as just its unequal outcomes. Yet economic and ethical liberals differ greatly on what should be the responsibility of individuals for themselves and towards others and what should be the purpose of government and the extent of its intervention in economic and social affairs. In short, one defines the difference between public and private sectors narrowly; the other defines it broadly.

Hence, economic and ethical liberals also reach very different political conclusions, and advocate significantly different policy principles, in response to the central questions of social policy in a liberal society: how to protect the persons and property of individuals against the attacks of others while preserving the rights of alleged attackers; what to do about ensuring that competition is fair and equality of opportunity is realized; and what to do about those who for some reason unrelated to their efforts as individuals are unable to provide for the basic material, and perhaps higher, needs of themselves and their families.

Communitarianism: Conservative and Radical

Communitarian ideologies start from the premise that humans are social beings. The concept of atomistic individualism that is central to thinking in the liberal tradition is rejected in communitarian ideology. Basic communities of family, neighbourhood, church, language, ethnicity, race, and class give meaning and order to human existence. Hence, for communitarians the central problem for politics and public policy is protection and development of these basic communities, including the state, within which individual and collective identities are formed and reformed.

The communitarian understanding of individuals as social beings has different political expressions, right and left, conservative and radical, depending on what is understood to be the place or relationship of individuals in the political community. For conservative thinkers on the right the political community is a hierarchical order in which individuals are unequal, governed by command and obedience based on relationships of legitimate authority. For radical thinkers on the left the political community is an egalitarian order in which individuals are equal, governed by cooperation and consensus based on relationships of democratic participation. Nonetheless, both conservative and radical communitarians agree on the priority of language and culture, which are intimately and inseparably related, in the formation of communities. Because linguistic and cultural communities are prior to individuals, their protection and development is the condition for the survival, belonging, esteem, and creativity of all living and future members of the community.

Thus, the protection and development of a cultural community is a collective right, which may take priority over the rights of individual members of the community.

States are the public institutions of communities; they are also territories. Along one line of communitarian thinking the coherence and integrity of the state derives from its foundation on a linguistic and cultural community, but the capacity of a state for purposive action provides the potential for protection and development of the language and culture that is its foundation. According to this communitarian view a regime of cultural and linguistic assimilation is an essential element in the formation, preservation, and development of the nation-state, within which people acquire consciousness of themselves and realize their individual potentials.

An opposing view of state and language among communitarians sees states as potentially supranational organizations of two or more cultural communities. The alternative to communal assimilation or separate states is a bicultural (or multicultural) political association of compartmentalized or segmented cultural communities within a single state. Such a political association might be organized as a federation based on territorial segmentation of cultural communities, or as a consociation constituted on the basis of status cleavages that run throughout the state. In either case, the mass of members of opposing cultural communities are generally isolated from contacts with each other as much as possible with respect to those aspects of their daily lives that are most likely to provoke conflict, and the task of bargaining and resolving intercommunity differences is reserved to a relatively small group of the communities' elites. For federation or consociation to work, state institutions and policies must create conditions for the survival and collaboration of majority and minority cultural communities. Domestic policies, especially education, must institutionalize segmentation by protecting basic collective rights and promoting segmented social organizations. Constitutional policies will define the relationship of state and citizens with respect to their basic communal identifications, designate policy fields subject to segmentation, and create parallel governmental organizations to administer segmented jurisdictions.

POLITICAL IDEAS AND EDUCATIONAL POLICIES IN CANADA

In this study of the historical development of elementary and secondary educational institutions and policies in Canada, I shall focus on the purposes of public education, institutions for educational governance, principles of educational policy design, and criteria of educational policy evaluation. I shall argue that educational politics and policies are constituted by consensus and difference in an ongoing dialogue about political principles. These principles shape what people perceive to be educational problems and what can and should be done about them by means of state action. Yet the dialogue of educational politics and the outcomes of educational policies in terms of programs and institutions also can affect the meaning of political principles. Public philosophy is a primary determinant of educational politics and policies, but educational politics and policies in turn can reconstitute public philosophy.

Public policies for elementary and secondary education in Canada have never been grounded on pre-existing consensual agreement. Both historically and currently, political struggles over educational policies in Canada engage fundamental divisions of religion, language, culture, and class. Political domination and grudging compromise pervade the history of Canadian educational policies, revealing the fragile foundations of the modern Canadian state, but educational policies also reveal an emerging basis for reconstructing the Canadian public philosophy and thus, perhaps, a hopeful prospect of political development and moral progress.

1

Principles of State Organization and Educational Governance

The central and continuing problem of educational governance is the establishment and functioning of state institutions, or the ordination and regulation of private institutions by the state, which will symbolize and integrate conflicting world-views, represent and reconcile general and particular interests, and make and implement coherent educational policies. Implicit in my argument is an assumption that institutional arrangements are properly understood as constitutive or framework policies. They are created in the prospect of dealing, or have emerged and become recognized retrospectively as dealing, with what is collectively perceived as a set of related problems or potential problems which require understanding, analysis, and action. Institutional arrangements for public decision-making thus incorporate the influences of both public philosophy and partisan doctrines, and their structure and functioning over time reflect changes in both public philosophy and partisan doctrines.

In describing and analysing the historical development of principles of educational governance in Canada I shall focus on three dimensions of state organization: the organization of central educational authorities, the relationship between central and local educational authorities, and the relationship between state authorities and educational interest associations. With respect to each of these dimensions of state organization, I shall describe a set of models or theories of state organization that have been and/or continue to be advocated in the Canadian political community as meeting the tests of good governance. Each of these theories or models comprises institutions and practices of educational governance that on their own terms purport to meet the requisite tests of public philosophy (legitimacy, justice), policy theory (feasibility, applicability), and program operations (effectiveness and efficiency).

CENTRAL STATE EDUCATIONAL AUTHORITIES

At the heart of the problem of central educational governance are normative and practical issues of institutional separation of educational politics, policy, and administration. One issue is the separation of partisan politics and educational policy-making. Some argue, for example, that the criterion for public policy in education must be the general public interest or common good, which requires effective insulation of policy formulation from the pressures of particularistic and partisan political interests. Others reply that the public interest has no meaning apart from the preferences of individual members of the political community; hence, there must be no institutional separation of educational policy from the democratic competition of party and group politics. Another issue concerns the separation of democratic politics and policy from educational administration. Some argue that educational policy must be a fundamental concern for any democratic community and therefore requires broad participation by citizens in its formulation, but the implementation of educational policy is best done by professional schoolteachers and administrators without interference by parents or politicians. Others reply that policy implementation inevitably incorporates political values; hence, educational administration should not be institutionally segregated from the democratic processes of educational politics and policy formulation.

Theories of politics, policy, and administration differ in the importance attributed to each of them as public functions, the knowledge and skills required to perform them, and the utility of their being exercised independently or jointly by different or the same officials. Politics, policy, and administration may be understood as public functions that require no special professional or technical knowledge in order to perform them successfully. What is required is general knowledge and understanding acquired from living in a political community. Politicians, policy-makers, and administrators should be representative of their political community, a condition that can be secured by democratic elections or, as in the case of juries, selection by lot. Alternatively, politics, policy, and administration may be understood as public functions that do require distinctive specialized knowledge for their effective and efficient performance. Politicians must have specialized knowledge and skills in order to articulate and harmonize public interests. Policy-makers must have specialized knowledge and skills to understand public problems, devise creative options for resolving them, and choose optimal courses of public action. Administrators must have specialized knowledge and skills to put in place and carry out the detailed programs of governmental activities to achieve the established goals of public policies. The specialized professional or technical knowledge and skills of politics, policy, and administration can be acquired by formal education or practical experience; they can be acquired and exercised either by the same persons having more than one public function, by different people having different public functions and acting jointly, or by persons who have different public functions and act independently of each other.

In Canada three theories of politics, policy, and administration have contended for predominance as public philosophies of central educational governance: parliamentary government, executive policy-making, and civic trusteeship. Each of these theories in turn has two versions, which give different weight to individual and collective responsibility in public decision-making.

Parliamentary Government and Ministerial Responsibility

According to the constitutional norms of liberal parliamentary government, both politics and policy are separated from administration, but no attempt is made to distinguish between politics and policy. The final determination of policy ultimately should reside collectively with popularly elected members of parliament. The executive authority of parliament, including the prerogatives of the crown, is exercised in practice by ministers, the political heads of governmental departments who are individually responsible to parliament for the specific policy directions and administrative implementation of their departments, and by the cabinet, the council of ministers that is collectively responsible to parliament for the government's policies and effectiveness and efficiency of administration. Administration may include giving advice to politicians in their capacity as policy-makers, but its essential task is efficient execution of the policy decisions taken by cabinet and ministers as ratified by parliament. Administration involves only routine implementation; the creative formulation of policy belongs to politicians. Efficient administration, however, may require skilled managerial, professional, and clerical employment, and that can only be assured by strictly separating administrative employment and practice from politics. If a neutral administration is not established, parliamentary government will remain stuck in a spoils system in which party machines dominate politics, direct policy, and make administration their dependent clientele.

Under liberal parliamentary government the conventions governing accountability of the political executive include both collective responsibility of the cabinet and individual responsibility of ministers. The political theory of parliamentary government, however, provides no principle to guide or define the proper balance between these essentially competing conventions. As a result the practice of parliamentary government may vary between two polar versions. On the one hand, the convention of ministerial responsibility may be paramount. As political heads of their departments ministers assume responsibility for the direction of policies within the jurisdiction of their departments. Overlapping jurisdictions or joint responsibilities among departments for policy development and implementation are assumed to be minimal. Collective responsibility of cabinet is reduced to a rule of ministerial logrolling by which ministers support each other's policies in return for support and acceptance of their own ministerial autonomy. On the other hand, the convention of collective responsibility may be paramount. The minister's authority is restricted to routine decisions. Initiation and control of policy development are shared with other ministers, either the cabinet as a whole or, more likely, a committee of the cabinet that includes the premier (or prime minister), the treasurer, and perhaps two or three other ministers whose departments are functionally or politically relevant to educational policy-making.

Executive Policy-Making: Departmentalized versus Institutionalized Cabinets

As a model of public policy-making and political accountability, executive policy-making conceives of policy as a public function that is continuous with both politics and administration, but politics and administration are separated. The key actors in this model are elected political executives. On the one hand, they are deeply engaged in politics through both their struggle for office and their leadership in forming public policy. Ministerial responsibility thus remains a central constitutional convention. On the other hand, they also have a close working relationship with administrative officials, who are assumed to make an important contribution to the formation of policy, as well as its implementation, but who are appointed on the basis of merit and hence remain outside the partisan struggle.

In contrast with the model of parliamentary government, in which administration has no functional implications for policy-making, in the model of executive policy-making administrative officials are assumed to have professional and technical knowledge and skills that are required for effective and efficient public policy-making. Formally, professional administrators remain advisers on matters of policy to ministers; in practice, their knowledge and skills have become indispensable for making good public policies. In this model public policy must be founded equally on the principles of political democracy and professional expertise, and in consequence a central problem of modern democratic government is the creation and preservation of a proper balance between political and administrative officials.

Writing about 'executive federalism' in Canada, Stefan Dupré has distinguished the 'departmentalized cabinet' from corporate policy-making in an 'institutionalized cabinet.'[1] In a departmentalized cabinet responsibility for policy-making is concentrated on individual ministers, deputy ministers, and a few senior officials. The convention of individual ministerial responsibility thus becomes the norm of policy-making practice. Under corporate policy-making in an institutionalized cabinet, the weight given to individual ministerial responsibility in a decentralized cabinet is shifted to collective ministerial responsibility. This emphasis on the institutionalization of cabinet properly focuses on the establishment of an effective system of cabinet committees, led by a cabinet committee on priorities and planning, and the reorganization of central agencies – in particular, the departments of the cabinet secretariat, provincial treasury, and governmental organization and management – as administrative support for cabinet in its exercise of collective planning and policy development. In effect, the institutionalization of corporate policy-making rests on a functional separation within the state bureaucracy between general policy priorities and development by central agencies and specific policy development and implementation by line departments.

Civic Trusteeship: Educational Governance by Non-Partisan Notables

In the political theory of civic trusteeship the public function of policy-making is separated from politics but not necessarily so clearly separated from administration. Advocates of civic trusteeship see politics as primarily a struggle for partisan position that should have minimal influence on the determination of public policies serving the general interest. The formation of public policy is best placed in the office of a pre-eminent statesman or council of civic notables who will rise above the particular interests of partisan and sectarian politics and make decisions in the public interest. The institutional separation of policy and administration from politics does not mean there will be no mechanism for public accountability. Policy-making authorities may be formally appointed by elected politicians and held answerable for their policies before a popularly elected, representative legislature. What is imperative is securing their autonomy from partisan politics by the terms and conditions of their appointment and the norms and practices of their public office.

Against the nineteenth-century liberal theory of parliamentary government and ministerial responsibility, conservatives, who defended the authority of the church in educational governance, and conservative liberals, who opposed the intrusion of partisan and sectarian politics in educational policy-making, advocated a model of public accountability based on civic trusteeship. Historically, the choice between corporate trusteeship in the form of a central board of education or individual responsibility in the person of a provincial chief superintendent appears to have depended on the perceived balance between the requirements for representation in policy-making and the pressures for political accountability to the legislature. Particularly where the educational authority of the church (or churches) was conceded as paramount, a board of education that included members of the ecclesiastical elites could serve to incorporate religious authorities in educational policy-making. Alternatively, a central board of education could be established, as J.S. Mill advocated, as 'a permanent board composed of people selected for their zeal for education and the amount of intelligent study they had given to their subject.'[2] Corporate trusteeship by such a civic elite, however, might then experience a recession of its policy-making authority by the iron law of oligarchy into the office of its secretary or chief superintendent.

CENTRAL AND LOCAL EDUCATIONAL AUTHORITIES

Democratic theories of state organization differ in their conceptions of politics, policy, and administration as public functions; they also differ in their understanding of the spatial or territorial dimension of politics, policy, and administration. Politics, policy, and administration may be understood as public functions that have no distinctive territorial dimension beyond the simple requirement that many public regulations and services must be implemented in different localities. Alternatively, politics, policy, and administration may each be seen as subject to important spatial or territorial variations, which must be taken into account in their institutionalization as public functions.

This potential spatial or territorial dimension to democratic politics, policy, and adminstration has special significance for understanding the formulation and implementation of public policies for elementary and secondary education in Canada. With only a few exceptions public elementary and secondary schools have been established historically as local institutions; while schools have grown in size and their catchment areas have expanded correspondingly, they have continued to function as local institutions.[3] Accordingly, once elementary and secondary education is incorporated into central state politics and the decision is taken to form a central state policy on providing elementary and secondary schools, the problem of local administration of state educational policy is necessarily encountered. Once central educational politics and policy are extended to the establishment of central state institutions for the governance of public education the problem arises of conceptualizing in theory and reconciling in practice the activities of central and local political, policy-making, and administrative institutions.

Theories of the relationship between central and local public authorities may differ about the direction in which authority to make and implement public policy is legitimated and power should flow, downward from the centre to localities (administrative agency) or upward from localities to the centre (communal autonomy). They also may differ about how decision-making authority should be divided between central and local authorities: vertically (policy tutelage), horizontally (fiscal equivalence), or concurrently (policy interdependence).

Administrative Agency: Local Governments as Agents of Central Governments

Local governments may be considered as territorial subdivisions serving as administrative agents of the central state. Popular control of public authority may be achieved by election of representatives to serve as legislators and executives at both central and local levels of government, but public authority is nonetheless strictly hierarchical. Central government is superior; local governments are subordinate.

In Anglo-American political thought the classic statement of this view is found in *The Constitutional Code* of Jeremy Bentham.[4] For Bentham the right and proper end of any government is the greatest happiness of the greatest number. Clearly much influenced by the structure of the modern French state, Bentham argued that this end of maximizing utility would be served best by a systematic hierarchy of legislative and executive agencies. The national ('supreme') legislature should be omnicompetent; to its power there should be no limits. Under its supreme authority Bentham proposed to divide the country into counties or districts of approximately equal size and establish in each a sub-legislature and a sub-ministry, including a sub-prime minister, as local legislative and executive authorities subordinate to the national legislature and executive. For administrative purposes each district would be divided into sub-districts, each with an elected local head under the strict control of the district executive. The district executive and sub-legislature would in turn be 'liable in all ways imaginable' to control by the national legislature and its executive.

In the Benthamite theory of administrative agency local governments were both representative and subordinate to ensure their accountability and efficiency. Local administration was not bureaucratic administration, but it had no distinctive territorial dimension. The enforcement of state regulations and delivery of public services was assumed to be essentially uniform across the sub-districts of the state.

Communal Autonomy: Neighbourhood Democracy and Confederate Communities

At the opposite pole from administrative agency lies a model of local autonomy, neighbourhood democracy, and confederate communities.[5] Local communities are seen as autonomous polities that have distinctive communal histories and identities. Such communities should be self-governing for many, if not most, public activities, including education. To deal with overlapping or joint activities they can constitute confederations of local communities by sending representatives to regional and/or national legislatures. Thus, local governments are seen as the primary public authorities, while regional and national legislatures are derivative institutions, depending for their legitimacy on the delegation of authority from local polities. The territorial dimension of politics, policy, and administration should properly and regularly have primacy over functional considerations.

Policy Tutelage: Centralized Policy and Local Administration

In contrast with a relationship of administrative agency in which school boards are strictly subordinate to the provincial department of education with respect to both policy and administration, or one of communal autonomy in which school boards are independent agents accountable to local communities, local educational administration may be subordinated to the central state in a tutelary relationship, which is based on a vertical division of authority between deciding the principles of policy and the details of their implementation. The basic premises of public decision-making are determined by central state authorities, which decide uniform policy goals and set guidelines and standards for policy implementation. Discretion over administration is accorded to local educational authorities within this centralized policy framework.

Such a view was advocated by John Stuart Mill, who is widely regarded as the classic theorist of Anglo-American local government. In addition to strictly local business, which should devolve on local authorities, and functions of universal concern, which require central superintendence of local administration, Mill identified an important group of public functions, including the administration of the poor laws, sanitary regulation, and apparently public education, which 'while really interesting to the whole country, cannot consistently with the very purposes of local administration, be managed otherwise than by the localities.'[6] For these functions, Mill argued, 'The authority which is most conversant with principles should be supreme over principles, while that which is most competent in details should have the details left to it. The principal business of the central authority should be to give instruction, of the local authority to apply it. Power may be localized, but knowledge, to be most useful, must be centralized.'[7]

In contrast with the Benthamite assumption of uniform implementation, Mill theorized local government as a creative adaptation of central policies to local circumstances. The principles of policy should be uniform throughout the state, but administrative management and practices are allowed to vary among localities. This creative adaptation of centrally determined policy principles through local democratic administration had important implications for democratic politics. In considering the institutional design of local government, Mill saw two primary issues: 'How the business itself can be best done; and how its transaction can be made most instrumental to the nourishment of public spirit and the development of intelligence.'[8] Mill, like Bentham, was concerned about the efficiency of local administration, but he also believed that participation in local government was crucial for the political education of citizens.

Fiscal Equivalence: Central and Local Governments as Coordinate Authorities

Central states and local authorities may be conceived as being essentially autonomous but complementary levels of government. As a principle of organization for central-local relations, fiscal equivalence assumes that the totality of governmental functions can be divided and conducted separately at different levels of government without significant overlapping of activities or much need for joint action.[9] The territorial distribution of benefits from the provision of different collective goods varies markedly from highly localized to universal. Only if there are several levels of government, and a large number of governments, can a proper symmetry be achieved between the boundaries of governmental agencies and the boundaries of the collective goods that governments supply.

The theory of fiscal equivalence opens the way to single-purpose agencies of local administration. In contrast with the assumptions of policy tutelage, the theory of fiscal equivalence asserts the impossibility of any simple, general territorial separation of policy (or politics) from administration. Because policies vary in the territorial scope of their impact, institutions and processes for policy-making and administration must be designed accordingly to reflect the territorial impact of each policy sector, which may or may not coincide with other policy sectors. Beginning from a state of multi-purpose administrative agencies, changes to existing policies and introduction of new policies are likely to result in the formation of new agencies for making and administering the newly constituted or reconstituted policy endeavours. Single-purpose agencies will tend to displace multi-purpose agencies.

Policy Interdependence: Central and Local Governments as Concurrent Authorities

In the model of policy interdependence, central and local public authorities are portrayed as separated institutions sharing powers to make public policy. In contrast with theories of administrative agency and policy tutelage, the theory of policy interdependence assumes that the public function of policy, as well as politics and administration, has an important territorial dimension. Against the theory of fiscal equivalence, the theory of policy interdependence holds that the territorial boundaries of public policies are not easily or permanently identifiable for allocation among agencies of government with appropriate territorial jurisdictions. Hence, central and local governments must have concurrent authority and decide jointly. Rather than the relationship between central and local governments in public decision-making resembling the 'layer cake' of administrative agency and policy tutelage or the 'neapolitan cake' of fiscal equivalence, in the theory of policy interdependence it is a 'marble cake.'[10]

Policy interdependence may be produced by constitutional design, but it can also emerge in practice, and become convention, from the interactions of intergovernmental politics. Policy interdependence requires that both levels of government have political resources that one level can use against the other to assert and preserve its relative autonomy. The political resources of local government may take the form of constitutional or statutory authority, supportive political-cultural beliefs, capacity to implement policy, or useful local knowledge. Inequalities of political resources can exist between levels of government but must not be cumulative. Reflecting contemporary pluralist theory that administration cannot be separated from politics and policy – they are a seamless web – central-local relations under policy interdependence are characterized as a process of intergovernmental bargaining and exchange rather than central planning and control.

CENTRAL STATE AUTHORITIES AND ORGANIZED SOCIETAL INTERESTS

Theories of public authority differ over the proper relationship between state agencies and organized societal interests. The legitimacy of intervention by organized societal interests may be viewed quite differently across the three public functions of politics, policy, and administration. Organized societal interests may be excluded entirely from any legitimate part in the public life of the community. They may be restricted to political action as 'pressure groups' or 'political associations,' expected to advocate the particular interests of their members in electoral campaigns and public debates and perhaps to make representations to policy-makers, but proscribed from any direct involvement in policy or administration. Where state organizational capacity is weak, however, or policy design and implementation depend on sectoral cooperation, organized interests may be accepted as legitimate participants in the design of public policies and even designated as agents of policy implementation.

Civic Trusteeship: Official Banishment of Organized Interests

As a model of legitimate relationships between state authorities and organized societal interests, civic trusteeship has both political liberal and conservative communitarian advocates. In the nineteenth century, federal and provincial cabinets in Canada generally comprised representatives of regional, religious, and ethnic interests who turned public policy-making into logrolling among particularistic interests. The cabinet in Canada historically operated essentially as a 'chamber of political compensation.'[11] At the same time the state's exclusive authority to control education was being strongly contested by Anglican and Roman Catholic church authorities. Conservative political liberals reacted against the press of partisan and sectarian politics on public education by advocating a model of political accountability based on civic trusteeship, which would isolate educational policy-making (and administration) from the press of particularistic interests. By contrast, Roman Catholic and Anglican communitarians who advocated church, not state, control of education saw a corporate form of civic trusteeship as a way to institutionalize church authority over the state educational organization and curricula.

Church authority over public education may be institutionalized in a model of corporate trusteeship, but this privileged position of denominational interests does not alter the central principle of civic trusteeship that separates politics and policy and thus aims to insulate policy-making authority from partisan and pressure politics. Civic trusteeship in both its political liberal and conservative communitarian versions implies the banishment of particularistic interest associations from any form of direct participation in policy initiation and formulation. Just as the state administration is expected to be a source of specialized scientific, professional, and technical advice without infringing on the prerogatives of making policy, so the policy-making authority will presumably welcome reasoned representations by educational associations as expressions of particular interests that merit consideration in the formulation of the general will. The requirement that policy-making be relatively autonomous from particular interests rules out, however, any operative functional partnership between the policy-making authority and pressure groups.

Parliamentary Government: Legitimate Representations by Organized Interests

The classical liberal theory of parliamentary government, which separates politics and policy from administration, admits a very restricted place for political associations and interest groups. Organized interests have a legitimate place in political campaigns, public debates, and representations to members of parliament. They have no legitimate place in making and implementing public policy. Moreover, the strict separation of administration from politics, routine business of administration, and requirements for uniformity in the application of policies mean that attempts to organize protective, or even professional, associations of central or local administrative officials would be strongly opposed. Hence, under a model of parliamentary government associations of school board members, educational administrators, or teachers are expected to function as professional or educational societies, not as pressure groups. Moreover, particularistic educational interests are likely to be seen as less important than common concerns and therefore justify the formation of omnibus educational societies comprising administrators, teachers, and trustees.

Executive Policy-Making, Sub-Governments, and Policy Communities

Reconceptualizing the public function of central departmental officials to include their participation in policy-making implies rethinking the potential contribution of local administrative officials. If central administrative officials make a functionally specialized and important contribution to the formation of public policies, then a plausible argument can be made that a similarly distinctive contribution to policy-making might be made by school trustees and teachers, who know the conditions of local administration. The legitimation of a policy-making role for central educational officials thus creates a precedent initially for the representation of policy advice through associations of teachers and school trustees and eventually for the participation of representatives of both teachers and trustees in processes of central policy-making.

Thus, executive policy-making in a decentralized cabinet also can lead to the isolation and insulation of educational politics, policy, and administration in an educational 'sub-government' or 'policy community' that centres on the 'educational partnership' of departmental officials, trustees' associations, and teachers' unions.[12] As functional sub-governments are similarly constituted in other policy areas, provincial cabinet decision-making becomes either multilateral logrolling among the ministers who represent various sub-governments or bilateral bargaining between 'spenders' and 'guardians,' a minister and sub-government on one side and the provincial treasurer and/or premier on the other.

Corporate policy-making in an institutionalized cabinet is likely to change the relationship between state institutions and organized interests. If it works as intended, the introduction of corporate policy-making weakens functional sub-governments as centres of policy-making authority. Against multilateral logrolling among sub-governments and bilateral bargaining between spenders and guardians, the ideology, institutions, and practices of corporate policy-making attempt to erect a more comprehensive and anticipatory style of public decision-making in which public problems generated by sub-governments are centrally reviewed, a collectively determined governmental agenda sets priorities for policy-making, and sub-governments are forced to work within this collectively determined framework. Some organized interests may respond by redirecting their representations and advocacy towards central agencies, but they are less likely to be able, or even try, to establish a participatory role in setting the governmental agenda. Policy communities are forced to redefine their policy-making activities within a framework of centrally determined priorities, while at the same time mobilizing themselves as advocacy coalitions against central agencies and provincial cabinet. Alternatively, policy communities may simply disintegrate as functional partnerships erode as a result of the co-optation of state officials, both central and local, into institutions of corporate policy-making.

POLITICAL THEORY AND INTERPRETIVE ANALYSIS OF EDUCATIONAL GOVERNANCE

In this book I shall focus my analysis on three issues of educational governance: the organization of provincial political authority, the relationship of central and local educational authorities, and the relationship between central political authorities and organized educational interests with particular reference to provincial associations of teachers and trustees. In Canada political thinking about educational governance has been characterized, first of all, by conflicting ideas about who ought to discharge the public functions of politics, policy, and administration and whether the relationships among them should be separation or collaboration. There have been equally conflicting ideas about whether the public functions of politics, policy, and administration have a territorial dimension or not, and if they have, what are the implications for the organization of central and local educational authorities. Similarly, there have been conflicting beliefs about the legitimacy of organized educational interests and, assuming organization is accepted, about what are the legitimate roles of organized interests in educational politics, policy, and administration.

In order to interpret the principles of educational governance that have been incorporated in the organization and relationships of provincial political authorities, local educational authorities, and organized educational interests, I have constructed three typologies of educational governance. In each typology the models are intended to incorporate the main features of institutional options that constitute the relevant range of political thinking about educational governance in Canada. These typologies in turn will be used as conceptual frameworks to describe and interpret historical institutions and practices of educational governance, which vary across provinces and over time.

Prevailing principles of educational governance vary in Canada from one political era or provincial arena to another, but they are embedded historically in two shared traditions of political thought. Particularly in setting out basic concepts and models for analysis of state organization, but also in devising typologies of educational policy design, I have drawn extensively, both explicitly and implicitly, on the classic texts of Anglo-American and French political theory as exponents of these two traditions. In part, this is the result of their being read by Canadians. Consider, on the one hand, the works of such Anglo-American political theorists as John Locke, Edmund Burke, James Madison, Thomas Jefferson, Jeremy Bentham, James and John Stuart Mill, T.H. Green, and John Dewey; on the other hand, there are the classic works of French theorists such as Jean-Jacques Rousseau, Baron de Montesquieu, Joseph de Maistre, and Alexis de Tocqueville. These luminaries of Anglo-American and

French political theory are the educators of Canadian political intellect, the grand masters of analysing public problems, designing institutions and policies, and thinking about legitimacy and justice. Directly or, more often, indirectly their works form the core of the political education of people who have comprised the public life of Canada, or at least the book-learning part of their political education. More importantly, these classic political theorists have looked deeply and clearly into the two political traditions. Their writing is an encapsulated expression of the dilemmas and possibilities of politics and policy-making in Canada. Their interpretations are essential for us to recover now the historical meaning of our public philosophies, institutions, and policies.

2

Principles of Educational Policy Design

The design of educational policies begins with ideas about what educational problems are and what, if anything, it is possible to do about them by collective action. In each of the three areas of educational policy examined in this study of elementary and secondary education in Canada basic differences of political principles have been important determinants of policy design. Political liberals and conservative communitarians have fought bitterly over the design of policies that have determined the place of religion in public education. Because of basic differences in their conceptions of equality of opportunity, political, economic, and ethical liberals, have been divided over the organization and curricula of secondary schools. Political liberals, ethical liberals and conservative communitarians have advocated very different approaches to regulating the official language of instruction in public schools. In order to interpret the historical development of educational policies in Canada, consideration must be given to the ideological structures that underlie educational policy design.

DOCTRINES OF CHURCH AND STATE IN EDUCATION

Political ideologies of church and state in education have been constructed from positions taken on five basic issues concerning the place of religion in public life in general and in public schools in particular. These issues concern the separation of church and state, the recognition of an established church, the inclusion of religious education as a necessary part of any school curriculum, the possibility of religious education being separated as a subject from other subjects of the school curriculum, and the possibility of general religious principles being articulated independently of denominational doctrines. Agreement or disagreement on each of these issues, taken in turn, results in five distinct conceptions of the place of religion in public schools.

Conservative Regimes of Church-State Coexistence: Established Church and Concurrent Endowment

The first issue is the separation of church and state. For conservatives who defend the inseparability of church and state, the church is a spiritual and supernatural society directly ordained for the eternal salvation of its members, while the state is a human and natural society established for the temporal good of its members.[1] These two sovereignties can coexist because they do not belong to the same human order, but in certain realms such as education, marriage, and the family their mutual dependency is patent and their powers and responsibilities must be integrated in public institutions. According to this view religious education must not only be a part of each school's curriculum, it must permeate each school's culture. Moreover, religious principles cannot be understood in isolation from church doctrine; religious education invariably must be denominational education. Because of the inseparability of church and education, educational governance must be accountable to the authority of the church, not the state.

From an assumption that church and state are inseparable in education and that denominational instruction must permeate each school, at least two different types of state educational regimes can be created. On the one hand, in states where a church is established, public schools can be claimed as institutions provided by the state but controlled by the established church. The problem with this policy option is the opposition of dissenters and unbelievers, who must either subject their children to unacceptable denominational indoctrination or else establish their own voluntary schools outside the state system and who, in either case, must pay through general state taxation for the support of established church schools. Alternatively, where establishment is absent or opposed successfully by dissenters, each religious denomination can claim concurrent state endowment for its own system of schools. This policy option will be unacceptable to the advocates of an established church; the requirement to replicate school facilities for each denomination makes it relatively expensive and inefficient, particularly a problem in sparsely populated areas; and it is criticized as making schools a divisive force rather than an integrating public institution.[2]

Political Liberal Regimes of Church-State Separation: Secular, Non-Denominational, and Reserved Public Schools

The separation of church and state is a basic tenet of political liberalism. In contrast with the view of church and state as two mutually dependent sovereignties governing different orders of human being, liberalism assumes the distinction and separation of spiritual and temporal affairs. Religious belief belongs to the private rather than the public domain. A church, as John Locke defined it, is 'a voluntary society of men, joining themselves together of their own accord in order to the public worshipping of God in such manner as they judge acceptable to Him, and effectual to the salvation of their souls.'[3] Against conservatives, liberals are agreed that public schools must be subject to public accountability, but they have been divided about the place of religious education and observance in public schools. Three types of state educational regimes can be derived from the separation of church and state depending on the response to three related issues about the place of religion in schools.

For those liberals who advocate a strict separation of church and state and who hold that religion should have no place in the school curriculum, public schools must be secular schools. According to this view, religious teaching can, and should, be separated from instruction in other subjects. Jeremy Bentham, for example, excluded religion from the curriculum of his chrestomathic school on the grounds of 'necessity' (the greatest number of children possible was needed for economies of scale), 'needlessness of opposite course' (day school for six hours left time for religious teaching in home and church), and 'innoxiousness of the course taken' (no instruction in school would be repugnant or disrespectful to religious believers).[4] John Stuart Mill in his 1849 'Speech on Secular Education' argued, 'Education provided by the public must be education for all, and to be education for all it must be purely secular education'; otherwise, minority rights cannot be respected.[5]

The majority of nineteenth-century liberals rejected the solution of strictly secular public schools. They insisted on separation of the state from the church, understood as denominational organizations, but they also were committed to founding public institutions, including public education, on religious principles. In this 'conservative liberal' view a free and ordered public life is inconceivable unless it is grounded on a common commitment to basic religious principles, and public schools have a pre-eminent public obligation to incorporate that common commitment in their organization and convey it through their teaching. Underlying this view is an assumption that basic religious and moral principles can be articulated and taught independently of denominational doctrines. Public schools should be non-denominational schools, teaching common religious principles and beliefs while excluding the doctrines and liturgies of particular denominations. Denominational instruction may be provided at home or in church, or it may be given at school outside the official curriculum during released time or in extra classes before or after school. In practice, however, non-denominational schools were non-denominational Christian schools. As such, as J.S. Mill argued, they were unacceptable to non-Christians and unbelievers. More importantly in terms of the numbers of their opponents, non-denominational schools were unacceptable to Roman Catholics and many Anglicans who refused to admit any distinction between church doctrine and true Christian belief.

Against the advocates of non-denominational public schools, liberals who believed in the separation of church and state but who were also committed to denominational religious education made their case for denominational public schools. In their view education was a proper responsibility of the state, schools were necessary public institutions, state financial aid was essential to their establishment, and state control was required to ensure public accountability. Nonetheless, rejecting church management and control of education did not necessitate banishing denominational religious instruction and observances from public schools. Rather than teach no one's religion in non-denominational or secular schools, public schools could teach everyone's religion by designating the particular denominational religious instruction and observances to be offered in each school and permitting students to enrol in schools according to their denominational affiliations.

A policy of reserving schools for denominational instruction would not be acceptable to those who reject the separation of church and state and insist on the superiority of the church in matters of education. In predominantly liberal societies, however, where the separation of church and state is a deeply ingrained principle of public philosophy, supporters of church schools may well prefer denominationally reserved schools to voluntary church schools with no, or at best inadequate, state aid. Denominational public schools also would not be acceptable to liberals who hold that religious belief and observance belong strictly to the private realm and hence have no legitimate place in public schools. Denominational public schools duplicate expensive facilities and fail to capture economies of scale in mass education. By segregating students in schools by denomination they perpetuate denominational divisions, undermining the social and political unity of a liberal society. Because schools are not reserved for members of smaller denominational groups or unbelievers, the rights of individuals professing minority religious beliefs are inevitably threatened by a system of denominational public schools; offering a conscience clause to allow minority believers and unbelievers to withdraw from denominational religious teaching and observances does not, in principle or in practice, remedy the resulting discrimination.

FORMATIVE PRINCIPLES OF SECONDARY SCHOOL ORGANIZATION

The basic issues of educational curriculum and school organization concern who learns what, how.[6] Philosophies of education and theories of learning specify, and justify, what constitutes good learning activities and appropriate learning groups. A philosophy of education is needed to provide guidance in determining the social purposes of education, the types and quality of schooling to be provided, and the best allocation of education among particular social groups. A theory of learning is needed to provide understanding of the growth of individual capacities, the contribution specific learning experiences can make to educated human action, and the most effective and efficient organization of instruction. In any political community the collective philosophy of education and theory of learning must be vital subjects of public deliberation and argument that are grounded in the fundamental beliefs and commitments of a broader public philosophy and hence can provide warrants for collective judgments about the effectiveness, efficiency, legitimacy, and justice of educational policies.

Viewed in this broad context of state functions serving human needs, education is always instrumental, but the purposes it serves vary with individuals, over time, among communities, and between levels of education. At the elementary level of education, learning is always focused on basic economic, social, and political competencies, individual responsibilities, and collective identifications. At the secondary level of education, however, especially as it has developed since the nineteenth century, these social purposes have become more refined and specific, and greater importance is given to preparation and selection for participation in the work force. Canadian public policies for educational curriculum and school organization in the twentieth century have been marked by their growing assumption that the focus of schooling, if not its main aim, is preparing young people for work. Schools are understood to provide general knowledge and skills as a base from which students can acquire specific knowledge and skills. As the occupational relevance of specific technical knowledge has increased with the advance of technological production and bureaucratic organization in business and government, schools increasingly have been expected to provide students with both general and specific knowledge and skills.[7]

Educational policy-making attention has shifted accordingly from elementary to secondary school curriculum and organization as the functional and distributive implications of state secondary educational policies have become political priorities. On the one hand, the actual and potential contribution of secondary education to material production and economic power has been recognized by public planners and policy-makers, as well as business interests, in advanced industrial countries. On the other hand, in contrast with mass elementary education, secondary education with its more occupationally specific knowledge and skills does bestow economic advantages on the individuals who get it. Access to secondary school has become increasingly an important condition for access to better jobs, and that raises difficult issues of accessibility and quality of secondary education: what types of secondary schooling should be provided and who should get what?

Educational Differentiation and Selection in Secondary Courses, Programs, and Schools

Policies for educational curriculum and school organization make differentiations among individual courses, programs, and schools. They specify categories of learners who will take prescribed courses, enrol in authorized programs, and attend designated schools. The hard administrative issues of educational curriculum and school organization concern the effectiveness and efficiency of actual or proposed differentiations among learning activities and learning groups. Are the contents of courses, the requirements of programs, and the organization of schools effective in providing individual students with prescribed knowledge and skills and efficient in their utilization of scarce material and organizational resources? The even harder political issues of educational curriculum and school organization concern the legitimacy and justice of actual or proposed differentiations among learning activities and learning groups. Are differences among learning groups, courses, programs, and schools based on criteria that can be justified by recognizably good and generally accepted reasons? Are the rights of individual students respected in the procedures used to assign them to learning groups, and are their needs met in the educations they then receive?

Both educational and social criteria are employed to differentiate secondary education. Courses, programs, and occasionally even schools are differentiated between the traditional humanities subjects, such as classical languages and literature, English (or French) language and literature, history, art, and music, and science subjects, such as physics, chemistry, biology, and mathematics. Some schools may also offer courses and programs in the social sciences of economics, geography, political science, and sociology. Courses, programs, and schools may focus on academic education, conveying human knowledge and culture abstractly as represented in the accumulation of insights, inventions, and discoveries that comprise the established disciplines of human inquiry, or they may focus on teaching applied technology, occupational trades, practical skills, and performance arts that are immediately applicable to the material and cultural reproduction of society through human work and social practices. Courses, programs, and schools may be differentiated according to their level of difficulty (basic, general, advanced) and by their intended relationship to further education (preparatory, terminal). Entry to courses, programs, and schools may depend on the educational achievements of students, such as obtaining high standing in examinations or providing a practical demonstration of their skills; it can also depend on the social characteristics of students, such as class, ethnicity, language, religion, and sex.

A complex array of educational criteria and social characteristics forms the basis for differentiating courses, programs, and schools and then selecting and assigning students to the resulting educational groupings, but most of these criteria are not unique to secondary education. For example, categorizations among schools based on religion, language, race, and sex are not limited to secondary schooling. Since the late nineteenth century, however, the most socially distinctive and politically controversial differentiations concerning secondary education have arisen from the educational definition of occupational classes and consequent structuring of social mobility. Educational careers have been progressively delineated as economic careers. Secondary education is designed to be preparation and selection not so much for specific occupations but rather for general categories or classes of occupations, such as professional, managerial, creative, technical, or manual workers. Workers in these occupational classes have varying prospects of material rewards, different amounts of freedom in choosing how and when to do their work, and vastly different degrees of economic power. Hence, the distribution of economic welfare, opportunity, and freedom becomes closely dependent on the distribution of educational opportunities.

Whichever criteria are employed to differentiate secondary schools, programs, and schools and whether students are assigned selectively to the categories created, or not, difficult educational and political issues may be expected to arise. Unrestricted entry that ignores previous educational achievements hinders the ordering of educational experiences and building on prior learning. Enrolment without reference to the social characteristics of students can undermine the achievement of essential social purposes through education, such as creating class consciousness, promoting ethnic or linguistic identities, preserving religious communities, or reproducing sex roles. When students are assigned selectively to courses, programs, and schools, however, the rules for restricting enrolments, and their results, can and often will be challenged on the grounds of educational effectiveness and efficiency as well as social legitimacy and justice.

In principle, the results of public policies that differentiate secondary courses, programs, and schools in terms of career tracks to occupational classes could range from completely differentiated systems in which differentiated schools offer differentiated programs and courses, to completely classless or undifferentiated systems in which all secondary schools offer the same program comprising the same set of courses.[8] In practice, where policies of class differentiation and selection in secondary education are politically contested, the issue having priority is almost certain to be differentiation by schools, simply because the structuring effects of separate schools are more visible and the results of initial selection are more difficult to rectify subsequently. Where public policy opts for undifferentiated schools, then class differentiation among programs within schools will tend to emerge as an important political and educational issue. Only when schools and programs are both undifferentiated is the differentiation of courses likely to emerge as a major controversy that extends beyond the circles of professional educators.

Institutionalizing Educational Differentiation: Five Types of Secondary School Organization

Based on this apparent hierarchy of political issues arising from educational differentiation and selection and taking account of the basic dichotomy between sectors of state and private education, the history of politics and policies for secondary education in the Canadian provinces can be analysed in terms of five types of school organization. Each type implies a distinctive understanding of the relationship between class structure and secondary education. Each type is also legitimized by a different concept of educational equality. Accordingly, each generates a distinctive pattern of political contestation about who should be the recipients of secondary education, what are the desirable characteristics of secondary education, and what should be the social processes for determining the distribution of secondary education.[9]

First, secondary education can be organized as an 'exclusive sector' of schools for the elite. In the usual form of exclusive sector, secondary education is provided by independent schools while public schools offer only an elementary education, perhaps including some provision for advanced, practical education in higher grades. Secondary education is limited to those students whose parents can afford to pay the requisite fees, essentially middle-class and upper-class families. Schools divided by class select and prepare students for economic careers in occupational classes based on their families' class membership. In the extreme there is simply no circulation between classes; both the existing class structure and its distribution of membership is isomorphically reproduced from generation to generation. Hence, secondary education as an exclusive sector is not only class-specific, it is also class-divided and class-confirming.[10] The legitimacy of secondary education as an exclusive sector will depend on acceptance of a concept of segmental equality by which claims for educational equality might be made within the public or private educational sector but not between them. Even so, claims for justice are likely to focus on the exclusionary features of the private sector; and a marginal equality may be attempted by state grants to independent schools and scholarships for a few very talented students whose parents cannot afford to pay fees.

Second, 'partite systems' are organized by differentiating public schools in terms of educational tracks that correspond to occupational classes and economic careers. The provision of secondary education for all young people means that secondary education is, at least in principle, inclusionary rather than exclusionary. Within the state sector, state-maintained and state-managed schools offer educational programs that lead to different occupational classes. These programs are thus class-specific; since students in different tracks are physically and socially isolated from each other in different class-specific schools, they are also class-divided. Partite systems are not in principle class-confirming, however, since the allocation of places in state secondary schools is determined by free choice or open competition. Usually partite systems allocate students to class-specific schools on the basis of a competitive examination that follows a common elementary or primary education. Hence, the legitimacy of a partite system will depend on acceptance of this competition for places as embodying an equality of opportunity in which all students are assumed to have essentially the same means or instruments (in terms of educational preparation) to demonstrate their merits and win places in their preferred schools. Critics are likely to attack the fairness (justice), as well as the effectiveness and efficiency, of the competition for places. They will also question the long-term consequences for societal integration of the physical isolation of students in different educational tracks.

Third, 'multilateral schools' resolve the priority issues of the partite systems by enrolling all students in unified schools. They differentiate educational tracks within these schools, however, and selectively allocate students, or guide their choices, among the various programs that are offered. Multilateral schools are multi-class institutions in which class-specific education is preserved in separate educational tracks. Class divisiveness between students who are enrolled in class-specific programs is assumed to be remedied by the physical proximity, and hence social integration, that results from attending the same school. As with partite systems, the allocation of students among programs in multilateral schools may depend on free choice or open competition, but distribution by student preference is much more likely to be found in multilateral schools than it is in partite systems. Multilateral schools assume the legitimacy of a segmental equality in which claims for equality are made within programs but not between them, and they also assume the educational effectiveness and efficiency of designing a small number of educational tracks (perhaps three or four) for students to follow. Critics of multilateral schools attack the fairness and efficiency of competitions which determine the assignment of students to tracks. Where entry depends on students' choices rather than open competition, they question the ability of young people to make a major career choice as early as the outset of secondary school, as well as the fairness of expecting them to make such a choice. Critics may also focus on the narrowness of the educational tracks that are offered to students in multilateral schools. Both partite systems and multilateral schools make only slight provision for individual differences among students; they are much too restricted in the variety of individual preferences, purposes, and needs that they can accommodate.

Fourth, in a system of 'comprehensive schools' there are no differentiations among schools and no predetermined programs differentiated within schools. Subject to their possessing the prerequisite qualifications, students are permitted to choose their courses according to their interests and abilities. As a result, in comprehensive schools programs are differentiated individually by the courses each student, with whatever guidance given by teachers, chooses to take. Equality of opportunity in competing for places in class-specific schools or programs is here replaced by 'person-regarding' equality in which students are treated neither identically nor interchangeably: all are assumed to derive equal value from their individual educational careers.[11] Individually chosen programs will still lead students into different occupational classes, but secondary education will be structurally classless rather than class-specific. The legitimacy of comprehensive schools depends on acceptance of a concept of person-regarding equality as the central consideration in designing and distributing secondary education. Advocates of any form of class-based secondary education will be unwilling to accept such a premise. Even among those who do accept classless education in principle, difficult questions are likely to arise about the basis on which person-regarding equality should be conceived – students' current preferences, their eventual ends, or their individual needs – which carry different implications for personal choice versus professional guidance in designing individual programs.

Fifth, 'uniform systems' are undifferentiated among schools, programs, and courses. Comprehensive schools assume that students have many different interests and abilities that should be accommodated through corresponding diversity in their education. A uniform system rests on the assumption that there is one worthwhile education that is known or can be specified, and that education ought to be given in all schools to all students. As with comprehensive schools, uniform systems in principle are classless, but the person-regarding equality of comprehensive schools is replaced by a concept of lot-regarding equality.[12] In a comprehensive school all students in principle should receive equal value in their educations but their educational lots would not be interchangeable. In a uniform system, where the one best educational program is followed by all students, no student would gain or lose value by exchanging his or her educational lot for that of any other student. Advocates of uniform systems commonly recognize that, for all students to follow essentially the same courses and program in a unified school, compensatory and remedial educational activities will be required to take account of individual differences in learning ability and experiences. Critics who support comprehensive schools reply that compensatory or remedial activities can never be effective in overcoming the range of individual differences that must be accommodated. Along with the advocates of class-specific secondary education, they also contend that uniform systems fail to take account of the complexity of the occupational class structure in advanced capitalist societies, and they dismiss as hopelessly naive the notion that one best secondary education can any longer, if it ever could, be defined and taught.

Exclusive sector, partite system, multilateral schools, comprehensive schools, and uniform system are five types of educational institutions that take different approaches to organizing the relationship between secondary education and class structure and make different assumptions about the meaning of equality in education. Using these types as a conceptual framework, we can undertake an empirical analysis of the history of policies for secondary school organization in Canada, the forms of differentiation and the results of selection over time, and the evolving ethos of educational equality. In doing so, however, we shall find that ideal types of secondary school systems may provide a framework for policy analysis and a focus for political advocacy and contestation, but they are rarely fully realized in practice. To understand the politics of state secondary education, it is necessary to know the distinctive mix of types of secondary schools in each province and, if possible, to identify the 'hegemonic school' that both incorporates the prevailing consensus and focuses the political controversies surrounding secondary education.

CONCEPTS OF LANGUAGE, STATE, AND EDUCATION

Like education, language is both an instrument and a symbol. A language is a means of communication among people; it is also a badge of collective identity. Like education also, but at a more basic level, language constitutes both individual and collective identities. The concepts people have, and those they create, come from their language. Hence, their very understanding of the world, the way people see themselves and others, is conditioned by the language they speak.

Language is a shared value. Any standard language, as opposed to a dialect, fulfills several functions: as a medium of formal and official communication, linking speakers of different dialects and vernaculars across a wider territory; as the working language of technical and scientific communication; and as the foundation of cultural expression and creativity in poetry, fiction, and drama. A standard language has value because of these functions. A parochial dialect or vernacular will have value as a means of communication within a particular group, but a standard language will be more widely valued because it can function generally throughout a wider community. A standard language rests on its acceptance and use as both social norm and common practice by the members of a community. Underlying a standard language, as William Coleman has pointed out, 'a certain degree of loyalty toward the standard language must exist among members of the community. They must take pride in it and must be aware that the language is a standard with specified norms and codes.'[13]

Language is also a world-view. That is, a language is not simply a means to express or convey thoughts and experiences to others; it determines the very categories of thought and experience by which humans perceive and understand the world in which they live. Thinking requires language, but there are no private languages.[14] As Charles Taylor has so perceptively remarked, 'The language I speak, the web which I can never dominate or oversee can never be just *my* language, it is always largely *our* language.'[15] The meanings of words are not unique to each person but derive from their usage in a linguistic community. Thus, thoughts never belong simply to isolated individuals; they are a product of membership and interaction in a linguistic community. Edward Andrew concludes that Aristotle was fundamentally correct: 'the community is prior to the individual. This does not mean that the end of human life is to subordinate individuals to the collectivity but that the pre-condition of a "human" life for individuals – the exercise of *logos* in practical and theoretical matters – is participation in a linguistic community.'[16]

Implicit in each of these concepts of language is a different understanding of the relationship between individual and community. In the concept of language as shared value individuals are repositories of values and beliefs that may be common to other individuals, or shared with others, or not. Communities are formed by individuals who have found agreement, or somehow created it, among themselves based on certain common or shared dimensions of their lives. Hence, communities are products of the thoughts and values of prior individuals. By contrast, in the concept of language as world-view individuals are inseparably identified with linguistic communities. Membership in a particular linguistic community is an essential determining condition of human existence. Hence, linguistic communities are prior to, and greater than the sum of, the individuals who belong to them.

The alternative principles or criteria for incorporating individuals in linguistic regimes are territoriality and personality.[17] Under the principle of territoriality one official language may be imposed by the state throughout its territory. Alternatively, two or more languages may be recognized by the state as legitimate public languages, but their public status and use will vary among districts, regions, or provinces of the state. Certain territories are designated as unilingual in one language; other territories are unilingual in another language; and/or still other territories are designated as bilingual districts, regions, or provinces. Under the principle of personality, however, the speakers of each publicly recognized language are entitled, at least in principle, to use their own language anywhere within the jurisdiction of the state in a regulated set of public spaces, for example, addressing the legislature or courts of law, dealing with government agencies, or choosing the language of instruction in schools.

Each concept of language, as either shared value or world-view, accords with fundamentally different ideological assumptions of liberalism and communitarianism. When these opposing ideological doctrines of human language are combined with territoriality and personality as alternative principles of incorporation in linguistic regimes, four basic types of linguistic regimes can be distinguished in states that encompass two or more language groups: majority will, linguistic choice, communal assimilation, and linguistic consociation.

Political Liberalism: The Official Language as Majority Will

A concept of language as shared value fits the conventional assumptions of liberal political thought. For many liberals a public language has some value as a symbol of common culture or political community, but essentially a common language is a public good, which is needed as a means of communication to effect economic and political exchange. Efficiency in communication dictates the adoption of one common language in the public life of the community. Choosing the language of the majority as the official or standard language of public life corresponds with liberal concepts of economic efficiency, political democracy, and social justice. The majority language is already more widely understood than any other language, it meets the liberal democratic test of majority preference, and in a calculus where each citizen's preferences are equally weighted it maximizes total utility ('the greatest happiness of the greatest number' as Bentham expressed it).[18]

In a democratic-majoritarian liberal society the official language for purposes of law, legislature, courts, and contracts will be the language of the majority. Other languages may be freely spoken by individuals who share them as private values, and liberal values of respect and tolerance for the private values of all individuals demand respect and tolerance for the private use of minority languages. Minority languages are not public values, however, and hence merit no recognition or protection in public institutions or public policy. Accordingly, in a majoritarian liberal society the language of instruction in all public schools is the majority language. Other languages are properly restricted, depending on public policy, to being used as transitional languages of instruction for children whose home language is not the majority language or taught as subjects of study.

Ethical Liberalism, Minority Rights, and Linguistic Choice

Liberal democracy rests on the will of the majority; it also fears the tyranny of the majority. Public policies must be founded on the values of the majority, but they should also respect and, if possible, reconcile the values of individuals who comprise minorities. Hence, an official language policy in a liberal democracy should balance majority will and individual choice. While one branch of liberal political thought emphasizes the prerogatives of majority will in the construction of public institutions and the design of public policies, another branch of liberal thought advocates the priority of individual choice and equal opportunity. For these liberals language is not simply a preference; it is a core or primary value and hence intimately connected to achievement of individual development. Equality of opportunity for people who choose to speak a minority language demands more than simply a *laissez-faire* policy of permissiveness and tolerance for their privately using it; it requires positive measures to create conditions that will permit minority-language speakers to live in their language, if they so choose, to the greatest extent possible. Nonetheless, the desirability of maximizing individual linguistic choice does not make the use of a minority language in the public institutions of a liberal society a natural right to which individuals can lay an absolute claim of justice. In a liberal society the protection and development of minority languages by public policy will be contingent on the number of minority languages and the numbers who speak them.[19]

A liberal regime of linguistic choice in education requires replacing the territorial principle of majority-will liberalism with the principle of personality. Under a liberal regime of linguistic choice all students, or the parents of each child, should be as free as public policy can provide to choose the language of their instruction in school. Accordingly, in a liberal society that gives priority to linguistic choice rather than majority will, the language of instruction in public schools will not necessarily be the language of the majority. The liberal democratic state may properly require the teaching of the majority language in public schools, but a requirement that schools teach the majority language does not entail that the majority language be the language of instruction. In an ideal situation where numbers warrant, a regime of linguistic choice would include not only majority-language and minority-language schools but also separate bilingual classes or schools for both majority and minority students. All public schools would be open to any student regardless of his or her mother tongue or home language; all young people would have opportunities to acquire proficiency in one or more languages, as they choose. Given proficiency, both majority-language speakers and minority-language speakers would be free to choose among majority-language, minority-language, and bilingual schools.

Communitarian Linguistic Regimes: Communal Assimilation versus Communal Consociation

A concept of language as world-view fits the assumptions of communitarian political thought. Language and culture are held to be intimately and inseparably joined together in the formation, preservation, and development of communities. Hence, states as the public institutions of communities must act to protect and develop the language and culture that is the foundation of both its integrity and legitimacy as a state and the identity, self-esteem, and creativity of its people.

For communitarians who assume an identity between state and nation, public education in general and the language of instruction in particular are powerful instruments of communal assimilation. Public education cannot be content with teaching the communal language simply as a medium of communication, but instead must aim to assimilate young people into the linguistic community's distinctive world-view and way of life. Advocates of communal assimilation as the linguistic regime tend to treat minority-language speakers at best as invisible and inaudible, at worst as threats to the survival and integrity of communal language, traditions, and culture who must be assimilated into the linguistic community.

In states where two or more languages are officially recognized, a linguistic regime based on communitarian principles may be constituted as a communal consociation. The principle of personality establishes equal collective linguistic rights in education throughout the state. Both majority-language and minority-language education will be available to majority-language and minority-language speakers, respectively, throughout the state rather than simply in those territories defined as majority or minority linguistic homelands. In contrast with the liberal regime of linguistic choice, a communitarian regime of communal consociation assumes that majority-language and minority-language schools, if not legally closed to speakers of the other language, at least will be focused in their purpose on communal assimilation.

Mixed Linguistic Regimes: Linguistic Federations and Mixed Consociations

Beyond these pure types of linguistic regimes states can authorize two or more official languages of instruction in public schools by constituting some combination of liberal and/or communitarian linguistic regimes as a linguistic federation. Using the principle of territoriality a linguistic federation might be constructed by drawing district, regional, or provincial boundaries in order to maximize linguistic homogeneity. Then each district, region, or province would be authorized to establish a linguistic regime of communal assimilation or majority will based on its hegemonic language. Alternatively, each of the basic types of linguistic regimes established in one territorial jurisdiction of the state might be combined with one or more of the other basic types established in other jurisdictions. Although unlikely in practice, it is conceivable in theory that all four pure types of linguistic regimes might be included in a linguistic federation that comprised at least four jurisdictions.

In addition to linguistic federations, two general types of mixed linguistic consociations can be distinguished, on the basis of statutory or constitutional protection on one side for either majority or minority collective rights respecting the language of education, while a reciprocal protection of collective rights is unavailable (often by choice) to the other side. In one type minority collective rights are protected by provision for schools that are open only to the children of one minority linguistic group. The protection of minority rights in turn can be based on either territoriality or personality as the principle of incorporation. In a minority-rights linguistic regime schools for majority-language speakers and other minority-language speakers are not similarly restricted. The language of instruction in schools other than those of the protected minority may be the language of the majority, or may vary in a regime of linguistic choice. In the other general type of mixed linguistic consociation, majority collective rights are protected by provision of schools that are open only to the children of majority-language speakers. By contrast schools for minority-language speakers, whether unilingual in the language of the dominant minority linguistic group or multilingual in a regime of (minority) linguistic choice, are open to the children of all minority-language speakers. Whether they will be equally open to the children of majority-language speakers will depend on how aggressively the linguistic majority determines to pursue a policy of (majority) communal segmentation.

INTERPRETIVE ANALYSIS OF EDUCATIONAL POLICY DESIGNS

In this book I shall limit my analysis of educational policy design to the establishment of religion in public education, the organization and curricula of secondary education, and the official language of instruction in public schools. By thus narrowing my analysis, regrettably but necessarily I shall slight such important subjects of educational politics and policy as early childhood education, private schools, post-secondary education, Native education, and multicultural education. Nonetheless, these three areas of educational politics and policy do permit us to confront basic historical and contemporary issues and ideologies in Canadian public education. Around religion in public schools, language of instruction, and secondary education, the basic political ideas and oppositions have formed and reformed, political consensus or compromise achieved or policies imposed, and political principles advanced and reconstituted. Looking beyond the educational politics and policies of religion, language and secondary education would doubtless broaden and enrich my study of public educational policy in Canada, but it would not change my interpretation in its essentials.

In Canada, political thinking about educational policy has been structured by conflicting principles or doctrines concerning the proper relationship of church and state in public education, the best organization and curriculum for secondary schools, and the appropriate language of instruction in public schools. Each of these contending principles or doctrines of educational policy in turn is grounded in a more complete liberal or communitarian world-view.

The interpretation of policy principles as elements of rival political ideologies is admittedly problematic. Where policy designs are the result of political compromise or historical evolution, participants in policy-making are unlikely to have articulated explicit ideological justifications and explanations for the outcomes. Where policies have been explicitly chosen, the ideological assumptions of policy design may remain unstated and unexamined, perhaps for the good reason that everyone involved at the time simply took them for granted and got on with the practical details. Even where ideological assumptions have been explicitly stated, perhaps fervently promoted, in the course of making educational policy, contemporary analysts cannot assume that the meaning of political language travels unchanged across time or that in our own time policy-makers and scholars share the same understanding of ideological structures.

Here I have proposed three typologies of educational policy designs that are meaningful in the terms of conflicting political ideologies. I do not claim that educational policy-makers would use the same language to describe their policy options, choices, and outcomes. I hope that many would do so, of course, and that their numbers would increase as we come closer to our own time. My primary concern, however, is that policy-makers over time would at least admit to the accuracy of my translation of their work: 'This is not how I would have said it, but I understand what you mean.'

By describing and examining the principles of those educational policy designs that were chosen among rival courses of collective action, or that emerged from interactive policy-making or historical evolution to be retrospectively ordained, historical and contemporary political arguments about public education can be situated in the context of greater public debates between liberals and communitarians – and among themselves – about the best organization of public institutions and best courses of collective action. In making this kind of interpretation I shall endeavour to show the changing ideological foundations of educational policy designs, not only in order to interpret the history of educational policies in Canada, but also to understand the changing political meanings of public education in Canada.

3

Foundations of Public Education: Religion, Language, and Public Schools

When public policies to expand and extend elementary and secondary education were initially formulated from the 1840s to the 1870s, there was little or no opposition to the principle of establishing schools as public institutions. The primary issue in the foundation of state educational regimes was the place of religious instruction and observance in public schools. The movement for public education was led by political liberals, for whom public schools constituted an essential public institution in the formation of a new political nationality. These political liberals, however, were divided between those who were committed to non-denominational Christian education in public schools and those who wanted a strict separation of church and state in education. Against the non-denominational or secular schools advocated by political liberals, religious conservatives, mostly Roman Catholics but also Anglicans, fought to preserve public education as publicly supported denominational education. Out of the conflicts and compromises of political liberals and religious conservatives, four types of educational regimes were constructed during this period, and these rested on very different assumptions about the purposes of public education, the place of religion in public schools, and the relationship of church and state in education. At the end of the nineteenth century the issue of language of instruction in public schools was confronted and had similarly divisive results.

REGIMES OF CHURCH AND STATE IN NINETEENTH-CENTURY EDUCATION

Which great social institution, church or state, should exercise ultimate authority over the guidance of learning? Conservatives, liberals, and conservative liberals held fundamentally antagonistic principles concerning the relationship of church and state in educational governance and school organization. In the various political outcomes conservative institutions were protected, liberal principles were imposed, and conservative-liberal compromises were made, resulting in four quite different educational regimes: concurrent endowment in Newfoundland and Quebec; unofficially reserved schools in the Maritime Provinces; separate districts divided between non-denominational (majority) public schools and denominational (minority) public schools in Ontario, Saskatchewan, and Alberta; and non-denominational (but not secular) public schools in British Columbia and Manitoba.

Concurrent Endowment of Confessional Systems in Quebec and Newfoundland

Colonial governments in British North America followed both British and American models in their early support for education. On the one hand, under framework statutes in New Brunswick (1802), Nova Scotia (1808 and 1811), and Upper Canada (1816), non-denominational common schools that followed the models of the town schools of Massachusetts (the parishes of New Brunswick and Nova Scotia) and the common schools of New York (Upper Canada) were built and supported by local voluntary effort and funds with minimal official aid or direction. On the other hand, district schools in Upper Canada (1807) and grammar schools in Nova Scotia (1811) and New Brunswick (1816) followed a British model to provide a socially exclusive elementary and secondary schooling for the children of the colonial upper class – government officials, military officers, lawyers, doctors and merchants. These schools, while nominally free of church control, in practice operated under Anglican or, occasionally, Presbyterian church influence with a clergyman or minister usually appointed as headmaster.[1]

The British influence was also evident in several schemes of concurrent endowment. In Newfoundland, for example, the schools of the Anglican Newfoundland School Society, the Orphan Asylum and Presentation Convent schools of the Roman Catholic church, and the Presbyterian Free School at Harbour Grace were beneficiaries of specific grants under the first education act passed in 1836. In Upper Canada, Reverend John Strachan was unsuccessful in his bid for establishment of the Church of England, but colonial governmental support was extended to a number of voluntary societies, including the National Society for Promoting the Education of the Poor in the Principles of the Established Church. Roman Catholic Bishop Alexander Donnell was also allowed by colonial authorities in the 1820s and 1830s to allot part of the colonial appropriation for priests to teachers in Roman Catholic church schools.

The Society for the Propagation of the Gospel established a few schools in New Brunswick; and schools of the National Society, introduced in 1818, flourished for a couple of decades – indeed, there were still eleven National schools in the province in 1871. In Lower Canada the Royal Institution for the Advancement of Learning was proclaimed in 1802, apparently to promote a school system controlled by an established Church of England. During its twenty active years beginning in 1818 it set up eighty-four schools, but in spite of offers to divide between Protestant and Roman Catholic committees in 1826 and again in 1829 it failed to gain any support from the French Catholic majority in the colony.

These early experiments with concurrent endowment ended in the Maritime provinces and Upper Canada with the founding of state school systems. Church involvement in school administration and curriculum was replaced by state control, and settlements on the place of religion in mass education were worked out inside the state sector. In Quebec and Newfoundland, however, concurrent endowment was transformed into schemes of state provision that left effective control of education in the hands of denominational hierarchies.

In Quebec the Roman Catholic and Protestant confessional school systems originated in legislation for separate denominational districts that was passed during the first session of the legislative assembly of the United Province of Canada. The School Act of 1841 provided that inhabitants of a parish in Canada East (Quebec), or a township in Canada West (Ontario), who adhered to a confession different from the majority might choose their own trustees and then establish and maintain one or more common schools for the dissenting minority separate from the majority's common schools. When the reformed School Act specifically for Canada East was passed in 1846, the provisions of the 1841 School Act for common and separate school districts were retained substantially unchanged outside the cities of Montreal and Quebec: the common schools in principle provided schooling that was non-denominational; in practice they were Roman Catholic in character and management while the separate schools were Protestant. In Montreal and Quebec City, however, school boards were officially divided by denomination: one, Roman Catholic, elected by Catholic property owners, managed schools for Catholic children and levied taxes for their support on Catholic residents; the other, Protestant, administered Protestant schools.

The transformation of separate denominational districts into two confessional systems began with the reconstitution of provincial government in Quebec following Confederation. The first step was separation of the Council of Public Instruction into Roman Catholic and Protestant committees in 1869.

Then after strong and persistent opposition by the Catholic bishops to any state control of education, the education portfolio was dropped from the cabinet, and the Council of Public Instruction was given full independence and authority over provincial education in 1876. From then until the reform of 1964 the Quebec Department of Public Instruction operated as two sections under a common superintendent and separate Roman Catholic and Protestant secretaries, who were responsible respectively to the Roman Catholic and Protestant committees of the Council of Public Instruction.

The first education act in Newfoundland, An Act for the Encouragement of Education, in 1836 provided for the distribution of public grants to voluntary denominational schools and authorized the establishment of interdenominational district boards to operate non-sectarian elementary schools. The experiment with interdenominational schools was short-lived. The Education Act of 1843 directed that Catholic and Protestant boards be established in each of the nine school districts, the entire public grant be divided in each district in proportion to the denominational affiliations of the local population, and all interdenominational schools built under the 1836 act be transferred to the management of a denominational school board. The formation of sectarian Protestant boards then became the main political issue until 1874, when Newfoundland was divided into Roman Catholic, Anglican, and Methodist school districts with twenty-three to twenty-five school boards each throughout the island; the Free Church of Scotland and the Congregational Church were each given two district boards, in St John's and Harbour Grace; and one board covering the whole of Newfoundland was authorized for the Kirk of Scotland. The Salvation Army was recognized as a separate denomination for educational purposes in 1892, the Seventh Day Adventist Church in 1912, and the Pentecostal Assemblies of Newfoundland in 1954.[2]

Minority Denominational Districts in Ontario, Saskatchewan, and Alberta

The Act for the Establishment and Maintenance of Common Schools in Upper Canada (1843), which separated the educational governance of Canada West from Canada East, incorporated the three basic principles of Ontario's separate school regime: secular central governance, non-denominational common schools, and separate schools for denominational minorities. Although the principle of ministerial responsibility was not yet accepted practice, the act named the provincial secretary as chief superintendent, with powers to apportion the education grant, administer the act, and report to the assembly; an assistant superintendent was authorized as administrative head of the education office. The act prohibited any child in a common school from being required 'to read or study in, or from, any Religious Book, or to join in any exercise of Devotion or Religion, which shall be objected to by his Parents or Guardians.'[3] It also gave more specific terms than did the 1841 act for the establishment of separate schools. Where the teacher of the district common school was Roman Catholic, Protestant residents might apply to have a separate school with a Protestant teacher; where the teacher was Protestant, Roman Catholic residents were entitled to apply for a separate school with a Roman Catholic teacher. At least ten residents together with the names of three trustees were required in order to make an application for a separate school. Separate schools were subject to the same inspections and regulations as common schools and were entitled to a share of the public appropriation according to the number of children in attendance.

The 'school question' was a deeply divisive issue in Canada West from the 1840s to the 1860s, embedded in the struggle for responsible self-government, emergence of competitive party politics, and creation of federal union. Catholic and Anglican conservatives committed to church control of education opposed liberals who were advocating non-denominational Christian common schools. Between them were a group of conservative liberals and liberal conservatives – notably Robert Baldwin, Francis Hincks, William Draper, and John A. Macdonald – who wanted common public schools with non-sectarian religious education but accepted the necessity of some sort of separate provision for Roman Catholics. Nonetheless, the central figure in the founding of Ontario public education was Egerton Ryerson, a conservative liberal and devout Methodist who was dedicated to non-denominational common schooling.[4] Appointed as assistant superintendent for Canada West in 1844 and holding office as administrative head until 1876, Ryerson established a strong central supervision of common schools while protecting and clarifying the place of separate schools. For example, in 1849, when a reform government led by Louis-Hippolyte LaFontaine and Robert Baldwin passed an education act that strengthened local educational governance, secularized the common schools, and abolished separate schools, Ryerson refused to administer the new act and submitted his resignation. The government retreated. An order-in-council authorized Ryerson to administer the schools under the 1843 act until 1850 when a new act, framed by Ryerson and Hincks, affirmed both the non-denominational character of common schools and the minority right to separate schools. In 1853, again on Ryerson's recommendation, separate schools were given an equal share of provincial school grants, according to their average attendance, and their supporters were effectively exempted from taxation for common school purposes and prohibited from voting in elections for common school trustees.

Separate schools acquired constitutional protection in Ontario through section 93 of the British North America Act,[5] but unfriendly provincial governments and adverse court decisions stunted their growth for many years. The rapid increase of widely held business corporations in the late nineteenth century created problems in determining ownership for purposes of distributing business property tax revenue between common and separate school boards. After 1886 Ontario companies and corporations had the option of supporting separate schools, but given the difficulty of making an exact division of ownership on a denominational basis few corporations made a declaration. Limited in their access to business tax revenue, separate school boards also were restricted by provincial education regulations from expanding into secondary education. In 1926 the Board of Trustees of the Roman Catholic Separate Schools for School Section No. 2 in the Township of Tiny launched a court action seeking to establish a right under the BNA Act to conduct its own secondary schools, gain exemption for separate school supporters from supporting public secondary schools, and receive an equitable share of provincial grants for secondary education. The trial court's judgment, upheld on appeal to the Judicial Committee of the Privy Council, recognized that a few separate schools before Confederation were giving instruction beyond the elementary stage in their 'fifth book' classes, but it concluded that no separate secondary schools existed in law prior to 1867 and consequently no right to separate secondary schools could be claimed under section 93. Departmental regulations were revised to recognize grades nine and ten, the equivalent of former 'fifth book' classes, for the purposes of provincial grants and municipal taxes, but extending separate school education to include the senior secondary grades remained a bitter, unresolved issue of educational politics in Ontario until the 1980s.

The ordinance of 1884 that provided for public education in the North-West Territories was patterned on the Manitoba School Act, which in turn had been based on the Quebec model of concurrent endowment. The territorial board of education was divided between Roman Catholic and Protestant sections, and provision was made for denominational school districts throughout the territory. Through a series of amendments culminating in a 1901 ordinance, the last education act before Saskatchewan and Alberta were granted provincial status in 1905, the system of territorial separate schools and religious instruction became virtually identical to the pre-Confederation policy in Canada West of separate denominational districts. All schools were now centrally administered by a commissioner of education who was a member of the territorial executive committee, denominational appointees to the Council of Public Instruction were merely advisers and had no vote, in each school district one school was designated as the common school, and a separate school was organized only where the denominational minority voted for it. The local board of each common school was authorized to direct that its school be opened with the Lord's Prayer, and the last half-hour of each day could be devoted to religious instruction from which children were excused at the request of their parents.

Separate schools in the North-West Territories were elementary schools. No provision for separate secondary schools existed in law in 1905 that could have been covered by the constitutional protection, equivalent to section 93 of the BNA Act, given to minority educational rights in the Saskatchewan Act and the Alberta Act. In Saskatchewan, the Secondary Education Act of 1907 made no provision for separate high schools, nor for tax exemption for their supporters if separate high schools were established. In the cities and towns of Alberta, however, as high schools were organized by gradually consolidating secondary classes from elementary schools, they were administered by public and separate school boards, and in both cases they were supported by student fees, municipal taxes, and provincial grants.

New Brunswick, Nova Scotia, Prince Edward Island: De Jure Non-Sectarian, De Facto Reserved Public Schools

After Confederation the first great controversy over public policy towards denominational schools arose in New Brunswick. In defining the duties of teachers the Parish School Act of 1858 had been explicitly non-denominational in its provisions for teaching religious principles common to Christian believers, ensuring that religious exercises were not compulsory, and prohibiting the use of the Bible as a means of inculcating specific doctrines. In practice, according to testimony given in *Maher* v. *The Town of Portland,* about 250 schools in Roman Catholic districts had been granted public support under the 1858 act while teaching denominational doctrine and using denominational books and prayers.[6] The Common Schools Act of 1871 appeared to put an end to this practice by requiring 'that all schools conducted under the provisions of this Act shall be non-sectarian.' According to the regulations issued by the Board of Education in November 1871 teachers were authorized to open and close their schools by reading from either the 'Common' (King James) or Douay version of the Bible and repeating the Lord's Prayer but could not compel the attendance at these exercises of any pupil against the wishes of his or her parents or guardians. In addition, no emblems or symbols distinctive of any national or other society, political party, or religious organization could be exhibited in the classroom or on the person of any pupil or teacher, although the latter prohibition was soon amended to exclude 'any peculiarity of the teacher's garb, or to the wearing of the cross or other emblems worn by the members of any denomination of Christians.'

Roman Catholics pressed their case against the 1871 act without success. The federal government professed sympathy for their plight but declined to disallow the legislation. A resolution in the provincial assembly to revert to the 1858 act was defeated twenty-four votes to twelve in 1874, and at the ensuing provincial election only five of the forty-one members who were elected favoured denominational Catholic schools. When the act was challenged as unconstitutional, the Judicial Committee of the Privy Council ruled that whatever privileges Catholics enjoyed in practice under the 1858 act they did not have any privileges or rights in law; hence, they had no protection under section 93(1) of the BNA Act.

Riots in Caraquet in January 1875, at the time of the annual school meeting, ended with two men being killed and nine men charged with murder.[7] The following summer, while the Caraquet rioters were awaiting trial, the five Catholic members of the legislative assembly approached the government to negotiate a compromise. Four concessions were approved by the provincial cabinet (although they were not made public until eighteen years later). These concessions provided the basis for a de facto system of Catholic reserved schools in New Brunswick: first, with the consent of school trustees, children might attend any school in the school district; second, teaching licences would be issued to members of a religious order if they had a certificate from the superior of the order, thus obviating the need to attend the provincial normal school program and take the regular examinations for certification; third, textbooks would be edited or annotated so as to avoid giving offence to Catholics; and, fourth, trustees were empowered to approve denominational religious instruction after school hours. When this policy was legally tested in 1896 in *Rogers et al.* v. *The School Trustees of School District No. 2 of Bathurst*, an action by Protestant ratepayers against the school board's policy to rent a convent school from the Sisters of Charity, the trial court held that the non-denominational provision of the Common Schools Act was not violated by the employment of members of a religious order as teachers, permitting them to wear the garb of their order while teaching, and holding Roman Catholic religious exercises before or after school hours. No appeal was lodged.

As in New Brunswick, Nova Scotia entered Confederation with a state school system that was non-sectarian in law but in practice incorporated substantial provision for denominational teaching. During consideration of the education bills of 1864 and 1865, Roman Catholic Archbishop Thomas C.

Connolly expressed his concern to the premier, Charles Tupper, that without separate schools provided in law Roman Catholics could not be assured of fair treatment. Tupper replied that the education act would be administered by the provincial cabinet, and since Catholics would always be well represented in cabinet their interests would be protected. In 1865 an amendment to give Nova Scotia separate schools was formally proposed in the assembly, but Tupper threatened to withdraw the bill rather than accept such an amendment. The archbishop again raised the possibility of extending the educational rights of denominational minorities in Canada East and Canada West to Nova Scotia in a letter to Tupper on the eve of Confederation; again Tupper rejected the idea. The initiative in finding an approach that would satisfy Catholics in practice without offending Protestants by amending the law was taken by William Henry, a Protestant who represented the predominantly Catholic constituency of Antigonish in the assembly. Under his proposal all common schools would be non-denominational in law, but local agreements would be condoned so that some schools would be reserved as Catholic schools.

In Prince Edward Island, as in New Brunswick, the school act of 1861 authorized Bible reading in common schools and permitted teachers to open their schools each day 'with reading of the Sacred Scriptures by those children whose parents or guardians desire it, without comment, explanation or remark thereupon by the teachers.' The same provision was retained in the act of 1877 with the addition, again following New Brunswick's law of 1871, that 'all schools conducted under this Act shall be non-sectarian.' In spite of the addition of the 1877 declaration of non-sectarianism, no attempt seems to have been made to bring the practice in PEI schools into line with the letter of the law. In predominantly Catholic communities, such as Souris, Tignish, North Rustico, and Morell, the schools reflected the Catholic character of their communities. 'These schools, although public, provided an atmosphere in which Christian values and education in the faith could develop.'[8] In Charlottetown and Summerside, as in the cities of Nova Scotia and New Brunswick, designated elementary schools were reserved for attendance on a voluntary basis by Catholic children.

Non-Sectarian Public Schools in British Columbia and Manitoba

The public schools of British Columbia were non-denominational from the outset. The first education act of the new province of British Columbia in 1872 followed an 1865 ordinance of the colony of Vancouver Island in making an explicit commitment to non-sectarianism: 'All Public Schools under the provisions of this Act shall be conducted upon strictly non-sectarian principles.

The highest morality shall be inculcated, but no religious dogma or creed shall be taught.' The clergy were no longer free, as they had been under an 1869 colonial ordinance, to visit schools before or after school hours to give denominational instruction, and four years later they were declared ineligible to hold positions in the school system as superintendents, teachers, or trustees. There were occasional representations over the next century from Roman Catholics seeking state aid to independent Catholic schools, but the non-sectarian principle of public education was not challenged.

The Manitoba School Act of 1871 followed the Quebec model by dividing the board of education between Catholic and Protestant sections, each with twelve school districts to administer, and splitting the provincial grant between them. The basis for this denominational (and in effect linguistic) duality eroded over the next two decades as English-speaking Protestant settlers, especially from Ontario, transformed the demographic composition of Manitoba. Within two decades Roman Catholics comprised only one-fifth of the provincial population.

In a period of growing provincial assertiveness and polarization between French and English, Catholic and Protestant, which began with the Métis rebellion of 1884 and the hanging of Louis Riel in 1885, the Liberal government of Thomas Greenway in 1890 passed the Manitoba Public Schools Act. This act abolished Roman Catholic school districts, established all public schools as free and non-sectarian, and prohibited religious instruction and observances except outside regular school hours, at the option of school trustees. When the constitutionality of the act was tested in the courts, the Supreme Court of Canada unanimously ruled that the act did prejudicially affect rights and privileges with respect to denominational schools that Roman Catholics had enjoyed by practice in 1870. The Judicial Committee of the Privy Council, however – in a judgment described by Schmeiser as 'difficult to justify, to say the least' and 'probably the most extreme example of judicial amendment of the Canadian Constitution'[9] – reversed the Supreme Court and upheld the act.

The Roman Catholic minority then appealed to the Governor General in Council to protect its right of denominational education, and the Conservative federal government's response became a main issue in the election of 1896, which was won by the Liberal party led by Wilfrid Laurier. Unwilling to force a federal remedy on the Manitoba government, primarily because of the long-term threat such action could pose for provincial rights in Quebec, the Laurier government secured only minor concessions: religious instruction was permitted during the last half-hour where authorized by the school trustees or requested by parents, and the employment of a Catholic teacher could be requested for every twenty-five Catholic pupils in a rural school or forty in an urban school. Such Catholic schools as remained did so as voluntary schools without the benefit of state aid.

LANGUAGE OF INSTRUCTION: ASSIMILATION VERSUS SEGMENTATION IN NINETEENTH-CENTURY SCHOOLS

In contrast with religion, the official language of instruction in public schools was not at first a major issue of educational governance or school organization. Indeed, Canadian public education in the nineteenth century was remarkably permissive about the language of instruction in schools. An 1841 act authorized payment of grants in Nova Scotia to schools using English, French, Gaelic, or German as the language of instruction. In Canada West the Council of Public Instruction in 1851 amended the regulations governing teachers' qualifications so that knowledge of French or German might be substituted for English, and both French and German were accepted as languages of instruction in the common schools of French-speaking and German-speaking communities. French was recognized as an official language of instruction in Manitoba (1871) and the North-West Territories (1877). The exception was British Columbia where English was de facto, if not de jure, the official language of instruction after 1872; nor did informal practices of bilingual schooling develop within the public schools.

Because the language of instruction was generally left to be determined by local school boards, ethnic minority groups living together in small communities and thus constituting linguistically homogeneous school districts could educate their children in their own language. In communities where the total population was large enough to support more than one school, schools might be reserved in practice for attendance by children of different mother tongues. Finally, because often there was a close correlation between language and religion, the exercise of minority denominational rights by Roman Catholics resulted in separate schools for French-speaking children, while separate schools for Protestants were English-speaking.

Communal Consociation in Quebec

The dream of Louis-Joseph Papineau and the *Patriotes* to create a French-Canadian republic modelled on the United States of America collapsed with the defeat of the 1837 rebellion. The initial policy response recommended by

Lord Durham was assimilation, and English was made the official language under the 1840 Act of Union, only to be revoked eight years later. As responsible government evolved in the 1840s, a policy of collaboration came to prevail over one of assimilation. As Eric Waddell has argued, the framework for a persistent dialectic in Quebec political debate was thus created in the 1830s and 1840s: 'One segment has persistently argued in favour of collaboration and the legitimacy of existing structures – hence rights for French Canadians within the framework of a bilingual country. A second segment has gravitated toward the creation of a French state and a separate political destiny for Quebec – hence toward unilingualism and the transformation of existing political arrangements.'[10]

From the 1840s to the 1950s the segment advocating collaboration prevailed, and this was reflected in the establishment and development of public schools. Public education in Quebec was segmented by mutual consent on the basis of religion and language. Public education became a communal consociation, constitutionally divided between Roman Catholic and Protestant segments and concomitantly divided between French-speaking and English-speaking segments.

The number of French-speaking Protestants in Quebec was minuscule in the nineteenth century. Hence, in Protestant schools the language of instruction was invariably English. Because of the relatively large number of Irish Catholics who emigrated to Lower Canada from the 1840s to the 1860s, English-speaking Catholics became a strong minority in the Roman Catholic sector of Quebec public education and constituted a majority in several school districts. Throughout the nineteenth century English-speaking Catholic children attended bilingual elementary schools in which teaching was done in French for half of the day and English for the other half.[11] During the 1930s English Catholic education became an essentially autonomous system with the appointment of an English Catholic school inspector in the Department of Public Instruction, the opening of the first English Catholic public high school (D'Arcy McGee) in 1931, and approval of separate regulations for English Catholic schools by the Catholic committee of the Council of Public Instruction in 1939. As one study of public education in the 1930s concluded, the principle of policy that determined the language of instruction in Catholic schools was communal autonomy: 'School boards decide the main language of instruction in each school by engaging either English-speaking or French-speaking teachers. Where English-speaking Catholics are in the majority, they run their own school. Neither the government nor the department of Public Instruction intervenes in matters of language, except to maintain the rights of the minority, whether Anglophone or Francophone.'[12]

Majority-Will Liberalism in Ontario and the Prairies

French-speaking minorities in Ontario and the West were not as fortunate as the English Catholics of Quebec. The British North America Act had attempted to balance the interests of English and French Canadians in the Maritimes, Quebec, and Ontario, but the influx of British and other non-French immigrants into Ontario, Manitoba, and the North-West Territories upset the equilibrium and reopened the question of English-French coexistence. After 1885 the change in ethnic composition resulting from European immigration raised fears among Canadians who identified with British ethnic groups for the preservation of the British character of Canada, and the potential fragmentation of public education became another rationale for questioning special privileges enjoyed by French minority groups. The fears and tensions of the period were soon expressed in the schools, and previously permissive policies were altered to make English the language of instruction.

The first official change of policy was taken in Ontario. In 1885 a regulation of the Ontario Department of Education required that English be taught in all schools without specifying the amount, and by 1890 bilingual schools were understood to be English-language schools in which French and German were taught only in the early years of school and then merely as a supplementary subject. A renewal of tensions between English and French in 1910–11 resulted in the promulgation of Regulation 17 in 1912; it reaffirmed the policy of restricting the use of French as a language of instruction and communication to the first form (grades one and two).[13] The next year the regulation was revised to permit the chief inspector to approve the use of French beyond the first form in the case of pupils who were unable to speak and understand English. French also could be taught as a subject of study beyond the first form if it had been offered previously, but it could not be taught for more than one hour a day without the permission of the chief inspector. When French-speaking trustees tried to protest by closing Ottawa's separate schools, an appeal to the courts by English Catholics established that section 93 of the British North America Act gave constitutional protection for minority rights to denominational schooling but did not confer any language rights in education. Throughout the 1910s and 1920s a large number of schools openly defied Regulation 17 and functioned as French-language schools,[14] and in 1927, following yet another departmental investigation that found poor quality and high attrition in French-majority schools, bilingual schools were again recognized in Ontario.[15]

In Manitoba, French lost its status as an official language in 1890. Although the status of French as a language of instruction was left unresolved, the abolition of Roman Catholic schools, which were virtually synonymous with French schools since 1871, was a frontal attack on French education. The 1897 federal-provincial compromise over denominational schooling included a provision that in schools in which ten pupils spoke any language other than English, parents could petition the school board to employ a bilingual school teacher and conduct instruction in both languages. As Manitoba was settled over the next two decades by many immigrants with mother tongues other than English or French, school districts faced growing difficulties in providing adequate schooling in two or three languages in addition to English.[16] The problem was compounded by the rise of ethnic prejudices during the First World War, fears for national integration, and genuine concerns about the economic prospects of immigrants who lacked competence in English as the working language of the province.[17] In 1916 the Liberal government of T.C. Norris repealed the bilingual clause and made English the official language of instruction in public schools. As with denominational instruction in Manitoba schools, minority-language instruction was restricted to the last half-hour of the school day where parents requested it and the local board approved.

In the schools of the North-West Territories, following the lead of Manitoba, French lost its official status in 1892. The education act, which replaced the dual confessional Board of Education with a non-denominational Council of Public Instruction, also required English as the language of instruction except for a proviso, as in Ontario, that local school boards might permit a primary course to be taught in French.[18] In Saskatchewan even this concession was withdrawn in 1930, as a result of a vitriolic campaign against francophone separate schools by the Conservative government of James Anderson, and school boards were only permitted to have French taught as a subject for no more than one hour a day.

Bilingual Schools in the Maritimes

The common school acts in Nova Scotia (1864), New Brunswick (1871), and Prince Edward Island (1877) contained no provisions for an official language of instruction, but the bias of public education was heavily towards English. There were Acadian schools already operating in each of the Maritime provinces, however, and in contrast with the fierce struggles over language of instruction in Ontario and the Prairies the continued use of French as a language of instruction in Acadian districts aroused little controversy in the Maritimes. On PEI a compromise in 1882 allowed the use of French textbooks in Acadian schools, and bilingual teachers were permitted to use French as the language of instruction during the first years of elementary schools. In New

Brunswick English was a compulsory subject in all schools, but it was taken for granted that French would continue to be used as a language of instruction in Acadian schools.[19] Regulations provided for bilingual elementary schools to use French as the initial language of instruction, with English taught as a subject until francophone children had the facility to continue their schooling in English. Relaxation of the regulations gradually extended French as the language of instruction to all grades in bilingual schools, and the first Acadian inspector was appointed in 1901. Similarly, in Nova Scotia the 'Acadian Regulations,' which followed from the investigation of a 1902 commission on bilingual schools, provided for daily instruction in speaking and writing English while permitting general education to be carried on concurrently in French. So far as was practicable, only bilingual teachers were to be hired to staff bilingual schools, and an official 'Bilingual Visitor' was appointed by the Department of Education in 1908 to inspect Acadian schools.[20]

RELIGION, LANGUAGE, AND THE FOUNDATION OF EDUCATIONAL REGIMES

The foundation of public education in the mid-nineteenth century was rent by passionate religious oppositions. Roman Catholic and Anglican conservatives demanded church control of education. Utilitarian liberals in the tradition of Jeremy Bentham and James Mill would settle for nothing less than strict separation of church and state. Liberal conservatives and conservative liberals, comfortable with social hierarchy and capitalist markets while bending to the necessities of limited popular government, sought some middle ground for reconciling mass education with Christian education in common schools.

Especially when compared with the uniformly non-denominational educational regimes of Australia, New Zealand, and the United States, or even the modest differences between England and Scotland, the diversity of Canadian educational institutions for dealing with religion in public education is striking. Catholic conservatives got their confessional system in Quebec. A strict liberal separation of church and state was recognized with little debate in British Columbia and then imposed with little concern for constitutional niceties in Manitoba. Liberals in the Maritimes insisted on formal separation of church and state in law; then in good conservative fashion they made accommodations with the Catholic hierarchies in practice. In Ontario, and by extension in Saskatchewan and Alberta, conservative liberals defended common and separate schools as an essential compromise against both conservative demands for confessional systems, as in Quebec, and liberal demands to abolish separate schools entirely. Finally, section 93 of the BNA Act ensured that future generations would never, or at least not easily, escape the multiform heritage of mid-nineteenth century school politics.

Institutional arrangements about the place of religion in public education were paralleled by diverse provisions and practices regarding the official language of instruction in public schools. In British Columbia, English unilingualism was never a major issue. In Quebec, public education, legally divided by religion, was also divided by language between French and English, but within the French Catholic sector the communal autonomy of English Catholics was recognized and respected. In the Maritime provinces bilingual elementary schools were not legally guaranteed, but with relatively little political controversy educational regulations facilitated provision of bilingual elementary education in Acadian districts. In contrast with the lack of prominence of bilingualism as an issue in Maritime educational politics, in Ontario French bilingual schools were fiercely attacked and severely restricted from 1885 to 1927. Bilingual schools did survive, however, and gain formal recognition in Ontario school regulations, in contrast with Manitoba where legal recognition of bilingual schools was rescinded in 1916. In Alberta and Saskatchewan, French also was restricted to use as a transitional language of instruction in elementary schools in 1892, and later rescinded entirely in Saskatchewan.

In sum, between the 1840s and 1930s four types of religious and linguistic regimes were established in Canadian public education. First, in Quebec the three main religious and linguistic communities of French Catholics, English Catholics, and English Protestants were officially separated with relatively little political controversy in a conservative regime of communal consociation. Second, in British Columbia liberal ideas about non-denominational Christian education in public schools and the majority language as the official language of instruction easily prevailed. A liberal regime of non-denominational and unilingual common education also was established in Manitoba, but there the liberal educational regime was imposed by a Protestant, English legislative majority that overturned the original regime of communal consociation based on the model of Quebec. As a result, the legitimacy and justice of the liberal regime in Manitoba were much more persistently contested than was the case in British Columbia. Third, in the Maritimes religion and language were deeply divisive political issues in the formation of nineteenth-century educational regimes, but conservative-liberal accommodations were achieved that formally entrenched non-denominational Christian education in provincial statutes governing public education, but made important concessions in practice by reserving schools for Roman Catholic children in city school districts and conceding linguistic and religious autonomy to school boards operating in

Acadian communities. Fourth, in Ontario, Saskatchewan, and Alberta there was constitutional protection of separate schools for Roman Catholic or Protestant minorities, although this was restricted to elementary education in Ontario and Saskatchewan. After an initial period of communal autonomy in Ontario and official bilingualism in the North-West Territories, English was established as the official language of instruction in public schools; French was grudgingly tolerated and officially recognized, if at all, only as a transitional language of instruction in the first years of elementary school.

In retrospect, what is striking about this diversity of institutional arrangements for religion and language of instruction in nineteenth-century public education is the apparent weakness of political liberalism as a national political ethos or public philosophy. In eight of nine provinces the establishment of public educational institutions and policies was motivated by liberal political ideas, but no dominating common principles gave consistency and coherence to the construction of public educational regimes across the regions of Canada in the mid-nineteenth century. The four types of educational regimes rested on quite different combinations of liberal, conservative, and conservative liberal ideas about the purposes of education, the place of religion in schools, the relationship of church and state, and the relationship of language and community. Moreover, while the educational regimes of Quebec and British Columbia achieved legitimacy essentially without much difficulty, those in the Maritimes did so only after prolonged and painful political struggle. In Ontario and the Prairie provinces Roman Catholic and francophone minorities never did concede either the legitimacy or the justice of the nineteenth-century liberal educational regimes.

4

Foundations of Public Education: Secondary School Organization and Curriculum

Before regimes of public education were established from the 1840s to 1870s, secondary education in the Canadian colonies was provided by a diverse assortment of grammar schools, academies, and classical colleges. Little thought was given to their relationship to the common schools. Grammar schools typically provided their own preparatory classes; academies and classical colleges took pupils who already had received an elementary education. Grammar schools, academies, and classical colleges all charged relatively high fees and hence were beyond the means of all but upper-class families.

Introduction of state elementary education, if only because of its principle of universality, raised directly as a matter of public policy the organizational relationship between elementary and secondary schools and the proper boundaries between public and private institutions. Two very different paths were taken.

In Ontario and the Maritime provinces direct state aid for private schools was terminated, all grammar schools and many academies were incorporated into the public educational regime, and a de facto policy of exclusive sector was transformed into a remarkably consensual commitment to uniform state secondary education. In the western provinces, where essentially there were no pre-existing grammar schools and academies, public secondary schools were founded from the outset as uniform institutions.

In Quebec and Newfoundland, by contrast, elite independent schools maintained their hegemony over secondary education until the 1960s. Within the confines of these confessional systems state support for universal elementary education was expanded upward to higher or superior elementary grades, but it was balanced by state aid to independent secondary colleges, which effectively preserved the institution of secondary schools as an exclusive private sector.

UNIFORM SECONDARY SCHOOLS IN ONTARIO, THE MARITIMES, AND THE WEST

Grammar schools and academies were alike in their reliance on fees, subscriptions, and endowments and hence in their clienteles, the children of upper-class families. They differed slightly in their form of governance and curriculum. The establishment of a grammar school in each district or county of the colony was authorized by statutes in Upper Canada (1807), Nova Scotia (1811), New Brunswick (1816), and Prince Edward Island (1825). Grammar schools were governed by boards of trustees appointed by the lieutenant-governor in council. Academies were privately established by subscribers living in the same town or belonging to the same church who desired a secondary education for their children. The curriculum of the academies was at first somewhat broader and more practical than that of the grammar schools, which focused on English grammar and composition, Greek and Latin, and mathematics, but as grammar schools widened their curriculum to include history, modern languages, and natural sciences these differences in curriculum disappeared by mid-century. Grammar schools were conceived as providing boys a classical alternative to the basic education of the common schools, and hence they also provided preparatory elementary education of their pupils. Academies, by contrast, admitted pupils who had already received an elementary education, and they typically enrolled both boys and girls.

Collegiate Institutes, High Schools, and Uniform Secondary Education in Ontario

From 1853 to 1855 the policy of secondary education as an exclusive sector was abandoned in Canada West. Authority to appoint the trustees of grammar schools was transferred to county councils, and county or town councils were empowered to fund grammar schools by local property taxation. Grammar schools were placed under the regulatory authority of the Council of Public Instruction, which now prescribed the course of study and textbooks and required that pupils be admitted only after passing an oral examination by the principal on common school subjects. Thus, the function of grammar schools as institutions for public education was restricted to providing a second stage of education for pupils who had completed successfully the program of the common schools. Following this reform of the grammar schools, academies either transferred to the public sector and officially became grammar schools, or they became marginalized in the small private sector. In 1871 the Act to Improve the Common and Grammar Schools of Ontario strengthened local financial support for state secondary schools and reduced the size of their fees. County councils were required to contribute an amount equal to at least one-half of the provincial grant, and secondary school trustees were authorized to levy supplementary rates through the municipality in which the school was located. The same act made state secondary schools legally coeducational institutions.

In 1871 two types of secondary education were conceived that derived from the expectations, if not the practices, of former academies and district (grammar) schools. Based on the tradition of the academies, the English and commercial course was designed to educate pupils 'not only for Commercial, Manufacturing and Agricultural pursuits, but for fulfilling with efficiency, honour, and usefulness the duties of Municipal Councillors, Legislators and various public officers in the service of this Country.' Deriving from the tradition of the district schools, the classical course emphasized 'the languages of Greece and Rome, of Germany and France, the Mathematics, etcetera, so far as to prepare youth for certain Professions, and especially for the Universities.'[1] The 1871 act also proposed two types of secondary schools, one for university preparation and the other for education that stopped at the secondary school. Collegiate institutes were intended to provide an intermediate education between common schools and the universities, offering a program of classical and modern languages and having at least four full-time teachers as well as a minimum of sixty pupils studying Latin and Greek. High schools were intended to provide a terminal, general course for those not bound for university. Their curriculum included English, commercial subjects, and natural science with an emphasis on agriculture.

The intended differences in curriculum between collegiate institutes and high schools did not last. On the one hand, high schools took full advantage of a change in departmental regulations that permitted them to include classical subjects in their curriculum, and the general course became increasingly academic. On the other hand, collegiate institutes soon acceded to pressure that they offer a general course. Thus, collegiate institutes and high schools converged towards providing a uniform secondary education.

By 1883 the academically-oriented programme was dominant in both, and the only differences between them were that the high schools had smaller enrolments and the collegiate institutes had a specified number of specialist teachers on their staffs. Whether the reason for the breakdown of this distinction was a desire for the greater prestige (and larger subsidy) that accrued to the collegiate institute, or a determination in the smaller towns to prevent the larger ones from supplying more than their share of the university students, or a deep-rooted belief in academically-oriented secondary education, or a combination of all these, the consequence was that the collegiate institute pattern became the norm, and for over twenty years no attempt was made to develop any of the secondary schools into the type of institution that combined general education with some vocational elements.[2]

Uniform Secondary Education outside Ontario

As in Ontario, the curriculum of high schools in the Maritimes, Protestant Quebec, and the West in the late nineteenth and early twentieth centuries was strongly academic and uniform. Courses of study were designed to prepare students for entrance to arts, science, law, medicine, and engineering programs at colleges and universities or to teacher training at provincial normal schools. The required subjects invariably included as core subjects English language, composition, and literature; English, Canadian, and ancient history; Latin, Greek, and French or German; arithmetic, mathematics, algebra, and geometry; and natural sciences. Optional subjects by the turn of the century commonly included bookkeeping, household science, and manual training, but their orientation also was academic rather than practical, giving them little if any vocational value.

Under the 1893 curriculum revision in Nova Scotia, for example, the high school program was divided into four years and grade twelve subjects into four groups: general including English, classical, scientific, and modern languages. All candidates were required to take subjects in the general group, they could choose between the classical or scientific group, and courses taken from modern languages made up the balance.

Similarly, the course of study at the High School of Montreal, which opened in 1843, was uniform and academic: Latin, English, arithmetic, history, geography, writing, and religious instruction in all classes of the six-year program; French and mathematics in the last three years; and Greek in the last two years. After the school was taken over by the Protestant Board of School Commissioners in 1870 there were recurring disputes about whether to establish a commercial department, and in 1891 the high school began to offer classical, science, and commercial programs as options.

In Saskatchewan the course of studies fixed by departmental regulations under the Secondary Education Act of 1907 was also traditional and academic in its orientation. The subjects taught included English and rhetoric; commercial education; ancient, medieval, and modern history: natural sciences; mathematics and physics; and ancient and modern languages. Instruction in agriculture, household science, manual industrial and physical training, music, and art was also available in some schools.[3] In practice, however, enrolments in secondary courses were dominated by pupils preparing for matriculation (university entrance) and teachers' training (normal school entrance).[4]

External Examinations: Setting Standards and Measuring Achievement

An important feature of the uniform secondary education that emerged in Canada in the latter part of the nineteenth century was external examination of pupils at the two critical junctures – first, the end of elementary school and entrance to high school and, second, the end of high school and entrance to university.

Written examinations for high school entrance administered by departments of education were introduced as secondary education began to expand in the last quarter of the nineteenth century. Universities administered their own entrance examinations until after the First World War, when joint matriculation boards were established representing universities and departments of education. In British Columbia, for example, university and departmental examiners began operating as a single board of examiners in 1918. Prior to 1918 they had met for purposes of liaison, but matriculation examinations were conducted by the University of British Columbia while all other external examinations at high school entrance and each grade level were set by the board of examiners of the Department of Education. Similarly, universities in Ontario administered their own entrance examinations until 1919, when the matriculation board was reorganized to include representatives of the Department of Education. Henceforward the combined matriculation and departmental examinations were administered by the registrar's branch of the department.

Beginning with the province of Ontario in 1904, the curricular and pedagogical impact of high school entrance examinations was moderated by systems of accreditation that permitted pupils from accredited elementary schools to enter high school without taking the provincial examinations. High school entrance examinations ended in all provinces between 1930 (Alberta) and 1950 (Ontario) without controversy. Departmental matriculation examinations, by contrast, were retained in all provinces until the late 1960s and early 1970s, and their abolition remained a recurrent issue of educational politics from the 1970s to the 1990s.

Secondary Education in Rural Areas

High schools separate from elementary schools were limited to cities and larger towns. In rural areas secondary education was provided through secondary departments of elementary schools. As the economic and social value of secondary education was increasingly recognized, these combined elementary-secondary schools were formally recognized as an important means of making secondary education available in rural areas.

In response to pressure from rural communities for improved secondary facilities, elementary school authorities in Ontario were authorized to establish continuation classes in 1896 for grades nine and ten, usually with a separate teacher, but sometimes under the supervision of the elementary school teacher in charge of the other grades of the school. In 1908 schools having such classes were formally recognized as continuation schools. The number of such schools reached a peak of 220 in 1930.

In Manitoba elementary schools were distinguished on the basis of the number of teachers or rooms devoted exclusively to high school work: collegiate departments (three high-school rooms or teachers in an elementary school building of at least seven rooms), high school departments (two high school rooms or teachers), and intermediate departments or continuation schools (one high school room or teacher). When statutory provision was made for secondary education in 1890, there were three collegiate departments and twelve one-room high schools. Winnipeg Collegiate Institute, which opened in 1892, was the first exclusively secondary school. By 1930, when there were twenty-two collegiate institutes, there were still 125 one-room and forty-seven two-room high schools, as well as eleven collegiate departments.[5]

In Saskatchewan under the Public Schools Act elementary schools that had a separate room for pupils above grade seven were called continuation schools; if students in grade eight were in a room separate from students in grade nine to twelve, they were high schools. In 1908, when there were 734 pupils enrolled in collegiate institutes or high schools under the Secondary Education Act, 663 pupils were enrolled in the secondary grades of high school and continuation schools operating under the Public Schools Act, and 180 were doing high school work in ordinary elementary schools. By 1927 there were 6,785 pupils enrolled in collegiate institutes and high schools under the Secondary Education Act, but there were 9,210 pupils enrolled in high schools and continuation schools operating under the Public Schools Act and 4,123 pupils doing high school work in elementary schools.

EXCLUSIVE SECTORS IN CATHOLIC QUEBEC AND NEWFOUNDLAND

In contrast with the uniform organization of secondary education in the Maritimes, Protestant Quebec, Ontario, and the West, the Roman Catholic segment of Quebec education functioned from the middle of the nineteenth century until the 'Quiet Revolution' of the 1960s as two complementary sectors – public elementary schools and private classical colleges. Similarly, in Newfoundland the confessional organization of colonial education was based on a split between mass elementary education in school districts organized throughout the province and elite secondary education in denominational academies located in St John's.

Quebec: Elementary Schools and Classical Colleges

In Quebec the classical colleges were founded under the auspices of the Roman Catholic church, with direction and teaching by members of religious orders. Classical colleges were founded and maintained initially without assistance of the state. Consequently, their independence in constructing programs, setting regulations, deciding teaching methods, and appointing teachers was established early. In spite of considerable diversity in their situations, the colleges all followed the traditional educational formula inherited from the Collège des Jésuites, and the consistent educational philosophy and hierarchical organization of the Roman Catholic church served as unifying factors in maintaining the integrity of this formula over time and among colleges. The academic independence of the colleges was further modified beginning in 1863, when five colleges affiliated with Université Laval, agreeing to accept the program of the university's faculty of arts and the regulations for its *baccalauréat ès arts*. In 1920, when Université de Montréal formally separated from Laval, some classical colleges began to affiliate with Montréal. The course of studies for the *baccalauréat ès arts* gave pre-eminence to literary humanities and philosophy, but after 1925 the establishment of science faculties and schools at both Laval and Montréal caused a greater emphasis on teaching mathematics and sciences in the classical colleges. By the 1940s the first four years at the classical colleges were generally regarded as secondary education (corresponding to the American and English-Canadian high school) and the last four years as college years.[6] In 1952 the classical course, which had been divided between humanities and sciences for its final two years since the end of the Second World War, was further diversified by the introduction of a Latin-sciences course, without Greek, running parallel to the Latin-Greek course after the first two years. Broadening the curriculum of the classical colleges to make more room for science and mathematics did not change the basically academic, elitist character of the classical colleges. They remained, as before, the formative institutions for the intellectual, professional, religious, and political elites of Quebec.[7]

Classical colleges took pupils following their elementary education, which was usually acquired by attending public schools. Within the state sector no provision for post-elementary general education existed until the four-year, terminal *cours primaire superieur* was introduced in 1929.[8] In 1935 a four-year science course was started that aimed to prepare pupils directly for higher studies in colleges or university. With the addition of a twelfth year to the science course in 1939, university science faculties began to accept students directly from the public schools without requiring them to take the traditional *baccalauréat ès arts*. Beginning with Arvida in 1944, a number of public school commissions also introduced classical courses corresponding to the first four years of the classical-college curriculum, thus providing a non-science route to higher education through the state schools. In May 1951 the Roman Catholic committee of the Council of Public Instruction created a sub-committee on the coordination of educational levels in the state sector, and its report in 1953 led to a reorganization of Roman Catholic state secondary education. A new program was prepared for secondary grades eight and nine to twelve and put into effect between 1956 and 1960. State secondary schools would now offer six courses for boys – general, commercial, scientific (sciences-mathematics and sciences-letters), classical, agricultural, and industrial – and five courses for girls – general, commercial, scientific, classical, and family arts. State secondary education was thus officially established in Quebec in 1956, but school commissions were not legally required to provide it until 1961.

Newfoundland: Elementary Schools and Denominational Academies

In Newfoundland the Education Act of 1843 provided for the establishment of a non-denominational college in St John's that was intended to offer elementary and secondary education. Against the opposition of both the Anglican and Roman Catholic bishops and the competition of the Church of England Academy (which was opened in 1844, according to Bishop Feild, 'to mitigate the evil of a public academy on liberal principles'), the non-denominational college attracted few students. In 1850 the college was divided into three denominational divisions.[9] The Church of England Academy absorbed the Anglican division in 1852, the Roman Catholic Academy was opened in 1856, and the Newfoundland Wesleyan Academy in 1859. These academies or colleges augmented their government grants by charging relatively high fees, a practice that limited their enrolments to children of upper-class families. Offering both elementary and secondary education, the colleges functioned as day schools for the children of the St John's commercial and professional elite and boarding schools for the children of prosperous outport merchants. As S.J.R. Noel has observed, 'The old Newfoundland educational system was often defended as representing the triumph of religion over the state; what it also represented, in practice, was the triumph within each denomination of class interests over religion.'[10]

Children whose parents were unable to afford the fees of the denominational academies attended elementary schools, and secondary education outside the church colleges in St John's remained largely undeveloped until after the Second World War. With increased road construction, regional or central high schools became feasible. In 1953 the Newfoundland government announced a new grant program to assist school boards to build 'regional' high schools, defined as schools having at least eighty-one pupils in grades nine to eleven, and later 'central' high schools, which were required to have at least forty-one pupils in grades seven to eleven. By the early 1960s over two-thirds of the secondary school students in Newfoundland were attending central or regional high schools, a development which also changed the position of the denominational academies in St John's. Increasingly the church colleges came to serve only students living in the capital city, and in due course each church transferred control of its college to its St John's school board. The denominational academies became either elementary or junior high schools, and new large high schools were opened by each of the denominations in the capital area. By the early 1960s the Newfoundland secondary school curriculum was still remarkably narrow and academic in its orientation, and a large proportion of pupils were being educated in combined elementary-secondary schools, but the institution of an exclusive secondary sector within a denominational framework had come to an end.

POLITICAL PRINCIPLES OF NINETEENTH-CENTURY SCHOOL ORGANIZATION AND CURRICULUM

For nineteenth-century political liberals public schools constituted a public institution essential for giving young people a basic practical education and teaching them the political liberties and (especially) civic obligations of citizens in a liberal-democratic political community. Public schools were instruments for shaping what Egerton Ryerson called 'the state of the public mind.' He believed that 'it is on Canadian self-reliance, skill and enterprise – in a word, on Canadian patriotism – that depends Canadian prosperity, elevation and happiness.'[11] Teaching such patriotic virtue was the great task of the public schools.

To achieve the purposes of civic education, public schools should be uniform in organization and curriculum. A common program would be followed by all pupils, progressing from lower grades to higher grades, in accordance with externally determined standards and externally administered tests of achievement. In the Maritimes, Protestant Quebec, Ontario, and the West, as public education was expanded in the latter part of the nineteenth century to include both elementary and secondary education, these basically liberal principles of school organization and curriculum were preserved and extended upwards from elementary schools to secondary schools. Initial efforts to create a significant class distinction within the public sector between elite academic and mass general secondary schools, in particular, the distinction projected between collegiate institutes and high schools in Ontario and the Prairies, quickly failed.

Secondary education as it developed in the late nineteenth century thus became overwhelmingly uniform in its theory and practice. In marked contrast with the diversity of educational regimes based on religion and language, public secondary schools in cities and larger towns offered an academic course of study that showed little variation from one province to another. With minor differences in timing, the passages from elementary to secondary and secondary to post-secondary education were everywhere guarded by written external examinations administered by provincial departments of education for high school entrance and jointly by the departments and universities in the case of matriculation. To be sure, at the deeper level of substantive criteria of political judgment, there was no consensus in Canadian public philosophy and policy development about either the meaning or the realization of legitimacy and justice in public education. Outside of Catholic Quebec and Newfoundland, however, there was widespread agreement on what meaning to give to the instrumental criteria of educational effectiveness and efficiency. No doubt the original public elementary and secondary schools fell far short of these aspirations, but the founders of this educational regime – politicians, superintendents, trustees, teachers, and parents – had few doubts or disagreements about what was needed for optimal school organization and curriculum.

During the founding period of public education in the second half of the nineteenth century the greatest differences in secondary school organization were not found between provinces but within them, between urban and rural areas. In rural areas 'continuation' or 'superior' schools struggled to provide their students with the minimum core of the approved academic program. Obviously, these combined elementary-secondary schools in rural areas could continue to be educationally effective only as long as the secondary curriculum remained narrowly academic and uniform. As course offerings became more diverse the educational advantages of large, specialized urban secondary schools would raise hard questions about equality of educational opportunity for urban and rural residents.

Quebec and Newfoundland remained impervious to these liberal ideas about the organization of secondary schools and the design of curricula. Against the liberal priority on creating a new political nationality, religious conservatives defined the purposes of public education in terms of reproducing denominational communities and saving Christian souls. The conservative educational regimes of Quebec and Newfoundland were thus built on the rock of religion, but they also institutionalized and legitimated a class division between mass elementary and elite secondary education that was absent in other jurisdictions. This does not mean that uniform secondary schools had no class bias. Indeed, they were excessively academic, highly selective, and strongly devoted to preparing their students for university and teacher's college. Yet the basic liberal principle of uniform secondary organization was fundamentally different from the conservative principle of an exclusive sector. In the liberal vision secondary schools were public educational institutions, extensions of the common elementary schools, in which every young person, however unlikely in practice, in principle might aspire to enrol, as a right and practice of citizenship. Herein lies the germ of a liberal concept of equality of opportunity in public education. The logic of that liberal principle would eventually transform the provision of public secondary education in Canada.

5

Political Authority and the Foundations of Public Education: Governing Schools in Nineteenth-Century Canada

Colonial government and politics in the British North American colonies were elitist, corrupt, and oppressive, culminating in 1837 in brief rebellions in Lower and Upper Canada. Over the next three decades responsible self-government was achieved in each of the colonies, and a difficult experiment with a formally united but politically segmented government in the two Canadas was developed into a continental federation. The struggle for responsible government and the campaign for public education were intersecting political movements in the middle of the nineteenth century. Advocates of responsible government campaigned for public education as an essential part of nation-building. Promoters of public education, in turn, found that their proposed regimes for governing public schools were necessarily shaped by the emergent liberal principles of political authority.

The first issue of political authority and educational governance in the founding of public educational regimes in British North America was the constitution of central educational authorities. For liberals the achievement of responsible government established the principle of ministerial responsibility, both collective and individual. Under a constitution that endowed provincial governments with jurisdiction over education, provincial regimes of public education ought to be subject to the authority of provincial legislative assemblies through the cabinet collectively and a minister individually responsible for education. Against this liberal theory of ministerial responsibility, conservatives and many conservative liberals, who were suspicious of partisan politics and desirous of protecting the influence of church authorities in public education, advanced a theory of civic trusteeship. Responsibility for educational policy and administration should be separated from partisan politics and given to a non-partisan, independent board of civic and clerical leaders and a provincial superintendent, who would be the executive officer of the board rather than the deputy of a cabinet minister.

A second issue of educational governance was the relationship between central and local educational authorities. None of the colonial or provincial governments attempted to administer local schools directly, but, with the exception of Quebec and Newfoundland, local school boards in rural areas were subjected to strict regulation by provincial departments of education. In urban areas local educational authorities were better able, and willing, to resist being reduced simply to administrative agents for provincial departments. City school boards thus generated an alternative approach to constituting the relationship of central and local authorities as an intergovernmental partnership in which the function of policy-making was centralized in provincial departments of education, but the discretionary powers of administration were decentralized to relatively autonomous school boards.

CENTRAL EDUCATIONAL AUTHORITY: MINISTERIAL RESPONSIBILITY VERSUS CIVIC TRUSTEESHIP

In the late nineteenth century in all provinces except for Quebec and Newfoundland the issue of ministerial responsibility versus civic trusteeship was resolved in favour of the conventional liberal model of cabinet government. Four patterns can be observed. First, in Ontario, central educational governance evolved along the lines of a classic utilitarian liberal argument for public accountability, beginning with civic trusteeship exercised by a central board, turning to a chief superintendent who fused policy-making and administrative authority, and ending with ministerial responsibility under parliamentary government. Second, in the Maritime provinces, the original principle of central educational governance was collective responsibility under a model of parliamentary government. Central educational authority was assumed by a board comprising the members of executive council with the superintendent of education as secretary, an arrangement that lasted until the 1930s and 1940s. Third, in the western provinces, central educational governance initially was established as a form of civic trusteeship with authority lodged in central boards of education. In the 1870s in British Columbia and the 1890s in Manitoba and the North-West Territories, these central boards were replaced by committees of the executive council, followed by the introduction of ministerial responsibility. Fourth, in Quebec, a quarter-century of experience with a model of civic trusteeship, in which the superintendent of education had responsibility for policy and administration, ended at Confederation with the appointment of a minister of education responsible to the legislative assembly for provincial education. The requirements of relating church and state in Quebec education, however, soon brought a return to civic trusteeship under central confessional committees comprised of members of the clerical and lay elites. Similarly, in Newfoundland, attempts to establish a central educational authority based on ministerial responsibility were successfully resisted by church authorities; central educational authority was settled on a corporatist central board of education comprised of state officials and denominational superintendents.

Civic Trusteeship in Ontario: Central Boards and Chief Superintendents

In the colonies of Canada East and Canada West, central boards of education were established, on the model of the Irish national commissioners, as independent councils of prominent clergymen and laymen that normally reported to the legislative assembly through the provincial secretary. The classic defence of an independent board was given by the Reverend John Strachan, president of Upper Canada's General Board of Education. He held that the efficiency and effectiveness of schools depended on the quality of their supervision.[1] Routine administration might be left in the hands of locally elected trustees, but general supervision and regulation should belong to those qualified: clergymen and professional men. In order to preserve elite values, an efficient educational system needed central supervision, whether by a board of education or a chief education officer. However, the General Board that existed in Upper Canada for a decade after 1823 more resembled the conciliar administration of an eighteenth-century monarchical government than it did a civic trusteeship. The board over which Strachan presided included two members of the legislative council, the attorney-general, the surveyor-general and the Reverend Robert Addison. It was abolished following attacks on the conservative policies of the 'Family Compact' by liberal educational reformers who feared that the General Board gave the colonial government 'power and bias over the minds of their children.'[2]

Egerton Ryerson was deeply critical of partisan politics. The Common Schools Act of 1843 had moved towards ministerial responsibility by naming the provincial secretary as chief superintendent with powers to apportion the education grant, implement the act, and report to the assembly. As the assistant superintendent for Canada West from 1844, Egerton Ryerson worked with a sympathetic conservative liberal ministry to strengthen central administrative supervision of colonial schools, and he promoted the re-establishment in 1846 of a central board, to which he would be responsible as superintendent, as a buffer between educational administration and colonial politics. Liberal Reformers, in turn, continued to be critical of the independence of the board and superintendent from the ministry and legislative assembly. Back in power in 1850, they renamed the General Board as the Council of Public Instruction and made the chief superintendent 'responsible to, and subject to the direction of, the Governor General, communicated to him through such Department of Her Majesty's Provincial Government, as by the Government, may be directed in that behalf ...'[3] What the Reform ministry added to the emerging structure of public education in 1850 was political accountability of central governance of education, but not yet explicit ministerial responsibility through a minister of education.[4] Thus, in the 1850s in Canada West, the Council of Public Instruction formally had responsibility for making general regulations, approving textbooks, and classifying teachers, and the education office headed by the chief superintendent administered the council's policies. 'In fact, however, the situation was rather different. The records of the council are incomplete, but from the minutes and the surviving internal correspondence there is no evidence, for the 1850s at least, to suggest that it ever initiated any policies except those recommended by Ryerson.'[5] This ambiguous arrangement apparently worked because of Ryerson's close personal connections with such leading politicians as W.H. Draper, Francis Hincks, and John A. Macdonald. In the 1860s, however, Ryerson found himself not above politics, as he had hoped the chief superintendent would be, but increasingly isolated from the centre of power in the cabinet. Ryerson reluctantly became an advocate of ministerial responsibility, but it was not established until 1876, following his retirement.

Perhaps because Egerton Ryerson was such a towering figure in the history of the foundation of public education in Ontario, the assertion of ministerial leadership following Ryerson's retirement was particularly striking. Adam Crooks (1876–83) and especially George P. Ross, who was minister of education (1883–99) and then premier (1899–1905), set the political and policy direction of Ontario education during their tenure of office.[6] The office of superintendent was abolished. As deputy minister, John George Hodgins (1876–89) provided his ministers with the routine administrative and clerical support that formerly he had given to Ryerson for thirty years. Hodgins's successor as deputy minister, John Millar, was a professional educator, but by now the relationship of the deputy to the minister was established: 'it was the minister, and not the deputy, who was the professional authority.'[7] Following the classic nineteenth-century liberal model, the public functions of educational politics and policy had been cleanly separated from both provincial and local administration and placed in the office of minister of education.

The Maritime Provinces: Executive Councils under Parliamentary Government

In the British North American colonies of Nova Scotia, New Brunswick, and Prince Edward Island, the original central governing agencies for education tended to follow the British approach of governing education through a committee of members of the privy council. Perhaps because their executive councils were relatively small, the Maritime governments named the entire executive council as the board of education or council of public instruction, rather than appointing a privy council committee for education. The Nova Scotia Board of Education established in 1841 (after 1864 the Council of Public Instruction) comprised members of the executive council with the premier as its president, and beginning in 1850 the chief superintendent of education served as a member and secretary. New Brunswick's Board of Education, which was created in 1847, comprised the lieutenant governor and executive council; the chief superintendent was added as secretary following the establishment of that office in 1852; and the president of the University of New Brunswick became an ex officio member of the board under the Common Schools Act of 1871. In Prince Edward Island the Board of Education, which had served as the central governing body since 1852, was replaced under the Public School Act of 1877, which formally created a provincial system of public schools as well as the office of provincial chief superintendent. Henceforward, the Prince Edward Island board comprised the executive council, the principal of Prince of Wales College, and the chief superintendent. Collective ministerial responsibility continued on the Island until 1931 and still longer in New Brunswick (1936), and Nova Scotia (1949), when a minister of education was given individual responsibility in cabinet and legislative assembly for provincial education.

Thus, as state school systems became established in the Maritime provinces the political and policy functions of provincial education were assumed by cabinets collectively responsible to the provincial assemblies. The provincial administrative function, which consisted mainly of energizing local school boards, writing regulations, and inspecting schools, was exercised separately from policy by provincial superintendents, with the aid of inspectors, who were appointed by, and responsible to, the cabinets.[8] Provincial superintendents who pressed beyond their administrative role into the realm of educational policy leadership found themselves out of office. In New Brunswick Marshall d'Avray, who was superintendent from 1854 to 1858, was dismissed because of his progressive and enthusiastic advocacy of public schools and replaced by the brother of Charles Fisher, the new government leader. As superintendent and principal of the normal school Alexander Forrester made an important contribution to the design of the 1864 Free School Act in Nova Scotia, but the Tupper government passed over him and appointed his subordinate, Theodore Harding Rand, as superintendent in 1864. When Rand attempted to assert his policy-making autonomy from the cabinet (Council of Public Instruction) as provincial superintendent, he was abruptly dismissed in 1870 by the Liberal government of William Annand.[9] Rand subsequently served as superintendent in New Brunswick from 1871 to 1884, but controversial issues of educational politics and policy, mainly the place of religion and language of instruction in public schools, were the preserve of cabinet.[10] By the 1870s, cabinet ministers in the Maritime provinces, acting collectively as councils of public instruction, were firmly in command of both educational politics and policy, leaving administration to their provincial superintendents.

Central Boards and Executive Councils in the Western Provinces

Each of the western provinces briefly relied on central governance by an independent central board of education before moving to ministerial responsibility. When the central boards were abolished, the common approach at first was to adopt the British and Maritimes model and simply make the provincial executive council the board of education or council of public instruction. More quickly than the Maritimes, however, the western provinces established individual ministerial responsibility for their provincial departments of education.

In British Columbia the Public Schools Act of 1872 provided for the executive council to appoint a board of six and a superintendent who would be chief administrative official and chairman of the board. When superintendent John Jessop and the board of education resisted changes to the 1872 act proposed by the government of G.A. Walkem, elected in 1878, the government reduced the superintendent's salary from $2,000 to $750, thus forcing Jessop and the board to resign. The government then transferred the board's duties to the cabinet, with the superintendent as its executive officer. The minister in cabinet responsible for education was the provincial secretary until 1891, when it became customary to designate a minister of education, but the Department of Education was not officially established until 1920.

In Manitoba the School Act of 1871 provided for a Board of Education of ten to fourteen members. The first board comprised eight clergymen and four lay members, as well as two superintendents who acted as joint secretaries. In practice the board functioned as two separate committees, one English-speaking Protestant and the other French-speaking Roman Catholic, until 1890, when the legislative assembly terminated state support of French-speaking Roman Catholic schools. The Board of Education became an advisory body, and central control of public schools as well as direction of the newly established Department of Education was given to a committee of five cabinet ministers. This arrangement continued until 1908, when a minister of education as political head and deputy minister as permanent administrative head were appointed.

The Board of Education established in the North-West Territories in 1884 also comprised six Protestants and six Catholics appointed by the lieutenant-governor in council. As in Manitoba, each section controlled its own schools, licensed its teachers, selected textbooks, and appointed its own school inspectors. 'The Board of Education remained independent of the assembly and was periodically criticized for the kind of irresponsibility which, it was alleged, indefinite lines of political responsibility made inevitable.'[11] This independent dual board of education was terminated by the school ordinance of 1892 in favour of a Council of Public Instruction, which was essentially a political body comprising the territorial executive committee plus four non-voting members (two Protestant and two Roman Catholic) appointed by the territorial executive.[12] The council's quorum consisted of the chairman (F.G. Haultain, who was 'premier' and the dominating leader of the territorial executive committee) and one other member of the executive committee; the Council of Public Instruction in its entirety met only at the discretion of the territorial executive. The council was reorganized in 1901 as the Department of Education with Haultain as commissioner responsible to the territorial assembly and a deputy commissioner (J.P. Calder) as administrative head. The next year D.J. Goggin resigned as superintendent, and he was not replaced. This model, minister of education as political head and deputy minister as administrative head, was continued when the provinces of Saskatchewan and Alberta were constituted in 1905.

Civic Trusteeship versus Ministerial Responsibility in Quebec and Newfoundland

Two provinces were exceptions to this trend to ministerial responsibility. In both Quebec and Newfoundland (except under the British commission of government from 1934 to 1949) parliamentary government was the norm, but the liberal principle of ministerial responsibility proved to be incompatible with the reconciliation of church and state authority in the governance of education.

Canada East initially followed a pattern similar to Canada West under

Ryerson. Dr Jean-Baptiste Meilleur was the first superintendent of education from 1842 until he resigned, because of political pressures, in 1855. Meilleur's successor was Pierre-Joseph-Olivier Chauveau, who resigned his seat in the legislative assembly to become superintendent and held the office until 1867. At Confederation Chauveau was propelled by the federal Conservative party leaders Macdonald and Cartier into becoming the first premier of Quebec, and Chauveau also assumed the office of minister of public instruction. Behind this facade of liberal parliamentary government, however, public education in Quebec remained fundamentally divided by religion and language. Church and state cooperated to overcome local resistance to public education in the 1840s and 1850s, but clerical opposition to political control of public education prevailed in the 1860s and 1870s. Separated between Roman Catholic and Protestant committees in 1869, the Council of Public Instruction regained its independence from the Quebec government; and the office of minister of public instruction was dropped from the cabinet in 1875.[13]

No permanent central administration existed in Newfoundland until 1920, when a minister of education was appointed and a Department of Education was established.[14] The churches successfully resisted this attempt to impose a secular central administration on denominational local boards and schools; and in practice the Anglican, Catholic, and Methodist superintendents maintained their former control.[15] The Education Act of 1927 abolished the post of minister of education and substituted a denominationally representative Bureau of Education comprising twelve members, including the prime minister, the three superintendents, and a secretary of education. Under the British Commission of Government, which governed Newfoundland from 1934 to 1949, the offices of superintendent were abolished in 1935 and replaced by secular officials in the Department of Education. Again the churches strongly resisted, and to secure their cooperation the commission agreed in 1937 to appoint denominational executive officers within the Department of Education. The former bureau became the Council of Education chaired by the commissioner for home affairs and education. It included the secretary for education as vice-chairman and nominal administrative head of the Department of Education and the four executive officers within the department representing the Church of England, the Roman Catholic Church, the United Church of Canada, and the Salvation Army – 'the recognized representatives on educational matters for their respective religious denominations within the Department.'[16] When Newfoundland entered Confederation in 1949, the commissioner and secretary of education were replaced by a minister and deputy minister, respectively; the denominational basis for the central governance of provincial education remained unchanged.

CENTRAL AND LOCAL AUTHORITIES IN THE GOVERNANCE OF NINETEENTH-CENTURY EDUCATION

As public education was established and developed in each of the Canadian provinces in the nineteenth century, the dominant model of governance provided for provincial control of educational policies and local management of schools. At the outset the relationship between central and local educational authorities in nineteenth-century Canada was conceived as a form of policy tutelage. In rural areas of the Maritimes, Ontario, and the West the expansion of provincial departments of education in the late nineteenth and early twentieth century soon transformed central policy tutelage into close bureaucratic regulation. In urban areas, however, larger and more diversified school districts were able to gain a degree of administrative autonomy against the bureaucratization of provincial departments of education. Similarly, in Quebec and Newfoundland the domination of the churches over educational policy provided the basis for a relationship of 'clerical' tutelage between central denominational boards and local school trustees that lasted until the 1960s.

Tutelary Superintendents and Bureaucratic Regulation

The model of local educational governance developed in the Maritimes, Ontario, and the West involved four main elements: small school districts, essentially the attendance area of an elementary school, with three residents elected as local trustees; financing primarily derived from revenue raised by local property taxation; provincial regulation of curriculum, licensing of teachers, and inspection of schools; and relatively small provincial grants designed to stimulate development of local schools.

The basic unit of local administration was a small school district that was independent of other local governments. The annual school meeting of resident property owners elected three trustees, usually one each year for a three-year term, who were authorized to build and maintain a school and appoint and dismiss teachers. Operating costs of the school were paid primarily by a levy on local property voted at the annual school meeting. Capital costs were financed by issuing school debentures and usually required approval by a vote of local ratepayers. The boundaries of school districts were determined by the distance children could be expected to walk to school, somewhere between nine and twenty-five square miles. In rural school districts the pupil population was usually very small, often not many more than the ten to fifteen pupils required under provincial law as the minimum for establishing a school district. Most schools had one room and one teacher. In Nova Scotia there were 1,769 school districts operating in 1895 and 1,758 in 1939, of which 83 per cent employed only one teacher. New Brunswick in its 1871 Common Schools Act replaced parish districts with 1,426 small school districts, approximately the same number that existed in 1944. In Ontario there were 4,400 school districts operating in 1870 and over 6,000 in the 1930s. In the western provinces the number of school districts rose rapidly with settlement. In Manitoba, for example, the number of districts was 774 in 1891 and 2,270 in 1936; in Saskatchewan there were 869 districts in 1905 and 5,146 in 1937.

Local property taxation provided 80 to 90 per cent of school board revenues from the late nineteenth century until the 1950s, but there was considerable variation among the provinces in the ease with which the property tax was established as the primary source of school finance. In Ontario, compulsory local property assessment was included in the 1850 act as an alternative to fees and voluntary subscriptions. Largely as the result of an energetic, persistent campaign by the provincial superintendent of education, Egerton Ryerson, 96 per cent of Ontario's school districts had voluntarily adopted compulsory assessment by 1871, when provincial legislation finally terminated the local option. Provincial grants for teachers' salaries in Prince Edward Island were conditional on the adoption of compulsory local assessment after 1852, although the condition was not strictly enforced until 1877, and in any case the provincial grant directly to teachers (based on two-thirds to four-fifths of a provincial minimum salary scale) covered 70 to 80 per cent of the costs of education in the nineteenth century and 30 to 40 per cent prior to the Second World War. In New Brunswick the option of compulsory assessment included in the 1852 act was little used, and the provincial share of school financing was 44 per cent in 1871.[17] Even after the 1871 act made compulsory assessment the required method for local school finance, difficulties in implementing the law continued for several years, and at the turn of the century the provincial government was still the source of 27 per cent of school board revenues. Under the British Columbia Public Schools Act of 1872, the provincial government paid all operating costs and local boards built the schools. The cities of Vancouver, Victoria, Nanaimo, and New Westminster were required to pay one-third of teachers' salaries beginning in 1888, and one-half in 1891, in addition to the total costs for school sites, buildings, and maintenance. The provincial government then extended this requirement to other urban centres (1901) and rural municipalities (1906), although not to the smallest rural school districts, with the result that the provincial share of the costs of education declined steadily from 79 per cent in 1899–1900 to 30 per cent in 1932–3.[18]

Provincial departments of education in the nineteenth century closely regulated the activities of school boards, setting out procedures for annual school meetings, budget preparation, and grant requests and standards for school site selection, construction, maintenance, and equipment.[19] Departmental regulations also determined who taught school and what they taught. Provincial training colleges educated teachers, and provincial licences were required to teach in public schools. To ensure that young people attended school, provincial legislation set minimum requirements for school attendance. In 1871, for example, Ontario children aged seven to twelve were required to attend school four months a year; by 1921 children eight to sixteen were required to attend elementary school for the full school year.[20] Provincial regulations authorized textbooks and determined courses of study at every level. Provincial inspectors regularly visited schools, observed and questioned pupils and teachers, and reported their findings and recommendations to the provincial superintendent. Provincial examinations at the end of elementary school and high school determined who was eligible to proceed to the next stage of education. In his survey of Canadian education at the end of the First World War, Sandiford concluded

> The course of study throughout any province is remarkably uniform. The department of education takes pride in making it so. The syllabus is seldom suggestive; it is almost invariably prescriptive and frequently restrictive, that is, subjects outside the official syllabus may not be taught ... A few enlightened inspectors permit teachers to fit the course of study to local conditions, but this is the exception and against the rule; no latitude in regard to the course of study is the order of the day.[21]

Provincial grant policies were calculated to expand local financial support for schools, and in particular for projects favoured by the provincial department. Flat grants helped school boards to meet their basic costs of paying teachers and maintaining schools, and there were special grants for poor districts. Most provinces also required municipalities to establish municipal school funds, sustained by a levy on local property, from which grants were made to school districts located within municipal boundaries. Provincial departments of education employed an extensive array of percentage grants to stimulate local expenditures in support of favoured school improvements, especially libraries and laboratories, pupil conveyance, more highly qualified teachers, and more specialized curriculum developments such as manual training and domestic science.

A tenuous balance of regulation and stimulation characterized the original relationship between central governance and local administration in nineteenth-century Canadian public education. Under the model of tutelary superintendence, first developed by Ryerson in Canada West and subsequently applied in all provinces except for Quebec and Newfoundland, the educational duties of local school trustees and teachers, and the penalties for failure to perform them, were defined by the central authority.[22] The procedures for informing and regulating local administration succeeded in bringing a large realm of educational activity under central supervision. Bruce Curtis has summarized the effect of the Common Schools Act of 1850 in Canada West:

> Hundreds of thousands of students, over five thousand teachers, fifteen thousand school trustees, hundreds of township school superintendents, members of county, town, city, village and township councils, justices of the peace, clergy and others in Canada West were implicated in educational organization and practice by the time of the first systematic revision of the Act in 1871. Much of this educational activity was framed and regulated by less than ten people working out of the education office in Toronto, in conjunction with the nine members of the Council of Public Instruction and the staff of the Normal School.[23]

The chief superintendent's control depended in part on his authority to disburse and withhold school funds on the basis of local performance, but it also depended on the willingness of local officials to comply with central directives. Ryerson's role as superintendent has been well described as 'the public instructor' of teachers and trustees.[24] He attached enormous importance to informing and advising local authorities, explaining their responsibilities, and arbitrating local disputes. There was a pronounced difference in spirit, if not in practice, between this tutelary central superintendence and the Benthamite model of administrative agency, let alone the Weberian model of bureaucratic administration. Similarly, chief superintendents in other provinces depended ultimately on their powers of persuasion and leadership rather than the imperatives and sanctions of bureaucratic regulation.

Thus, the regulations of these tutelary superintendents were intended to impose a central vision of educational progress and prohibit anti-educational behaviour by local trustees and teachers, but they also were designed to inform and persuade trustees and teachers, who had limited skills and little knowledge, what needed to be done to maintain their schools and teach their pupils. Similarly, percentage grants were intended to stimulate reluctant local boards and ratepayers to expand the quantity and quality of the schooling in their districts. In cities and towns, as local professional school administrations became established central departmental supervision could be slowly reduced. In small school districts, however, where local professional administration was not feasible, the unending cycle of poorly qualified teachers and trustees turned tutelary superintendence into a permanent condition of administrative agency that would only be escaped by fundamentally reorganizing the basic unit of rural school administration.

Administrative Tutelage in Urban School Districts

In cities and towns the original provisions for small school districts were very soon abandoned in favour of integrated school boards with jurisdiction over all elementary and, eventually, also secondary schools within the municipal boundaries. In 1847 school sections in the cities of Canada West were amalgamated under city school boards, with their members at first appointed by municipal councils and then, after 1850, elected. The Winnipeg school board, originally established as Winnipeg Protestant School District Number 10 with three elected trustees in 1871, was expanded to twelve elected members in 1876 and given authority to appoint, and pay, its own school inspector. Trustees on the four city school boards established in 1888 in British Columbia initially were appointed, four by the city council and three by the provincial cabinet; after 1901 they were elected. In the Maritime provinces, by contrast, the joint appointment of city and town school boards by municipal councils and the provincial cabinet continued until the reorganization of regional school divisions in New Brunswick (1967) and Prince Edward Island (1972), while in Nova Scotia an amendment to the School Board Membership Act in 1978 provided for one-third of urban trustees to be elected.

These larger urban school districts operated rather differently from the small rural districts. They were authorized to establish their own administrative staffs, headed by a city inspector or superintendent, and consequently were exempted from provincial inspection. For example, the Toronto board appointed James L. Hughes as its first professional inspector of schools in 1874. A disciple of Friedrich Froebel, the German educational theorist who was founder of the kindergarten, Hughes worked tirelessly until his retirement in 1913 to improve school attendance, raise teachers' qualifications, establish kindergarten classes, and introduce manual training to the senior elementary curriculum. Similarly, cities and towns in Manitoba were authorized to appoint their own inspectors in 1876, and British Columbia cities were authorized to appoint superintendents under the 1901 act.

In comparison with rural school districts, city and town school districts had important political and educational resources: sizeable population and an adequate tax base, civic leadership concerned to promote local educational expansion, several schools including both elementary and secondary education, and a small but growing cadre of professional staff. City and town school boards did not easily or quickly escape the confines of provincial departmental regulation in the late nineteenth and early twentieth centuries, but they provided the nascent model of a functional partnership between central authorities and school boards that later became the norm for school district reorganization in rural areas.

Clerical Tutelage in Quebec and Newfoundland

As the first superintendent in Canada East Jean-Baptiste Meilleur, like Ryerson in Canada West, seems to have conceived the relationship between the central educational authority and local school commissions as one of policy tutelage. Like Ryerson, for example, Meilleur was a forceful advocate of compulsory local property taxation to finance public schools. A provision for compulsory property taxation was imposed in 1841, removed in 1845, restored in 1846, and again made optional in 1849. During what is known as 'la guerre des éteignoirs,' taxpayers resisted the 1846 law by withdrawing children from school, electing unqualified commissioners, threatening opponents, and even burning schools. The resistance eventually faded, thanks to the leadership of the superintendent of education and the influence of the church – for example, the archbishop of Quebec imposed an interdict on one parish until compulsory taxation was accepted – and compulsory property taxation became effective throughout Canada East during the 1850s.[25] Meilleur's advocacy of compulsory rates weakened his political authority as superintendent, however, and, following his resignation because of political pressures in 1855, the central educational authority proved increasingly unable to enforce its will against church authority, whether wielded against the centre or through local school commissions.

With the establishment of the confessional Council of Public Instruction as central governing authority, school commissions in Quebec came to enjoy considerable administrative, educational, and financial autonomy.[26] They determined the school tax rate based on the valuation of property within their districts; appointed, paid, and dismissed teachers; and under the supervision of the Catholic and Protestant denominational committees of the council regulated courses of study in their schools. Under the Catholic committee of the Council of Public Instruction the majority of school commissions acquiesced to direction by the church; and issues of power, influence, and control over local education rarely arose: 'it was clear to those concerned that the Church was the ultimate moral and temporal authority in all matters related to Quebec education.'[27] The relationship of Catholic school commissions and the

Catholic committee fitted, with little controversy, in both law and practice, a model of clerical tutelage. By contrast, the Protestant committee of the Council of Public Instruction operated more as a council of civic notables drawn from the Quebec Protestant community. The Protestant committee represented the common interests of the Protestant school commissions and coordinated their few joint enterprises, leaving Protestant school commissions with substantial communal autonomy.

The government of Newfoundland first appointed inspectors in 1843 to visit schools and make reports on their condition, 'the character and description of the master or mistress,' and the proficiency of their pupils.[28] Inspection was sporadic, however, until 1858, when two inspectors, one Roman Catholic and the other Protestant, were appointed and regular annual reports were submitted to the legislature. After the 1874 act divided the Protestant school boards between Anglican and Methodist (and after 1892, Salvation Army), the work of inspection was carried out mainly by the denominational superintendents. Their reports were filled with recommendations for improving Newfoundland schools, but their practical emphasis was examination of pupils and correction of teachers.[29] The 1920 act that established the Department of Education authorized eleven supervising inspectors, but no appointments were made until 1935.

Hence, during most of the pre-Confederation era school boards in Newfoundland were highly autonomous of state control. Legislative grants were divided among school boards on the basis of denominational affiliations reported in the census. In their annual reports denominational superintendents criticized weak teaching, poor learning, and inadequate facilities, but there was no direct institutional mechanism for enforcement of public accountability. Indeed, except for the personal influence of denominational superintendents and, in the case of Roman Catholic school boards, the hierarchy of the church, no means of central regulation existed until the formation of the Bureau of Education in 1927. Members of school boards were appointed by the government on the recommendation of denominational superintendents; the Education Act required that one be the most senior clergyman of that denomination in the school district. The boards were empowered to run elementary education within their districts and, subject to the approval of the superintendent, establish high schools. Boards were authorized to appoint and dismiss teachers and prescribe courses of studies and textbooks, but the Council of Higher Education, established in 1893 and comprising the denominational superintendents and the heads of denominational colleges in St John's, prescribed the syllabus and set external examinations for upper grades in all schools.[30]

LIBERAL PUBLIC PHILOSOPHY AND THE GOVERNANCE OF NINETEENTH-CENTURY PUBLIC EDUCATION

The British North America Act (now the Constitution Act) of 1867 provided that the colonies of British North America would 'be federally united into one Dominion under the Crown of the United Kingdom of Great Britain and Ireland and with a Constitution similar in Principle to that of the United Kingdom.' Section 93 of the BNA Act assigned to provincial legislatures exclusive jurisdiction to make laws in relation to education. The constitutional entrenchment of education in the jurisdiction of the provinces opened the way for different paths of provincial institutional and policy development. That potential for difference was certainly realized in distinctive regimes of education based on religion and language. In forms of governance, however, as with school organization and curriculum, there was much less variation. Outside Quebec and Newfoundland, educational governance in Canada was founded on a liberal theory of political accountability based on parliamentary government and ministerial responsibility and a liberal concept of local governments as the administrative agents of central authorities.

Liberal principles of parliamentary government and ministerial responsibility determined the constitution of provincial educational authority in the nineteenth century, but there were subtle regional variations in patterns of constitutional development and conceptions of political accountability. Egerton Ryerson succeeded for a time in sustaining a conception of civic trusteeship that purported to separate colonial educational policy, lodged in a central board of education and the office of chief superintendent, from partisan legislative politics. Following Ryerson's retirement, however, central educational authority in Ontario was quickly reconstructed on the conventional liberal principle of individual ministerial responsibility. In the western provinces the original models of civic trusteeship were replaced first by collective ministerial responsibility and then by individual ministerial responsibility. In the Maritimes, from the outset, central educational authority focused political accountability collectively on the executive council acting as a council of public instruction, and the introduction of individual ministerial responsibility was delayed until the 1930s and 1940s.

Quebec and Newfoundland were exceptions to the hegemony of political liberal ideas in the constitution of central educational authority. Liberal ideas were certainly evident in the original design of Quebec education, the commitments of the first superintendents, the campaign for compulsory local taxation, and the introduction of ministerial responsibility in 1867. The liberal project soon foundered, however, as the Council of Public Instruction, divided between Roman Catholic and Protestant committees, took control of central policy-making and superintendence, and the office of minister of public instruction was dropped from the provincial cabinet. Similarly, in Newfoundland a belated attempt in 1920 to establish ministerial responsibility for education soon collapsed under pressure from the entrenched regime of denominational educational authorities.

Local school boards were not initially conceived as administrative agents of provincial departments of education. In the first phase of the foundation of education, working with a theory of civic trusteeship, central boards of education and their chief superintendents tended to assume a role of educational leadership and local stimulation. In this view, school boards were political institutions of local communities rather than administrative agents of provincial departments of education. The central board and chief superintendent provided policy direction and legal framework, but the priority of central educational authority during the pioneering phase of the establishment of public education was to stimulate local communities to elect trustees, build schools, hire teachers, enrol their children, and vote tax levies.

The triumph of ministerial responsibility and the subsequent expansion of provincial departments of education beginning in the late nineteenth century altered the relationship between central and local educational authorities. Central leadership gave way to central regulation. Communal autonomy, for example, with respect to language of instruction, was steadily eroded by the proliferation of provincial departmental regulations, implemented by cadres of provincial inspectors, which aimed to control all phases of local education. In cities, where school boards had their own professional administrative staff, local authorities exercised marginal discretion in managing their schools. In rural districts school boards were strictly supervised administrative agents of provincial departments of education.

The liberal constitution of local educational authorities in the nineteenth century thus incorporated a severely restricted conception of local democracy, which gave priority to efficiency and effectiveness of school boards as administrative agents of provincial departments rather than democratic participation of citizens in their local self-government. In the twentieth century administrative efficiency and effectiveness would be the motives for reorganizing small rural school districts into large school divisions. That reorganization would also expose the tension between local administration and local democracy inherent in liberal theories that combine parliamentary and local government.

6

Economic Liberalism and Secondary Educational Policy: Occupational Selection and Accessibility of Education

Public education can be designed as civic education to serve the formation of political nationality and the preservation of political order. Especially under the liberal democratic conception of political order based on representative government, public education is assigned the vital task of teaching the moral standards of the community and the rights and duties of democratic citizenship. Public education also can be designed to serve the requirements of industrial expansion. An industrial economy needs workers able to apply the latest advances in modern technology, managers with specialized professional education and skills to organize production, and researchers who can create new technology. The educational purposes of civic education and occupational selection are not incompatible; on the contrary, at least during an early stage of industrial expansion and economic nationalism, they can be highly complementary.

Historically, the Canadian political ethos assumed that national wealth and individual opportunity depended mainly on the promotion of economic progress and preservation of social order. Access to land and natural resources, opportunities for investment and employment, and protection of life and property were the essential elements of economic wealth and opportunity, at least until the first decades of the twentieth century. From this political liberal perspective public education certainly served the cause of social order, but was not expected to make an important contribution to increasing either national economic wealth or individual economic opportunity.

With industrialization came demands for reforms that would fit public education to the requirements, and opportunities, of the new occupational structure. From the economic liberal perspective the main purpose of the state school system was no longer simply the education of virtuous citizens; it must now include responsibility for the distribution of occupational opportunities.

Policy-making attention shifted correspondingly from elementary to secondary and then to post-secondary education, levels which were seen to be more concerned with communicating knowledge and skills specific to different occupational classes. At the same time, the nineteenth-century liberal idea of individual economic opportunity was redefined to include educational opportunity. In contrast with mass elementary education, secondary education with its more occupationally specific knowledge and skills did bestow economic advantages on the individuals who got it. As access to secondary school increasingly became an important condition for access to better jobs, the accessibility of educational opportunities for anyone able to benefit from them came to be regarded as an integral part of the meaning of equal opportunity.

A public policy of uniform secondary education, which was adopted incrementally in the late nineteenth century, prevailed in all provinces except Quebec and Newfoundland by the turn of the century. As the idea of designing secondary education for occupational selection gained ground in the twentieth century, this policy of uniform secondary education was challenged successively by advocates of partite systems and multilateral schools. These very different types of secondary school organization each claimed to secure educational effectiveness and efficiency, but they incorporated a concept of educational justice as segmental equality that was very different from the equal educational lots of uniform secondary organization and curriculum.

MASS SECONDARY EDUCATION AND EQUAL OPPORTUNITY: PARTITE SYSTEMS AND BILATERAL SCHOOLS

Two closely related but distinct approaches to reform of secondary education were promoted in the early twentieth century. First, in concert with business interests and organized labour, educational reformers who wanted to reorganize public education to fit the needs of occupational selection for an industrial economy campaigned for vocational secondary education as an alternative to academic secondary education. Focusing on the organization of secondary education in city school districts, their preferred model was a partite system, in which specialized vocational secondary schools were educational institutions separate from conventional academic high schools. Second, as enrolments in academic high schools continued to expand, educational reformers who were concerned to adapt the secondary curriculum to fit the needs of mass education pressed their case to develop a general secondary program as an alternative to the traditional academic program. Essentially these reformers proposed to combine academic and general programs in bilateral secondary schools.

Despite considerable initial success in several Canadian cities, the development of specialized vocational schools was stunted between the wars by their failure to meet basic political and educational tests of efficiency, effectiveness, legitimacy, and justice. At the same time general secondary education remained largely undeveloped as an alternative to the academic program. Only when the three streams of academic, general, and vocational education were combined in the concept of multilateral secondary schools was a proposal for educational reform reached that was sufficiently potent to displace uniform education as the hegemonic form of secondary school organization and curriculum in Canada.

Secondary School Organization for Occupational Selection: The Concept of Partite Systems

The leading advocate of partite systems was John Seath, superintendent of education in Ontario. In his 1911 report on industrial education Seath urged the inclusion of manual training and household science as general subjects in elementary school.[1] For the relatively small number of young people who would remain in school after age fourteen, Seath proposed two types of vocational programs in addition to the academic secondary program. First, 'general industrial schools' would provide a two-year basic course in wood and metal shop work, English, practical mathematics, and science, followed by 'special industrial school,' which would offer specialized courses in trades and industrial occupations. Second, 'technical high schools' (or technical departments) would prepare students for jobs requiring specialized technical knowledge and responsibilities greater than those of skilled mechanics. Their curricula would involve two years of common technical education and two years spent in specialized courses. Seath was adamant that industrial education be strictly segregated from academic programs.

> The mathematics, science, English, and work-shop courses must be wholly separate from the corresponding classes in the academic High Schools, and must be taught by teachers who have been specially prepared for the work. At present, in the so-called technical High Schools and High School departments, these subjects are almost invariably taught by the ordinary members of High School staffs, whose chief duties and whose ambitions are connected with the academic work of the school. They do not possess the special knowledge that would enable them to correlate the subjects with the practice of the industrial school; and, even if they did acquire this knowledge, it would be futile to expect them as a class to be zealous for a department in which they have no vital interest. As a matter of convenience and economy, the industrial classes we are

now contemplating might be taken in the same building as one of the other schools; but they should be under the control of an independent principal ... The future of the industrial school should not be imperilled by intimate associations, with schools whose main object hitherto has been the preparation for the professions and the universities.[2]

In its 1913 report Canada's Royal Commission on Industrial Training and Technical Education strongly recommended expansion of industrial training and technical education in Canadian high schools. In part, its argument rested on the imperative of economic growth. When apprenticeship was disappearing and major industrial nations such as Britain, Germany, and the United States were rapidly improving their technical schools and colleges, continued industrial expansion in Canada depended on transforming Canadian secondary education from its heavily academic orientation to a balance of academic and technical education.[3] The commission also argued that the needs of individuals for knowledge and skills in their future vocations or occupations should be taken into account in determining courses of study. For the commission, secondary education was understood as comprising two types, both having a distinctive occupational orientation. The prevailing secondary education provided preparation for entry to 'the learned professions, other professional occupations, or the leisure class'; but secondary vocational education also should be provided for 'those persons who are to follow manual industrial occupations, producing occupations such as agriculture, conserving occupations such as housekeeping, and commercial and business occupations.'[4]

The royal commission left no doubt that its argument rested on a fundamentally different conception of equality of opportunity in education from that inherent in uniform secondary education.

Sometimes an idea prevails that a scheme of education provides equality of opportunity by letting all who desire have access to the same classes. Equality of opportunity, to mean anything real, must have regard to the varying needs, tastes, abilities and after lives of the pupils. To be able to attend schools, whose courses are provided chiefly for those whose education can be continued until 18 or 20 years of age, does not ensure any sort of equality of preparation for occupation or for living to those who are compelled to leave at 14. Equality of opportunity to enter a school designed to prepare leaders, is not what is needed and is not what is wanted by the parents of most of the children. Equality of opportunity, to be sincere and operative, must offer opportunities of education which will serve the pupils not all the same thing, but will serve them all alike in preparing them for the occupations which they are to follow and the lives which they are to lead.[5]

According to the commission, 'The ideal or perfect system would provide for the participation in the opportunities for education of all individuals according to their ability, the occupation they are to follow, and the place they are to occupy in the State.'[6] The commission recognized that technical secondary education could be provided through a technical department of a general high school or in a separate technical high school.[7] It did not state a preference for partite systems as opposed to multilateral schools in its report, but in the early twentieth century city school boards and superintendents, as well as provincial departments of education, clearly favoured separate academic and vocational high schools.

Partite Systems in Canadian Cities

Among the provinces Ontario had by far the most developed system of vocational high schools.[8] Ontario's Technical Education Act of 1897 authorized the trustees of any high school board or board of education to establish a technical school or change an existing high school into a technical school. Based on John Seath's extensive survey of technical education in the United States and Europe, the Industrial Education Act of 1911 provided for general industrial training for early school-leavers, establishment of technical schools or technical departments in high schools, and provincial grants for both day and evening technical classes. Within the framework of the 1897 and 1911 acts, the Toronto board of education took the lead in establishing separate technical and commercial high schools. The Toronto Technical School, which had begun operation in 1891 under a board of business and labour leaders separate from the public school and collegiate institute boards, was brought under the authority of the Toronto board of education in 1904. Toronto Central Technical School was opened in 1915, the following year commercial classes were consolidated in the Central High School of Commerce, and after the First World War Danforth Technical School and Eastern High School of Commerce were added. Outside Toronto, separate vocational high schools were established in Hamilton, London, Brantford, and Ottawa. Under the provisions of the 1911 act there were eleven technical and industrial day schools operating in Ontario by 1918 and sixty-two in 1939.[9] Enrolments in technical secondary courses reached 30 per cent of the total enrolment in secondary schools between the wars.[10]

Outside Ontario, there were only two separate vocational high schools in the Maritime provinces before the Second World War – vocational schools were established in Carleton County (1918) and Saint John (1926) under the New Brunswick Vocational Education Act of 1918 – and none in Quebec. In the four western provinces vocational high schools were established in each of the main urban centres. The Winnipeg school board had started a commercial department in the Winnipeg collegiate institute in 1896, and, in response to the recommendations of the Commission of Inquiry into Aims and Methods in Industrial Education appointed in 1910, as well as pressure to expand facilities for secondary education, two technical high schools (Kelvin and St John's) were opened in 1912. The academic programs consistently proved more attractive to students, however, and the Winnipeg technical schools soon lost their distinctiveness as specialized technical high schools.[11] Vancouver (later King Edward) High School introduced a commercial program in 1905 and soon added classes in manual training (1908) and domestic science (1909). In 1918 the commercial course was relocated in the Fairview High School of Commerce, and in 1921 the technical program was transferred to the new Vancouver Technical School.[12] In the early 1920s technical high schools were also opened in New Westminster, Victoria, and Trail. By 1913 Calgary had organized a commercial department in its high school, and a technical high school opened in Edmonton, with an enrolment of twelve students. Subsequently, in Calgary, Edmonton, and Lethbridge one high school in each city concentrated on commercial training and another focused on technical subjects such as carpentry, electricity, metal work, and drafting. In Saskatchewan the Vocational Education Act, which was passed in 1919 as a response to the availability of federal categorical grants, offered to pay school boards 50 to 75 per cent of equipment costs and 50 per cent of teachers' salaries if they established commercial, industrial, or home economics courses. Four city high schools did add such courses to their academic programs in the 1920s, and technical collegiate institutes were opened in Regina, Saskatoon, and Moose Jaw in the early 1930s. Their total enrolments remained fairly flat over the years, however (1931–2, 2,989; 1941–2, 3,103; 1951–2, 2,705), and Saskatchewan in 1945 became one of the first provinces to make an official commitment to multilateral secondary schools.

Political and Educational Deficiencies of Partite Systems

Separate academic, commercial, and technical secondary schools had strong advocates among Canadian educators in the 1910s and 1920s; nonetheless, they failed to gain general acceptance as public educational institutions. Because partite systems were not feasible outside larger cities, their potential for expansion was strictly limited. A survey of educational needs carried out by the Canada and Newfoundland Education Association in 1943 remarked that across Canada only fourteen cities had populations over fifty thousand.[13]

In small cities and towns, technical and commercial education could be provided, if at all, only by setting up vocational departments in academic high schools and collegiate institutes. During the 1920s and 1930s expansion of vocational education occurred primarily through the formation of technical and commercial departments in academic high schools. In larger cities, where there were specialized technical and commercial high schools, they were generally stigmatized as inferior to academic high schools. Parents and students quickly understood that the programs offered in both academic and vocational secondary schools were class-specific and class-defining and that economic opportunities were consistently superior for graduates of academic programs. As a consequence, enrolment demands on academic high schools continued unabated and specialized technical and commercial high schools were pressed to extend their offerings to include more academic secondary education.

Thus, specialized vocational and academic high schools in partite systems failed the tests of effectiveness and efficiency. From the outset educational planners and policy-makers recognized that for reasons of effectiveness and efficiency partite systems were necessarily restricted to large cities. As professional experience with vocational schools and departments as instruments of mass secondary education was acquired through the 1920s and 1930s, educational planners and policy-makers also came to realize the enduring public resistance to vocational secondary education. As long as high school entrance examinations were designed to set basic minimal standards for continuing to secondary education rather than select an academic elite, parents and their children who had a choice between academic and vocational secondary education overwhelmingly opted for academic schools and programs. To counter this parental and public prejudice many professional educators began to see multilateral schools with separate academic and vocational departments as a way to bring all students into the same school and thus facilitate their guidance into academic or vocational programs, whichever was judged appropriate to their abilities.

For parents and their children, specialized vocational high schools in partite systems also failed the tests of legitimacy and justice. Outside the closed circles of professional educators and business and labour interest associations like the Canadian Manufacturers Association and the Trades and Labour Congress, which supported separate vocational high schools, partite systems were seen as foreclosing economic opportunities for those who chose vocational rather than academic education. As long as parents and children were free to choose, they opted overwhelmingly for the superior economic opportunities offered by academic secondary education. Accordingly, where educational choices within partite systems were restricted, whether by intent through organizational design or by lack of parental resources, the partite system's failure of the test of legitimacy was compounded by the perceived injustice of its distribution of educational opportunities.

Academic versus General Programs in Bilateral Schools

Egerton Ryerson had expressed doubts about the utility, even the feasibility, of converting grammar schools, with their aristocratic and academic bias, into high schools serving all classes. Over the last quarter of the nineteenth century many other professional educators criticized the narrow academic curriculum of public secondary schools and their fixation with preparing students for matriculation examinations. The expansion of secondary school enrolments early in the twentieth century heightened these longstanding concerns about broadening the secondary educational curriculum beyond preparation for university and normal school. No one advocated termination of academic secondary education. Rather, the reformers argued, the curriculum of secondary schools should be broadened to provide a general secondary education appropriate to the needs, aptitudes and interests of the majority of students, for whom high school was the last stage of formal education.

In addition to the development of separate vocational programs, programs that differentiated between academic and general education were introduced from the 1910s to the 1930s. In Ontario the regulations for secondary school programs were revised to recognize seven programs: matriculation, normal school entrance, general, commercial, manual training, household science, and agriculture. Significantly, the most controversial changes were the separation of matriculation from normal school entrance and dropping Latin and a modern language as compulsory for normal school entrance.[14] A major revision of Alberta's curriculum in 1922 provided for six courses: normal school entrance, university matriculation, agricultural, commercial, technical, and general. Perhaps the strongest attack on the academic high school came from Putman and Weir in their 1925 report on schools in British Columbia: 'So far it has been a class institution with a mathematical and literary bias.'[15] According to them, secondary schools had to broaden their programs of pre-vocational training beyond a narrowly academic program leading to law, teaching, medicine, engineering, banking, and nursing. Secondary schools had to respond to the technical needs of modern society, take responsibility for vocational misfits, and teach that all work was honourable. Putman and Weir's recommendations for change emphasized a reorganization of school grades from eight grades in elementary schools and four in high schools to six in elementary schools, three in junior high schools, and three in high schools. Junior high ('intermediate') schools would offer a common program of basic subjects plus options to meet the 'varying powers and widely different tastes' of students aged twelve to fifteen; senior high schools would provide a common core with optional subjects in a four-track curriculum comprising general, normal school entrance, commercial, and university matriculation programs. In the subsequent revision of British Columbia's curriculum in 1929–30 a credit system was implemented, which differentiated between junior matriculation (requiring provincial departmental examinations and restricting students to six to twelve elective credits out of 120) and a general course (which had no external examinations and provided for seventy-four elective credits).

Despite the diversity of secondary school programs formally recognized in provincial regulations, in practice most secondary schools in the 1920s and 1930s offered only academic programs that led to matriculation and normal school entrance. Rising enrolments in secondary education continued to be concentrated in these academic programs. In Alberta, for example, in spite of its being based on an unprecedentedly wide consultative process, the 1922 revised program found little acceptance.[16] There were separate commercial and technical high schools in Calgary, Edmonton, and Lethbridge, but everywhere else in the province high schools provided a combined normal school entrance and matriculation course and possibly a general course.[17] The numbers of diplomas granted in the different courses in 1935 show the persistent academic bias of secondary education in Alberta between the wars: normal entrance, 1,532; university matriculation, 745; technical, 7; agricultural, 0; commercial, 117; and general 57. In Manitoba a high school leaving course was instituted as part of the curriculum revision of 1928, but it won little acceptance outside Winnipeg. In rural areas schools were too small to offer more than one course so they chose to offer the university entrance program.[18]

In the Maritime provinces secondary education continued to be almost exclusively academic until after the Second World War. Departmental policies from the 1930s to the 1950s aimed at building rural and regional high schools, not to provide distinctively rural or occupational education, but to offer rural children an academic education comparable to that available in urban centres. The 1933 curriculum revision in Nova Scotia did add a number of electives to what had been an extremely rigid, academically oriented program. Industrial arts, home economics, commercial subjects, and agriculture were among the new options, but these subjects were regarded as part of the student's general education until 1942 when a specifically vocational commercial program was introduced. In Prince Edward Island students who wished to continue into secondary education after ten years of elementary school enrolled in a three-year academic program at Prince of Wales College. Revision of the New Brunswick curriculum in 1939 established three options to the academic program – home economics, agriculture, and industrial – but the new programs remained primarily academic in focus, restricted in their vocational options, and limited in their availability to urban centres until after the Second World War.

OCCUPATIONAL SELECTION AND ACCESSIBILITY OF EDUCATION IN MULTILATERAL SCHOOLS

During and immediately following the Second World War, official policy studies undertaken as part of planning for the post-war reconstruction of Canadian education unanimously condemned the segregation of academic and vocational education, domination of mass secondary education by a narrowly academic curriculum, and systemic inequalities in the provision of education that resulted from failure to provide programs appropriate to the needs of different types of students. As Canadian educational policy-makers became more concerned about the implications of partite systems for equalizing educational opportunity between urban and rural schools, as well as the adverse impact of class-divided schools on social integration, they turned with remarkable uniformity across the provinces to multilateral secondary schools.

Policy Convergence on the Concept of Multilateral Schools

In 1945 a special select committee of the Manitoba legislative assembly on education reported that almost every brief presented to it had been critical of the existing school curriculum. The complaints fell into two main groups: those concerned with equality of opportunity and those concerned with the differentiation of educational programs and practical relevance of school to life.

> In its consideration of the relation of the present programme to the needs of the pupil and of the community, the Committee found that despite all efforts to provide differentiation by means of 'options,' despite the fact that only a small percentage of the pupils proceed to the University, the college-preparatory course of the academic type still holds the field, even in face of a persistent demand for a more realistic and relevant programme. It found that within the schools, the academic tradition still prevails, maintained by the vigorous use of prescription and examination; mathematics with the traditional content, is still taught in the traditional divisions; general science is gaining ground at the elementary levels, but physics and chemistry, narrowly prescribed to

chapter and paragraph of an authorized text, reign almost unquestioned for higher grades. Despite earnest efforts of reformers to induce a wider view of education than that indicated by the study of closely detailed 'subjects' the pressure continues to be towards academic form whatever the more immediate needs of the pupils may be.[19]

The Royal Commission on Education in Ontario reached a similar conclusion in 1950. 'Evidence we have received indicates that the departmentalization of secondary education into academic and vocational education has led to invidious comparisons, in some cases a stigma has been attached to pupils attending particular types of schools. This must be rectified.'[20] According to the commission, many optional subjects had been introduced into the secondary school curriculum in Ontario, but with little effect. Analysis of secondary school examination statistics revealed that relatively few students took any examination subjects other than English, history, mathematics, science, French, and Latin. The commission concluded:

It might well be argued that, in practice, there is little more adaptation and selection of courses under our present programme than there was in the grammar schools of our forefathers. This 'choice' of subjects suggests only one conclusion: in Ontario, as elsewhere, the work of the secondary schools is dominated by requirements for entrance to the university. For the few who continue their education at university this is perhaps not unreasonable; but for the vast majority of students who ... complete their formal schooling during, or at the end of, the secondary school stage, the effect is bad. The needs of members of the latter group are so different from those of the former that no common course, crowned by uniform external school examinations, can do justice to both.[21]

The problem of Canadian secondary education, according to wartime and post-war reappraisals, was not a concept of equality of educational opportunity that focused on providing a diversity of programs to meet the needs of different types of students.[22] It was institutional. The policy of partite systems had proved inadequate on both territorial and class dimensions of equality. On the dimension of territorial equality, specialized vocational high schools were feasible only in urban centres. A policy of partite systems inevitably entailed inequalities in the provision of education between urban and rural areas. As for class equality, the segregation of students between academic and vocational high schools erected a barrier to the transfer of pupils from one course to another and had the result of stigmatizing vocational courses, which were segregated from the more prestigious academic course. As the educational policy committee of the Canada and Newfoundland Education Association commented on the partition of secondary education between academic and vocational high schools, 'such a division in education means the acceptance of a division of young people into two groups – the majority who would be given a practical training and the minority who would be educated as an intellectual elite.' The committee concluded, 'many believe that such a classification of schools and young people is based on an aristocratic concept incompatible with modern democracy.'[23]

A national survey of educational needs by the Canada and Newfoundland Education Association recommended in 1943 that the establishment of 'composite' high schools offered a solution to the problem of providing for curricular diversity in secondary schools located in smaller centres. In addition, the survey committee argued, 'Operating such a composite high school is a further step in the direction of democracy, whereas the separating of pupils in different kinds of school leads to a distinction between classes almost at the threshold of life. Schools of this type should be set up all over the country for the purpose of training truly democratic citizens.'[24] Although it did endorse a proposal of the Winnipeg school board to establish a vocational-technical high school, the 1944 select committee on education in Manitoba recommended as general provincial policy 'the establishment of a new type of school, the Composite High School, in such administrative areas as may desire to provide differentiated courses related to their needs.'[25] Similarly, the Royal Commission on Education in Ontario concluded that the best form of organization for secondary education was the multilateral secondary school with separate divisions for university preparation and vocational training.

At the end of the 1950s royal commissions in Manitoba, British Columbia, and Alberta assessed the state of secondary school organization and curricula, and all three found that vocational programs were being neglected. According to the Manitoba Royal Commission on Education, 'the dominant problem in the field of secondary education continues to be that of providing equality of opportunity.' As the commission put it, 'If equality of opportunity is to be one of the guiding principles of our educational system, the curriculum must include sufficient variety and flexibility to educate every child to the limit of his capabilities.'[26] No one disputed the importance of the matriculation program, according to the Alberta royal commission, but it was unrealistic to assume that every student was competent to follow it: 'The school should nurture and develop a wider variety of talents ... Excellence must be achieved not only in the matriculation program but in the fine arts, business education, and other vocational fields as well.'[27] Similarly, the Royal Commission on Education in British Columbia found that 'present school programmes do not adequately meet the needs of pupils of widely different levels of ability.' There were obvious limits to the provision for individual differences, 'because no public school system can provide a separate programme for each pupil, and the organization of the educational system should not be thrown into confusion by an overemphasis upon individual differences. In fact pupils are sufficiently alike that a more realistic concept for fashioning a school programme is that of group differences rather than individual differences.'[28] To accommodate such group differences, the Manitoba and British Columbia commissions both recommended that senior high schools should become multilateral schools. The Alberta commission proposed composite high schools in urban areas with regional vocational schools to serve rural areas.

Implementing the Concept of Multilateral Schools

Despite growing professional and political support for the concept of multilateral secondary schools, the vast majority of high school students in Canada continued to attend academic high schools in which their choice was limited to matriculation or general programs. The number of multilateral secondary schools rose steadily, but their rate of development varied considerably across provinces until the 1960s. Then, pushed by the need to expand facilities to accommodate a rising population of secondary students and helped by the new pot of federal funding for technical and vocational secondary education, multilateral schools rapidly became the hegemonic form of secondary education in eight of ten provinces. Although there was considerable variation in organization, as much within provinces as among them, the preferred model was a multilateral or 'composite' secondary school with a core of common courses in junior high schools and separate academic, general, and vocational educational programs in senior high schools.

Prior to the 1960s multilateral secondary schools were most widely established in the West, and here Saskatchewan gave the lead.[29] The Co-operative Commonwealth Federation government elected in 1944 adopted as its general policy the recommendation of the Canada and Newfoundland Education Association in favour of composite high schools.[30] By the mid-1950s there were thirty-nine high schools, enrolling about 39 per cent of the total secondary school population, which offered both academic and vocational courses. Seventeen of these thirty-nine schools were new composite schools built since the end of the war with financial aid under the Dominion-Provincial Vocational Schools Assistance Agreement (1945), and thirteen others resulted from extensions built to accommodate vocational classes in existing academic high schools.[31] In other western provinces the record was less impressive. A decade after the first composite high school was opened at Dauphin, twenty-eight high schools in Manitoba offered the commercial course, three offered home economics, and three the industrial course.[32] In Alberta there were ten fully composite high schools, which enrolled about 25 per cent of secondary students in the province, and the high school curriculum was still dominated by matriculation and general programs – 43 per cent of secondary students were enrolled in the matriculation program, 45 per cent in the general course, and only 11 per cent in technical, commercial, or homemaking programs.[33] Similarly, in British Columbia, the Royal Commission on Education, which reported in 1960, found that outside Vancouver most British Columbia high schools offered only an academic program and a general program.[34]

Outside the West, New Brunswick was the only province where composite high schools were well established as policy prior to the 1960s.[35] Based on a 1939 revision of the provincial curriculum into academic, home economics, industrial, and agricultural programs and the introduction of county school finance boards in 1943 to provide a consolidated tax base, New Brunswick had ten urban and twenty-four rural composite high schools in 1950. Ten more urban and twelve more rural composite high schools were opened during the 1950s. In Ontario vocational high schools declined in favour of composite schools – there were twenty-two fully composite high schools and eighteen vocational high schools in 1938–9; forty composite and fifteen vocational high schools in 1960–1 – but enrolment in composite secondary schools increased only slightly from 17.3 per cent of total enrolment in secondary programs in 1938–9 to 19.8 per cent in 1950–1 and 20.1 per cent in 1960–1.[36] The provincial policy set out in Nova Scotia's Vocational Education Act of 1953 established a partite system. Academic high schools operated by local school boards provided matriculation and general programs; vocational programs were restricted to regional vocational high schools, which operated under separate boards appointed by the province and supporting municipalities.[37] In Quebec the reorganization of the Catholic secondary curriculum in 1956 resulted in the introduction of vocational programs in secondary schools, but these programs were not substantially different from the general program and did not attract many students.[38] In Newfoundland and Prince Edward Island public secondary schools offered academic programs; vocational training was conducted in provincial trade schools and thus segregated from secondary education.[39]

The most dramatic change of policy in the early 1960s was made in Ontario. The minister of education, John Robarts, announced in August 1961 that the three existing secondary programs (general, commercial, and technical) would be reorganized into arts and science; business and commerce; and science, technology, and trades.[40] All three branches would be offered in the majority of secondary schools, thus establishing the composite school as the dominant organizational form in Ontario. Addressing the legislative assembly, Robarts explained that the 'Reorganized Plan' was intended to rectify inadequacies of the previous curriculum in relation to the diverse needs of young people, give secondary school students better occupational preparation, reduce the number of drop-outs, and shift the emphasis from what had been in many schools a single program option.[41]

Secondary school curricula in other provinces were similarly reorganized as multilateral programs in senior high schools. In Saskatchewan, for example, school grades were reorganized in 1964 from eight elementary and four secondary to six primary, three junior high, and three senior high. Senior high schools would offer a three-year matriculation course for university preparation with general course electives, a three-year preparatory course for technical institutes, a four-year combined preparatory course for university or technical institutes, an occupational preparatory course, and an adult high school course.[42] When the new British Columbia curriculum was implemented in 1965, the former university program became the academic and technology program, with separate streams for arts, science, and technology. The old general program was replaced by five programs leading to a regional vocational school, institute of technology, or directly to employment: commercial, industrial, community services, agriculture, and visual and performing arts. The Nova Scotia government announced in 1966 that it was adopting a policy of 'comprehensive' secondary education divided between junior and senior high schools, with four programs at the senior high school level: matriculation, general, business education, and vocational. Regional vocational schools would continue as separately governed institutions, but consultative committees were established to foster the operation of these schools as part of the secondary system.

Federal Government, Occupational Selection, and Accessibility of Education

The British North America Act of 1867 assigned general legislative and administrative jurisdiction over education to the provinces, but did not erect any constitutional impediment to federal expenditures for educational purposes where the provinces agreed to accept federal aid or federal transfer payments were made directly to individuals. Outside of provision of elementary and secondary education in the three areas where the federal government does have constitutional jurisdiction – public education in federal territories, federal schools for defence establishments, and federal schools for Native children – the intervention historically by the federal government into provincial jurisdiction over elementary and secondary education has consisted of a series of incentive grants designed to promote the expansion of vocational education in state elementary and secondary schools.

The Royal Commission on Industrial Training and Technical Education was appointed by the federal government in 1910 after several years of representations by business associations and trade unions, which urged federal action to promote vocational education. The final report of the royal commission recommended an annual federal contribution of three million dollars to a Dominion development fund that would be used to subsidize provincial initiatives to expand vocational education. The first response by the federal government was a program of conditional aid to agricultural education through the Agricultural Aid Act of 1912, which provided half a million dollars; the next year the Agricultural Instruction Act extended the total aid offered to ten million dollars over a ten-year period. In 1919 the federal Technical Education Act provided for a further ten million dollars over ten years. Only Ontario had used its entire allotment when this act expired in 1929, however; four extensions, until 1944, were required before all provinces had claimed their shares. The Vocational Education Act of 1931, which authorized $750,000 annually, was not implemented because of the fiscal crisis caused by the Great Depression. The Vocational Training Co-ordination Act of 1942 provided for agreements between the federal Department of Labour and provincial departments of education, under which thirty million dollars was made available to the provinces for vocational secondary schools, including ten million for capital expenditures between 1945 and 1952 and two million annually for maintenance and operating costs.

Undoubtedly the single most influential intervention by the federal government in support of vocational secondary education came in 1960; it was also the last. The Technical and Vocational Training Assistance Act authorized extensive programs of federal aid towards capital costs of building and equipping facilities for secondary, post-secondary, and adult vocational training. Under this act $950 million in conditional federal aid was transferred to provincial governments to add vocational departments to existing academic high schools and build new composite high schools to accommodate the expanding secondary school enrolments of the 1960s. The Adult Occupational Training Act, which replaced TVTA in 1967, included no provision for federal aid to vocational education in secondary schools. Under the 1967 act federal aid became restricted to adult occupational training, through programs negotiated with provincial agencies, mainly directed at unemployed workers in the regular labour force and delivered through post-secondary community colleges.

MULTILATERAL SECONDARY SCHOOLS: EDUCATIONAL IDEOLOGY AND POLITICAL CHOICE

In the 1950s and 1960s the multilateral secondary school was not a new policy option. Curricular distinctions among general, matriculation, commercial, and technical programs dated from the beginning of public secondary education in the late nineteenth century. The introduction of vocational departments in academic high schools and academic courses in vocational high schools in practice blurred the formal distinctions of partite systems. Moreover, a considerable debate over the relative merits of partite systems versus multilateral schools had engaged professional educators in the United States and to a lesser extent Canada since the turn of the century.

What emerged in the late 1950s and early 1960s was a strong consensus within provincial educational policy communities across the country that equality of opportunity in education – understood as young people freely choosing to enrol in secondary programs, subjects, and courses appropriate to their individual interests, needs, and abilities – required a commitment to the institutionalization of multilateral or composite secondary schools as the hegemonic form of Canadian secondary education. Without such a policy commitment student choices would inevitably continue to be distorted by a combination of strong social pressures to choose the academic program and poor accessibility of alternative vocational programs.

What is remarkable is not simply that such a policy commitment was made, and effectively implemented, but that an essentially similar policy commitment was made and implemented in eight of ten provinces. By the mid-1960s only Newfoundland and Prince Edward Island held out against the national trend to multilateral secondary education.[43] In part, this convergence of secondary school organization and curricula on multilateral secondary education was caused by the availability of federal funding to pay for operating and capital expenditures of secondary technical and vocational education. Nonetheless, federal funding under the Technical and Vocational Training Assistance Act (1960) did not force provincial departments of education to build composite high schools. TVTA funding could just as easily have been used to build separate vocational secondary schools and develop partite systems. The choice of school organization for vocational secondary education belonged to provincial officials and school boards, and they chose multilateral schools.

7

Occupational Selection and Accessibility of Education: Institutional Reforms and Public Resources

As public secondary education became a recognized instrument for occupational selection and training, a low level of public concern about inequalities among school districts, which had characterized the general attitude towards the original public elementary schools, was replaced by a growing belief that environmental factors – in particular, urban residence and taxable property, both unrelated to individual merit – were having a chronic adverse impact on the creation and distribution of educational and occupational opportunities. Expansion and reorganization of uniform secondary schools into multilateral high schools, which would equalize educational opportunities, were seen to depend on consolidation of small school districts into larger regional educational authorities and establishment of provincial equalizing grants. From the 1930s onwards district reorganization and provincial financing were central issues of educational policy in Canada, culminating in a burst of institutional reform during the 1960s that largely succeeded in realizing the goal of equal access for rural and urban pupils to secondary schooling.

The allocation of public resources and institutional reforms that were needed to equalize occupational selection and the accessibility of education altered provincial approaches to governing education. Provincial governments permanently expanded their commitment of public resources to elementary and secondary education. Reorganization of school districts and reform of provincial financing of education gradually modified the working relationship between provincial departments of education and school boards, from one of administrative agency to one of policy tutelage. During the 1960s the federal government also gave an important financial boost to the reorganization of secondary education in multilateral schools. In contrast with the provincial governments, however, the federal government simply facilitated the completion of a trend in policy development that was already in progress, and then retreated from any permanent role in elementary and secondary educational policy.

ACCESSIBILITY OF EDUCATION AND INSTITUTIONAL REFORMS

In contrast with partite systems, which were restricted to large cities, building and operating multilateral or composite secondary schools was feasible in smaller cities and towns. Beginning in the 1920s and 1930s improvements in rural roads and school busing made it increasingly practical to equalize educational opportunities by transporting rural pupils to multilateral schools located in regional centres. The introduction of regional multilateral secondary schools depended on two basic institutional reforms in order to equalize conditions between rural and city school districts: first, consolidation of small rural school sections into larger regional or county school divisions, at least for purposes of secondary education; and, second, provincial equalization of financial capacities between poor rural districts that had to rely primarily on farm property assessment and relatively wealthy city districts where the tax base included sizeable business as well as residential property.

Reorganization of School Districts

From the late 1930s to the early 1970s the basic unit of local administration in Canada was transformed from small districts based on school attendance areas to large regional or county school districts. In these large school districts elected boards of five to fifteen members had local jurisdiction over several thousand pupils, a hundred or more elementary and secondary schools, and an array of specialized educational services. Supported by their extensive professional and administrative staffs and more highly qualified and organized teachers, regional and county school boards increasingly assumed active responsibility for managing local schools. Detailed regulations of departments of education gradually were rewritten into general guidelines; provincial inspectors became program advisers and curriculum consultants. In effect, as the nascent model of nineteenth-century city school administration became generalized, central-local relations in Canadian educational administration were transformed from administrative agency to policy tutelage.

Virtually from the outset Egerton Ryerson had been dissatisfied with the attendance areas of elementary schools as the basic unit of local administration. At his urging, the possibility of forming township school areas in Canada West by a favourable vote of ratepayers in local districts was included in the 1850 act, but very few township units were formed until the 1930s.[1] Legislative attempts to facilitate voluntary consolidation of rural school districts were similarly ineffective in other provinces. Professional educators pointed to the widening gap between urban and rural schooling as evidence for the need to amalgamate small rural districts. They argued that larger school districts would result in more specialized educational programs, more enlightened political leadership, and greater financial support for schools. Rural school trustees and ratepayers stubbornly resisted the increased costs of consolidation and loss of control over their local schools, and initial legislative attempts to impose reorganization were turned back by provincial assemblies that were dominated by the representatives of these rural interests.

School district reorganization in Canada was shaped by three major social changes: the fiscal crisis of the Great Depression, the planning for reconstruction after the Second World War, and the post-war boom in the school population, which began to reach secondary schools in the late 1950s, but the impact of each varied markedly from one province to another. Shifts in governing parties facilitated reform in several provinces, although there appears to be no obvious ideological connection among the election of the populist, right-wing Social Credit party in Alberta in 1935, the social-democratic Co-operative Commonwealth Federation elected in Saskatchewan in 1944, the Conservative government that won power in Manitoba in 1958, and the Liberal government that initiated Quebec's 'Quiet Revolution' in 1960. In any case, reorganization was also carried out by incumbent governments – a re-elected Coalition government kept its campaign promise and implemented reorganization in British Columbia in 1946, the Conservative government that introduced county districts in Ontario for secondary education in 1964 and for elementary education in 1968 had held office since 1943, and the 1967 reorganization of school districts in New Brunswick was part of a fundamental reform of local government carried out by an incumbent Liberal government.

Underlying the variable impact of social changes and the particularities of partisan commitments, two commonalities of school district reorganization reveal the basic concerns of the emerging policy paradigm. First, reorganization was aimed at establishing regional or county districts for local administration of secondary education. In some provinces reorganization was initially restricted to secondary education – Manitoba in 1958, Ontario and Quebec in 1964 – although elementary education was eventually also assigned to the regional or county boards. Second, reorganization was aimed at establishing regional or county districts for local administration of rural education. In several provinces reorganization was initially restricted to rural school districts – Alberta in 1936, Nova Scotia in 1942, Saskatchewan in 1944, Manitoba in 1958, Ontario in 1964 – although subsequently they also integrated and rationalized the administrative organization of urban education.[2] In effect, district reorganization in Canada was driven by a concern to make the educational (and hence occupational) opportunities of large city high schools available to rural students.

Equalization of Provincial Funding

District reorganization created client populations large enough to sustain functionally specialized educational programs and facilities, but full equalization of rural and urban secondary education still required equalization of fiscal capacities across city, regional, and county school districts. In the nineteenth century special municipal and provincial funds were used to assist poor districts, but they were exceptional measures of public charity. Between the 1930s and the 1960s equalization grants became a uniformly integral part of provincial educational policies, and the main burden of financing elementary and secondary schools was assumed by provincial governments.

A weighted population grant was the instrument first used to promote equalization.[3] Under this type of grant the total amount of provincial aid was distributed to each school district in proportion to a measure of population – such as number of pupils, classrooms, or teachers – that was adjusted to take account of local resources, usually by reference to the district's assessed property valuation per pupil compared with the average in the province. A good example was the weighted grant introduced in British Columbia in 1933 to replace the flat grant per teacher that had served as the provincial general grant since 1906. The new basic provincial grant to each district was the product of the number of teachers and the provincial grant per teacher ($780 for each elementary teacher, $1,100 for each junior high school teacher, and $1,200 for each high school teacher) less the yield of a one (in cities 1.25) mill tax in the district. In Alberta, a daily grant per teacher weighted by the value of local assessment was introduced as an addition to the flat grant for rural districts in 1942. The population base of this equalizing grant was changed to the number of classrooms beginning in 1946, when towns became eligible for the grant. In 1955 a weighted grant per pupil was added; both continued in effect until a foundation program (see below) was introduced in 1961.

A more complex instrument for attempting to equalize fiscal capacity among local school districts was the foundation program, or fixed unit equalizing grant, which established both the unit cost of an educational program to be provided equally in every school district and a mandatory local property tax rate to be applied to the equalized assessed valuation in every school district. The provincial grant paid to each district would be the difference between its expenditure for the foundation program and its revenue from levying the mandatory tax rate.

Nova Scotia and British Columbia were the first provinces in Canada to use a fixed unit equalizing grant. Under the Nova Scotia plan introduced in 1942, rural municipalities assumed financial responsibility for a 'minimum programme of education,' defined rather crudely by the province in terms of a minimum salary scale for teachers and annual maintenance rates of $125 to $150 for each classroom. The Department of Education paid as an equalization grant the difference between the cost of the minimum program and the yield of a uniform school tax in each municipality. In 1955, following the recommendations of the Pottier commission, the costs of providing the foundation program were redefined to include teachers' salaries, allowances for principals, and the cost of school maintenance, transportation, and tuition and boarding. The grant was extended to both rural and urban school districts.[4] In British Columbia the plan recommended by the Cameron commission in 1945 covered allowances for teachers' salaries, supervision, and maintenance; an allowance for transportation costs was added to the basic grant structure in 1955.[5] These allowances on current expenditures comprised the basic provincial program, and the share of each school district was the yield of a five-mill tax on local property. Fixed unit equalizing grants were introduced to allocate provincial funding to school districts in Alberta (1961), Quebec (1965), Manitoba (1967), and finally Saskatchewan (in 1970 to replace the variable percentage 'general formula grant' that had been used since 1957).

Ontario was the only province in Canada to use a percentage equalizing grant to finance its school districts. A percentage equalizing grant defines a 'key district,' usually set up as a district with assessed valuation per pupil equal to the provincial average. The percentage of expenditures paid in other districts is adjusted according to the ratio of their assessed valuations per pupil to the assessed valuation per pupil in the key district. An approximation of the formula for this grant can be obtained by using schedules that set out the specific percentages of approved expenditures to be paid to districts in different categories of wealth. Such schedules were used in Ontario from 1944 to 1964. In 1968, after an interlude in which a fixed unit equalizing grant was used to finance ordinary expenditures, the province adopted a standard version of the percentage equalizing formula to determine the amounts of the provincial grants.

As with the reorganization of school districts, the introduction of foundation programs as the mechanism of provincial financing of education implied a shift in the relationship between provincial departments of education and local educational authorities, from administrative agency to policy tutelage.

The reorganization of small rural school boards into county and regional school divisions made strict provincial regulation of school boards administratively inefficient as well as politically difficult. As the counterpart of district reorganization, the specification of provincial grants to school boards in terms of foundation programs focused provincial departments on the task of creating the policy framework within which local authorities could exercise administrative discretion. By defining what costs of elementary and secondary education were approved, provincial policy-makers continued to determine what the basic elements of publicly provided elementary and secondary education should be. With appropriate provision for provincial oversight, however, the details of implementation could be left with increasing confidence to cadres of professional educational administrators employed by city, county, and regional school boards. In this emerging form of policy tutelage, strict administrative subordination of local school boards to provincial policies and administrative directives was replaced by a territorial demarcation between policy at the centre and administration in the localities. In a situation analogous to the model advocated by J.S. Mill, the principles of policy continued to be established uniformly by provincial departments of education, but administrative management and practices were allowed to vary to fit local circumstances and preferences.

ACCESSIBILITY OF EDUCATION AND THE ALLOCATION OF PUBLIC RESOURCES

Over the first three decades of the twentieth century education became one of the leading sectors of the Canadian public economy. Throughout this period teachers formed much the largest group of public employees. By the 1920s government expenditures on education continued to surpass expenditures on all other social activities and had come to rival government expenditures on economic activities. Public education declined in relative importance during the Great Depression and the Second World War. During the 1950s and 1960s, however, education regained its place as a substantial and prominent part of the growing public economy. The proportion of public resources allocated to public education increased in all provinces, and there was significant narrowing of interprovincial differences in average size of schools, expenditures per pupil, and pupil/teacher ratios.

Expansion of Education in a Liberal Public Economy

The 'public economy' comprises the mobilization of resources, production and distribution of goods and services, and redistribution of income through the public sector. In Canada, as in other advanced industrial countries, the size of the public economy relative to the national economy increased markedly in the twentieth century until the 1970s. Total government expenditures rose from 17 per cent of gross national product in 1913–14 to 40 per cent of gross domestic product in 1975–6 (Table 7.1). During the same period total government employment increased from 4.6 per cent to 21.2 per cent of the labour force.

In terms of the relative size and functional distribution of government expenditures and employment (Table 7.2), the development of the Canadian public economy has followed a typical liberal pattern. Military activities of the state have been relatively small, except during wartime. In the early twentieth century, during the first stage of industrial expansion, state economic activities were quite extensive in order to promote private capital accumulation. Expenditures on social activities were relatively small until the Great Depression. After the Second World War spending on economic activities remained relatively high, at least until the 1980s, but economic activities were increasingly outweighed by rising social expenditures, first on education and more recently on health and social welfare.

The commitment of state resources to elementary and secondary education did not simply follow the trend of expansion of the public economy after the Second World War. As the indicators of state expenditure and employment in Table 7.1 show, from 1950–1 to 1970–1 public elementary and secondary education was a leading sector in the expansion of the public economy. Table 7.3 shows that public elementary and secondary education accounted for 31 per cent of total provincial and local expenditures in the 1920s, ranging from one-fifth of the public economy in British Columbia to nearly one-half in Saskatchewan. Education then declined sharply as a percentage of total provincial and local expenditures during the Great Depression, recovered somewhat during the Second World War (except in Prince Edward Island), and then increased markedly in the 1950s and 1960s in the public economies of all provinces except for Newfoundland.

Tables 7.4 and 7.5 show the extent to which this expansion of state expenditures on public elementary and secondary education was attributable to the replacement of local taxation by provincial grants. Provincial grants rose from about 15 per cent of the combined current revenues of public school boards (from local taxation and provincial grants) on average in the 1930s to over 40 per cent of total school board revenues in the 1960s and over 60 per cent in the 1970s. Provincial governments thus became the main source of funding for elementary and secondary education, but there continue to be substantial

TABLE 7.1
Historical expansion of public elementary and secondary education in the Canadian public economy, selected fiscal/school years, 1913–14 to 1989–90

Fiscal/ school year	Elementary and secondary ex- penditures / GDP labour force (%)	Elementary and secondary ex- penditures / total government expenditures (%)	Full-time teachers / labour force (%)	Full-time teachers / total government employment (%)	Total government expenditures / GDP (%)	Total public employment / labour force (%)
1913	1.9*	11.2	1.6	35.9	17.0*	4.6
1926	2.5	18.0	1.8	38.0	14.1	4.7
1937	2.2	10.2	1.7	38.0	21.4	4.3
1950	1.6	8.2	1.7	15.9	20.0	12.2
1955	2.1	9.2	2.0	15.3	22.6	15.3
1960	3.2	11.8	2.3	13.0	26.8	18.2
1965	3.8	13.5	2.7	13.8	28.2	19.6
1970	5.0	14.7	3.2	14.8	34.3	20.1
1975	4.4	11.3	2.7	12.7	40.0	21.2
1980	4.3	10.8	2.2	11.1	39.6	20.3
1985	4.3	9.2	2.0	10.3	45.6	19.4
1989	4.1	9.3	2.0	10.1	43.8	20.0

* Based on Gross National Product

TABLE 7.2

Functional distribution of government expenditures, selected fiscal years, 1913–14 to 1990–1 (%)

	1913	1926	1937	1950	1955	1960	1965	1970	1975	1980	1985	1990
Administration, law and order	32.4	23.8	17.5	7.7	9.2	10.4	9.2	11.3	11.2	10.5	9.6	9.7
Defence and international assistance	5.8	2.5	3.5	15.1	25.5	15.0	10.5	6.3	4.7	4.6	5.0	5.1
Economic activities	31.7	16.0	11.9	16.1	16.0	20.3	21.2	17.8	20.2	19.8	16.1	13.2
Social activities	6.4	15.1	32.4	26.1	23.3	25.7	29.5	34.0	37.4	35.9	36.3	38.3
Education	15.8	18.4	11.5	10.7	10.6	14.6	17.3	19.0	14.8	13.7	12.7	11.9
Debt charges	7.9	24.3	23.1	11.2	7.7	7.6	10.0	10.4	9.6	13.2	17.9	20.3
Other	*	*	*	13.1	7.7	6.4	2.3	1.1	2.1	2.3	2.5	1.6
Totals												
%**	100.0	100.0	100.0	100.0	100.0	100.0	100.0	100.0	100.0	100.0	100.0	100.0
$millions	442	785	1,177	4,139	7,026	10,784	17,207	31,965	71,997	131,758	224,496	309,501

* Included in general administration

** Percentages may not add to 100 because of rounding.

TABLE 7.3

Government expenditures on public elementary and secondary schools as percentages of total provincial and local government expenditures, selected fiscal years 1913–14 to 1989–90

Fiscal year*	New-foundland	Prince Edward Island	Nova Scotia	New Brunswick	Quebec	Ontario	Manitoba	Saskat-chewan	Alberta	British Columbia	Canada**
1913		34.5	28.6	27.4	17.1	26.1	20.8	22.7	14.7	8.5	18.6
1926		41.7	28.0	25.9	31.2	29.5	34.5	48.7	32.6	20.9	31.1
1937		17.3	15.5	14.0	14.1	20.3	19.5	10.9	27.1	16.6	17.3
1937		15.8	15.0	13.4	15.0	21.2	19.5	12.1	24.9	17.2	18.2
1950	18.2	15.1	20.1	21.0	17.1	22.2	24.5	26.2	22.5	17.2	20.9
1955	22.3	15.8	26.3	20.3	23.7	22.4	26.1	23.8	23.0	22.9	23.7
1960	24.2	20.2	25.8	22.4	24.5	24.8	24.3	27.9	25.5	23.4	25.5
1965	20.1	22.0	27.3	23.8	28.4	29.4	27.6	26.4	28.3	25.1	28.7
1965	14.4	17.1	21.0	18.8	23.1	24.9	23.0	21.2	21.7	21.7	23.6
1970	18.6	18.1	19.7	22.7	25.3	23.5	22.7	23.5	20.4	21.8	23.6
1975	17.4	16.1	19.1	18.1	20.6	18.7	17.3	17.6	16.5	16.7	19.0
1980	17.1	17.8	18.1	19.3	19.0	21.4	17.8	16.3	12.6	15.8	18.6
1985	17.7	15.2	17.3	18.2	15.4	18.2	15.9	14.2	12.9	14.1	16.2
1989	16.5	14.6	15.6	17.2	13.4	18.8	15.8	15.3	13.1	15.0	15.8

* The statistical series for provincial government expenditures is broken at 1937–8 and 1965–6. Hence, two sets of statistics are given for these fiscal years to permit comparison of long-term trends.

** Canada includes the Yukon and Northwest Territories and excludes Newfoundland before 1950–1.

variations in the proportion of elementary and secondary school costs funded by provincial governments. Indeed, provincial financial regimes for public education now divide at the Ottawa River. To the east, in the Atlantic provinces and Quebec, provincial governments supply 80 to 100 per cent of the revenues of school boards; in Ontario and the West (with the brief exception of British Columbia in the mid-1980s), the provincial share varies from 42 to 61 per cent.

In Canada elementary and secondary education has been, and remains, dominated by provincial governments and school boards. Table 7.6 shows that spending by the federal government increased during the 1960s because of the Technical and Vocational Training Assistance Act, then declined in the 1970s and 1980s to just under 3 per cent of total spending on elementary and secondary education. Fees as a source of funding for elementary and secondary education also declined on average from 3.4 per cent in 1955–6 to 1.8 per cent in 1975–6, then rose slightly in the 1980s. The decline in fees from the 1950s to the 1960s was mainly the result of the reform in Quebec that ended secondary education as an exclusive sector.[6] The slight rise in the proportion of expenditures covered by fees occurred as a result of the rise in importance of fees in four (British Columbia, Alberta, Manitoba and Quebec) of the five provinces that provide provincial grants to independent schools, and in Ontario, where the contribution of fees increased because of a rise in private-school enrolments in the 1980s and then decreased with the transfer of Roman Catholic secondary education from the status of fee-paying independent schools to state separate schools after 1984.

Resource Allocations and Client Benefits: Expansion and Convergence

The post-war expansion of elementary and secondary education resulted primarily from the sharp rise of the population in the schools during the 1950s and 1960s (Table 7.7), but there was also a marked expansion of public resources allocated per pupil. State expenditures per pupil provide a rough indicator of the levels of benefits accruing to persons in school from public resources allocated to elementary and secondary education. Expenditures per pupil have been consistently below average in the Atlantic provinces (Table 7.8). Historically British Columbia and Ontario were the leaders in spending per pupil, joined after the Second World War by Alberta and Saskatchewan. The Quiet Revolution transformed Quebec from among the lowest provinces to the highest province in spending per pupil by 1970–1, a position which it retained while British Columbia and Ontario both fell below the national average in the late 1970s and early 1980s. As Table 7.8 shows, except for the

TABLE 7.4
Current revenues of public school boards from provincial grants as percentages of total combined revenues from provincial grants and local taxation, selected fiscal years, 1890–1 to 1950–1

Fiscal year*	New-foundland	Prince Edward Island	Nova Scotia	New Brunswick	Quebec	Ontario	Manitoba	Saskat-chewan	Alberta	British Columbia	Canada*
1890		73	27	33	18	9	31			91	18
1900		77	24	28	14	10	21			78	19
1910		67	20	24	12	10	15	30	19	40	17
1920		58	11	12	6	10	11	13	11	34	12
1930		57	13	15	8	12	15	23	15	30	15
1940		60	19	17	10	14	16	28	18	28	16
1950	100	55	50	42	27	37	24	30	28	47	35

* Canada includes the Yukon and Northwest Territories and excludes Newfoundland before 1950–1.

TABLE 7.5

Current revenues of public school boards from provincial grants as percentages of total school board revenues from all sources, selected fiscal years, 1950–1 to 1989–90

Fiscal year*	New-foundland	Prince Edward Island	Nova Scotia	New Brunswick	Quebec	Ontario	Manitoba	Saskat-chewan	Alberta	British Columbia	Canada*
1950	76	50	51	42	27	38	24	28	28	46	35
1955	78	55	42	44	27	33	30	29	49	55	37
1960	87	62	45	33	30	37	45	41	50	47	39
1965	87	61	47	24	49	44	40	43	48	42	46
1970	92	74	56	100	57	51	50	45	58	57	55
1975	93	99	69	100	71	61	49	56	70	55	65
1980	90	99	77	100	88	51	44	54	60	55	66
1985	92	99	81	100	93	46	52	51	57	88	67
1989	92	100	81	99	91	42	50	49	54	61	61

* Canada includes the Yukon and Northwest Territories.

TABLE 7.6
Expenditures on public and private elementary and secondary education by source of funds, selected fiscal years, 1955–6 to 1989–90 (%)

Fiscal year	Source of funds: Local	Provincial	Federal*	Fees	Other	Totals: %**	$millions
1955	51.1	38.9	3.7	3.4	2.9	100	671
1960	49.7	40.7	3.9	3.3	2.5	100	1,314
1965	43.1	45.7	5.9	2.7	2.6	100	2,400
1970	35.1	54.1	6.6	1.9	2.3	100	4,880
1975	28.5	63.8	3.8	1.8	2.1	100	8,434
1980	25.6	67.0	3.6	2.0	1.9	100	15,051
1985	25.0	66.8	3.3	2.3	2.6	100	21,947
1989	30.7	61.0	2.7	2.6	3.0	100	28,254

* Federal expenditures from 1970–1 include federal grants to provincial governments under the official languages in education program.
** Percentages may not add to 100 because of rounding.

Great Depression there have been large increases in expenditures per pupil in public elementary and secondary education since the turn of the century. These increases are attributable in part to currency inflation, but there also were sizeable gains in real benefits per pupil, although the rates of increase have varied considerably over time (Table 7.9). From 1900–1 to 1915–16 the average annual increase in real per pupil expenditures was nearly 7 per cent, a level that was not reached again until the expansion of the late 1950s. The rate of increase in expenditures per pupil continued to rise, reaching nearly 10 per cent a year from 1965–6 to 1970–1 before falling in the 1970s and 1980s.

Pupil/teacher ratios are another measure of the allocation of public benefits to clients of public education, and to the extent that smaller classes are educationally more effective also a measure of quality. Pupil/teacher ratios in public elementary and secondary schools (Table 7.10) follow the same pattern as expenditures per pupil, falling early in the century from 40.0 in 1895–6 to 30.9 in 1915–16, decreasing again in the late 1960s, and showing only marginal improvement in the 1980s.

Young people going to elementary and secondary schools in Canada since

TABLE 7.7

Enrolments in public elementary and secondary schools as percentages of provincial population, selected school years 1920–1 to 1990–1

School year	New-foundland	Prince Edward Island	Nova Scotia	New Brunswick	Quebec	Ontario	Manitoba	Saskat-chewan	Alberta	British Columbia	Canada*
1920		19.8	20.9	19.0	19.4	21.7	21.1	24.4	23.5	16.4	20.9
1930		19.9	22.5	21.8	18.9	19.5	21.9	25.0	23.1	16.4	20.2
1940		19.1	20.2	20.1	17.7	17.0	18.0	22.5	20.5	14.6	18.0
1950	21.9	19.2	20.9	20.5	15.8	16.7	16.6	20.1	18.5	14.9	17.1
1955	24.7	21.5	22.6	22.9	18.6	19.2	18.8	20.6	19.9	17.3	19.4
1960	28.2	23.4	24.3	25.5	20.9	22.3	20.6	22.6	22.1	19.7	21.9
1965	29.7	25.6	26.4	26.8	23.9	25.0	23.1	24.9	24.8	22.5	24.5
1970	30.8	27.4	27.2	27.7	26.4	26.3	25.0	26.7	26.2	24.1	26.2
1975	28.3	23.6	24.4	24.4	22.1	24.1	22.3	24.0	23.9	22.0	23.3
1980	26.2	21.9	21.9	21.9	17.6	21.3	19.9	21.2	19.6	18.6	19.9
1985	25.0	19.7	19.8	19.9	15.9	19.4	18.7	20.1	19.0	16.9	18.4
1990	22.3	18.9	18.4	18.4	15.1	19.2	18.1	20.1	19.0	15.8	17.8

* Canada includes the Yukon and Northwest Territories and excludes Newfoundland before 1950–1.

TABLE 7.8

Government expenditures per pupil on public elementary and secondary schools, in current dollars by province, selected school/fiscal years, 1900–1 to 1989–90

School fiscal year	New-foundland	Prince Edward Island	Nova Scotia	New Brunswick	Quebec	Ontario	Manitoba	Saskat-chewan	Alberta	British Columbia
1900		8	9	9	7	11	16			31
1915		14	15	16	23	31	43	40	49	61
1925		26	32	43	39	65	60	62	66	75
1935		30	36	30	40	66	53	40	59	71
1945		34	63	55	71	98	92	85	96	107
1950	64	72	111	115	106	154	97	161	180	204
1955	98	96	144	132	166	222	189	229	287	302
1960	153	165	238	200	272	334	306	354	396	387
1965	202	276	309	278	474	490	448	456	506	509
1970	472	562	583	664	856	896	762	717	840	738
1975	1,152	1,269	1,268	1,221	1,714	1,420	1,390	1,306	1,447	1,480
1980	2,021	2,319	2,299	2,280	3,782	2,812	2,660	2,551	2,638	2,724
1985	3,221	3,238	3,829	3,988	5,204	4,360	4,353	4,053	4,608	3,926
1989	4,430	4,185	4,834	5,040	5,697	5,854	5,645	4,726	5,000	5,036

TABLE 7.9
Average government expenditures per pupil on public elementary and secondary schools, selected school/fiscal years, 1900–1 to 1989–90

School/ fiscal year	Average expenditure per pupil in current dollars	Coefficient of variability	Average real expenditure per pupil in 1986 dollars	Average annual increase during preceding period (%)
1900	10	0.41	160	–
1915	31	0.50	314	6.4
1925	55	0.30	394	2.5
1935	51	0.31	458	1.6
1945	84	0.29	597	3.0
1950	137	0.33	684	2.9
1955	201	0.37	927	7.1
1960	305	0.30	1,283	7.7
1965	456	0.28	1,745	7.2
1970	814	0.19	2,587	9.7
1975	1,465	0.11	3,196	4.7
1980	2,915	0.17	4,085	5.6
1985	4,420	0.14	4,510	2.1
1989	5,484	0.10	4,697	1.0

the 1950s have had smaller classes in larger schools. Table 7.11, which shows the average number of pupils per school by province, provides a rough indicator of the impact of policies to enlarge school districts and centralize elementary and secondary education in larger schools. The average size of Canadian schools roughly doubled in the 1950s and doubled again in the 1960s. Differences among the provinces resulted from the timing of provincial policies for district reorganization and school consolidation. Alberta and British Columbia were very much ahead of other provinces in moving to larger school districts and centralizing schools. With the exception of Prince Edward Island, which delayed major reorganization until 1972, all provinces had implemented effective policies of school consolidation during the 1960s. The average sizes of schools achieved by 1970 were generally maintained in each province through the 1970s and 1980s, but only as a result of further, often difficult and controversial, school closures and consolidations in response to declining school populations.

Expenditures per pupil, pupil/teacher ratios and average sizes of public schools vary among the provinces, but there is evidence of convergence over time. In Tables 7.9, 7.10, and 7.11 the coefficients of variability provide a measure of the relative dispersion among the provinces in their expenditures per pupil, pupil/teacher ratios, and average sizes of schools over time.[7] Variability

TABLE 7.10
Ratios of enrolments in public elementary and secondary schools to full-time teachers, selected school years, 1895–6 to 1990–1

School year	New-foundland	Prince Edward Island	Nova Scotia	New Brunswick	Quebec	Ontario	Manitoba	Saskat-chewan	Alberta	British Columbia	Canada*	Coefficient of variability
1895		40.0	41.4	34.6	27.0	54.0	34.8			43.3	40.0	0.20
1905		33.5	38.9	36.3	26.5	45.8	27.1	24.1	31.2	41.3	35.0	0.20
1915		31.3	36.2	34.9	25.4	41.0	34.7	22.4	21.5	31.3	30.9	0.19
1925	38.7	28.1	33.9	32.2	26.1	37.5	36.5	27.4	28.9	29.9	31.2	0.12
1935	34.4	27.7	31.9	34.1	24.9	31.5	35.1	30.0	28.6	29.5	29.2	0.10
1945	31.6	27.1	32.6	32.8	21.1	29.8	27.1	24.7	28.6	29.4	26.3	0.12
1950	31.7	26.2	30.3	27.1	24.0	29.3	25.8	23.2	25.6	27.6	26.7	0.09
1955	33.0	25.9	28.1	27.4	24.4	29.2	26.3	23.8	26.7	28.3	26.9	0.09
1960	29.9	25.3	26.9	26.0	24.0	28.2	25.4	24.2	25.0	27.1	26.1	0.07
1965	26.4	23.0	25.3	24.3	25.0	25.3	24.1	22.7	23.3	26.7	25.0	0.05
1970	25.0	19.1	21.5	22.3	20.4	21.7	21.4	22.5	20.9	24.4	21.6	0.08
1975	21.2	19.3	18.8	21.0	18.4	20.7	19.9	20.6	20.7	20.9	20.0	0.05
1980	19.2	19.6	17.5	19.9	16.4	20.0	18.3	18.9	19.2	19.4	18.7	0.06
1985	17.6	19.4	17.0	19.3	17.2	18.9	17.6	19.0	18.6	20.5	18.5	0.06
1990	15.9	17.9	16.2	16.5	17.7	16.6	16.6	20.7	19.0	18.7	17.4	0.08

* Canada includes the Yukon and Northwest Territories and excludes Newfoundland before 1950–1.

TABLE 7.11
Average size of public schools by province, selected school years, 1925–6 to 1990–1

Province	Average number of pupils per school			
	1925–6	1960–1	1970–1	1990–1
Newfoundland		103	195	239
Prince Edward Island	37	55	122	362
Nova Scotia	64*	134	301	312
New Brunswick	56*	111	305	315
Quebec	63	151	360	403
Ontario	90	186	420	404
Manitoba	73	122	348	281
Saskatchewan	44*	89	250	226
Alberta	43	244	335	310
British Columbia	92	255	353	330
Canada**	66	156	350	354
Coefficient of variability	0.30	0.43	0.28	0.18

* Average number of pupils per district
** Canada excludes the Yukon and Northwest Territories and Newfoundland before 1950–1.

among the provinces in expenditures per pupil decreased markedly during the first quarter of the century and decreased again after 1965–6. The historical variability among the provinces in pupil/teacher ratios has been lower than the variability of expenditures per pupil, but the coefficients of variability for pupil/teacher ratios show a similar decline early in the century, with essentially complete interprovincial convergence in the period since the Second World War. The rise in average size of schools from the 1920s to the 1950s was accompanied by greater differences among provinces (the coefficient of variability increased from 0.90 in 1925–6 to 1.35 in 1960–1), but during the 1960s variations among the provinces decreased as all provinces implemented essentially similar policies of district reorganization and school consolidation.

ACCESSIBILITY OF EDUCATION, INSTITUTIONAL REFORM, AND PUBLIC PHILOSOPHY

The rapid expansion of the population in school during the 1950s and 1960s and the increase of public resources allocated to public education transformed the place of elementary and secondary education in provincial public economies. The scale of educational benefits was historically unprecedented. While there continued to be variations among the provinces, there was also significant interprovincial convergence in important measures of the provision of education – average size of schools, expenditures per pupil, and pupil/teacher ratios. These trends of public educational provision signify the advent of a 'national policy' of public education based on the common commitment in all provinces to the principle of accessibility of education and a general consensus on the institutional conditions required to achieve it.

As leading educational issues from the 1930s to the 1960s the institutional reforms of school district organization and provincial educational financing were unique in Canadian educational politics and policy-making, because the opposing interests and ideologies were so ambiguous and ill-defined. In retrospect, two different public campaigns can be identified, each driven by a different criterion of political evaluation.

First, there was the campaign for public education to serve the requirements of industrial expansion by converting the curriculum and organization of secondary schools from academic and humanistic studies to more technical and scientific work. In this campaign professional educators and business interests joined together in giving new meanings to the criteria of educational effectiveness and efficiency. Public education in North America had always emphasized 'practical education,' and educators in Canada had eagerly combined forces with businessmen and politicians in the early twentieth century to expand the quantity and improve the quality of scientific and technical education in Canadian secondary schools. Here the principle was simply unquestioned by educational, business, and political elites; the issues were practical ones of how much and how quickly to expand state spending and educational activities in vocational training. Any opposition was never explicitly articulated or organized; it came from parents and students who resisted assignment into the technical and commercial tracks of secondary schools because that would end their chance for access to higher education and hence to professional and managerial occupations.

Then there was the campaign to make the advantages of secondary education accessible for all young people. Here the differentiation of academic and general secondary education was as important as the differentiation of academic and vocational secondary education. Not only effectiveness and efficiency of education, but also educational equality required the provision of different types of educational programs to fit the needs of different types of students.

Significantly, the problem of justice in provision of education was seen primarily in terms of territorial rather than class differences – young people in rural areas ought to have the same educational opportunities as young people in urban areas. In this campaign professional educators took the lead; business played little part. Professional educators pointed to the widening gap between urban and rural schooling as evidence for the need to amalgamate small rural districts. They argued that composite secondary schools located in much larger school districts would result in more specialized educational programs, more enlightened school trustees, and greater financial support for schools. The opposition was diffuse but identifiable: rural school trustees and ratepayers who stubbornly resisted the increased costs of consolidation and loss of control over their local schools and provincial legislative assemblies that were dominated by the representatives of these rural interests.

Concerns to overcome territorial inequalities between rural and urban public school districts were predominant, but a significant change in perception of the relationship between class and education also occurred between the wars. Before the First World War professional educators were overwhelmingly committed to partite systems with separate schools providing different types of educational programs. Educational surveys during and after the Second World War continued to advocate separate academic, general, and vocational programs or 'tracks' for different types of students, but now, it was believed, the differentiation of education should take place within schools rather than between them. Educational programs might be class-defining and class-specific, but not schools.

Education for occupational selection was conceived within the constitutional framework for public education that had resulted from conflicts and compromises of nineteenth-century political liberals and religious conservatives. Economic liberal thinking about accessibility of education began from political liberal assumptions about the place of religion in public education and the majority language of instruction. As a consequence, outside Quebec and Newfoundland, the benefits of expansion and diversification of public education from the turn of the century to the 1960s were not much extended to Catholic separate schools, and French bilingual schools. Indeed, the reorganization of public school districts, centralization of secondary schools, and introduction of multilateral curricula greatly increased pressure on the meagre resources of separate and bilingual schools, widening the gap in educational opportunities between their students and those enrolled in public schools. Working from economic liberal ideas of occupational selection and educational accessibility, over the first seven decades of the twentieth century educational policy-makers certainly reached a more nearly national policy than did nineteenth-century political liberals, but the stubborn injustices of religion and language that were incorporated in the nineteenth-century educational foundations were not thereby removed.

8

Economic Liberalism and the Governance of Education: The Foundations of Educational Policy Communities

In the late nineteenth century a liberal model of parliamentary government and ministerial responsibility, either individual or collective, emerged as the accepted theory of public authority and political accountability for public education in all provinces except for Quebec (and Newfoundland). In the early twentieth century, as the functional contribution of senior administrative officials to policy was increasingly recognized as legitimate, ministerial responsibility evolved into a model of executive policy-making that assumed a sharing of responsibility for policy-making between political and administrative heads of government departments. Given this basic alteration in the prevailing theory of political accountability, the reorganization of school districts and equalization of provincial funding created conditions conducive to a modification of intergovernmental relations between provincial departments of education and local school boards, from administrative agency to policy tutelage. Provincial organizations of teachers and trustees became accepted as legitimate channels for representation of advice to official policy-makers and often enjoyed close relationships with ministers and officials. They were not yet, however, regarded as legitimate participants in educational policy-making, which remained the preserve of premiers, ministers, and senior departmental officials.

EDUCATIONAL POLITICS, POLICY, AND ADMINISTRATION: FROM PARLIAMENTARY GOVERNMENT TO EXECUTIVE POLICY-MAKING

Organization charts are notoriously unreliable as guides to actual bureaucratic relationships, but in the case of provincial departments of education from the turn of the century to the 1960s they present consistent and compelling evidence about the pattern of educational policy and administration. A combination of formal authority, professional experience, and longevity in office gave the senior administrative official – variously designated as chief superintendent, chief director, deputy minister of education, or some combination of these titles – domination over departmental administration and policy. The deputy ministers' wide span of control ensured their control over the administrative routine of their departments and presented formidable barriers to political interference in administration. Their position as administrative masters also ensured their involvement in educational policy-making. Moreover, deputy ministers were experienced professional educators, who typically had long careers first as a teacher and principal, then inspector, and finally chief inspector or assistant deputy minister before becoming deputy minister. Those who became deputy ministers typically retained the office for many years. After the Second World War, as public education expanded rapidly, the growing importance of their policy function was confirmed by reorganizations that aimed to protect their ultimate administrative authority while enlarging their time for policy-making. The usual result was not only an increased administrative responsibility for assistant deputy ministers and divisional directors, but also an extension of the policy function to a wider group of senior managers. The pre-eminence of the deputy minister remained undisturbed.

Departmental Organization and the Authority of Deputy Ministers

In the last quarter of the nineteenth century, departments of education varied in size, but except in Quebec and Newfoundland their administrative organization was very much the same, based on a simple division of activities between school inspection and clerical work. In Ontario, which had the largest department, the staff in 1867 consisted of the chief superintendent, a deputy superintendent, a grammar school inspector, three clerks, and a messenger; in the 1890s the central office still had fewer than twenty employees and only two new offices: inspector of public libraries and registrar. At the turn of the century the education office in New Brunswick comprised the chief superintendent of education, eight school inspectors, and four clerks. In British Columbia the superintendent of education was supported by four inspectors of schools and two clerks.

From the late nineteenth century to the Second World War the pattern of departmental expansion consisted of adding new branches or divisions to the existing organization. Departments acquired responsibility for curriculum design and school supervision in the areas of secondary and vocational education, and they began to provide new provincial educational services, such as correspondence courses, textbook distribution, and special education.[1] By the 1940s provincial departments of education typically had twelve to fifteen officials who reported directly to the chief superintendent, chief director, or deputy minister of education.[2] These included the superintendent or chief inspector of elementary schools, superintendent or chief inspector of secondary schools, director of curriculum, director of technical and vocational training, director of teacher training or principal of the provincial normal school, supervisor or principals of provincial schools for blind and deaf children, director of the correspondence school, registrar of teacher certification and departmental examinations, textbook bureau manager, school attendance officer, director of school administration, librarian, and departmental administrative officer or accountant.

The lines of departmental policy and administration all ran directly into the office of chief superintendent, chief director, or deputy minister of education.[3] After the Second World War organizational critiques of provincial departments of education became focused on reducing the deputy ministers' span of control to free them from administrative routine and allow more time for their policy function. The underlying administrative thinking is well reflected in the 1950 report of the Royal Commission on Education in Ontario. The Hope commission recommended that the deputy minister be the chief executive officer of the department and the minister's chief educational adviser. 'Since in the new organization the Deputy Minister should be freed so far as possible from routine duties in order that he may devote his efforts to educational statesmanship,' an associate deputy minister should be appointed as 'executive assistant to the Deputy Minister' with responsibility to coordinate the work of senior officials of the department.[4] Lines of responsibility within the department should be clearly defined by reorganization into seven divisions, each headed by a superintendent.[5] As another example, the Manitoba Royal Commission on Education, which was chaired by a former deputy minister, R.O. MacFarlane, recommended reorganizing the department into six divisions with the three most senior officials – the directors of school administration and curriculum and the chief inspector – reporting directly to the deputy minister, and the directors of research, vocational education, and professional and special training reporting through an assistant deputy minister. Again, the rationale for these changes was the pressure of the deputy minister's role in executive policy-making: 'At present the Deputy Minister is seriously over-worked. He should be kept as free as possible from all routine duties in the first instance, so that he has time to carry out the functions which he alone can perform. These are, managing the Department, planning administration and educational policy, and advising the Minister.'[6]

From the 1940s to the 1960s there were no attempts to reorganize departments in the Maritime provinces, and organizational changes in Ontario and the West were marginal. They aimed to narrow, if only slightly, the deputy minister's span of control by reorganizing departments into seven to ten directorates, thus reducing the number of officials reporting directly to the deputy minister, and by appointing associate or assistant deputy ministers. In Alberta in 1945 the deputy minister, G. Fred McNally, reduced his span of control to nine by consolidating several branches under two senior officials as director of school administration and a chief superintendent of schools, who eventually became associate deputy minister in 1970. When C.F. Cannon became chief director of education in Ontario in 1956, two deputy ministers were appointed, one responsible for elementary education and the other for secondary education. In British Columbia the office of assistant deputy minister of education (before 1953, deputy superintendent) was split in 1958, and assistant superintendents of education for instructional services and administrative and school board relations were appointed, thus reducing the span of control exercised by the office of deputy minister and superintendent to nine branches. The reorganization implemented in Manitoba by the Roblin government in 1960 followed very closely the recommendations of the MacFarlane commission by setting up six directorates for administration, instruction, curriculum, special services, teacher training, and vocational training, with the last three reporting to the deputy minister through a new office of assistant deputy minister. A very similar reorganization was carried out in Saskatchewan in 1962 where the chief superintendent of schools, the registrar, and the directors of school administration, curriculum, and special education reported through an assistant deputy minister. The directors of teacher training, vocational education, continuing education, and provincial educational services (northern education, the school for the deaf, the correspondence school, and the textbook bureau) were directly responsible to the deputy minister.

Premiers, Ministers, and Deputy Ministers as Executive Policy-Makers

Deputy ministers of education dominated departmental administration and policy, but they were subject to strong political and policy direction from provincial cabinets. The case of Ontario is instructive. The Ross government was defeated in 1905 by the Conservatives led by James P. Whitney, who came into office with a strong commitment to educational reform. The minister of education from 1905 to 1918 was Robert Pyne, a doctor who was a friend of the premier and who had served as trustee on the Toronto public and high school boards. The deputy minister, who remained in office until 1934, was

A.H.U. Colquhoun, a former journalist and also a personal friend of Whitney. The Whitney government revived the office of superintendent of education and appointed John Seath, a senior high school inspector. By all accounts Seath, who held the office until his death in 1919, had a domineering and authoritarian personality, not unlike Ryerson or Ross, but he also had Premier Whitney's backing.[7]

The development of provincial educational policy in the twentieth century increasingly depended on some such collaboration of politicians and administrators in executive policy-making as had occurred in Ontario under Whitney, Pyne, and Seath. On the one hand, ministers of education, if not always unwilling, were simply unable to master the details of policy and administration required to dominate their departments in the way George Ross had been able to do in late nineteenth-century Ontario.[8] Three ministers of education in the first half of the twentieth century had professional experience comparable to Ross: J.T.M. Anderson, minister of education in Saskatchewan from 1929 to 1934; George Weir, minister of education in British Columbia from 1933 to 1941 and again from 1945 to 1947; and Woodrow S. Lloyd, Saskatchewan minister of education in CCF governments from 1944 to 1960.[9] In contrast with Ross, however, Anderson, Weir, and Lloyd as ministers worked with deputy ministers who were experienced professional educators.[10] On the other hand, provincial government in Canada is usually 'premier's government.'[11] Not all premiers dominate their governments, but most do. Hence, in judging the relationship between educational politics and policy it is essential to consider the relationship not only of ministers and deputies but also of premiers and deputy ministers of education. In fact, from the turn of the century to the 1940s there were several cases where premiers retained the office of minister of education for themselves: A.C. Rutherford (1905–10) and William Aberhart (1935–43) in Alberta; Walter Scott (1912–16), W.M. Martin (1916–21), and J.T.M. Anderson (1929–34) in Saskatchewan; John Bracken in Manitoba (1922–3); and in Ontario G. Howard Ferguson (1923–30), George S. Henry (1930–4), and George A. Drew (1943–8). Where premiers did not personally assume the education portfolio, by all accounts their political strength would still be an effective countervail to even the most entrenched deputy ministers of education. Thus, from civic trusteeship and ministerial policy-making in the nineteenth century, central educational policy-making in the first half of the twentieth century became jointly conducted by premiers and their ministers of education on one side as politicians and chief superintendents, chief directors, or deputy ministers of education, with increasing support from assistant deputy ministers and divisional directors, on the other side as administrators.

FOUNDATIONS OF EDUCATIONAL POLICY COMMUNITIES: THE POLITICAL ORGANIZATION OF TEACHERS AND TRUSTEES

The expansion of secondary education, consolidation of schools, reorganization of school districts, and equalization of provincial funding created both institutional conditions and political resources that facilitated the political organization of teachers and trustees. At the same time, the displacement of civic trusteeship and parliamentary government by the theory and practice of executive policy-making also contributed to legitimizing the political organization and policy advice, if not participation in policy-making, of representatives of teachers and school trustees.

Formation of Provincial Teachers' Organizations

The provincial organization of teachers in the nineteenth century took the form of teachers' institutes and omnibus general educational associations.[12] Teachers' institutes were organized by provincial departments of education as a way of providing poorly qualified teachers with some elementary training. The educational associations, bringing together teachers, school trustees, provincial officials, and interested citizens, were also promoted by departmental superintendents and inspectors, usually with some university president or civic notable as head.[13] These organizations aimed at educational, especially professional, improvement and gave teachers little opportunity to discuss, let alone influence, the policies most affecting their professional lives: salaries, pensions, and tenure. In spite of much dissatisfaction with these strictly non-political associations, in the period before the First World War teachers were either unable or unwilling to establish their own political organizations. According to Paton, 'Nowhere in Canada in the first decade of this century were teachers strongly organized in occupational groups; nor did they have any clear aims regarding professional recognition. They respected and followed, almost without question, their superiors in education; they knew their proper places and, in general, refrained from any kind of self-assertive action.'[14]

The rapid organization of teachers' unions in all provinces except Quebec between 1914 and 1920 no doubt can be explained by the conjuncture of a decline in the material position of teachers during the war and expansion of elementary and secondary education.[15] From the outset these teachers' unions had both professional and political objectives. The Saskatchewan Teachers' Alliance, for example, originated from a rejection by the minister of education of teachers' tenure and salary grievances. The constitution of the

Ontario Secondary School Teachers' Federation included professional objectives, to discuss and promote the cause of education in secondary schools, raise the status of the Ontario teaching profession, and promote a high standard of professional etiquette, but it also referred to more political objectives to secure material conditions essential to professional service and a larger voice for teachers in educational policy and administration. In its 1921 policy statement the Alberta Teachers' Alliance set out demands for material benefits such as tenure protection, sick leave, and a pension scheme, but also political objectives, such as larger administrative units, collective bargaining, and representation of teachers on committees controlling conditions of work.

As Table 11.1 suggests, provincial organization of teachers, as well as school trustees, has been determined also by the divisions of religion and language that are so deeply embedded in the history of Canadian educational politics. These associations have tended to form at critical points of political and policy change, when members of a minority group both fear change and perceive opportunity for collective action. The Ontario English Catholic Teachers' Association, for example, was organized at the same time as Ontario teachers' associations became linked in the OTF. The Provincial Association of Catholic Teachers in Quebec was formed in the early years of the Quiet Revolution, as the issue of language in public education suddenly became a high priority. In New Brunswick, sections of francophone teachers and trustees that had formed inside the New Brunswick Teachers' Association and the New Brunswick School Trustees' Association became independent organizations in the late 1960s at the same time as elementary and secondary education was being fundamentally reformed.

Official Recognition of Provincial Teachers' Organizations

The establishment of provincial teachers' organizations between 1914 and 1920 did not immediately result in their acceptance by the ministers and departmental officials as official representatives of teachers' interests, with a right of access to the policy-making inner circle, if not to participate in policy-making, at least to advise. That recognition was won gradually by a combination of political pressure by teachers' organizations and changing personnel and outlook on the side of official policy-makers.

Perhaps the best indicator of official recognition was provincial legislation providing for automatic membership in provincial teachers' unions. With membership dropping and provincial organization split between the Saskatchewan Teachers' Alliance and the Rural Teachers' Association, the minister of education (who was also premier) promised a provincial statute requiring compulsory membership if the two organizations would reunite and increase membership to 70 per cent of the province's teachers. With help from provincial inspectors who canvassed for members the goal was met, and the Saskatchewan Teachers' Federation Act of 1935 required all provincially licensed teachers to belong to the federation. The Alberta Teachers' Alliance gained compulsory membership following the election of the Social Credit government led by William Aberhart, who also served as minister of education. In Ontario, the establishment of the Ontario Teachers' Federation in 1944 resulted from a representation by three public school teachers' associations to the new Conservative government led by George Drew. The government apparently hoped to simplify the governance of provincial education by channelling all teachers' representations through a single organization, and the statute included provision for an annual consultative meeting with representatives of the OTF.[16] The British Columbia Teachers' Federation got automatic membership in 1947 when George Weir was minister of education for the Coalition government. The last provincial teachers' union to gain automatic membership was the Corporation des instituteurs et institutrices catholiques du Québec in 1960, at the outset of the Quiet Revolution that began with the death of Premier Maurice Duplessis.[17]

Provincial Organization of School Trustees

As with teachers, the historical organization of school trustees was motivated by the changing place of education in the public economy, but it was also a reaction to the provincial organization of teachers. In some cases departments of education actively promoted provincial organization of school trustees as a counter to provincial organization of teachers. The Alberta School Trustees' Association, for example, was an unassuming organization until its 1919 convention, at which the minister of education joined with the ASTA in a vigorous attack on the Alberta Teachers' Alliance.[18] In Ontario, the organization of the Urban School Trustees' Association (1920) and the Ontario School Trustees' and Ratepayers' Association (1921) both followed closely on the organization of three public school teachers' associations, and OSTRA at least was established with the active support of the Department of Education. The Associated High School Boards of Ontario was organized in 1932 to cut the costs of secondary education and counter the power of the OSSTF.[19] The Nova Scotia Association of Urban and Municipal School Boards was organized in 1954, in order to provide collective defence against pressure for collective bargaining and provincial salary scales by the Nova Scotia Teachers' Union, which had gained compulsory membership in the previous year. In several provinces official recognition of teachers' associations by provincial statutes conferring automatic membership was followed by comparable status for provincial associations of schools trustees.[20] On the verge of collapse because of falling membership during the Depression, the Alberta School Trustees' Association was granted automatic membership, with a provision for opting out, in 1939. The Manitoba Association of School Trustees was incorporated during the war years at the same time as the Manitoba Teachers' Society. The provincial act that provided for the federation of six trustees' associations in the Ontario School Trustees' Council was inspired by the trustees' desire to counter the teachers' federation and the department's aim to create a unified channel of representation for trustees.[21]

Institutionalizing Educational Policy Communities: The Introduction of Collective Bargaining

From the 1940s to the 1960s the key policy development which transformed relationships between organized teachers and school boards in provincial educational policy communities was the trend to collective bargaining. During the 1920s and 1930s, teachers' unions and their local affiliates had pressed school boards for voluntary recognition as bargaining agents. Most school boards refused to recognize teachers' unions, however, and continued to determine teachers' salaries and working conditions either by negotiating with teachers individually or unilaterally setting salary schedules. Beginning in the 1940s three approaches to collective bargaining were taken: inclusion of teachers under provincial labour relations acts, protection of teachers' rights to bargain collectively under specific legislation or sections of the eduction act, and voluntary recognition by school boards.

In the 1940s, as reformed provincial labour relations acts required employers to recognize trade unions and accept collective bargaining, teachers' unions in Alberta, Quebec, and Manitoba altered their strategy to press for statutory recognition of their right to bargain collectively under provincial labour relations legislation. The Alberta Industrial Conciliation and Arbitration Act (1938) did not include teachers within its definition of 'employee.' Troubled negotiations with school boards and strong representations to the government by the Alberta Teachers' Association secured an amendment to the act in 1941, making the ATA the first teachers' union in Canada to get the right to bargain collectively. The Quebec Labour Relations Act (1944) did not exclude teachers, and during the 1950s a few local Catholic teachers' unions became certified. Formal recognition of the teachers' right to bargain was incorporated by an amendment to the Quebec Labour Code in 1965. Collective bargaining was standardized throughout the province, and beginning in 1967 the major items of salaries and working conditions were negotiated by centralized bargaining involving representatives of the Ministry of Education and provincial associations of school trustees and teachers. Local branches of the Manitoba Teachers' Society also qualified as bargaining units under the Manitoba Labour Relations Act of 1948, and most applied for certification. Strong resistance to collective bargaining by school trustees, which included the formation of the Manitoba Urban School Trustees' Association in 1952 specifically to combat collective bargaining, eventually led to an agreement between trustees and teachers in 1956, as a result of which the Public Schools Act was amended to provide for collective bargaining with compulsory arbitration.

As an alternative to using provincial labour relations acts, when school boards refused to bargain voluntarily teachers' unions pressed for specific statutory recognition of their right to collective bargaining. In Saskatchewan the CCF government sought to avoid certification of teachers under the provincial labour relations law by encouraging voluntary collective bargaining.[22] When that failed, the Teachers' Salary Negotiation Act passed in 1949 guaranteed teachers' right to bargain with school boards. School boards in Nova Scotia also were opposed to collective bargaining, and voluntary teacher-trustee negotiations were severely restricted until a threat to strike by Sydney teachers produced an amendment of the Nova Scotia Teachers' Union Act to provide for compulsory collective bargaining. In British Columbia, following the reorganization of school districts in 1946, most school boards had voluntarily agreed to bargain collectively with teachers, but, when twenty-six districts refused to negotiate in 1958, the Public Schools Act was amended to guarantee teachers the right to bargain collectively regarding salaries but not working conditions.[23]

In Ontario and the Atlantic provinces other than Nova Scotia, teachers were excluded from provincial labour relations acts, and collective bargaining remained strictly voluntary or non-existent until the late 1960s and early 1970s. Following the incorporation of the Ontario Teachers' Federation (1944) and the Ontario School Trustees' Council (1950), the federations of trustees and teachers evolved informal procedural agreements to govern voluntary local bargaining. This voluntary regime was remarkably effective until it broke down under a wave of strikes in the early 1970s, and a regime of compulsory collective bargaining with mediation and conciliation by the provincial Educational Relations Commission was introduced in 1975. By the 1960s most school boards in New Brunswick had also voluntarily granted bargaining rights to their teachers, but, when provincial education was reorganized, the right of collective bargaining was legally recognized and negotiations were centralized under the Public Service Labour Relations Act (1968). By contrast, there was no history of voluntary bargaining prior to the statutory provisions for collective bargaining that were passed as parts of major reorganizations of public education in Prince Edward Island (1972) and Newfoundland (1973).

Outside of Newfoundland and Prince Edward Island, the trend to collective bargaining from the 1940s to the 1960s slowly institutionalized a relationship of consultation, negotiation, and exchange between organized teachers and school trustees at both the local and provincial levels of educational administration. Until the mid-1960s, all three approaches to implementing collective bargaining fixed negotiations at the local level between school boards and local affiliates of provincial teachers' unions. Provincial organizations of teachers and trustees represented their sectoral interests to provincial governments, whose legislation set the framework for collective bargaining. They negotiated informal agreements to guide local bargaining and provided support services to their affiliates during negotiations. Provincial organization of teachers and trustees and local collective bargaining were both facilitated by departments of education, but departments were officially isolated from the details of collective bargaining. The one exception was Saskatchewan where the Saskatchewan Teachers' Federation had a close relationship with the CCF government, and Department of Education officials annually met with representatives of the STF and the SSTA to negotiate provincial guidelines for local bargaining.[24] In other provinces regimes of collective bargaining institutionalized the relationship of policy tutelage that had become the norm for structuring relationships of department, teachers, and trustees in provincial educational policy communities. Working out the details of educational administration might increasingly be left to bargaining between school boards and teachers' unions, but establishing the policy framework and setting the limits for local bargaining remained firmly the preserve of the departments of education.

EXECUTIVE POLICY-MAKING AND THE GOVERNANCE OF EDUCATION: POLICY COMMUNITIES AS HIERARCHIES

Educational expansion in the first seven decades of the twentieth century increased the importance of education in the public economy of Canada; it also hastened the reconstitution of provincial governance of education from ministerial policy-making under parliamentary government to executive policy-making by premiers, ministers, and deputy ministers of education. As provincial departments of education expanded their administrative functions, the deputy minister became an increasingly influential administrative official, whose professional contribution to educational policy-making could not be disregarded or slighted by premiers and ministers. At the same time the policy function of premiers (when they wanted to exercise it) and ministers of education (when premiers let them exercise it) was unchallenged in either theory or practice by deputy ministers, who continued as professional administrators to respect the paramountcy of the principle of ministerial responsibility. From around the turn of the century to the 1960s, outside Quebec and Newfoundland, provincial educational policy was made in highly centralized sub-governments, which joined provincial premiers and ministers of education as politicians with deputy ministers and assistant deputy ministers as administrators.

Educational expansion also affected the potential for political organization by teachers and school trustees. Larger school districts had the local political leadership and cadres of professional administrators that permitted, even necessitated, a reduction in administrative surveillance by provincial departments of education. More teachers working together in larger schools transformed their potential to organize. As teachers organized successfully, school trustees reacted defensively by forming, or reforming, their own provincial associations. The expansion of provincial departments, and the institutionalization of a policy function in the structure of provincial administration, facilitated the recognition of provincial organizations of teachers and trustees as channels of advice to provincial policy-makers, but neither organized teachers nor organized trustees were incorporated as participants in provincial policy-making. Just as the theory and practice of executive policy-making fitted neatly with a shift in the relationship of provincial authorities and local school boards from administrative agency to policy tutelage, so it encouraged the policy sub-governments of premiers, ministers, and deputy ministers to concede a function of policy advice to organized teachers and trustees, but without thereby giving them a place at the decision-making table.

Educational politics, policy, and administration became increasingly isolated in educational policy communities that were hierarchically structured. At the apex they were dominated by sub-governments of premiers, ministers of education, and senior officials of departments of education. These sub-governments accepted, even encouraged, institutionalized channels of advice by representatives of provincial trustees' associations and teachers' unions. Provincial federations of local home and school or parents and teachers associations were also encouraged as channels of policy advice, as well as instruments for mobilizing public support for education, and they were similarly excluded from provincial policy decision-making. Even business interest associations, which had been highly influential in promoting vocational secondary education and articulating new criteria of educational effectiveness and efficiency early in the century, were increasingly marginalized as the focus of educational policy communities shifted from occupational selection to accessibility of education after the Second World War.

The institutionalization of state-society relations in the form of policy communities was certainly not unique to educational governance. Indeed, its emergence in the governance of public education must be attributed as much, if not more, to general trends in principles of policy-making institutions and theories of political accountability in Canada as to pressures unique to educational governance. The hierarchical policy communities that had been tentatively formed between the wars and became the established pattern of educational governance in Canada outside of Quebec and Newfoundland after the Second World War were simply particular expressions of a much more broadly based evolution in Canadian public philosophy about the proper meanings and interrelationships of politics, policy, and administration. At the same time, the obvious importance of education as an area of public policy in Canada, especially at the provincial level, meant that ideas and practices in educational policy communities were crucial in constituting the broader postwar trends of executive policy-making in provincial sub-governments, policy tutelage in relationships between central and local authorities, and domination by state authorities inside hierarchical policy communities.

9

Ethical Liberalism and Person-Regarding Education: Ideologies and Policies of Comprehensive Secondary Education

The ideal of ethical liberalism is a society founded on the principle of universal human development, in which all persons have equal opportunities to develop fully their special abilities and participate freely in the political, economic, social, and cultural life of their community. Ethical liberal aspirations for universal individual self-development presuppose the creation of an educative society. Its foundation is what I call 'person-regarding' education.

Policies for person-regarding education shift the argument for accessibility of education, from a criterion of equal educational opportunity in order to pursue economic success to a criterion of individual self-development. 'Child-centred' or 'student-centred' schools are seen to contribute to individual development by providing learning experiences that meet the complex needs of each person in school while de-emphasizing the ranking and competition that inevitably accompany the function of selection. As the Provincial Committee on Aims and Objectives of Education in the Schools of Ontario argued in its seminal report, 'A school should serve all its children comfortably and humanely in its on-going child-centred programs and a learning experience should be found to match the needs of each.'[1]

Beginning in the 1930s and culminating in the late 1960s and early 1970s, an ethical liberal commitment to public schooling as individual development challenged the economic liberal view of education as occupational class selection. As the educational objectives of economic liberalism approached realization in the form of composite schools, district reorganization, and financial equalization, an ethical liberal conception of person-regarding education seemed set to become the hegemonic ideology of Canadian educational policy communities. Provincial commissions on education articulated comprehensive visions of provincial education based on ethical liberal principles. Official statements of the aims of education were rewritten, and fundamental curricular reforms were achieved as provincial examinations were dropped and credit systems with individual timetables and subject promotion replaced more occupational class-structured programs.

IDEOLOGIES OF COMPREHENSIVE SECONDARY EDUCATION: PERSON-REGARDING EDUCATION IN OFFICIAL POLICY STUDIES

Multilateral schools accommodate all persons in state secondary education within the same building, but they create internal differentiations among academic, general, and vocational educational programs and allocate students among them according to their aptitudes, abilities, and achievements. Comprehensive schools attempt to provide equally broad opportunities for academic, general, and vocational education for all students without differentiating them by program. The ideal of comprehensive education is person-regarding equality without class-specific or class-defining school organization.

As practical experience with multilateral secondary schools revealed the persistent institutional barriers and educational stigmas of differentiated programs, the educational ideal of ethical liberalism was redefined as comprehensive education. Three provincial reports on education dominated educational policy analysis and development in the 1960s and early 1970s: the Royal Commission of Inquiry on Education in the Province of Quebec, chaired by the Right Reverend Alphonse Marie Parent, which was appointed by the Liberal government of Jean Lesage in 1961 and whose final report was issued in five volumes from 1963 to 1966; the Provincial Committee on Aims and Objectives in the Schools of Ontario, chaired by Mr Justice Emmett Hall and Lloyd Dennis, which was appointed by the Conservative government of John Robarts in 1965 and issued its report entitled *Living and Learning* three years later; and the Commission on Educational Planning in Alberta, with Walter H. Worth as the lone official commissioner, which was appointed by the Liberal government of H.E. Strom in June 1969 and reported to the Conservative government of Peter Lougheed in 1972. Each of these commissions began from a fundamentally ethical liberal ideal of education as person-regarding and proceeded to make proposals for a comprehensive reform of school organization and curriculum in their respective provinces. Their recommendations for educational reform in turn became the framework for educational policy development in the late 1960s and early 1970s, with an influence that was not limited to Quebec, Ontario, or Alberta but reached across the country.

Ethical Liberalism and the Quiet Revolution: The Parent Commission in Quebec

According to the Royal Commission of Inquiry on Education in the Province of Quebec democracy is not simply a political structure but 'essentially and fundamentally a spirit, a frame of mind, a way of life. It is based on the participation of the greatest number, individually and in groups, in the conduct of a common enterprise, on respect for the rights of the person, on the equality of all within the diversity of occupations and abilities.'[2] In such a democratic society education is essential and must be equally accessible to all. 'Such is the two-fold prior condition for any hope of attaining equality in the life of the community, an equality based, not on uniformity, but on diversity.' Hence education in a modern democratic society 'must be sufficiently varied to afford opportunities for fulfilment to personalities and intelligences of every kind'; as much as possible it must be accessible even to those living in sparsely populated areas; and all students should be able to continue their studies to the most advanced level they can reach, taking into account their capacities and their academic achievements.[3] The fundamental challenge for educational policy-makers was the transformation of public education into a coherent and integrated system which would provide for varieties of intelligence and diversity of aptitudes.

The Parent commission held that major educational reforms in contemporary societies are the result of efforts to overcome the fragmentation of knowledge and culture among humanities, science, technology, and popular culture.[4] Divisions among these separate domains of knowledge are replicated in educational systems that lack coherence, erect barriers between educational programs, and allocate students by socio-economic status. An activist pedagogy, which would focus on the child and the adolescent and subordinate individual competition to collective solidarity, should be implemented.

> The school environment is competitive, and it is perhaps impossible for it to be otherwise. But educators have often carried competition to the point where the school has become a place of bitter rivalry. Educational experts and psychologists today recognize that this constitutes a grave danger to the intellectual and emotional equilibrium of child and adolescent. A child consistently out-distanced by competition will often react through pathological and anti-social behaviour. The effort today is to replace this competition with a greater degree of community feeling in work, with team spirit and a sense of solidarity. Hence we are moving in the direction we desire, toward a less individualistic school, a school better attuned to the requirements of social life, more concerned with the shaping of future citizens.[5]

Making secondary education truly accessible to all young people entailed both diversification and integration of educational programs.

Obviously secondary education cannot be the same for everyone. All will participate but not all will start out with the same talents, the same preparation, the same interests, the same needs. All will not persevere to the end, and all will not seek identical training. Some intend to pursue later studies that vary greatly from each other and require widely different preparation. A great number of young people need, above all, together with a store of general knowledge, immediate training for some occupation or other which will allow them to earn a living. The responsibility of secondary education is to receive the many thousands of students coming to it from the elementary schools, accepting them all, and making certain that each receives the preparation for life best suited to his tastes and abilities.[6]

The provision of general, scientific, classical, industrial, agricultural, and family arts programs in Quebec secondary schools had given some recognition to this need, but these programs had to be rethought and coordinated into a harmonious whole. General secondary education should lead gradually to specialization, and a flexible system of electives was needed so that students were not forced prematurely or irrevocably into making final choices among educational programs.

To attain these objectives, the Parent commission proposed to reorganize Quebec public education into six years of elementary school, five years of secondary school, and two years of post-secondary 'institute.' Secondary education from years seven to eleven would be comprehensive education. In the seventh and eighth years students would combine basic subjects with a number of technical electives in order to explore the various domains of human knowledge. From the ninth to the eleventh years students aiming at job preparation and those intending further academic or technical studies would concentrate their electives accordingly, but predetermined curricular tracks would disappear.

In the classification of secondary students, there will be a considerable departure from traditional procedures, in order to give this course the diversity and flexibility it needs. The division from the very beginning into five or six completely distinct courses will disappear. Each student will be expected to take, at each stage in the programme, a given number of basic courses common to all, but he will have the right to choose a certain number of other courses from a list of electives. The number of the electives will increase as the student moves through the various stages of his course. So there will no longer be, as there are in the traditional school, groups of students compelled to follow the same programme. Quite the reverse; the grouping of students will be highly fluid, changing in accordance with individual learning speeds and the choice of electives.[7]

The twelfth and thirteenth years were proposed as being separately organized in 'institutes' which would combine pre-university and vocational education. At this level the Parent commission concluded that there could be no question of presenting a single program for all students.[8] Hence, the institutes would be composite or multilateral institutions, preparing some young people for the pursuit of higher education and simultaneously offering others both general education and technical and vocational instruction leading to various kinds of employment.[9]

Aims and Objectives of Person-Regarding Education: The Hall-Dennis Committee in Ontario

Like the Parent commission, the Provincial Committee on Aims and Objectives in the Schools of Ontario acknowledged the interdependence of the worlds of work and learning, the need to reconcile civic and occupational education with the goals of individual development, and the potential conflict between the needs of individuals and the needs of the community. The Hall-Dennis committee also rejected individual competition in favour of collective solidarity dedicated to universal individual development: 'When schools exhibit a small selected honor roll of students, a price is paid by those who did not make it. Concern should always be felt for the non-team members, the unhonored, the absentees, and the corridor wanderers. A school should serve all its children comfortably and humanely in its on-going, child-centred programs and a learning experience should be found to match the needs of each.'[10] According to the committee, 'How to provide learning experiences aiming at a thousand different destinies and at the same time to educate toward a common heritage and common citizenship is the basic challenge to our society.'[11] In its recommendations the Hall-Dennis committee attempted to create a balance among conflicting aims and objectives by adopting John Dewey's ideal of 'the child in society,' but, consistent with its overriding commitment to person-regarding education, 'where conflict remains, the committee tends to side with the individual.'

The Hall-Dennis committee advocated fully comprehensive public education. The committee was disturbed to find 'still some evidence of educational practice in Ontario that reflects a tendency to segregate students for instruction' and strongly rejected such class-specific and class-defining educational programs. 'Separate classes for the intellectually superior, separate schools for vocational and academic students, and separate curriculum categories all tend to keep alive the idea that the academically endowed are in some way superior to their vocationally-oriented peers. The practice is sufficiently prevalent to cause the Committee to deplore such survival of class distinctions, and to advocate schools that will accommodate students without invidious distinctions.'[12]

To realize its ideal of comprehensive education, the Hall-Dennis committee advocated 'a learning continuum,' a unified school period of thirteen years without horizontal or vertical divisions such as elementary and secondary or academic and vocational. In the intermediate (eighth to tenth) and senior (eleventh to thirteenth) years students would choose their courses from a great number and variety of offerings from the three broad areas of communications, environmental studies, and humanities.[13] There would be individual timetables, promotion by subject, and no designated programs or grades. The primary purpose of secondary schools would be integration of general, academic, and vocationally oriented education, leaving training for specific trades or occupations to post-secondary institutions.

Education in the Person-Centred Society: The Worth Commission in Alberta

The 1972 report of the Commission on Educational Planning in Alberta was constructed on the basis of an ethical liberal theory of a hierarchy of basic individual needs. In future the people of Alberta would have rising expectations for the satisfaction of their basic needs – physical, security, social, and self-actualization – and they would face increasing risks of failure to meet these needs. In this situation of rising expectations of need satisfaction and increasing threats of need frustration, argued the commissioner Walter H. Worth, Albertans had to make a choice of futures between a 'second-phase industrial society' and a 'person-centred society.' A second-phase industrial society would be characterized by the dominance of materialist values, concentration of power in a professional and intellectual elite, and reliance on economic efficiency as the principal criterion of good social organization. A person-centred society, by contrast, would be a significant departure from past trends.

> The goals of the [person-centred] society include making economic growth meet human needs, achieving advances in knowledge and aesthetics and controlling social problems so that individuals may progress toward their goals of self-fulfillment. The industrial system is subservient to, and responsible for serving these larger purposes of the society. The over-arching goal is the cultivation and enrichment of all human beings.[14]

In a person-centred society education would be central. Historically, schooling in Alberta had been residual (assigned tasks that other institutions such as home and church had relinquished) and adjustive ('Preparing persons to fit into our society and stimulating their interest in movement up the socio-economic ladder have become central goals of our educational system'[15]). As education became recognized as a lifelong process and the occupation of the student became accepted as a valid one, there would be 'new approaches to education which emphasize the development of self-learning skills in the person and creation of conditions which foster spontaneous learning,' and there also would be 'more diversity in educational pursuits together with less emphasis on grading, credentials.'[16] Thus the commissioner conceived Alberta's potential future as an educative society.

> The scope of the total educational enterprise, embracing a variety of institutions, agencies and resources, will grow until it permeates the entire social fabric. The intent will be socially responsible individualization that helps set loose the creativity, inventiveness and uniqueness of all individuals throughout their lives ... The traditional boundaries of educational institutions will be extended so that the concerns and resources of the total community are available to teachers and students for learning experiences.[17]

In the educational system of a person-centred society the basic assumption of teaching would be that 'the learner learns by doing.' Controlled course offerings, stereotyped teaching methods, limited learning resources, and inflexible scheduling of conventional public education made for homogeneity and rigidity, which stifled learning and teaching. The content, methods, and organization of public education should be transformed 'from conceiving of schooling as shaping the individual's behavior to fit predetermined roles, to the view that recurrent education seeks to help the learner acquire the knowledge, skills, attitudes and interests that will enable him to constantly influence his environment to achieve his purposes.'[18] The strategies and tactics of teachers should be concerned to develop learning environments in which opportunities to explore, seek, and test were the essential ingredients of teaching methods and learning transactions. 'But it is the learner who is to explore, to seek, to test; and it is the teacher whose methods must be formed by these objectives.'[19]

POLICIES AND POLITICS OF COMPREHENSIVE SECONDARY EDUCATION

The theory of person-regarding education attained a considerable ideological hegemony over elementary and secondary educational policy-making in the late 1960s. Over the next two decades its influence persisted in shaping perceptions of educational problems, analysis of policy options, and proposals for collective action. Ideological hegemony, however, did not easily or necessarily translate into policy practice. In particular, the reform of secondary education based on principles of person-regarding education aroused strong opposition, which forced compromises over principles and retreats on policies.

Policy Design and Implementation of Comprehensive Secondary Education

In May 1965 the Quebec Ministry of Education issued Regulation 1, which implemented the Parent commission's recommendations for years one to eleven. The second part of the regulation, covering years seven to eleven, specified that secondary education would not be differentiated by program. Students would determine their individual programs from a set of graduated optional subjects and would be promoted by subject. Following the recommendations of the Parent commission, however, provision was made for a short vocational program, to be completed in secondary IV (year ten), and also a long vocational program, usually to be completed in secondary V but occasionally extending into secondary VI depending on the area of vocational specialization. In practice, as Regulation 1 came into effect in schools, three-quarters of secondary students opted for the general program, one-fifth enrolled in the long vocational program, and only 5 per cent opted for the short vocational program.

In Ontario a grade-thirteen study committee recommended in 1964 that the provincial departmental examination at the end of grade thirteen be abolished. The 1965 provincial examination results were combined with teachers' class marks and weighted initially at 75 per cent and subsequently at 65 per cent of the final mark. Provincial examinations were finally abolished completely after the 1967–8 school year. During 1967–8 six secondary schools in Ontario experimented with individual timetables for students, promotion by subject, additional optional courses, and some bridging of the barriers between the four-year and five-year programs and across the three branches of the 'Reorganized Plan.' The next year, twenty high schools had introduced some form of non-grading, and eighty more followed in 1969–70, when guidelines for a more flexible system were issued by the Department of Education in Circular H.S.1.[20] Circular H.S.1, as issued in 1969–70 and revised in 1970–1, presented curricular guidelines in two parts. The first part provided guidance for the implementation of the new secondary school organization and curriculum. Under these revised guidelines, branch or program classification of students was to be replaced by individual curricular choices based on broad areas of study. A credit system would facilitate flexible schedule patterns and give students greater freedom of choice among an expanded range of subject offerings. Course outlines prepared by the Department of Education would provide a framework within which courses of study could be developed at the local level to meet the needs, aptitudes, and interests of individual students. The second part of Circular H.S.1 in 1969–71 outlined a more traditional alternative curriculum involving required and optional subjects and retaining the four-year and five-year programs in arts and science; business and commerce; and science, technology, and trades. In 1971–2 all public secondary schools in Ontario were required to adopt the credit system.

In each of the western provinces secondary education became structured by a credit system, which established various provincial requirements regarding general education and course distribution and excluded vocational streaming, whether between different types of secondary schools or within different branches of composite schools. Revised provincial objectives for secondary education emphasized general rather than specialized education and focused on students as individuals. According to a departmental handbook on secondary education in Manitoba, for example, 'A definite attempt is made to provide differentiation to meet the needs, interests and abilities of students.' Similarly, official objectives in Alberta referred to organizing and equipping secondary schools to serve 'the needs of every individual': 'This will be brought about through increased flexibility in organization of staff and students, through the use of a greater variety of instructional and learning experiences, and through new concepts in building design.'[21] Within the framework of a credit system, senior high school students in each of the Prairie provinces were required to take courses in social studies, mathematics, and science in grade ten (Saskatchewan) or grades ten and eleven (Alberta and Manitoba) and English in all three years. In British Columbia all students had 'general education constants' in English, social studies, and physical and health education. Optional credits were chosen from a range of courses offered at each grade level in language arts, second languages, social studies, natural sciences, mathematics, fine arts, home economics, and industrial, agricultural, and business education. Provincial departmental examinations were eliminated in British Columbia (1967), Manitoba (1970), and Alberta (1972). They were retained in Saskatchewan on a limited basis for students, usually those attending small rural high schools, whose teachers lacked the subject qualifications required for accreditation.[22]

In the Maritime provinces general educational objectives were restated to correspond to the ideals of person-regarding education. A revised departmental statement on organization of instruction in New Brunswick schools, for example, expressed the intention to help each person in school to become 'a happy, well adjusted, productive individual – the best person he is capable of becoming.'[23] In Prince Edward Island the statement on educational philosophy issued by the department's educational planning unit made individualization of education the central aim of the entire school system.[24] Provincial departmental examinations were ended in Prince Edward Island in 1970 and in New Brunswick and Nova Scotia in 1972. Students in senior high schools were required to take fifteen course credits, promotion by subject was introduced, and except for required courses in English or French (depending on the student's mother tongue) students were free to construct individual timetables. The list of course offerings in all senior high schools continued to be fairly traditional: English or French as a first language, French or English as a second language, mathematics, biology, chemistry, physics, geography, history, physical education, music, art, home economics, and industrial and business education. Additional electives such as other languages might be available in larger schools, but in general Maritime high schools offered fewer courses and less variety than was found in other provinces. In Nova Scotia and Prince Edward Island distinctions between academic and vocational students disappeared within senior high schools, but both provinces continued to operate separate regional vocational schools. In New Brunswick, although ministry guidelines encouraged provision for 'cross-setting' of courses, the majority of pupils continued to progress through senior high school in one of the three available programs: college preparatory, general educational, and occupational or practical.[25]

In Newfoundland, as in Quebec, the persistence of the denominational system had severely retarded secondary school reorganization and curricular reform. The reorganization of secondary education that began in 1969 was based on the the report of Royal Commission on Education and Youth chaired by Phillip Warren. The Warren commission recognized that a remarkable expansion in provision for secondary education had occurred in the late 1950s and early 1960s, but that much greater effort was required in order to bring the standard of secondary education in Newfoundland up to that prevailing in other provinces. The commission recommended continuing consolidation of schools, in order to expand as many regional and central high schools as possible to 300 and 500 pupils respectively, and more flexibility in the curriculum to meet the diverse needs and abilities of students.[26] The commission supported the recommendation of the provincial committee on curriculum for a three-year high school program with subject promotion and courses divided in difficulty between advanced (A) level and ordinary (O) level. Except for a terminal 'practical' program, designed to provide instruction in trades and general education for those without the ability or inclination to continue in a matriculation or general program after grade seven or eight, the Warren commission recommended against incorporating vocational education into the high school curriculum. Instead, vocational education would be given in six regional community colleges built to serve as an educational level between high school and university.[27]

To summarize, in the late 1960s and early 1970s comprehensive education had gained ascendancy in principle and increasingly in practice in educational policy-making in all provinces, and vigorous programs of school reorganization and curricular reform were launched in each province to implement it. Acceptance of the principles of comprehensive education and concrete measures to implement it in school organization and curriculum perhaps can be judged according to the following scale: (1) commitment to the principles of person-regarding education in statements of the aims and objectives of public education, (2) termination of provincial departmental examinations, (3) abandonment of any official recognition of programs based on a differentiation between academic and vocational tracks, (4) implementation of a credit system with individual timetables and promotion by subject, and (5) no required subjects. An official commitment to comprehensive education was made in each of the provinces in the late 1960s and early 1970s. All provinces except for Quebec and Newfoundland had ended provincial department examinations for matriculation at the end of senior high school. In the Atlantic provinces, official recognition of distinctive academic and vocational schools or tracks remained part of the provincial curriculum, but this had disappeared in other provinces. Only Ontario implemented a credit system with no required subjects for secondary school graduation.

Political Counterattacks and Policy Dilutions

Comprehensive secondary education became the dominant ideal of Canadian educational policy-makers in the late 1960s and early 1970s, but it was never uncontested. Increasingly in the 1970s and continuing through the 1980s, the principles and practices of comprehensive secondary education were vigorously attacked by advocates of a revisionist version of uniform education. As a result, official commitment to person-regarding education wavered, and the practices of comprehensive secondary education were considerably diluted. By way of illustration, consider the cases of the three provinces in which the seminal official policy studies based on the educational ideas of ethical liberalism had been produced: Ontario, Alberta, and Quebec.

In Ontario reorganization of secondary schools according to the principles of comprehensive education was hardly in place when the Ontario Teachers' Federation in 1973 presented a brief to the minister of education that called for a return to compulsory subjects because of 'the lack of any defined core of knowledge, skills or attitudes in the new programme.' Beginning in 1974–5 Ontario secondary students were required to take six compulsory subjects (four English courses and two Canadian studies courses). From 1977–8 the compulsory core was increased to nine credits and broadened to include compulsory credits in mathematics and science, and in 1979–80 it was again expanded to thirteen courses and broadened to include required credits in the arts and physical and health education. Following a major secondary education review in 1980–1, a revised secondary curriculum was introduced, beginning with the students entering grade nine in 1984–5 which made sixteen of the thirty credits required for the new Ontario Secondary School Diploma compulsory.[28]

In Alberta school boards and teachers had wide freedom in the 1970s to develop their own curricula and determine appropriate textbooks and pedagogical resources. Beginning in 1980 with the social studies curriculum, courses of study in all secondary grades and subjects became more prescriptive.[29] Teachers were no longer permitted to use textbooks and resource materials not on the prescribed or recommended lists without approval of their school boards, and school boards in turn had to seek approval for all exceptions from the Department of Education. Beginning in 1984, students graduating from grade twelve were required to take standardized provincial examinations covering their three years of work in senior high school in English, history and social studies, mathematics, biology, chemistry, and physics.[30] Beginning in 1986–7 instructional time allocated to core academic subjects of English, mathematics, social studies, and sciences was increased from 50 per cent to 65–75 per cent in grades seven to nine. In senior high school, under revised diploma requirements phased into effect from 1988–9 to 1992–3, mandatory core subjects were increased to sixty-two of the 100 credits required for the general diploma and seventy-six of the 100 credits required for the advanced diploma. 'Exploratory subjects' developed at the local level were eliminated, and a much narrower range of optional courses was prescribed by the department.[31]

In Quebec, many parents reacted negatively to the new comprehensive secondary schools, especially those located in rural areas.

> The contrast between the small local school, where everyone was known, and the large, impersonal and often distant comprehensive school was indeed a major one. In addi-

tion, the system of electives, options, subject promotion and streaming created major difficulties within the schools themselves. Some of these difficulties were of an administrative nature, such as devising individual timetables for every student, but there were also problems of a more personal sort. In such a large organization, with students in different groups for different subjects, it was often difficult for the students themselves to relate personally to any of the teachers or even to their own peers. These difficulties eventually led to the charge that the comprehensive schools lacked adequate supervision and had become too impersonal and anonymous.[32]

The Green Paper issued by the Parti Québécois government in the fall of 1977 recognized that in spite of efforts to improve schools and modernize education there were serious complaints which needed to be addressed.

People complain that many secondary schools have degenerated into teaching factories, that they have become depersonalized ... People claim that widespread and continuous experimentation, absence of detailed programmes and progress reports on pupils have created impromptu teaching to the detriment of any sort of learning process ... People complain that the school and the teachers demand too little of the pupils, that in some institutions there is a lack of rules of discipline and of the work ethic ... In short, many parents and educators feel that our schools have no coherent educational plan and that the training of our children is deteriorating.[33]

The Parti Québécois Green Paper advanced suggestions for greater uniformity and central control of curriculum and school organization, more detailed educational objectives and programs, and more systematic evaluation of learning outcomes. Bill 71 passed in December 1979 reinforced the authority of the minister of education to regulate curriculum organization and content, and 'régimes pédagogiques' covering elementary and secondary education were approved by the Quebec cabinet in February 1981. Under the new régime pédagogique for secondary education regular programs and courses were prescribed by the minister of education. School boards were permitted to design special programs for their own schools, but these had to be approved by the minister. Every course was required to have at least one approved textbook, and all textbooks and teaching materials were subject to approval by the minister. Over the full program of secondary studies 152 of 176 credits were compulsory.[34] In general there were no options during the first cycle (secondary I and II), one option in secondary III, two in secondary IV, and three in secondary V. Ministry examinations at the end of secondary education would evaluate achievement in subjects required for the school leaving certificates, with the final mark determined equally by the results of school evaluations and ministry examinations, and the passing mark was raised from 50 to 60 per cent. With respect to vocational education, in January 1987 amendments to the secondary régime pédagogique terminated both the short and long vocational programs and introduced two new certificate programs that eliminated vocational training before age sixteen. As Henchey and Burgess have concluded, the régimes pédagogiques for primary and secondary education represented a major retreat from the freedom, individuality, and choice envisaged in the Parent report.

> The major thrust of the proposals in the Green Paper, the Orange Paper and the *régimes pédagogiques* had been in the direction of the scientific and technological management of education. This was the educational philosophy which valued the standardization of timetables, terminal behavioural objectives, detailed curriculum guidelines, and systematic and objective evaluation. It was a world-view based on rationality, coherence, consistency, and systems; it was an orientation not peculiar to Quebec, but one which reflected a general trend of back-to-basics, of increased accountability and of competency-based approaches to learning.[35]

SECONDARY EDUCATION AND THE IDEOLOGIES OF LIBERALISM

Post-war educational politics and policy-making were driven in large part by the ideology of economic liberalism, with its strongly utilitarian view of secondary education and emphasis on equality of opportunity for individual economic achievement. But post-war public education in Canada was also shaped by the ideology of ethical liberalism and its ideal of 'progressive education' or person-regarding education, which aimed at achieving an educative society and individual self-development in the broadly humanistic sense, not simply economic success.

The ethical liberal commitment to educational individuation has a conception of justice as person-regarding equality, in which the distribution of educational benefits is not exactly the same for each person but varies according to the educational needs and abilities of each individual and, hence, has equal value for each person. This ethical liberal conception of educational justice differs fundamentally from the lot-regarding equality to which nineteenth-century political liberals were committed: all children should have the same basic education, so no one in school would have any reason to exchange educational lots with any other person in school. The ethical liberal conception of educational justice appears at first sight to differ much less from the ideas of economic liberals who advocate differentiation of schools and/or courses in order to provide for individuals with different educational needs. Economic liberals, however, perceive the educational needs of individuals primarily in terms of their future membership in occupational classes. As a consequence, the economic liberal conception of educational justice is reduced to a form of segmental equality, in which educational segments are broadly defined by the occupational class structure of capitalist industrial economies and equality is claimed (if at all) only among persons within the same segment, not between segments. For economic liberals, whether secondary educational tracks are organized in partite systems or multilateral schools, they are class-defining and class-specific. For ethical liberals, at least in principle, comprehensive secondary education should be neither class-defining nor class-specific.

Ethical liberals and economic liberals also differ in their conceptions of educational effectiveness and efficiency. Economic liberals judge public secondary education in terms of its contribution to industrial expansion and occupational selection. Educational effectiveness and efficiency are partly defined in terms of individual economic success, but these standards of educational policy evaluation also have a collective dimension. From its early articulation around the turn of the century, the economic liberal conception of economic progress has consistently assumed a strong interdependence among individual opportunity, educational accessibility, occupational selection, industrial expansion, and national wealth. Ethical liberals evaluate the effectiveness of education in terms of its capacity to achieve the full development of each young person in school. Provision for individual development cannot ignore the condition that young people must learn to live and work in their society. Classrooms cannot be isolated from workplaces and communities. Nonetheless, the ultimate test of education for ethical liberals is teaching each person to the greatest extent and in the best way that they are able and willing to learn.

Ethical liberals differ from political and economic liberals in their vision of the transformative power of public education in democratic societies. Political and economic liberals share a view of public education as serving to socialize young citizens and future workers to existing liberal-democratic and capitalist market institutions. Ethical liberals are committed to the ideal of a democratic educative society. They see reform of education as the precondition for reform of society. If schools can be created as truly democratic educative societies, then children who have lived and learned in such schools, will in time, as adults, will transform their neighbourhoods, workplaces, and political communities. Probably it is this radical liberal vision of public education as an instrument of democratic transformation that most decisively divides ethical liberal advocates of person-regarding education from their economic and political liberal critics.

Since the mid-1970s, a confrontation between narrowly economic and broadly humanistic conceptions of collective educational need and individual educational opportunity has been the principal ideological division in Canadian educational politics and policy-making. Certainly, fundamental reforms of school organization and curriculum were achieved during the 1960s and 1970s that made both elementary and secondary education more person-regarding. In spite of budget constraints in the 1980s educational policy-makers continued to design programs to meet the individual needs of students who were academically or vocationally oriented, physically or mentally handicapped, artistically talented, or intellectually gifted. Yet the implementation of curricular reforms in secondary education was scarcely started before complaints about lack of structure and standards and demands for getting 'back to basics' were being made, not only by business interests but also by many parents and teachers. This opposition was persistent and effective. Secondary educational policy development was characterized from the mid-1970s to the mid-1980s by an incremental retreat from the high ideals of comprehensive secondary education. Until the late 1980s, however, ethical liberals might concede the loss of a few battles over policy; at least they had won the war of ideology. What changed was the appearance in the late 1980s and early 1990s of several official policy studies that forcefully articulated an alternative liberal educational ideology, including strands of both political and economic liberalism, to meet the educational challenges of the new global economy.

10

Ethical Liberalism and Cultural Community: Religion and Language in Person-Regarding Public Education

Modern liberalism, both as political theory and as public philosophy, is often criticized as protecting and promoting the dignity and autonomy of individuals at the expense of the human associations and communities that are the social preconditions for individual well-being and self-development. In a persuasive defence of liberal conceptions of individualism, community, and culture, Will Kymlicka has argued that membership in a cultural community does have an important place in liberal thought as an individual good and hence as a criterion for evaluating distributive justice. Kymlicka builds his argument on a distinction between two different types of community. On the one hand, there is the political community, within which individuals exercise the rights and responsibilities entailed by the framework of liberal justice. People who reside within the same political community are fellow citizens. On the other hand, there are cultural communities, within which individuals form and reform their goals and ambitions. People belonging to the same cultural community share a language and history that define their collective identity.[1]

The congruity of political and cultural communities seems to be assumed by most contemporary liberal theorists, for example, John Rawls and Ronald Dworkin, as it was by classical liberal theorists from Locke to Bentham. Kymlicka argues, however, that in the liberal writings of J.S. Mill, T.H. Green, Leonard Hobhouse, and John Dewey human freedom was tied to the existence, and consciousness, of membership in a common culture. In their theories, commonality of language and history, shared membership in a cultural community, does not constrain individuality; it enables individuals to make meaningful choices about how to lead their lives. These theorists of ethical liberalism 'were as much concerned with the value of individual liberty as anyone before or since. Yet they recognized the importance of our cultural membership to the proper functioning of a well-ordered and just society, and hence they had a different view of the legitimacy of special measures for cultural minorities.'[2]

From an ethical liberal perspective, regard for the educational development of individuals requires regard, not only for the educational implications of their membership in the political community, as political and economic liberals assumed, but also for the educational implications of their membership in the cultural community (or communities) in which they are born, grow, and learn to make choices about the conduct of their lives. In order to meet properly the educational needs of each person in school, public education in a multidenominational and officially bilingual political community ought to incorporate the religious and linguistic communities that constitute the cultural foundation of individual educational development. For Canadian educational policy-makers, undertaking official commitments to the principles and policies of person-regarding education involved reopening fundamental questions about the language of instruction and the place of religion in public education.

SECULARIZING AND PLURALIZING RELIGION IN PUBLIC EDUCATION

Four regimes of religion in public education were established in nineteenth-century Canada: state-supported confessional systems in Quebec and Newfoundland; minority denominational separate schools in Ontario, Saskatchewan, and Alberta; de facto reserved schools in the Maritime provinces; and non-denominational common schools in British Columbia and Manitoba. They remained essentially unchanged until the 1960s. Since then, however, changes in educational policies have altered the systems of concurrent endowment, made state public schools more strictly non-denominational, and pluralized religious education, while at the same time state aid for public and private schools serving minority denominations has been increased. These policy changes have been affected by the general trend of post-war educational reform up to the 1960s, which took a strongly utilitarian view of education and put the emphasis on equality of opportunity for individual economic achievement. Reorganization of secondary education, formation of large school districts, and expansion of provincial funding inevitably impinged on the organization of denominational schools and the place of religion in public schools. Resolution of the issues of religion in public education, many of them freshly restated but essentially still unresolved from the nineteenth century, also resulted from commitment to the principles of person-regarding education.

Secularizing the Central Governance of Confessional Systems in Quebec and Newfoundland

The Parent commission created an agenda for educational reform as an essential component of Quebec's 'Quiet Revolution.' On the controversial matter of religion in public education, the commission recommended secularizing both central governance and local administration of public schools, as well as introducing an option for parents and students between denominational and neutral schools.[3]

From its establishment in 1964 the Quebec Ministry of Education combined denominational and functional principles of organization. Under the deputy minister, there are two associate deputy ministers, one Catholic and the other Protestant, and four assistant deputy ministers responsible for administration, labour relations, primary and secondary education services, and educational planning and curricular development. The Superior Council of Education became strictly an advisory body to the ministry, but it can take the initiative in conducting educational inquiries and also submits an annual report to the National Assembly on the state of Quebec education.[4] Associated with the council but operating independently in their jurisdiction over religious and moral education, the Catholic and Protestant committees each have fifteen members representing church authorities, parents, and educators. The denominational committees set the criteria for recognizing educational institutions as Catholic or Protestant, and they determine curricula and teachers' qualifications for courses in religion and morals.

The Parent commission recommended that Catholic and Protestant school boards should be replaced by secular school boards that would operate both French and English, denominational and non-denominational ('neutral') schools. This recommendation was not immediately implemented, in part because it encountered objections on the grounds of language as well as religion. First elected in 1976 on a Quebec nationalist platform that included implementation of the Parent commission's recommendation, and re-elected in 1981, the Parti Québécois government tabled a White Paper in June 1982, which proposed to abolish denominational school boards. Outside Montreal, regional boards would administer the schools of both languages and both denominations in their districts. Each school would be governed by a council of parents, teachers, and (at the secondary level) students that would determine whether its school would be Catholic, Protestant, multi-faith, or neutral in its orientation and would have the authority to choose textbooks, set budgets, and hire and evaluate staff. On the island of Montreal denominational boards would be replaced by eight French-language and five English-language boards. In order to allay opposition to the reorganization and meet the constitutional requirements of section 93, the government amended Bill 3 before its passage in 1984, so as to put school boards throughout the province on a linguistic basis, not just on the island of Montreal, and restrict the denominational boards of Montreal and Quebec City to their 1867 jurisdictions, areas now covering very few schools.

Challenged by the Quebec Association of Protestant School Boards and the Montreal Catholic School Commission, Bill 3 was judged by the Quebec Superior Court to be unconstitutional under section 93 of the Constitution Act, 1867; the Liberal government elected in 1985 chose not to appeal the decision. Instead, in December 1987 the Bourassa government introduced Bill 107, which followed in its essentials the Parti Québécois government's legislation: outside Montreal and Quebec, school boards would be either French or English, not Roman Catholic or Protestant; school councils would decide whether their schools would have a religious status, or not; and the school boards of Montreal and Quebec City, specifically protected under section 93, would continue to operate as Roman Catholic and Protestant boards alongside the new secular French and English boards.[5] Referred to the courts following its passage by the Quebec National Assembly in December 1988, Bill 107 was upheld as constitutional by the Quebec Court of Appeal in September 1990 and by the Supreme Court of Canada in June 1993. Thus, in the early 1990s, 150 years after its foundation, local school administration in Quebec passed an historic turning point in its organizational ethos from religion to language.[6]

In Newfoundland the report of the Royal Commission on Education and Youth in 1967 also recommended wide-ranging reforms to modernize school curricula, raise teachers' qualifications, improve educational facilities, and increase financial support. With respect to the central governance of education, the royal commission proposed to reorganize the Department of Education 'on a functional rather than a denominational basis,'[7] abolish the Council of Education as the central policy-making agency, and transfer the denominational superintendents to denominational advisory bodies outside the department. The churches would continue to control religious education programs and the distribution of any denominationally specific grants, but the primary locus of church control of education would be the district and school, not the provincial, level.

The Department of Education and Youth Act of 1968 implemented a functional reorganization of the Newfoundland department as recommended, and also established denominational education committees (later councils) and the Denominational Policy Commission. The denominational education councils were responsible for establishing, modifying, and dissolving the boundaries of school districts; allocating the province's capital grant for school construction to their various school boards; training, certifying, and recruiting teachers; selecting the appointed members of school boards; and developing and administering religious education.[8] Along with the minister, deputy minister, and an assistant deputy minister, the three executive directors of the Integrated, Catholic, and Pentecostal education councils comprised the Denominational Policy Commission, which advised cabinet on all educational policies affecting any right or privilege of any religious denomination constitutionally protected under the Terms of Union. If the commission was not unanimous in its recommendations, any denominational council might make separate recommendations to the cabinet. With respect to policies that did not impinge on denominational rights, there was a larger general advisory committee that also included the executive directors. Thus, Newfoundland established a secular central administration that nonetheless remained strongly corporatist in its organization. As before, the linking officials were the executive directors of the denominational education councils.

At the same time as the central governance of Newfoundland education was reformed in the 1960s, the denominational structure of local administration was simplified. In a context of increasing public concern about the adverse impact of denominational divisions on the costs, quality, and accessibility of education, the Anglican and United churches in 1963 established a liaison committee to facilitate common policies between their school boards. In 1967 an integrating committee, which now included the Salvation Army, undertook to unify these three Protestant systems. Two years later the Avalon Consolidated School Board united adherents of the Anglican church, the United church, the Salvation Army, and the Presbyterian church in integrated schools and became the prototype for similar boards throughout the province. Thus, Newfoundland public education became essentially a dual confessional regime, divided between Integrated school boards (eighteen districts, 324 schools, and 56.2 per cent of total enrolment in 1989–90) and Roman Catholic school boards (twelve districts, 181 schools, and 38.6 per cent of enrolment).[9]

Secularizing Public Schools in the Maritimes

In the Maritime provinces, district reorganization and school consolidation in the 1960s and 1970s created large, heterogeneous schools and made it difficult to preserve the informal practice of reserving schools for Roman Catholics. In New Brunswick, for example, the change was quite abrupt. In 1967 school districts were reduced in number from 433 to thirty-three and subjected to a high degree of provincial control. Within a decade enrolment in Catholic 'rented buildings' had fallen to 4 per cent of total provincial enrolment.[10]

Regional schools raised difficult issues about denominational religious instruction and observance for multidenominational student bodies. The historically accepted practice of conducting religious education outside the regular school program also was complicated by the constraints of bus schedules, availability of alternative extracurricular activities, and shortages of qualified teachers. Moreover, Catholic parents were less insistent on Catholic education for their children. In their survey of francophone parents in New Brunswick, Pierre Michaud and Lionel Desjarlais found religious education to be among those educational objectives having a larger variance, implying a lack of consensus among parents. Many parents still see a role for the school in religious education, but many others believe that religious instruction and observances belong in church, not school. If this evidence is representative of opinion in the Acadian community, it indicates an important evolution of values compared with the pre-1967 period, when the slogan of the most influential francophone educational organization, l'Association acadienne d'éducation, was 'Dieu et langue à l'école.'[11]

Full Funding for Roman Catholic Separate Schools in Saskatchewan and Ontario

In Saskatchewan and Ontario the constitutional protection of separate Catholic schools extended only through elementary schools. As the expanded postwar school population passed through the primary grades and began to reach secondary schools, the financial pressures of capital expansion, teacher shortages, and curriculum diversification renewed demands for recognition and funding of separate secondary schools as state-provided schools. In Saskatchewan the demand encountered little resistance. In 1964, following a brief campaign by a coalition of Catholic school supporters (and with a provincial election on the horizon), a bill introduced by the New Democratic party government to recognize separate secondary schools as eligible for full provincial funding was approved unanimously by the legislative assembly. In Ontario the issue proved to be much more controversial.

In the late 1960s a coalition of Ontario Catholic school supporters, including parents, students, teachers, and trustees, organized a public campaign to secure full state funding for grades nine through thirteen. During the 1971 provincial election both the Liberal and New Democratic parties committed themselves to full funding. The governing Conservative party under its new leader William Davis stoutly defended the historical restriction. The Conservative government easily won re-election, in part because of its stand on the separate-school issue, and state aid for separate schools disappeared from the provincial public agenda for the next decade. Then in June 1984, on the verge of his retirement as premier and party leader, Davis announced that as a result of 'a careful and fresh review' full funding would be introduced over a two-year period beginning in September 1985. Appearing before the legislative committee that reviewed Bill 30, the premier explained his discomfort with the 1971 electoral campaign decision and the contradiction of unequal funding between public and separate school education in terms that reveal an essentially ethical liberal commitment to person-regarding education.

What is the date when people leave in June? When does the secondary school fold up? The 18th? It is hard to explain the logic to [Catholic] youngsters, many of whom came from families who chose this province as their home ... that when they left on June 18, having successfully completed grade 10, if they got their marks, with a public investment by the people of this province, something had happened between June 18 and September 5 in the same calendar year whereby they then had to start to pay fees. It was hard to explain the logic or the fairness of this, because we have encouraged children to stay in the same educational environment. I am not going to quarrel for a moment that their educational purposes would not have been well served by going to Brampton Centennial Secondary School some 10 blocks away. But at the same time, you have to talk about logic in some of these decisions; you have to talk about the equity of it ... I am not minimizing for a second the complexity of the issue, nor am I minimizing its sensitivity ... I am not in any way minimizing the difficulty facing government. But I also hope, and I like to believe, that this province is mature and tolerant and that this province understands that if we really believe in some of the things we say – when we look at our multicultural policy, when we want to make people retain some of the things that are dear to them – we recognize the equity and the logic in a matter of conscience that this is the time for this very fundamental change in policy ... We are talking about rights. We are talking about children. We are talking about their educational program.[12]

When the constitutionality of Bill 30 was referred to the Supreme Court of Canada in *Re The Metropolitan Toronto Board of Education et al. and the Attorney General of Ontario et al.* in 1987, the court held that not only was the bill constitutional, but also the right of Roman Catholic school supporters to have their children receive instruction at the secondary level had been wrongly restricted by the decision of the Judicial Committee of the Privy Council in *Tiny*.

Extending State Aid to Private Schools

Beginning in the 1960s Quebec and the four western provinces have developed programs of financial assistance to private schools that provide support mainly to voluntary denominational schools.

Since 1967 public funding has been available in Alberta for private schools that meet certain conditions: the Alberta curriculum must be taught, the teachers must have Alberta teaching certificates, the students must write provincial examinations, the schools must be open to regular inspection and conform to provincial standards, and the parents of the students must be residents of Alberta. Grants to private schools can be as much as 75 per cent of the basic provincial foundation program. In 1968 Quebec began giving financial aid to private schools that were designated as operating in the public interest, a term defined primarily by the extent to which their curriculum coincides with the provincial curriculum. Such schools receive grants equal to 80 per cent of average costs per pupil in equivalent public schools, and schools not meeting the public-interest criterion may still be eligible for a 60 per cent grant. In British Columbia, following ten years of lobbying by the Federation of Independent Schools, the Social Credit government in 1977 fulfilled its campaign promise to assist independent schools by paying part of their operating costs and their teachers' salaries. Public funding for private schools can be as much as 30 per cent of the grants made to public schools. Beginning in 1980, Saskatchewan granted private secondary schools 55 per cent of their average costs per pupil and, for those that had been in operation for at least five years, 10 per cent of approved capital costs. Finally, after several years of providing assistance in kind for transportation, textbooks, vocational education, and even school facilities, Manitoba in 1981 began to give private schools financial aid similar to that provided in the other western provinces.[13]

In Ontario the campaign for state aid to private schools was invigorated by the Conservative government's decision to extend full funding to separate schools, and a provincial commission reported in favour of such a program in October 1985.[14] Opposition to the commission's recommendation was fragmented and desultory, and the unwillingness of the Liberal (1985–90) and New Democratic (post-1990) governments to implement it seems to have been more a result of the provincial budget deficit rather than any principled opposition to state aid for private schools.[15] Even worse financial straits make the development of state aid programs unlikely in the Maritime provinces.

Pluralizing Religious Education and Observance in Public Schools

Denominational religious instruction is constitutional in all schools in Quebec and Newfoundland and in separate schools in Ontario, Saskatchewan, and Alberta. In public schools outside Quebec and Newfoundland religious education typically has been left to the discretion of local boards. Ontario, however, was an exception. A campaign for compulsory religious instruction by the Ontario Religious Education Council, an alliance of eight Protestant denominations, began in 1927, and by the Second World War it had succeeded in getting about 10 per cent of school boards voluntarily to adopt compulsory programs of religious instruction. During the war the Conservative premier, George Drew, increasingly identified his party's educational policy with teaching basics, loyalty to the British Empire, and commitment to the Christian religion.[16] Following its re-election the government issued a regulation requiring two half-hour periods of religious instruction in elementary schools each week. The curriculum focused on the life and teachings of Jesus as well as Old Testament stories.

Through the 1950s and 1960s the Ontario regulation became increasingly controversial. In 1969 a provincial commission chaired by Keiller Mackay recommended its elimination in favour of informal moral or ethical education that would permeate the entire curriculum and encourage pupils to make their own value judgments and moral decisions,[17] but no action was taken by the government. Following the proclamation of the Canadian Charter of Rights and Freedoms, the constitutionality of the regulation was challenged. In *Corporation of the Canadian Civil Liberties Association et al.* v. *Minister of Education and Elgin County Board of Education*, the divisional court held that the provincial requirement for religious education did not necessarily violate the charter, but that the Elgin County board's exclusively Christian course of studies certainly did. Subsequently, the board revised its program to focus on world religious beliefs and practices, but a unanimous decision of the Ontario Court of Appeal in January 1990 found that the Elgin County board's curriculum was not broad enough and the provincial regulation was inconsistent with constitutional guarantees of freedom of conscience and religion. The decision was not appealed. Under a new ministry regulation issued in December 1990, local boards were permitted to offer up to one hour of religious education a week as long as their courses do not promote any particular faith. Boards were also allowed to provide classrooms for voluntary denominational education before or after school, but they must provide fair access to all religious groups.[18]

At the time the charter was proclaimed in 1982, Ontario, British Columbia, and Manitoba all required religious exercises at the daily opening and/or closing of public schools. In other provinces they were optional, at the discretion of school boards.[19] With the support of advocacy organizations like the Canadian Civil Liberties Association, parents who opposed mandatory religious exercises in schools began legal challenges under section 2(a) of the charter, which guarantees individual freedom of conscience and religion.

In the first of these cases to reach the appeal court, *Zylberberg et al.* v. *The Director of Education of the Sudbury Board of Education,* the issue was recitation of the Lord's Prayer and reading from the Bible. The Ontario Court of Appeal in 1988 decided that peer pressure and classroom norms operate to compel members of religious minorities to conform with majority religious practices and hence the provincial regulation mandating religious exercises at the opening and closing of schools had the effect of imposing Christian observances on non-Christian pupils and religious observances on non-believers. In its judgment the court referred approvingly to the policy of the Toronto Board of Education, in order to show that religious exercises could be appropriately reflective of a multicultural, multidenominational society, and hence constitutional under section 2(a).[20]

The compulsory requirement for opening schools with prayers was also successfully challenged in British Columbia (*Russow and Lambert* v. *Attorney General of British Columbia,* 1989) where the British Columbia Supreme Court, citing *Zylberberg,* held that the provincial regulation was unconstitutional.[21] Manitoba then changed section 84 of the Public Schools Act to require that Christian exercises be held in every school unless the local school board each year voted otherwise. Simply providing for local discretion could not in itself save Christian religious exercises from challenges to their constitutionality, however; to be constitutional, religious exercises in public schools other than separate schools must be truly multidenominational or nondenominational. In August 1992, four years after the case was launched, Mr Justice Michael Monnin of the Manitoba Court of Queen's Bench found that morality and ethics have a place in public education but 'to prefer one religion over another, as is now being done in the school system of this province, contravenes the provisions of the Charter relating to freedom of conscience and religion.'[22] Section 84 was unconstitutional.

MAJORITY-WILL UNILINGUALISM, MINORITY RIGHTS, AND LINGUISTIC CHOICE

By the 1930s there were four types of linguistic regimes, which overlapped with religious regimes, in Canadian public education: English as the majority will, fortified and impassioned by the spirit of British-Canadian communal assimilation, in British Columbia and Manitoba; English as the language of the majority and also British-Canadian communal assimilation in Ontario,

Saskatchewan, and Alberta, with French permitted in elementary schools as a transitional language of instruction; English as the majority language in the Maritimes, with French as a limited minority right in Acadian districts; and a communal consociation of French Catholics, English Catholics, and English Protestants in Quebec. These regimes operated with relatively little questioning or disturbance until the 1960s. Then the impact of three interdependent historical developments changed the issue of language in public education.

First, as English-speaking Canada became increasingly non-British in ethnic origins, the vision of English as the language of British-Canadian communal assimilation faded to the margins of politics and policy, reduced to a small but vocal core of British-Canadian true believers. Outside Quebec the position of English as the official language of instruction came to depend simply on the political power and legitimacy of the majority will.

Second, inside Quebec a rise of French-Canadian nationalism in the 1950s resulted from a basic change in public philosophy. The 1960s and 1970s were characterized by a reformulation of ethnic identity among French-speaking Quebeckers in which language, province, and state replaced religion, race, and church as central elements of the symbolic order of French Quebec.[23] A commitment to the economic and political modernization of Quebec, which not only relied on the Quebec state as instrument but also infused the state with powerful emotions of Québécois nationalism, at once threatened the segmented consociation of Quebec public education. For the 'nouveaux clercs' of the Quebec state, both language and education were central policy problems in realizing their vision of becoming 'maîtres chez nous.' Inevitably, where language and education intersected in the issue of French and English as official languages of instruction in Quebec public schools the tension between the will of the francophone majority and the rights of the anglophone minority was most starkly confronted.

Third, French-Quebec nationalism and the resulting challenge to national unity revived the issue of linguistic equality in all provinces. The anglophone minority inside Quebec strenuously resisted any erosion of its 'historical right' to schools where English was the language of instruction. Francophone minorities outside Quebec pressed for full recognition of their right to have their children educated in elementary and secondary schools where French was the language of instruction. Ethnic minorities whose mother tongue was neither English nor French fought inside Quebec to preserve their right to send their children to schools where English was the language of instruction; outside Quebec they began to question both the majority's imposition of English as the language of instruction and the recognition of French as the only minority right. From the 1960s, then, linguistic regimes of majority will, communal assimilation, and communal consociation, which had governed the language of instruction in public education since the nineteenth century, were hard pressed by claims for minority rights and linguistic choice.

Public Education and Federal Language Policy

The federal Royal Commission on Bilingualism and Biculturalism was appointed in 1963 'to inquire into and report upon the existing state of bilingualism and biculturalism in Canada and to recommend what steps should be taken to develop the Canadian Confederation on the basis of an equal partnership between the two founding races, taking into account the contribution made by the other ethnic groups to the cultural enrichment of Canada and the measures that should be taken to safeguard that contribution.'

To the Royal Commission on Bilingualism and Biculturalism equal partnership between the official languages meant the provision of opportunities for individuals, wherever they might reside in Canada, to work, study, and live creatively in either English or French. However much the principle might have to be modified in practice by the constraints of language-group distribution, the aspiration should be joint usage of French and English throughout Canada: 'Living in French must be made possible in every part of Canada where there are enough French-speaking people.'[24]

With respect to languages other than the official languages of English and French, the commission held that cultural pluralism was an enriching treasure for all Canadians: 'The presence in Canada of many people whose language and culture are distinctive by reason of their birth or ancestry represents an inestimable enrichment that Canadians can not afford to lose.'[25] Because of the interdependence of language and culture ('Language allows for self-expression and communication according to one's own logic'), the commission considered the teaching of languages other than English and French in provincial educational systems to be an important element of any program to preserve non-British, non-French cultures. The commission made a distinction, however, between learning the official languages and opportunities for learning other languages. While there must be 'a systematic approach to teaching the second official language to members of both the major linguistic communities,' the commission did not recommend the same degree of development for teaching other languages in Canada: 'rather, we recommend that there be opportunities to study many languages within the context of the public education system.'[26] In effect, what the commission proposed was a regime of linguistic choice, where numbers warrant, with priority given to English and French as the official languages of Canada.

The standards of public policy proposed by the commission directly expressed its guiding principle of equal opportunity for individual development between speakers of both official languages. 'Equal partnership in education implies equivalent educational opportunities for Francophones and Anglophones alike, whether they belong to the majority or the minority in their province.'[27] Because equal partnership was taken to mean linguistic choice for individuals, in the commission's analysis the crisis of ethnic relations in Canada was mainly an issue of individual rights rather than one of collective rights or group status. Taken together the commission's recommendations expressed a strong belief in the generosity of the majority and the legitimacy of minority rights, which together formed the core of the commission's understanding of the principle of equality: 'The principle of equality implies respect for the idea of minority status, both in the country as a whole and in each of its regions ... Recognizing the rights of a linguistic minority does not reduce those of the majority: with a little good will, the rights of both can be exercised without serious conflict.'[28]

The regime of linguistic choice envisaged by the Royal Commission on Bilingualism and Biculturalism became the foundation of federal language policy. The commission's major recommendations for a federal official languages act, commissioner of official languages, bilingual federal public service, and constitutional protection for language rights formed the primary elements of federal language policy from the late 1960s to the early 1990s. Two of these elements of federal language policy impinged significantly on public education in Canada: the provision for advancement of English and French implied in the Official Languages Act and the protection of minority language rights in education under section 23 of the Canadian Charter of Rights and Freedoms.[29]

Beginning in 1970 federal aid for official languages in education was distributed under bilateral agreements with provincial governments, which provided 9 per cent of the teaching costs of programs giving 75 per cent of their instruction in the minority official language, 5 per cent of the average annual cost of programs having less than three-quarters of their instruction in the minority official language, 1.5 per cent of the average cost of French and English minority-language and second-language programs, to offset administrative costs, and 10 per cent of provincial operating grants, plus 8.5 per cent of capital grants, paid to minority-language and bilingual post-secondary institutions. When these bilateral agreements (renewed in 1974) expired in 1979, the federal government reduced funding to the provinces by about 20 per cent. Grants for official languages in education then continued under annual interim arrangements until a protocol for bilateral agreements was signed in 1983 between the Department of the Secretary of State and the Council of Ministers of Education, Canada. Under the protocol, subsequently renewed in 1985 and 1988, federal support was provided for infrastructure support, program expansion and development, teacher training and development, and student support.

From the outset federal aid to provincial governments for advancement of official languages in education has been the largest item in the federal budget for promotion of official languages, amounting to over 40 per cent of total federal expenditures on official languages programs. As Table 10.1 shows, the largest beneficiary among the provinces has been Quebec, where the entire English-language educational system is eligible for federal aid to minority-language education. In addition, all students in English-speaking elementary schools study French as a second language, and in French-speaking schools elementary students above grade four and all secondary students study English as a second language. Under the five-year protocol (1988–93), for example, the minimum levels of funding established at the outset for infrastructure support gave Quebec $81.43 million or 47 per cent of guaranteed funding, compared with $46.95 million (27 per cent) for Ontario and $18.88 million (11 per cent) for New Brunswick.[30]

Section 23 of the Canadian Charter of Rights and Freedoms made a major advance in minority linguistic rights in Canada by establishing parental rights with respect to the language of their children's primary and secondary school instruction. Under section 23 the exercise of minority-language educational rights is restricted to parents who are citizens of Canada. Three types of claimants are defined. First, parents whose first language learned and still understood is English and who reside in Quebec have the right to have their children receive primary and secondary school instruction in English; parents whose first language learned and still understood is French and who reside outside Quebec have the right to have their children educated in French. Second, parents who have received their primary school instruction anywhere in Canada in English and who reside in Quebec have the right to have their children educated in English; parents who reside outside Quebec and who received their primary school education in French have the right to have their children receive primary and secondary school instruction in French. Third, where one child has received or is receiving primary or secondary school instruction in French or English, the child's parents have the right to have all their children educated in the same language. For all three categories of claimants minority-language educational rights apply wherever 'the number of citizens who have

Table 10.1
Distribution of federal government transfers to public elementary and secondary education under official languages in education programs, selected fiscal years, 1970–1 to 1989–90 (%)

Province	1970	1975	1980	1985*	1989*
Newfoundland	0.3	0.4	0.4	0.9	0.7
Prince Edward Island	0.2	0.2	0.3	0.5	0.8
Nova Scotia	1.6	1.2	1.2	1.9	2.2
New Brunswick	8.3	7.2	7.8	8.7	8.4
Quebec	54.0	61.6	57.6	43.3	36.5
Ontario	29.9	24.1	26.2	32.1	36.7
Manitoba	1.5	1.6	1.9	4.0	4.9
Saskatchewan	0.9	0.7	0.6	1.3	2.3
Alberta	1.7	1.4	2.0	3.5	4.8
British Columbia	1.6	1.6	2.2	3.5	4.2
Yukon and NWT				0.3	0.3
Canada %**	100	100	100	100	100
$thousands	47,018	99,202	113,243	118,989	127,010

* Fiscal years 1985 and 1989 include transfers under infrastructure support programs only. Allocations among levels of education are not possible under program expansion and development, teacher training and development, and student support.

** Percentages may not add to 100 because of rounding.

such a right is sufficient to warrant the provision to them out of public funds of minority language instruction.'

The initial impact of the Canadian Charter of Rights and Freedoms on minority-language education was greatest in Quebec. There the courts held that sections of Bill 101 (Charte de la langue française) restricting English-language education violated minority-language rights protected under section 23 of the charter. Subsequently, section 23 has proved important primarily in establishing that minority-language educational rights include the right of participation in school governance. L'Association canadienne-française de l'Ontario and l'Association des enseignantes et des enseignants de l'Ontario based their argument on section 23 of the charter, and in 1984 the Ontario Court of Appeal held that the right of French-language schools included the right to manage them. In March 1990 the Supreme Court of Canada ruled in *Mahé* v. *Alberta* that section 23 of the charter confers a general right to minority-language education. Where the number of minority-language students is sufficiently large, the linguistic minority is entitled not only to a separate school but also to its own school board. According to the Supreme Court of Canada, where the number of students is not sufficiently large to warrant an independent school board, it may still be large enough to require establishment of a separate francophone school and representation of the linguistic minority on the existing school board. In the particular case at issue in *Mahé*, the court found that the number of students likely to attend the francophone school in Edmonton was insufficient to justify creating an independent francophone school board, but there was a sufficient number of students to warrant both a separate francophone school and a guarantee of representation for francophone parents on the Edmonton school board.

The *Mahé* decision set an important judicial precedent for claims to local self-governance, where numbers warrant, as an essential attribute of minority-language educational rights, but provincial governments were slow to respond. The first statutory amendment that provided for the establishment of francophone school boards conjointly with public school boards was introduced by the NDP government in Saskatchewan in September 1992 and passed by the legislative assembly in June 1993.[31] The government of Alberta in May 1992 introduced a bill to provide for francophone minority-language school boards, but the bill failed to pass before the assembly was dissolved for the provincial election of June 1993. Following the re-election of the Conservative government, passage of the School Law Amendment Act authorized the establishment of francophone school boards, and plans were initiated for three school boards in Falher–Peace River, St Paul–Bonnyville, and Edmonton to serve about 3,000 francophone students.[32] In Manitoba the Conservative government's bill to provide for French school boards was being considered by the legislative assembly when a judgment of the Supreme Court of Canada in March 1993 confirmed that the *Mahé* decision was applicable to that province and, hence, presumably to other provinces, notably Ontario, remiss in legislating full rights of local school governance to francophone minorities.[33]

Minority-Language Education in the Atlantic Provinces, Ontario, and the West

In its final report on the crisis of linguistic and cultural relations between French and English, the Royal Commission on Bilingualism and Biculturalism argued, 'The school is the basic agency for maintaining language and culture, and without this essential resource neither can be strong.' Hence, 'it must be accepted as normal that children of both linguistic groups will have access to schools in which their own language is the language of instruction.'[34] According to the commission, the exercise of that right required the establishment of parallel school systems in Ontario and New Brunswick, where the francophone minority-language groups were largest in number, and separate schools for francophones where their numbers warranted in the remaining provinces.

In New Brunswick, where approximately one-third of the population has French as their mother tongue, the royal commission's recommendation for parallel systems was adopted incrementally in the course of a decade of linguistic disputes over both central and local control of educational policy-making. As a result of the reorganization of school districts in 1967 predominantly English-speaking and French-speaking communities, which previously had operated as separate school districts, found themselves in the same school district. Especially in linguistically balanced towns such as Bathurst, Dalhousie and Grand Falls, prolonged struggles began over control of the school board and designation of the language of instruction, particularly in secondary schools. Francophone criticism was also directed at the predominantly anglophone composition of the provincial educational bureaucracy. The first step towards the creation of parallel anglophone and francophone educational systems was taken in 1973, with the appointment of separate anglophone and francophone deputy ministers. That was followed by separate anglophone and francophone divisions in the Department of Education for primary and secondary educational services. At the local level, the Bathurst and Dalhousie school districts were replaced by separate French and English districts in 1978; by 1981 all school districts were reorganized into parallel systems of English-language and French-language school districts.

Outside New Brunswick and Quebec provincial governments have been reluctant to accept language as a principle of educational governance. Prior to the Supreme Court's decision in *Mahé* v. *Alberta* in 1990, there were only four officially recognized French-language school boards. In Prince Edward Island the relatively small (one elementary school, one high school) regional administrative unit number five has operated as a French-language district since it was set up in 1972, and French is the operational language of the Argyle-Clare district school board in southwestern Nova Scotia. In Ontario Bill 75, introduced in 1985 by the new Liberal government, provided for the establishment of minority-language councils within public school boards and authorized the councils to govern minority-language schools in their districts, while sharing decision-making with the public school board in areas of common jurisdiction. Two exclusively French-language school boards were established in the national capital district and in metropolitan Toronto in 1988.

Although reluctant to accept language as a principle of local educational governance, governments in all English-majority provinces had made some provision for French-language elementary and secondary school instruction where numbers warrant even before the proclamation of section 23 in the

Canadian Charter of Rights and Freedoms. Ontario in 1968 established the right of Franco-Ontarian students, where their numbers warranted it, to receive their elementary and secondary school instruction in separate French-language schools or in separate French-language classes within English-language schools.[35] In 1967 an amendment to the Manitoba Public Schools Act permitted French to be used as a language of instruction for up to one-half of the school day, and in 1970 Franco-Manitobans gained minority-language school privileges similar to those available to Franco-Ontarians. Alberta removed its former time restrictions on instruction in French in 1968, permitting French at the discretion of local school boards for up to half the school day. An amendment to Saskatchewan's School Act that freed the Department of Education to determine the use of French by regulation resulted in a minority-language program under which the use of French varied from 100 per cent of instructional time in kindergarten to 50 per cent in grades five to twelve. British Columbia became the last province to make provision for minority-language education when the provincial curriculum was changed to permit the use of French as language of instruction in elementary grades, where numbers warranted, beginning in September 1978.

Despite official recognition of minority-language education, the number of minority-language schools and enrolments in minority-language programs have declined steadily since 1970–1 as percentages of the total number of schools and total enrolments. In part these national trends are affected by the sharp decline of anglophone schools and enrolments in Quebec, but the trend in other provinces suggests that minority-language educational programs have not reversed, although they may have slowed, the assimilation of francophone minorities outside Quebec.

In contrast with minority-language education, enrolments in programs in French as a second language have expanded steadily. Perhaps the most significant expression of the ideology of personal bilingualism in educational policy has been the rapid expansion of these programs. Here the phenomenon of French immersion programs is perhaps the key indicator. Beginning with the first experimental classes in St Lambert, Quebec, in 1967, enrolment in immersion programs increased to 37,835 in 1977–8 (0.8 per cent of total enrolment) and 288,050 in 1990–1 (6 per cent of enrolment). Despite its popular success and educational achievement, French immersion has its share of critics.[36] Nonetheless, the expansion and diversification of instruction in French as a second language in all provinces during the 1970s and 1980s stands as a powerful expression of the theory of person-regarding education and the institutionalization of linguistic choice, at least as regards education in the official languages.

TABLE 10.2

Enrolments in second-language programs, minority-language education and French immersion as percentages of total enrolments in public elementary and secondary education, selected school years, 1970–1 to 1990–1

School year	New-foundland	Prince Edward Island	Nova Scotia	New Brunswick	Quebec	Ontario	Manitoba	Saskat-chewan	Alberta	British Columbia
Second language*										
1970	37.1	46.9	33.8	45.5	53.8	38.7	38.6	34.3	32.6	27.7
1977	43.4	59.7	44.9	43.5	53.8	45.3	38.7	24.9	na	30.5
1980	48.4	59.0	51.0	45.6	54.0	47.7	40.6	23.8	na	36.2
1985	53.7	63.8	59.5	50.9	54.8	55.6	50.8	32.7	31.2	39.0
1990	58.2	63.1	60.8	57.4	58.3	56.6	55.3	60.4	38.0	46.3
Minority language**										
1970	0.1	2.6	3.4	34.5	15.7	5.7	4.2	0.3		
1977	0.1	2.3	3.0	32.7	16.4	5.3	3.7	0.6	na	
1980	0.1	2.1	2.8	32.3	14.0	5.2	3.2	0.6	na	0.1
1985	0.1	2.0	2.4	32.9	11.2	5.2	2.8	0.6	0.3	0.3
1990	0.2	2.3	2.1	33.4	9.6	5.0	2.8	0.5	0.5	0.4
French immersion										
1977	0.1	2.0	0.1	2.0	1.4	0.7	0.8	0.2	1.6***	0.2
1980	0.3	4.8	0.3	3.6	1.6	2.5	2.1	0.8	2.5***	0.9
1985	1.4	10.0	1.1	10.3	1.7	5.0	6.3	2.9	4.2	3.2
1990	3.7	13.8	3.2	12.9	3.0	7.0	9.9	5.4	5.8	5.4

* Francophone students taking English in Quebec, and anglophone students taking French in other provinces; includes enrolments in immersion programmes beginning in 1980–1.

** English in Quebec, and French in other provinces; years prior to 1980–1 include enrolments in immersion programmes.

*** French immersion includes minority-language education.

na Comparable statistic not available.

Majority Will and Minority Rights in Quebec Education

In 1968 the Royal Commission on Bilingualism and Biculturalism proposed Quebec as the standard for other provinces in recognizing and providing for minority-language education.[37] Over two decades later, in both law and practice, minority-language education in Quebec continued to be more generous and extensive than that in any other province except New Brunswick. Nonetheless, the trend of Quebec educational policies was retreat from communal consociation and constraint of English-language education. In the ensuing political controversy and public debate about French and English as languages of instruction, the right of the historical English community to preserve its English-language schools was recognized by all but the most extreme Quebec nationalists. Rather, the central issues of language in Quebec schools were the freedom of francophone parents to educate their children in English and the language of instruction for the children of immigrants.

Historically, non-English, non-French immigrants settling in Quebec usually opted to enrol their children in English-language schools. As the immigrant population increased rapidly during the 1950s and 1960s, especially in the Montreal area, English-language schooling in both the Protestant and especially the Roman Catholic sectors expanded correspondingly. Increasingly, in the 1960s Quebec nationalists identified the long-term linguistic incorporation of immigrants into French-speaking Quebec as being crucial for its survival and development as a modern francophone society in North America.

In 1967 the public (Roman Catholic) school commission of the Montreal suburb St-Léonard began a phased closure of its English-language schools, thus requiring English-speaking Catholics who resided in its jurisdiction, mostly Italian immigrants, to enrol their children in French-language schools. The Quebec Superior Court refused to overturn the board's action, on the grounds that neither Quebec provincial statutes nor Canadian constitutional law guaranteed instruction in English. Fierce opposition to the school board's proposal from both English and immigrant sectors of the community eventually led the Union nationale government to introduce Bill 63. Passed in 1969, the Loi pour promouvoir la langue française au Québec made French the official language of Quebec and gave priority to French as the language of instruction in Quebec public schools. All parents were given the legal right to have their children educated in French or English, whichever was their choice, subject to the condition that children receiving their elementary and secondary school instruction in English should acquire a working knowledge of French.

In effect, Bill 63 gave legal recognition to a regime of choice between French and English as the language of instruction.

The Liberal government of Robert Bourassa introduced Bill 22, Loi sur la langue officielle, which was passed by the Quebec National Assembly in July 1974. Bill 22 included a number of provisions intended to promote the use of French as the language of work in the province, but its primary target was public education. The act made French the official language of instruction in Quebec public schools. School boards were permitted to provide instruction in English only to those pupils who already had a 'sufficient knowledge' of English prior to their enrolment, and a permanent upper limit on English-language enrolment was set, equal to the number of students enrolled in English-language schools in 1975. The minister of education was authorized to develop language tests to be administered by school boards. Thus, the act aimed to redirect the enrolment of immigrant children from English to French schools, as well as curtail the enrolment of French children in English schools.[38] Testing young children, most of whom were of kindergarten age, aroused predictable controversy and opposition from the English and immigrant communities.[39] Bill 22 was attacked by immigrant groups as a discriminatory means of forcing them into the French sector, it was condemned by the English community as an infringement of its historical rights, and it was derided by Quebec nationalists as totally inadequate to ensure the predominance of French as the standard language of Quebec.

The Charte de la langue française (Bill 101), introduced by the Parti Québécois government and passed by the National Assembly in August 1977, responded to this nationalist criticism. Bill 101 went much farther than Bill 22 in making French the official language of the legislature and courts of Quebec, as well as the normal language of the workplace. With respect to public education, section 72 required that the language of instruction in kindergarten, elementary, and secondary classes be French. With limited exceptions, section 73 restricted entry to English-language schools to children whose mother or father had received elementary instruction in English in Quebec.[40] Bill 101 also provided the basis for the minority-language educational rights later incorporated in section 23 of the Canadian Charter of Rights and Freedoms. Sections 86 and 86.1 authorized the Quebec government to extend legal rights to English-language education where a 'reciprocity agreement' existed between Quebec and another province or 'where it considers that the services of instruction in French offered to French-speaking persons are comparable to those offered in English to English-speaking persons in Quebec.'

Bill 101 encountered angry opposition from non-French minority groups in Quebec, but initial rulings of the courts upheld the authority of the Quebec government to legislate with respect to the language of instruction in provincial education. With the proclamation of the Canadian Charter of Rights and Freedoms, however, the Protestant School Board of Montreal, the Quebec Association of Protestant School Boards, and parents of six children who had been refused permission to attend English schools launched another challenge against sections 72 and 73 of Bill 101 on the grounds that they violated the guarantee of minority-language educational rights in section 23 of the charter. In a September 1982 decision, which was subsequently upheld by the Supreme Court of Canada, the Quebec Superior Court ruled that the Quebec language charter's restrictions on English-language education did violate minority-language rights protected under section 23 of the Canadian Charter of Rights and Freedoms. The Quebec government failed to persuade the court, under section 1 of the charter, that the restrictions placed on English-language education were 'reasonable limits prescribed by law as can be demonstrably justified in a free and democratic society.' In fact, the Quebec National Assembly has never adopted section 23(1)(a) of the charter, which protects minority linguistic rights in education of Canadian citizens whose mother tongue is English, so the protection of the charter in Quebec extends only to Canadian citizens whose elementary school education was received in Canada in English. Since English-speaking citizens are tending to emigrate from Quebec rather than immigrate to it, the charter protects only a limited and currently declining group of Quebec anglophones.[41]

Linguistic Choice and Heritage Languages

Beginning in the 1970s, three types of provision for 'heritage' language instruction have been developed: bilingual programs within the regular public school system, which involve the use of a heritage language as medium of instruction for half of each school day; heritage languages taught as core subjects within the regular school curriculum; and heritage languages taught as subjects supplementary to the regular curriculum, in areas where there is demand for them, sometimes during regular school hours, but very often outside regular school hours.[42]

The most extensive development of instruction in heritage languages has occurred in cities of the Prairie provinces. In 1971 Alberta made it legal to teach in a language other than English for up to 50 per cent of school time. Bilingual programs combining English with French, Ukrainian, Hebrew, Yiddish, German, Chinese, Arabic, and Polish have been developed, primarily by the public and separate school boards of Edmonton and Calgary. In the late 1970s English-Ukrainian bilingual programs were started in Regina, Saskatoon, and Winnipeg; English-German programs were approved in both provinces in the early 1980s; and an English-Hebrew bilingual program was established in Winnipeg. These bilingual programs in the Prairie provinces all operate at the elementary school level, but several heritage languages also are taught as optional subjects at both the elementary and secondary levels. In Manitoba, since the 1950s, heritage languages have been offered as subjects in secondary programs where there is sufficient demand to support them, and heritage languages were introduced as subjects at the elementary level during the 1970s. In Saskatchewan, when a second-language requirement was introduced in 1967 for junior high school students, courses in German and Ukrainian were approved to meet the new requirement. In 1990–1 nine second languages other than English and French were being offered in Manitoba, two in Saskatchewan, and six in Alberta.

In the provinces of Ontario and Quebec instruction in heritage languages, which is organized as a supplement to the regular school program, has been provincially supported by financial assistance and curriculum development since 1977. The Ontario Ministry of Education extends assistance to instruction in forty-five heritage languages; but such instruction must be restricted to two and a half hours a week, carries no academic credit, and must be given outside of regular school hours or by lengthening the school day. In 1988 the ministry's regulations were changed to require school boards to introduce a heritage-language program where twenty-five or more parents with children in the board's schools requested it. Similarly, through its programme d'enseignement des langues et des cultures d'origine, the Quebec Ministry of Education supports one half-hour of daily instruction in minority languages beginning in first grade. Instruction is given in twelve heritage languages, usually but not always outside the regular school day.

Heritage-language education has expanded in Canada since the early 1970s, but tested against the standard of a regime of linguistic choice only a few cities in the Prairie provinces – Edmonton, Calgary, Regina, Winnipeg – would qualify for serious consideration. As Cummins and Danesi observe, the bilingual programs involving heritage languages in the Prairie provinces 'are unique in North America and demonstrate the educational feasibility of such an approach'[43] Nonetheless, enrolment in these programs is limited, in part because the populations of linguistic groups are not sufficiently concentrated to support bilingual heritage-language programs, in part because only a few school boards have been willing to commit the resources needed to operate them. Heritage-language programs in Quebec and especially Ontario involve sizeable enrolments, especially in the metropolitan areas of Montreal and Toronto, but instruction is restricted to one hundred hours a year that are supplementary to the regular school timetable. Provincial governments in the Atlantic provinces and British Columbia have no programs that provide direct support for instruction in heritage languages, although British Columbia gives some provincial funding indirectly through its program to encourage instruction in languages of the economically significant Pacific Rim.

Proponents of heritage language education stress the pain of linguistic and cultural assimilation, the collective political and cultural benefits of a tolerant pluralism, and the potential economic resource of multilingual skills. Opponents of heritage-language education stress the financial costs of multilingual education, its adverse impact on teaching other core subjects, especially English and French, and the dangers of segregating children into parochial linguistic and cultural groups. Cummins and Danesi conclude that far more could be done in Canada to establish

> alternative schools or programs where all Canadian students would have the opportunity to develop literacy and fluency in at least three languages. We have abundant research knowledge upon which to base such schools at the present time. We simply choose not to enrich our children. A major reason why we make this seemingly absurd choice is that to implement such trilingual schools would amount to an explicit valorization of multilingualism and an elevation of the status of minority groups whose languages would not be institutionalized within the mainstream educational system.[44]

CULTURAL COMMUNITY, EDUCATIONAL INDIVIDUATION, AND PUBLIC PHILOSOPHY

At first glance the diversity of institutional arrangements for Canadian public education appears to have changed little from the mid-nineteenth century to the late twentieth century. Indeed, if anything, the diversity seems even greater. The rigidly uniform secondary education of the nineteenth century has been diversified, first, by the establishment of differentiated, class-specific, and class-defining educational programs in partite systems and multilateral schools and, then, by adoption of the principle of person-regarding education in comprehensive schools. The de facto reserved school systems of the Maritime provinces have faded, and confessional education in Newfoundland and Quebec stands on the brink of historic change. Yet four models of religion in public education remain apparently in prospect – confessional and neutral schools in Quebec; public and separate schools in Ontario, Saskatchewan, and Alberta; non-denominational public schools in British Columbia, Manitoba, and the Maritimes; and 'interdenominational' schools in Newfoundland. Since the 1960s, because of official bilingualism and multiculturalism, language has become a recognized division of educational politics, policy, and administration in all provinces; but, as with religion, the linguistic regimes of public education vary markedly from New Brunswick and Quebec, on the one hand, to British Columbia and Newfoundland, on the other. Perhaps contemporary political oppositions are less intense than those of the nineteenth century, although even that is not certain with respect to issues of language.

Yet what is striking about the institutional arrangements for public education in the late twentieth century is not their persistent diversity but rather a nascent consensus on principles that legitimate public education. Recent educational conflicts and policy developments appear to revolve around three basic principles. First, education is an essential condition for individual economic opportunity and collective material prosperity; hence the purposes of education must give appropriate weight to the preparation of young people for work and the benefits of education must be equally accessible to all. Second, public schools serving a multicultural, multilinguistic, and multidenominational society must be inclusive, giving equal respect to all students regardless of their religion, language, or ethnicity. Third, because membership in a cultural community is a good for individuals, public education in a liberal political community must provide for the education of young people in their various cultural communities, for example, by extending state aid to minority-denomination and minority-language schools.

The first two principles of equal opportunity and equal respect derive from longstanding principles of liberalism, as argued from John Locke, the framers of the United States Constitution, and utilitarian liberals like Jeremy Bentham and James Mill to such contemporary liberal theorists as John Rawls and Ronald Dworkin. Although less well recognized as such, the third principle of communitarian justice is also a tenet of modern liberalism, but here it is the developmental or ethical liberalism of John Stuart Mill, T.H. Green, Leonard Hobhouse, and John Dewey to which reference must be made.

An ethical liberal concept of justice as person-regarding equality cannot separate individual development from the cultural communities within which people live and learn. Hence the pluralization of religion and language in contemporary public education in Canada, which has been justified by reference to a concept of justice as person-regarding equality, has also given legitimacy to political demands and policy responses on behalf of religion and language in public education that were fiercely opposed or rudely dismissed in political and economic liberal thinking. Under the influence of the principles of person-regarding education, public education in Canada became less class-specific and class-defining in educational organization and programs. At the same time it became both more multidenominational and less sectarian, and it became more linguistically diverse.

None of this was achieved without political conflict. Especially in Quebec, opposition to liberalizing confessional education has come partly from conservative Catholics concerned to protect confessional education, but more importantly from English-speaking Quebeckers, who have used the constitutional entrenchment of minority denominational education rights to defend their linguistic community. The francophone majority, which perceives itself as a minority struggling to preserve its language and culture in anglophone North America, has experienced severe but understandable difficulties in dealing with the demands for minority educational rights of English and other non-French cultural groups. Outside Quebec official recognition of denominational and linguistic pluralism in public education has been attacked as socially and culturally divisive, a threat to the integrity of the political community, and a drain on economic and educational efficiency.

Nonetheless, in sharp contrast with the incremental retreat from the ethical liberal policies of comprehensive secondary education, over the last quarter-century there have been continual incremental advances of ethical liberal principles in the construction of public policies about religion and language in public education. Progressive educational policies on secondary school organization and curricula, which have focused on the developmental needs and potential of each individual learner, have been increasingly contested. Progressive educational policies on religion and language, which have aimed to give proper weight and respect to the diversity of cultural memberships in a pluralistic society, gradually but steadily have become better institutionalized and more legitimate. Perhaps the greatest and most enduring achievement of ethical liberalism has been finding the principles and developing the policies from which historic issues of the legitimacy and justice of religion and language in Canadian public education at last can be laid to rest.

11

Ethical Liberalism and the Governance of Public Education: Policy Interdependence in Policy Communities

Two rival theories of public decision-making competed for predominance in educational governance in the late 1960s and early 1970s. One was the theory of 'rational management,' which envisaged public decision-making as comprehensive, anticipatory problem-solving. The other was the theory of 'participatory democracy' or 'neighbourhood democracy,' which envisaged public decision-making as decentralized, communal, deliberative judgment.

According to the theory of rational management, public decision-makers should start by making an extended analysis of their problem situation, then establish clear policy objectives, search widely for optional courses of public action to resolve their problem, assess prospective benefits and costs, and finally implement the course of action projected to maximize benefits or minimize costs. As a form of public decision-making, rational management presupposes the establishment of three types of public institutions, each making its own distinctive functional contribution to the process of rational decision-making: political institutions for articulating goals, assessing options in relationship to goals, and making policy choices; policy institutions for program planning and analysis; and administrative institutions for effective implementation of chosen courses of action.

In the theory of participatory democracy, local communities are assumed to be potentially autonomous polities that have distinctive communal histories and identities. Decentralization of public decision-making to local communities makes possible the inclusion of many more, if not all, citizens of the community, who deliberate together about their shared problems, form collective political judgments, and undertake common actions to implement their judgments. With respect to public institutions this theory of public decision-making presupposes the existence of a local assembly or town meeting as a forum for communal deliberation, close integration and joint action of public employees and citizens in forming judgments about communal policies, and considerable reliance for policy implementation on instruments of self-regulation and self-administration involving all members of the community.

In Canada the theory of rational management displaced conventional incremental decision-making as the norm, if not the practice, of public decision-making in the late 1960s and early 1970s. At both the federal and provincial levels of government, previously departmentalized cabinets were transformed into institutionalized cabinets, each with a formally elaborated set of cabinet committees backed by a phalanx of central agencies. The trends to rational management and institutionalized cabinets in provincial government necessarily affected the organization and functioning of provincial departments (now generally renamed ministries) of education, in particular with respect to their organizational capacities for educational planning and program evaluation.

Although perhaps lacking the generalized impact that the theory of rational management had on the norms and institutions of public decision-making in Canada, the theory of participatory democracy did have an important impact on the domain of educational policy and administration. The institutions and policies of person-regarding education implied a radically different regime of educational governance in which policy-making and administrative authority would be substantially decentralized from central authorities to local boards, school staffs, parent associations, and classroom teachers. By legitimizing local autonomy in educational policy and administration, the ideology and practices of person-regarding education constituted a potential counterweight to the trend to rational management.

The seminal official studies of public education that were based on a theory of person-regarding education advanced a model of policy interdependence and egalitarian decision-making that aimed to reconcile the theories of rational management and participatory democracy in the institutions and practices of educational policy communities. This distinctively ethical liberal attempt to adopt the radical communitarian concept of neighbourhood democracy without letting go of the utilitarian liberal concept of rational management proved to be an artistic triumph. A model of policy interdependence became the norm for relationships between provincial ministries of education and local school boards in the 1970s. Institutionalization of policy interdependence proved easier to conceive in theory than it was to achieve in practice, of course, and results varied among provinces. Moreover, when falling enrolments and fiscal austerity started to shift political priorities against education, it became no longer possible to disguise the inherent contradiction between the utilitarian liberal norms of rational management in institutionalized cabinets and the ethical liberal ideal of egalitarian decision-making in person-regarding educational policy communities.

POLICY INTERDEPENDENCE IN THE THEORY OF PERSON-REGARDING EDUCATION

Person-regarding education implies a massive decentralization of educational decision-making. The central assumption of person-regarding education is that children, their parents, and their teachers in local schools ultimately must have power to make decisions for the education of each person in school. The responsibility of higher policy-making and administrative authorities – the school's principal and its council, the local board of education, and the provincial ministry of education – should be restricted to providing a framework for decision-making by teachers and learners that incorporates the collective purposes of the political and cultural communities in which children live and learn, but which does not deny or frustrate the choice of each child's unique educational destiny.

In making their case for the reform of educational governance, the Parent commission, the Hall-Dennis committee, and the Worth commission all rejected the historical model of domination by a central executive in a relationship of administrative agency or policy tutelage. They each insisted on local autonomy and decentralized decision-making in public education, but they also eschewed any simple radical communitarian theory of neighbourhood democracy. Educational governance of person-regarding education was not simply a matter of empowering children, parents, and teachers in networks of autonomous micro-communities. Their official recommendations strove to balance the needs of individual and community by strengthening and integrating different levels of educational decision-making in a relationship of policy interdependence.

From Decentralization to Policy Interdependence: The Parent Commission in Quebec

In the seminal reports that advocated person-regarding education in Canada, the philosophical justification and political requirements for policy interdependence were most carefully articulated in the arguments and recommendations of the Parent commission for the reform of local educational administration in Quebec. According to the Parent commission, 'Decentralization can take two principal forms: leaving to subordinate agencies responsibility for certain decisions or the direction of certain sectors; or making these subordinate agencies party to the decisions of higher authorities.'[1] Historically the Quebec state had relied on the first method, with the result that school commissions had extensive autonomy. Now with the prospect of greater intervention by the central state in provincial education, the second form of decentralization had become necessary. Such a formula of public administration was new to Quebec, and 'to effect this, it is essential to lay a foundation in the form of suitable agencies, capable of participating in the responsibilities and decisions of the state.'[2]

The reorganization of local boards into regional commissions, the Parent commission argued, would 'make it possible to organize an elementary and a secondary education of good quality, and thus to eliminate the pronounced local discrepancies in elementary school services which are conspicuous today.'[3] By their jurisdiction over a relatively large territory and population, regional commissions would have sufficient flexibility to ensure for parents the choice of confessional or non-confessional education, as well as to protect linguistic dualism. Unified regional commissions would administer confessional and non-confessional, French and English schools simultaneously and hence secure the advantages of cultural pluralism for the general progress of Quebec education. Democratic openness and protection of minority representation, however, were essential if religious and cultural diversity were to be truly respected. Parents should be guaranteed a more active role in educational decision-making by ensuring their right to choose freely the type of education they want for their children. For each school there should be a school committee, comprising elected representatives of parents and staff. Members of regional school commissions would be chosen by an electoral college of school committee delegates, and a council of school development comprising representatives of regional school commissions would be formed in each economic region of the province to serve as an intermediary between the regional commissions and the provincial department of education. As for the working relationship among school committees, regional commissions, area councils, and the provincial department, the Parent commission clearly desired a form of policy interdependence.

> The new division of responsibilities which we propose presumes that the functions and powers of these various bodies be clearly foreseen and formulated in the Education Act. Each will then know its duties, and will be able to fulfil them in terms of joint action and an over-all policy. For each of these bodies ... will be closely linked to the others through the interplay of elections and by cooperation in the same educational work.[4]

From Policy Tutelage to Policy Interdependence: The Hall-Dennis Committee in Ontario

As with the Parent commission, the Hall-Dennis committee in Ontario supported the formation of larger units of local school administration as an administrative necessity, but the Hall-Dennis committee went much further in its recommendations for decentralizing educational decision-making. The Hall-Dennis committee accepted that to protect the interests and welfare of children in school the provincial department must retain a certain degree of regulatory authority, but in the past provincial regulation had covered too many areas in too much detail, from the square footage of classrooms to specifically prescribed curricula, school visits by provincial inspectors, and teacher certification. Such a 'gatekeeper' approach to provincial governance of education must be ended. 'In theory, then, each school board should establish its own priorities and exercise real autonomy. Only on such a principle can diversity be encouraged in cultural, architectural, curricular, and organizational matters.'[5]

In the 'domain of provincial policy' led by the minister and deputy minister, the activities of the Department of Education would be focused on legislative planning, research and development, and systems evaluation. In the 'domain of educational implementation,' school boards should have a degree of administrative and financial autonomy similar to that accorded to provincial universities. 'Larger and more responsible school boards should have far greater control and autonomy than has been possible heretofore. The fundamental role of the provincial authority should be to equalize educational opportunity by means of a redistribution of money to the local education authorities, while leaving most of the decisions concerning its expenditure to them.' In turn, school boards would be expected to decentralize decision-making to schools: 'Schools and their principals and staffs need considerably more autonomy than is usually granted by boards and superintendents. This relative autonomy should be extended in such matters as curriculum planning, school organization, staffing, and the disposition of supply budgets.'[6]

As school boards became larger in area and encompassed more schools, the Hall-Dennis committee also saw a developing need for school committees to provide a formal communication link between each school and the community it served.[7] The members of each school committee would be elected at a meeting of 'the school community.' The functions of school committees would include aiding the principal and staff in interpreting the school to the community, keeping the principal and staff informed of the needs of the community, supporting their school in its relationship with the school board, and stimulating an active local interest in the school.

Ethical Liberalism and Educational Planning: The Worth Commission in Alberta

The Worth commission on educational planning in Alberta reconciled its dual aspirations of rational management and participatory democracy in a concept of 'participatory planning.' On the one hand, rational planning and decision-making were dependent on the approach of systems analysis. 'The general stages of this analysis are conceptualization of the system – the entire provincial effort in education, a school system, an institution, a classroom, a learning group, an individual – in terms of its main structures and processes, specifying goals and objectives, generating and evaluating alternatives, and programming implementation.'[8] On the other hand, educational decision-making should seek to involve all citizens of Alberta. 'People must be more than mere clients of the educational system. They must share in determining it. If education truly is to benefit society, it must draw on all of society's strengths. Expertise, then, can be mobilized without granting educators and bureaucrats dominating roles because of their special credentials or strategic positions.'[9]

The lead roles in provincial planning belonged to members of the legislative assembly and cabinet, who had responsibility to decide broad social, economic, and educational goals and priorities. To support their leadership they needed a central planning agency to provide expertise in planning technology, coordinate sectoral planning, and organize information bearing on policy alternatives. The legislative assembly and cabinet also would have to rely heavily on various departments of government in planning for their respective areas of policy. In the domain of educational planning the departments of education and advanced education should have a joint planning unit, which would coordinate, support, and supplement the planning done by their operating divisions. 'Its prime objective would be to ensure the availability of data – the hard facts – that will enable legislators and departmental personnel to both make informed decisions and assess results.'[10]

The departments of education and advanced education would be expected to 'adopt a broad scale, open and pervasive approach to planning with all those involved and affected. Before enunciating policies that set the framework for the development and operation of educational programs and institutions in the province, inputs from the grass-roots level need to be deliberately sought and assimilated.'[11] In particular, the Department of Education should engage in continuing dialogue with 'stakeholder groups' such as the Alberta School

Trustees' Association, the Alberta Teachers' Association, the Alberta Federation of Home and School Associations, Unifarm, the Métís Association of Alberta, and students' organizations.

Public involvement in educational decision-making was more likely to occur in a system where effective central coordination was combined with decentralized control. If the humanist values of a person-centred society prevailed, 'then a large measure of self-determination will be possible among governing boards and institutions for schooling, for the individuals within them, and for those served by them.'[12] The provincial government should decentralize authority and place greater responsibility in the hands of locally elected boards. School boards in turn should ensure that decentralization of authority also occurred within their jurisdictions. Worth recommended the creation of school councils, which would be representative of parents, citizens of the community, school staff, and (at senior stages of basic education) students. 'The council should be a mature partnership among people which reflects not only responsiveness and influence, but essentially builds on respect, trust, the right of initiative, and a flexible formula for participation in policy decisions.'[13]

EDUCATIONAL GOVERNANCE IN THE 1970S AND 1980S: BETWEEN RATIONAL MANAGEMENT AND PARTICIPATORY DEMOCRACY

The concept of policy interdependence in educational governance, which was articulated in the Parent, Hall-Dennis, and Worth reports, promised to reconcile provincial planning and local autonomy. Three avenues of institutional reform were especially important.

First, as provincial governments initiated institutional and procedural reforms based on the theory of rational management, ministries of education moved with apparent ease to reorganize their basic functional divisions and focus on educational planning, policy analysis, and administrative support. Initially at least, there was a comfortable fit between officials in central agencies, who were moving to institutionalize provincial cabinets based on a theory of rational management, and officials in ministries of education, who were reorganizing their departments based on a model of policy interdependence.

Second, a shared focus on educational planning and a common commitment to an ideology of person-regarding education created the potential for interprovincial coordination among ministries of education. The organization and development of the Council of Ministers of Education, Canada, symbolized official awareness of not only an interprovincial convergence in public education that made national policy coordination conceivable, but also a growing provincial interdependence that made national policy coordination desirable.

Third, within provincial educational communities the key areas of policy that shaped the structure of educational governance were educational finance and collective bargaining. Institutional arrangements favouring policy interdependence were unevenly developed, ranging from moderately favourable in Ontario and the Prairie provinces, where pluralist networks predominated, through moderately weak in the Atlantic provinces and Quebec, where educational policy communities were typified by centralized concertation between provincial ministries and teachers' unions, to very weak in British Columbia, where the provincial ministry assiduously protected its historical domination of state-directed policy networks.

Institutionalized Cabinets and Reorganized Departments

Corporate executive policy-making based on the theory of rational decision-making became the leading doctrine of public authority and political accountability in the late 1960s and early 1970s. Initially, the requirements of corporate executive leadership and institutionalized cabinets fitted neatly with the reorganization of departments of education to emphasize broad issues of educational policy leadership. The shift from classical bureaucratic regulation, incremental analysis, and line-item budgeting to more comprehensive policy analysis, planning priorities, and program budgeting fitted the approach to educational policy and administration of reorganized ministries of education as they were advocated by the Parent commission, the Hall-Dennis committee, and the Worth commission. The basic functions of central governance were educational planning, program development, and administrative support.

Establishment of a ministry of education was the main recommendation of the Parent commission in the first volume of its report. With respect to the organization of the ministry, the commission recommended that under the deputy minister and (Protestant) associate deputy minister there should be three divisions, each headed by a director general: instruction, administration, and planning. The division of instruction would be responsible for curricula, inspection and examinations, and teaching personnel. The division of administration would encompass provincial administrative services to external institutions, including school commissions, provincial schools, higher education, private schools, and adult education. The commission reasoned that grouping pedagogical activities in a single division would facilitate communication and coordination among the primary, secondary, higher, and technical sectors: 'This close association will encourage discussion of common problems, such as the co-ordination of instructional levels and the organization of programmes. School commissions will be able to deal with one group of services only for all pedagogical matters at all levels, and with another group of services for all administrative questions, such as new construction, finance, etc.'[14] As for the division of planning, the royal commission insisted on the importance of this function in the new ministry.

In the past, institutions have come into being under the pressure of special needs and individual initiative without prior demographic or financial studies. Large business houses undertake extensive surveys before opening a branch in a town or in a neighbourhood. A similar regard for efficiency and future development is equally important in the field of education. The erection of an institution in a specific area, and the consequent investment of thousands if not millions of dollars, must not be left to chance. Prior investigations, including the study of population trends, finance and pedagogy, are dictated by the most elementary considerations of prudence.[15]

The initial organization of the Quebec Ministry of Education in 1964 indicated only a modest influence of the royal commission's recommendations on the ministry's internal division of activities. The Parent commission's advocacy of the new ministry's planning function was acknowledged with the formation of the directorate of planning, and, given the appointment of two associate deputy ministers, one for Catholic and the other for Protestant education, the royal commission's insistence on the principle of functional rather than confessional divisions was adopted. Missing from the new ministry's structure was the vertical integration of educational activities proposed by the commission. Instead, seven separate directorates were established for planning, curricula and examinations, school organization, higher education, continuing education, building and equipment, and finance, as well as a variety of departmental services such as personnel, legal, information, school publications, and school materials. The ministry's organization remained essentially unchanged until 1985, following the departure of college and university education to the Ministry of Higher Education, Science, and Technology. Then activities were grouped under four assistant deputy ministers, responsible for planning and educational development, administration, educational network services (réseaux), and labour relations.

In Ontario successive reports prepared by officials of the Civil Service Commission in 1962 and 1963 recommended reorganizing the Department of Education very much along the lines envisaged for the Quebec ministry by the Parent commission: abolition of the dichotomy between elementary and secondary education, consolidation of special subject branches into curriculum and supervision sections, and a clear separation of educational policy and programs from general administration.[16] In 1965 the Ontario Department of Education implemented a reorganization that reduced the department's educational activities to two functional categories, each headed by an assistant deputy minister: instruction, which encompassed elementary, secondary, and teacher education; and provincial schools and further education. A third deputy minister assumed charge of departmental and school administration, in which the significant change was the creation of a school administration branch to handle fiscal and administrative transactions between the department and the school boards.[17] Three years later the minister of education, William Davis, told the legislative assembly that a centralized system of education had served the province well historically, but put an undue emphasis on regimentation and conformity. The evolution of local educational authorities as responsible agents capable of assuming many of department's functions required a fundamental re-examination of the role of the department.

> It follows that the function of departmental officials is to develop and continuously review a comprehensive philosophy of public education. This educational planning – which must cover an extremely broad spectrum, taking into account the social and economic needs of all citizens – is then expressed as policy in two ways: through the medium of the educational laws ... and through the distribution of funds ... Being centrally located, the department is also specially qualified to be a resource centre for new information and a clearing house for worthwhile ideas emanating from within and outside the province.[18]

Under the reorganization of 1972 the division of instruction became that of 'education development,' which included a directorate of planning and research; the division of provincial schools and further education was dropped; and administration was split into two divisions, one for departmental services and the other to deal with school boards. This three-fold organization remained essentially unchanged until January 1987, when the ministry was reorganized into four major divisions (corporate planning and policy, learning programs, learning services, and administration) with a fifth assistant deputy minister responsible for Franco-Ontarian education.[19]

Departments of education in the Atlantic provinces all underwent major reorganizations in the early 1970s. The Nova Scotia Department of Education was reorganized in 1969–70 as part of the implementation of a provincial planning, programming, and budgeting system that had been introduced the previous year. Three assistant chief directors were given charge of divisions for education programs, planning and budgeting, and finance (which included public school operations).[20] In the New Brunswick Department of Education, when separate divisions of English and French educational services were formed in 1973, each having its own assistant deputy minister, a division of finance and administration headed by a third assistant deputy minister and an office of director of planning and development were established to serve both English and French education. In Prince Edward Island administrative reorganization followed from the work of the educational planning unit that was set up in the Department of Education in 1970.[21] In 1973 four major divisions were created: programs and services, administrative services, planning, and provincial libraries.[22] In Newfoundland two generations of departmental reorganization were accomplished in a span of three years. Following the recommendation of the Royal Commission on Education and Youth for a functional rather than denominational division of educational activities, the department was first reorganized in July 1969 into five divisions: instruction, supervision, administration, special education, and technical and vocational education, with a sixth division of physical education and youth added the next year.[23] Then, in 1972, instruction, supervision (renamed school services), and special education were consolidated under an assistant deputy minister; and a director of research and planning was appointed.[24]

In the West, two associate deputy ministers, one for education and one for administration, were appointed in Saskatchewan in 1969–70. Following the election of the NDP government led by Allan Blakeney in 1971, the office of associate deputy minister for administration was dropped; the two directors of administrative services and school administration, the associate deputy minister of educational programs, and the new director of research, planning, and development all reported directly to the deputy minister. Divisions of educational planning and research were created in Manitoba (1972) and Alberta (1974), and at the same time a basic separation of central administrative functions was made between educational programs and administrative services. In British Columbia, the six basic services (administrative, field, financial, instructional, post-secondary, special, and technical-vocational), which had been established under the direction of superintendents in 1971, were placed under the direction of two associate deputy ministers, one for educational programs and one for educational operations (finance and administration), in 1973.[25] A directorate of policy and planning, attached to the deputy minister's office, was not created until 1983 and became a major division of the ministry headed by an associate deputy minister in the reorganization of July 1987.[26]

From the turn of the century to the 1940s, departments of education were transformed from a simple dichotomy between inspectors and clerks to twelve or fifteen offices reporting to the deputy minister. From the 1940s to the

1960s administrative reorganizations aimed to reduce the deputy minister's span of control to six (the MacFarlane commission) or seven (the Hope commission) directorates. In the late 1960s and early 1970s provincial departments underwent another round of major reorganizations into two, three, or four major divisions, which were variously based on the functions of educational planning, program development, and administrative support. For the most part the forms of departmental organization adopted by the early 1970s remained essentially still in place in the early 1990s.[27] These reorganizations fitted quite well the conception of central educational governance in the theory of person-regarding education. They also corresponded to the conceptions of departmental organization and institutionalized cabinets in the theory of corporate executive policy-making. This coincidence of educational philosophy, departmental organization, and cabinet decision-making was not in evitable, however; it was contingent on a shared perception of educational purposes and public priorities. Once that shared perception faltered, the harmony of politics, policy, and administration would be broken.

Ideological Convergence and Interprovincial Organization: The Council of Ministers of Education, Canada

From the 1930s to the 1960s provincial educational authorities slowly moved towards similar policies of multilateral secondary education, school consolidation, district reorganization, and provincial equalizing grants. By the mid-1960s there was a growing awareness among provincial educational policy-makers of their common commitments to person-centred schools, multidenominational education, linguistic and cultural equality, and decentralization of educational decision-making. Hugh Stevenson has observed, 'While it is often done, no one is in an unchallengeable position to speak for "Canadian education": technically, it is safe to speak only of "education in Canada."'[28] Stevenson is correct: no single institution can speak for public elementary and secondary education in Canada. Nonetheless, the establishment of the Council of Ministers of Education, Canada (CMEC) did symbolize a nascent interprovincial convergence of educational purposes and policies in the late 1960s and early 1970s. As a form of provincial educational sovereignty-association, the CMEC also showed the way in which national coordination of educational policy-making could be institutionalized in Canada.

Beginning in 1960 ministers of education met annually in the Standing Committee of Ministers of Education a day or two before the convention of the Canadian Education Association in order to facilitate interprovincial communication and cooperation in educational policy-making. At their meeting in June 1967 the ministers of education agreed to establish the Council of Ministers of Education, Canada, as a permanent organization with a small secretariat located in Toronto. According to the 'Agreed Memorandum' the purpose of the CMEC would be 'to enable the Ministers to consult on such matters as are of common interest, and to provide a means for the fullest possible cooperation among provincial governments in areas of mutual interest and concern in education.' Meetings of the full council are held at least twice each year.[29] An advisory committee of deputy ministers serves as steering committee, with responsibility to prepare the agenda and documentation for each council meeting and make recommendations for CMEC action. Several committees and task forces are appointed under the aegis of the CMEC each year. Their membership is drawn from senior ministry officials in all provinces. 'The work of these committees is in itself important, since it covers a wide range of problems, but equally important is the fact that over one hundred senior officials from the provincial systems are brought together two or three times a year to exchange opinions about their work.'[30]

No doubt the most interesting and important manifestation of that national educational convergence in the early years of the council can be seen in the regional background reports that were prepared for the national education review carried out by the Organization for Economic Cooperation and Development in 1975. Overall management of this project was the responsibility of a coordinating committee of the CMEC comprising one representative from each region (the Atlantic provinces, Quebec, Ontario, and the West) as well as two representatives of the federal government. Each region appointed a director to be responsible for the production of a background report on education in that region. Taken together, the four regional reports, which covered elementary and secondary education in the ten provinces, showed both the residual historical diversity of educational institutions and practices and an unprecedented ideological convergence of educational purposes and policies. Significantly, the introductory background report chose to illustrate 'this unanimity of purpose' in elementary and secondary education by citing the Parent commission: 'In modern societies the educational system has a threefold goal: to afford everyone the opportunity to learn; to make available to each the type of education best suited to his capacities and interests; to prepare the individual for life in society.'[31]

Institutionalization of Policy Communities: Educational Finance and Collective Bargaining

During the late 1960s and early 1970s the normative relationship in educational policy communities shifted from administrative agency and policy tutelage to policy interdependence. As departmental inspection and examinations were abolished and provincial curricula were transformed from detailed prescriptions to flexible guidelines, local superintendents, program consultants, school principals, and classroom teachers progressively acquired greater professional autonomy to design educational programs specifically to meet the needs of their students. Reorganized departments of education oriented their activities towards broader issues of educational planning and program development. Within educational policy communities the structure of policy-making relationships among departmental officials and representatives of teachers' unions and trustees' associations was much less determined by unilateral assertions of regulatory authority by departments and defensive reactions by organized teachers and trustees. Policy networks involving departmental officials, organized teachers, and trustees became much more determined by provincial regimes of educational finance and collective bargaining. Based on whether educational finance and collective bargaining were relatively centralized or decentralized, four types of regimes can be distinguished in Canadian educational policy communities in the 1970s and 1980s.[32]

First, in Ontario and the Prairie provinces educational finance and collective bargaining were relatively decentralized. Elementary and secondary schools were jointly funded by provincial governments and local school boards. Provincial financing in each case stopped well short of full support (Table 7.5), requiring school boards to raise a considerable proportion of their budgets by municipal taxation, but also leaving a significant margin within which school boards were free to raise local funds to support educational programs above the provincial grant ceilings, or not. Provincial financing of elementary and secondary education was designed as either a foundation grant plan (the Prairies) or a percentage equalizing grant plan (Ontario), which protected a measure of policy and administrative autonomy for local school boards.[33] Collective bargaining was decentralized between school boards and local affiliates of provincial teachers' unions in Ontario, Manitoba, and Alberta. In Saskatchewan collective bargaining was divided between provincial and local negotiations: teachers' salary scales were determined at the provincial level, but several important items of working conditions were bargained locally.

Second, in New Brunswick and Prince Edward Island educational finance and collective bargaining were entirely centralized. In both provinces district reorganization rationalized the constitution and operation of school boards as administrative agents of the provincial ministries of education.[34] The two pro-

TABLE 11.1
Provincial organizations of teachers and school trustees, 1990

Province	Teachers' organizations	Trustees'' organizations
Newfoundland	Newfoundland Teachers' Association	Newfoundland and Labrador School Trustees' Association
Prince Edward Island	PEI Teachers' Federation	PEI School Trustees' Association
Nova Scotia	NS Teachers' Union	NS School Boards Association
New Brunswick	Association des enseignantes et des enseignants francophones du Nouveau-Brunswick; NB Teachers' Association	Association des conseillers scolaires francophone du Nouveau-Brunswick; NB School Trustees' Association
Quebec	Centrale de l'enseignement du Québec; Provincial Association of Catholic Teachers (Quebec); Provincial Association of Protestant Teachers	Fédération des commissions scolaires catholiques du Québec; Québec Association of Protestant School Boards
Ontario	Association des enseignantes et des enseignants franco-ontariens; Federation of Women Teachers' Associations of Ontario; Ontario English Catholic Teachers' Association; Ontario Public School Teachers' Federation; Ontario Secondary School Teachers' Federation; Ontario Teachers' Federation	Association française des conseils scolaires de l'Ontario; Association franco-ontarienne des conseils d'écoles catholiques; Ontario Public School Boards' Association; Ontario School Trustees' Council; Ontario Separate School Trustees' Association
Manitoba	Éducatrices et éducateurs francophones du Manitoba; Manitoba Teachers' Society Catholic	Association des commissaires d'écoles franco-manitobains; Manitoba Association of School Trustees; Manitoba School Trustees' Association
Saskatchewan	Saskatchewan Teachers' Federation	Saskatchewan School Trustees' Association
Alberta	Alberta Teachers' Association	Alberta Catholic School Trustees' Association; Alberta School Trustees' Association
British Columbia	BC Teachers' Federation	BC School Trustees Association

Source: Canadian Education Association, *The CEA Handbook 1990* (Toronto: Canadian Education Association, 1990), 215–17

vincial governments assumed full responsibility for financing all public schools. In both provinces the departments of education made all decisions to build schools, allocated teaching positions to the school districts, and appointed the superintendents who were chief administrative officers in each school district. The responsibilities of school boards were limited to hiring and dismissing staff for positions approved by the department and administering the district budget, following its approval by the department, within the guidelines established by the department. In both provinces provision was made in the school act for raising supplementary local funds, but school boards found these procedures extremely cumbersome and voters unwilling to give approval.[35] The terms and conditions of teachers' employment were bargained collectively at the provincial level. The New Brunswick Teachers' Association and the Association des enseignantes et des enseignants francophones du Nouveau-Brunswick acted as separate organizations on professional matters, but they were joined in the New Brunswick Teachers' Federation to negotiate one salary schedule and one set of working conditions.[36] Across the table in both provinces the employers' committee comprised representatives of the Treasury Board, the Department of Education, and the provincial school trustees' association.

Third, educational finance and collective bargaining were relatively centralized in Newfoundland, Nova Scotia, and Quebec, but school boards retained a small margin of local autonomy in financing elementary and secondary education. Provincial governments were directly (in Newfoundland and Quebec) or indirectly (in Nova Scotia) responsible for providing over 90 per cent of the revenues of school boards. Under the financial regime passed in 1979, which came into effect in 1981–2, Quebec school boards were prohibited from levying a tax greater than 6 per cent of their funded expenditures, or 2.5 mills (2.5 cents per $1000 of assessment), whichever was lower, unless the levy was approved in a local referendum.[37] In Newfoundland, the province in general paid the full costs of teachers, 90 per cent of transportation and construction costs, the full cost of textbooks from kindergarten to grade eight, and half the cost of textbooks for grades nine to twelve.[38] The 5 per cent of education funded locally was raised from school fees or local taxes levied by special local school tax authorities. Under the foundation grant plan introduced in 1982–3 the government of Nova Scotia provided over 90 per cent of school board revenues, 81 per cent contributed directly through provincial grants (Table 7.5), and 12 per cent raised by a mandatory tax on local property. Optional levies in Nova Scotia were subject to approval by the local governments of municipalities in which school districts were located and amounted to about 4 per cent of school board revenues. As for collective bargaining, in Newfoundland negotiations were centralized between the Newfoundland

Teachers' Association and an employers' negotiating committee comprising representatives of the Department of Education, the Treasury Board, and the Newfoundland and Labrador School Trustees' Association. Negotiations were bi-level in Nova Scotia, but, as in Saskatchewan, the most important items of teachers' remuneration and working conditions were negotiated at the provincial level, between the Nova Scotia Teachers' Union and an employers' committee that included representatives of the Department of Education and the Nova Scotia School Boards Association, with an official from the Civil Service Commission as negotiator. In contrast with centralized collective bargaining in the Atlantic provinces, where a single, hierarchical organization of teachers faced an alliance of provincial officials and representatives of school trustees, both sides were alliances in Quebec. The Quebec employers' negotiating committee comprised representatives of the Ministry of Education, Ministry of Social Affairs (whose member was the negotiator), and provincial associations of Catholic and Protestant school trustees; the teachers' committee represented the three (French Catholic, English Catholic, and Protestant) teachers' unions.

Fourth, in British Columbia, collective bargaining and educational finance were relatively decentralized during the 1960s, but both became increasingly subject to provincial control in the 1970s and 1980s.[39] As provincial expenditures on education rose sharply in the late 1960s, the Social Credit government imposed tighter fiscal controls on school boards. If a school district's budget exceeded 110 per cent of the cost of the basic provincial educational program, it had to be approved by the relevant municipal council(s), 60 per cent of the voters in a local referendum, or the provincial cabinet. In 1972 the floor for extraordinary approval of optional spending was reduced to 108 per cent of the cost of approved provincial programs, membership in the British Columbia Teachers' Federation was made voluntary, collective bargaining was abolished, and teachers' salaries were set by ministerial decree. Social Credit policies on educational finance and collective bargaining were major electoral issues in 1972. When the New Democratic party won the election, automatic membership and collective bargaining rights were restored to the BCTF, and school boards were given greater fiscal autonomy.[40] Although the Social Credit party regained office in 1975, no major changes to educational finance or collective bargaining were introduced until 1982. Educational finance acts passed in 1982 and 1983, again as part of a program of fiscal austerity, authorized the provincial cabinet to determine all tax rates and set expenditure levels for each school district's budget, and prohibited school districts from taxing non-residential property.[41] School boards in practice were administrative agents of the Ministry of Education until 1986–7, when boards were again allowed to tax residential property to provide optional local programs and services up to a ceiling of 110 per cent of approved provincial expenditures. At the same time the Teaching Profession Act of 1987 reinforced the decentralization of collective bargaining by weakening the position of the BCTF. A College of Teachers with membership mandatory for all teachers in public schools was established to regulate the teaching profession, and membership in the BCTF became voluntary. Teachers were given the choice to form a local union and bargain collectively with their local school board under the provincial Industrial Relations Act, form a local association with limited powers to bargain under the Public Schools Act, or not to bargain collectively.

In sum, the rhetoric of provincial educational governance may have shifted in general during the late 1960s and early 1970s from models of administrative agency and policy tutelage to the ideal of policy interdependence, but provincial regimes of educational finance and collective bargaining were not uniformly constructed to be conducive to decentralized decision-making. In Ontario and the Prairie provinces relatively decentralized regimes of educational finance and collective bargaining tended to support preconditions for policy interdependence involving departmental officials, organized teachers, and school trustees interacting across provincial and local levels of government. In New Brunswick and Prince Edward Island, however, centralization of educational finance reduced school boards to the status of administrative agents, and state capacity to act in key policy areas depended on concertation between the department and the teachers' unions, which was achieved by centralized collective bargaining. Similarly, in Newfoundland, Nova Scotia, and Quebec, although school boards retained a margin of local autonomy in educational finance, the financial dominance of the provincial government and centralized collective bargaining supported policy tutelage or administrative agency, not policy interdependence, as the prevailing mode of central-local relationships in educational policy communities. Finally, in British Columbia collective bargaining was decentralized but subordinate in a regime of educational finance that was increasingly centralized through provincial control of the fiscal framework within which school boards made their budgets. Thus, the ministry protected its historical relationship of policy tutelage in the British Columbia educational policy community and resisted any institutionalization of bargaining with either organized teachers or school boards.

INSTITUTIONALIZED CABINETS, EDUCATIONAL POLICY COMMUNITIES, AND FISCAL CRISIS

Policy interdependence as a form of educational governance proved easier to conceive in theory than to actualize in practice. As enrolments in elementary and secondary education declined in the 1970s and fiscal problems of provincial governments deepened, public policy priorities also turned against education. The vaunted harmony of partnership in educational policy communities was sorely tested.

Education in the Canadian Public Economy: Falling Demand and Lower Priority

In the late 1960s and early 1970s elementary and secondary education reached the peak of its importance in the Canadian public economy. Expenditures on elementary and secondary education in 1970–1 reached their highest level as a percentage of gross domestic product (5 per cent), and employment of full-time teachers also reached its highest level at 3.2 per cent of the labour force (Table 7.1). Total government expenditures on elementary and secondary education was 14.7 per cent of total government expenditures in 1970–1, the highest proportion since the 1920s, and employment of full-time teachers in public education constituted 14.8 per cent of total public-sector employment, the highest level since the mid-1950s. Similarly, enrolments in public schools as a percentage of total population had also reached a peak (Table 7.7).

From the middle 1970s policy priorities turned against education. As Table 7.2 shows, total public expenditures on education declined from 19 per cent of total government expenditures in 1970–1 to 12 per cent in 1990–1. At the same time spending on social policies, primarily health and welfare, continued to rise from 34 per cent to 38.3 per cent of total government expenditures. Perhaps even more important for understanding the shift of policy priorities against education, however, the percentage of total government spending on debt charges rose from 10.4 per cent of total spending in 1970–1 to 20.3 per cent in 1990–1.

For state elementary and secondary education, the shift in policy priorities reflected not only a shrinking clientele, but also less concern to improve the quality of educational resources. In the early 1970s enrolments began to decline (Table 7.7). Expenditures on elementary and secondary education declined in the 1970s and then levelled in the 1980s as a percentage of gross domestic product and total government expenditures (Table 7.1). Employment of full-time teachers in public education fell to 2 per cent of the labour force and just over 10 per cent of public-sector employment in the 1980s. Pupil/teacher ratios continued to decline after 1970–1, as enrolments fell faster than cutbacks in full-time teachers (Table 7.10), but average annual increases in real expenditures per pupil fell from 9.7 per cent in the late 1960s to 1–2 per cent in the late 1980s (Table 7.9).

Institutionalized Cabinets versus Educational Policy Communities

Once policy priorities shifted against education, the formerly comfortable relationship between institutionalized provincial cabinets and educational policy communities became more antagonistic. Ministries of education were weakened in their dealings with cabinets and their central agencies such as the premier's office and the provincial treasury. Tensions also mounted within educational policy communities between ministries on the one hand and trustees' associations and teachers' unions on the other hand, which put unaccustomed pressure on established norms of partnership in education.

The limits of policy interdependence in an era of fiscal austerity were starkly demonstrated in 1982–3. With economic growth stagnating, and inflation and unemployment running at 10 per cent, the federal government and all provincial governments except for the NDP government in Manitoba introduced compulsory public-sector pay restraints. Public-sector wage and salary increases were held well below the rate of inflation and collective bargaining was suspended for two years. Government-teacher relations became especially hostile in Quebec and British Columbia. In Quebec, when no agreement was reached and teachers went on strike, the Parti Québécois government passed legislation in February 1983 that ordered teachers back to work, cancelled their right to strike until the end of 1985, threatened dismissal without further recourse of any teacher who did not return to work, made teachers responsible to prove their own innocence if charged with failure to comply, made teachers' unions liable for ensuring the compliance of their members, and suspended protection of the Quebec Charter of Rights.[42] In British Columbia teachers took a prominent part in the 'Operation Solidarity' campaign conducted against the government by public-sector unions and engaged in a brief strike (8–13 November 1983), but the government made no concessions to the teachers' main demands to maintain existing levels of school funding and restore collective bargaining.[43]

In the end in both Quebec and British Columbia, as well as in other provinces, provincial cabinets decreed pay restraint and cancelled collective bargaining. Pressure campaigns and strike actions by teachers and other public-sector unions won few, if any, concessions. On the impact of compulsory pay restraint on relationships within the Quebec educational policy community, Henchey and Burgess have observed, 'Whatever pretense of partnership that may have previously existed was finally put to rest by Bill 111 (1983).'[44]

Although the level of hostility between teachers and government was especially high in Quebec, a similar lesson was probably drawn from the experience of public-sector pay restraint in other provinces.

PERSON-REGARDING EDUCATION, POLICY INTERDEPENDENCE, AND PUBLIC PHILOSOPHY

Person-regarding education implied a decentralization of educational decision-making. The seminal reports of the Parent commission, the Hall-Dennis committee, and the Worth commission recognized the necessity of local autonomy, but they were also influenced by the prevailing theory of rational public management. Hence they developed a concept of policy interdependence among levels of educational governance that attempted to integrate the utilitarian liberal theory of rational management and the ethical liberal theory of local democracy.

Initially, this concept of policy interdependence was quite successful in providing a model to reconcile the ideas and interests of central agencies with provincial ministries of education, provincial ministries with local school boards, and provincial ministries with organized teachers and trustees inside educational policy communities. In most provinces ministries of education hastened to rid themselves of detailed control over local administration and reorganized their activities into functional divisions of educational planning, program development, and administrative support. Within educational policy communities relationships of policy interdependence came to prevail as the norm, although institutional arrangements in the key areas of educational finance and collective bargaining varied among the provinces. At the national level recognition of interprovincial convergence in educational ideology and policy, as well as greater provincial interdependence in educational policy and administration, led to the institutionalization of interprovincial coordination in the Council of Ministers of Education, Canada.

The onset of declining enrolments and fiscal austerity altered the initially comfortable relationships between institutionalized cabinets and educational policy communities and put pressure on relationships within educational policy communities. As political and policy priorities shifted against public education, the contradiction in liberal thought between the utilitarian liberal theory of rational management and the ethical liberal theory of local democracy became increasingly evident. The situation was particularly trying for ministries of education. They found themselves squeezed between the established norms (if not always practices) of policy interdependence within educational policy communities and the ideology of rational management that operated within institutionalized cabinets and central agencies.

During the 1980s relationships within educational policy communities were also eroded by growing criticism of person-regarding education. The concept of policy interdependence that was advanced as the norm for relationships within educational policy communities presupposed common commitment to the principles of person-regarding education. Political and educational attacks on person-regarding education, especially on policies of comprehensive secondary education, created an ideological rift inside educational policy communities that contributed to the breakdown of consensus on the norms of policy interdependence. As a result provincial ministries of education came under pressure to rethink their responsibilities for giving central direction to elementary and secondary educational policy and administration.

12

In Pursuit of Educational Excellence: Public Education and Policy Analysis in the 1990s

Two decades after the reports of the Parent commission and the Hall-Dennis committee, public education in Ontario and British Columbia was subjected to unusually coherent and penetrating policy analysis in two official reports. The publication of George Radwanski's report on the problem of drop-outs in Ontario in November 1987 and Barry Sullivan's report as royal commissioner on education in British Columbia in August 1988 symbolized the new ideological divide in contemporary Canadian education.[1]

Working within the parameters set by Sullivan and Radwanski, reports on public education in Canada prepared by provincial governments, federal agencies, public institutes, and policy consultants in the early 1990s presented the attainment of 'educational excellence' as the central problem of public education in contemporary Canada.[2] They interpreted relatively high drop-out rates, widespread functional illiteracy, and mediocre results in international mathematics and science tests as evidence of the failure of public education. They believed these educational failures to be the result of muddled purposes, fragmented curricula, and inadequate accountability. Against the prevailing public philosophy and policy practices of educational pluralism and individuation, these reports advocated the externally established curriculum and standards of a uniform education transformed to meet the competitive demands of the new global political economy.

EDUCATIONAL PURPOSE AND PROBLEMS IN THE GLOBAL ECONOMY

Contemporary official studies of public education begin with the emergence of a new global economy driven by technological change, high productivity, and international competition. This economic transformation is seen as having profound implications for educational policy.

First, individual and collective economic well-being are now determined to an unprecedented degree by the type and quality of education provided at all levels. The only type of elementary and secondary education that is relevant in a technological society is a general, liberal education teaching basic knowledge and skills. Luckily, the historic purposes of elementary and secondary education – civic education, occupational selection, and individual development – can be achieved simultaneously in a general, liberal curriculum.

Second, the successes and failures, and thus the public problems, of education in technological society are measurable by the extent to which young people acquire the basic knowledge and skills that are the foundation for lifelong learning and work in technological society. What matters for public understanding of educational problems are the results or outcomes of education rather than the resources or processes devoted to it.

Third, an education relevant for technological society inevitably means putting limits on accommodation of individual differences. Restricting educational pluralism requires sensitivity to legitimate expectations for the protection and promotion of social diversity in educational institutions and curricula, but at the core or foundations of public education there must be a common curriculum.

Individual and Collective Educational Purposes

Current official policy studies accept that public education is a complex public enterprise with multiple social, economic, and political objectives. Nonetheless, it is argued, the design of educational policies must give priority to the external pressures of an increasingly competitive global economy. Excessive emphasis on the goal of individual self-development, which characterized the orientation of person-regarding educational policies in the 1960s, eventually will prove destructive of both individual and collective well-being as Canadians grapple with the economic realities of the 1990s and beyond.

Among the most forthright and influential critiques of recent educational policies in Canada was the 1988 report by George Radwanski, former editor-in-chief of the *Toronto Star*, to the Ontario Ministry of Education on the relevance of education and the issue of drop-outs. According to Radwanski, Canada and other advanced industrialized countries are undergoing a shift from the production of goods to the provision of services and from exploitation of material resources to reliance on human knowledge that involves 'a socio-economic transformation every bit as fundamental as the earlier shift from the agrarian to the industrial era.' Because capital and technology have a high degree of mobility in the new global economy, the key variable in determining the location of production is the quality of the work force. Hence, investment in the human capital of a better-educated work force is the single most important strategy for a society to compete effectively in a knowledge-intensive global economy. 'Education has long been recognized as an important contributor to economic growth, of course – but now it has become *the* paramount ingredient for competitive success in the world economy.'[3]

In its first report, *Competing in the New Global Economy* (1988), the Ontario Premier's Council similarly argued that the best hopes for the future prosperity of the province lay in moving to an economy based on production of goods and services with high wages and high value added. A critical determinant of Ontario's ability to make the transition to a higher value-added economy will be the education, skills, ingenuity, and adaptability of its workers. In its report issued in 1990, *People and Skills in the New Global Economy*, the council then focused on the role of the educational system, as well as issues of training in the workplace and adjustment of displaced workers. According to the council, 'Education is our major public investment in equipping people to face and shape change.' As a consequence, decisions over the form, content, and place of learning have become broad political issues involving many legitimate participants beyond teachers and students in classrooms. The educational system is designed to meet many social goals, but recognizing the broad social purposes of schools does not diminish the importance of schools in preparing students for the world of work. 'Among the many goals the education system is designed to meet, maintaining and enhancing Ontario's competitiveness in the new global economy should figure prominently.'[4]

Education has become the main determinant of collective economic well-being, but education also has crucial economic implications for individuals. Radwanski argued, for example, that in technological societies the career ladder has been truncated so that young people starting with inadequate education and few skills will be stuck in low-skilled, low-paid jobs and eventually become unemployable as those marginal jobs disappear because of automated and internationalized production. Hence, he concluded, the premises and priorities of child-centred education as set out in the report of the Hall-Dennis committee have lost their relevance. In advanced technological societies meeting basic needs for self-esteem and self-development depends on ensuring individual employability and earning power.

In this new economic environment, our young people will not long feel fulfilled, nor will their self-esteem long endure, if they find themselves unemployable or unqualified for other than the most menial, dead-end work because they lack the requisite knowledge or skills. And our collective sense of fulfillment and self-esteem as a society will scarcely be enhanced if our standard of living goes into steady decline because an under-educated population has made us uncompetitive in an increasingly rigorous global economy.[5]

In its 1992 report, *A Lot to Learn,* the Economic Council of Canada was equally blunt about the economic imperative that, according to the council, must determine contemporary educational policy-making. Better educated workers are the key to improved collective economic performance at a time when the Canadian economy is threatened by global competition, but better-educated workers also enjoy higher earnings, more secure employment, and more satisfying work. The vast majority of young people who pass through Canadian schools are ultimately destined for the labour market; their future economic, and social, well-being will depend on how well they can exploit their potential in the labour market. 'To improve productivity, trade performance, and innovation – to improve the overall competitiveness of a firm, an industry, or an entire economy – one of the critical factors is the enhancement of human skills. Indeed, individually and collectively Canadians face a painful choice: develop skills or accept low wages.'[6]

Recognizing the economic implications of educational policy-making in advanced technological societies does not mean that other social and political goals of education must be ignored, or even subordinated to economic goals. For George Radwanski, not only did education determine the competitiveness of the Ontario economy and the employability of individuals, but also the effective functioning of democratic government, and hence the overall quality of life enjoyed by all citizens, depended on having a knowledgeable and well-educated population. To strengthen Ontario as a free, compassionate, and truly democratic society the education of young people must prepare them 'for the requirements not only of the workplace but also of the marketplace of ideas ... Against this background, consequently, it becomes clear that a relevant education in today's circumstances is one that prepares young people for effective and satisfying participation both in an increasingly knowledge-intensive economy and in an increasingly complex society.'[7] The educational requirements for participation in the economy and in society are convergent, not competing. Elementary and secondary education will be most relevant to economic and social needs if schools provide young people with a high-quality general education.

In its 1992 report on the public school system of New Brunswick, the Commission on Excellence in Education also argued that the economic, political, and social purposes of education can be met by liberal education in which the emphasis is placed on teaching broad skills. In their view it made sense during a period of relative social affluence in the 1960s for educational reform to focus on the purposes of individual fulfilment and social equity. In the 1990s the context has changed. 'The traditional industrial basis of our prosperity is threatened, not by any one country or circumstance, but by a changing world economic order and our own declining productivity.' The decline of employment in resource-based export industries, on which the New Brunswick economy historically relied, and the growth of industries depending on highly skilled and well-educated workers require a renewed stress on the connection between educational and economic achievement, for both individuals and society.

Fortunately, this can be done without de-emphasizing the other traditional purposes of schooling. Such is the knowledge-intensive nature of the new economies that, for the most part, they require and reward the same kinds of knowledge, skill, and behaviour which are conducive to personal fulfillment and social literacy. There is no reason to abandon, or even compromise, a broad-based liberal education in pursuit of more vocational or technological training. On the contrary, what is needed is a re-discovery and re-affirmation of the essence, rigour, and goals of a liberal education: to equip students with enough fundamental knowledge and skills to think for themselves, to be flexible, adaptable, resourceful, inventive, and responsible.[8]

Educational Outcomes as Policy Problems

If the test of high-quality education is its usefulness for economic competitiveness and individual employability, then the public problems of education are best described and measured by the results of educational policies rather than allocations of public resources to educational activities or intrinsic properties of educational processes. The purpose of elementary and secondary education is acquisition of basic knowledge and skills. Hence, measuring the levels of knowledge and skills attained by young people during their schooling will provide the information necessary to evaluate how well those in school are being served by their education.

Among the official policy analyses carried out in the early 1990s, the report of the Economic Council of Canada was the most developed effort to evaluate public education in Canada on the basis of results or 'outputs' of education, rather than resource allocation or educational process. Measures of the quality of education were developed, with special emphasis placed on students' performance in acquiring foundation skills upon which subsequent learning and labour-market experience depend. In terms of duration of schooling, for example, the council found that Canada compares favourably with other countries, but about 30 per cent of Canadian students do not finish their secondary education. Composite scores from the Canadian Test of Basic Skills show a long-term decline in the performance of grade-eight students, especially in language skills. The national survey of literacy skills conducted by Statistics Canada in 1989 found that 28 per cent of Canadians aged sixteen to twenty-four lacked basic 'everyday' reading skills and 44 per cent were below that standard in numeracy. In international tests of achievement in mathematics and science the results of Canadian children at age ten compare favourably with those in most industrial countries. At age thirteen or fourteen, however, the relative position of Canadian students begins to deteriorate; by the end of secondary school the achievement scores of Canadians are well below the average level attained for industrial countries. In short, the successes and failures of public education are measurable by the extent to which young people acquire the basic knowledge and skills that are the foundation for lifelong learning and work in technological society. By this criterion, according to the council, the results of their analysis indicate serious shortcomings in Canadian elementary and secondary education.

Social Diversity and Common Education

The ethical liberal ideology of person-regarding education legitimated educational pluralism. Individual self-development through elementary and secondary education required taking account of individual differences of religion, ethnicity, mother tongue, and racial origin, as well as differences in abilities and interests. According to more recent official policy studies, however, individual and collective well-being in a technological society depends on universal provision of a general, liberal education teaching basic knowledge and skills. Restrictions on educational pluralism accordingly must somehow be reconciled with the educational expectations deriving from social diversity.

The 1988 report by Barry Sullivan on education in British Columbia showed greater willingness than other recent official studies of Canadian education to contemplate the implications of social diversity for education, but ultimately he insisted on the necessity of common education. Historically schools have been regarded as an instrument for assimilating immigrants into Canadian society, and immigrants themselves have seen schools as 'institutional gateways' to a better future. These broad objectives remain unchanged. Just as they did a century ago, schools still work to bring culturally and ethnically diverse people together for purposes of learning and provide them with opportunities for their fullest social and individual development, but in addition schools now are expected to sustain and nourish cultural diversity. Public schools are expected to foster positive intergroup attitudes, break down cultural stereotypes, and ensure equality of treatment and access for all minorities. Schools also are expected to preserve diverse cultural heritages through language instruction and studies in history, geography, art, music, and drama, and they must be prepared to deal with special learning problems faced by some minority groups. Somehow public schools must achieve these multicultural goals without sacrificing their larger purpose of providing education for a productive and socially responsible citizenry. This implies that schools and school curricula should be diverse enough to allow for individual interests, abilities, and differences, but the expression of such choice and diversity should not lead to social fragmentation.

> Strictures must therefore be placed to ensure that all youngsters are taught something about common values, social behaviour, and intellectual and other traditions which support the common good in community, province, and nation. Simply put, variation and autonomy in the character and governance of schools must, by necessity, co-exist with requirements which ensure that certain standards are met and that certain curricular elements form a part of every child's basic education.[9]

Sullivan's concern to reconcile common education and social diversity is unusual in official policy studies of public education in the late 1980s and early 1990s. More typical is a position which ignores the issue, or even dismisses it. This is the position taken by Radwanski, for example, when he says 'there are not different relevant elementary and secondary educations, depending on an individual child's aptitudes, interests or presumed career potential or intentions. There is, rather, only one kind of meaningful general education that is relevant to the needs of society and of the economy, and hence to the well-being of the young people who must participate in both. Our challenge is to define the necessary content of that education and to bring it into effect for all.'[10]

In their critique of the Radwanski report, Stacy Churchill and Isabel Kaprielian-Churchill have pointed out that its recommendations are 'notable for the absence of suggestions that the school curriculum should be adapted to the particular needs of any ethnocultural group.'[11] The French-language school system in Ontario is mentioned only twice, both times indirectly (pages 41, 49). The words 'racism' and 'multicultural' appear only on page 38, where an argument is made to remove these issues from the school curriculum to family and community. Other words and phrases not used by Radwanski include 'English as a second language' (ESL), 'Franco-Ontarian,' 'Native people,' 'Black,' 'visible minority,' and 'discrimination.'

Similarly, in an issues paper released by New Brunswick's Commission on Excellence in Education in December 1991 formal recognition was given to the principle that an 'education system is the creature of its society' and hence must 'reflect fundamentally its own character and values. In the case of New Brunswick that fundamental character includes, preeminently, two legally equal linguistic communities.'[12] The implication of this principle, however, is not the protection and promotion of cultural pluralism in public education but its containment ('To last, therefore, educational reform must be accompanied by comparable attitudinal and institutional reform in the rest of society'). No further reference is made in the paper to either bilingualism or any other ethnocultural dimension of education. Nor did the commission return to the issue in its final report, although the commission did recognize that children with special needs, learning disabilities, and special gifts or talents do present a challenge for educational programming.[13]

Much of the analysis as well as the most far-reaching recommendations of the Newfoundland and Labrador Royal Commission of Inquiry into the Delivery of Programs and Services in Primary, Elementary, Secondary Education dealt with the transformation of the confessional school system into an 'interdenominational' one, but the commission chaired by Leonard Williams also made a clear statement of what it saw as the social context of educational change in the 1990s, and articulated a coherent philosophy of education as the framework for its analysis. In its analysis of the context for change, the royal commission observed that, historically, education has been seen as both a public good essential to preserve good government, political stability, and social cohesion and an economic good essential to create an educated labour force responsive to the needs of business and industry. In addition, 'the trend to recognize individual needs and the trend toward cultural pluralism have led to an education system embracing various forms of accommodation.'[14] As a result, the principle that the needs of individuals and interest groups should be met by the educational system has become a public expectation, and some of the pressures for structural change come from groups currently disenfranchised. In large measure, however, provision of education in the future will be shaped by global pressures over which there can be little control and which will require comprehensive rethinking of educational policy and organization.

Coping with technological change and scientific innovation will require a sound set of basic skills which go beyond the necessary fundamentals of literacy and numeracy. They will require such new basics as critical and creative thinking, the capacity for independent learning, the ability to synthesize and communicate information, and innovative problem solving ... To use an industrial metaphor, we will be forced to *re-*

tool our schools to deal with new expectations for a new type of learner – one capable of responding to an ever-changing post-industrial, high-technology age. Much of the public criticism of education, which has emanated to a large degree from the business community, has centred on the need for a graduate who is not so much a storehouse of knowledge but a manipulator of knowledge, capable of responding to personal, social and business needs.[15]

PRINCIPLES OF CURRICULUM DESIGN AND SCHOOL ORGANIZATION

Fundamental agreement on the principles of curriculum design and school organization links together the analyses and recommendations of official policy studies of public education in the late 1980s and early 1990s. Elementary and secondary education in a technological society should be a common education teaching basic knowledge and skills to all young people. Language, mathematics, and natural sciences are the foundation for all learning and, hence, should be taught as core subjects or skills at all stages of elementary and secondary education. Progress of young people through the school system should depend on their demonstrated mastery of the knowledge and skills designated to be essential at each stage of schooling. At regular intervals in the schooling of each person there should be external evaluations to assess both the individual student's progress towards attaining specific educational targets and the success of the educational system in achieving its goal to give each person in school a relevant, high-quality education. Schools should be organized to teach the common curriculum in ways that facilitate the progress of young people from lower to higher levels of educational achievement, taking into account the developmental changes in young people between their entry into kindergarten and their completion of secondary school, and making use of pedagogical techniques appropriate to each person's learning needs.

Within this framework of general principles important differences can be detected in conceptions of basic knowledge and skills and proposals for school organization and transitions between stages of education, in particular, the transition from common education to diversified academic and vocational education and training.

Conceptions of Basic Knowledge and Skills

'If we are to have a system of education that focuses meaningfully on intended outcomes for all students,' George Radwanski argued, 'the unavoidable first step is to make hard choices – to pare the list of those intended outcomes to a manageable number that the schools can realistically be expected to bring about.'[16] What are the indispensable elements of educational content out of which the common curriculum should be shaped? For Radwanski there were twelve essential content areas: English (or French in francophone schools) language skills of reading, writing, speaking, and listening; ability to think clearly and learn effectively; mathematics; classic works of English (or French) literature and Canadian literature; the sciences; Canadian and world history; Canadian and world geography; Canadian government; a common program of study about work in society; French (or English in francophone schools); the arts; and fitness and health. Bringing students to the desired levels of knowledge and skills in these twelve essential content areas would fill most, if not all, available instructional time.

In Barry Sullivan's report as royal commissioner on education in British Columbia the proposed common curriculum was organized in four core areas: humanities (English, social studies, French), fine arts (music, art, drama, dance, theatre), sciences (mathematics, biology, chemistry, physics), and practical arts (physical education, industrial education, home economics, lifespan education).[17] Although it was more integrated and interdisciplinary than that proposed by George Radwanski, Sullivan's concept of the core curriculum was nonetheless a marked contrast to the three curricular categories set out by the Hall-Dennis committee twenty years previously – communications, environmental studies, and humanities – which were designed to break the hold of traditional subjects on elementary and secondary education. Sullivan, like Radwanski, accepted that historically evolved disciplines of human knowledge and inquiry have proved productive in making sense of the world and must constitute the basic elements of curriculum design. Traditional subjects should be integrated within core areas during the first years of schooling. In later years the curriculum would become more directly organized by academic disciplines, but without losing, it was hoped, the breadth and integration implied by the core areas.

Although Radwanski and Sullivan differed about the degree of subject integration, both envisaged the core curriculum as a liberal education comprising basic knowledge and skills organized in terms of traditional disciplines.[18] An alternative concept, more strictly defined by the acquisition of basic skills, was proposed in Ontario by the Premier's Council in its 1990 report on people and skills in the new global economy and by the Newfoundland and Labrador Royal Commission of Inquiry into the Delivery of Programs and Services in Primary, Elementary, Secondary Education. As the basis for its policy analysis the Premier's Council posited a hierarchy of skills. At the first level are five basic or foundation skills upon which all higher-order skills are founded: motor skills, mathematical literacy, reading and writing ability, capacity to learn, and interactive communication skills. The council's educational principles and policy recommendations followed from this hierarchy of skills. Schools should teach 'the foundation skills that constitute a platform for lifelong learning.'[19] For the Williams commission the crucial element of curriculum was a core based on language, mathematics, and science; high standards of achievement in these disciplines must be the primary aim at all levels of education, not because they are traditional subjects in a liberal education, but because they teach basic skills essential to further learning. 'Although the specific content of the curriculum is important, in a world of rapidly changing technologies and an unprecedented explosion of knowledge, learning how to locate, analyze and utilize information and how to think critically about it is also crucial. Now more than ever, the emphasis of education must be on acquiring process skills, as specific content becomes outdated with increasing rapidity, especially in the technical and scientific fields.'[20]

Content-Oriented versus Child-Centred Education

In the theory of person-regarding education the developmental needs and learning capacities of each individual determine, at least in principle if not always in practice, the choice of curriculum. In recent official policy studies of public education for technological society, the determination of a common or core curriculum is the first step. Once the overall content of elementary and secondary education has been established, then specific objectives can be set for each major stage of learning, appropriate curricular materials and learning activities can be developed, and effective pedagogical approaches can be chosen. In undertaking these more specific tasks of curriculum development, differences among young people in their needs, abilities, and interests should be taken into account. The organization of schools, pedagogical approaches, and transitions between major stages of learning should be designed to accommodate differences among children while bringing them all at the end of their studies to the achievement of basic knowledge and skills that all young people must have to live and work in a technological society.

Perhaps because the Hall-Dennis committee had such an impact on official educational ideology in Ontario, George Radwanski was scathing in his comments on the contemporary relevance of the Hall-Dennis educational philosophy. 'That report faithfully mirrored the flower-child, do-your-own-thing outlook of the 1960s in its belief that a relevant education was one in which content was of secondary importance, that the acquisition of specific knowledge should be subordinated to more abstract goals of individual self-fulfillment and self-esteem. But relevance is a moving target. Whether or not that view was ever valid, today it is dangerously outdated.'[21] Radwanski agreed that child-centred education can stimulate better learning, but 'process should not be confused with product.' Education in the first instance must be content-oriented; 'the whole object of the exercise is to develop each individual child by bringing him or her into possession of the specific knowledge and skills that every young adult coming into our society should have.'[22] The techniques of child-centred education – such as using the existing interests of learners to create new interests, supplementing book-based instruction by diverse learning activities, making learning as exciting and enjoyable as possible rather than mere drudgery, and fitting instructional methods as closely as possible to the learning style of each child – are means to that end. Thus content-oriented and child-centred education are complementary, not competing approaches. Once the content of common education has been determined, the full array of pedagogical methods and skills should be employed to bring each child into possession of that content.

In other official reports child-centred education is treated as more than pedagogical technique; it is recognized as the appropriate paradigm for early childhood and primary education, but should be progressively subordinated in the middle and higher years of elementary and secondary schooling to more traditional, subject-oriented teaching. Undoubtedly the strongest advocate of child-centred education during the early years of school was the Sullivan report. According to Sullivan, 'Teachers and schools must recognize the wide range that exists in students' abilities, interests, ambitions, beliefs, attitudes, and values. Curriculum must respond to it by providing variety and choice.'[23] In the primary years (kindergarten to grade three) subjects should be fully integrated within the four strand areas of humanities, sciences, fine arts, and practical arts. Primary schools should be ungraded, and developmental criteria should be decisive in the placement and progress of children at this stage of their learning. In the intermediate years (grades four to ten) teaching might continue to be organized by integrating subjects within strands, shift to an approach based on traditional subjects, or employ some combination of strand and subject organization. In the senior years (grades eleven and twelve) teaching would be organized by traditional subjects.

In defining the principles that guided its recommendations for reform of education in Newfoundland and Labrador, the Williams commission revealed its concern for education to be balanced between meeting individual needs and responding to technological change.[24] To achieve 'equity,' schools should provide for the diverse learning needs and interests of each child, but equity must be balanced by the requirements of 'quality.' 'Achieving a quality education will require that, regardless of interests, abilities or talents, every child is individually challenged to understand, meet and exceed the needs and expectations of society in a manner which is appropriate and realistic for the child.'[25] Similarly, a 'responsive' system will take into account the personal backgrounds and goals, individual characteristics and circumstances, and different geographical locations of all the children whose needs it must meet, but it also will respond to changing societal needs 'primarily arising from the business and political communities and often based on social concerns.' In making specific recommendations about school organization the Williams commission followed the model proposed by Sullivan to make child-centred education the paradigm for primary education and then shift progressively to organization by subject or discipline in middle and high school. The commission recommended that the primary level of education (kindergarten to grade three) be reorganized on a non-graded basis in order to be consistent with child-centred principles and practices, but elementary education (grades four to six) would shift from a child-centred approach to discrete courses and subjects.

The New Brunswick commissioners Aldea Landry and James Downey also accepted 'the need to acknowledge that children enter the education system at different stages of development, and that they develop skills in different ways and at different speeds.'[26] In making specific recommendations, however, they were more cautious than the Williams commission in their endorsement of the Sullivan model. For primary schools they proposed departmental assessment of the British Columbia model of an ungraded and integrated curriculum, but withheld recommending a full commitment to it pending further studies. Their curriculum for the middle years also closely followed the Sullivan report by suggesting an interdisciplinary approach to teaching, assigning each teacher at least two subjects with the same class, and experimentation with multi-grade and cross-grade classroom groupings.

Program Differentiation and Educational Transitions

Recent official policy studies of public education in Canada all have advocated a common curriculum for elementary education and at least a common core of subjects for all high school students. They have condemned homogeneous grouping by ability for instruction in elementary schools and recommended an end to the practice of streaming high school students into courses differentiated as advanced, general, and basic. Secondary education raises the issue of transition from a common curriculum to diversified programs, however, and here opinions have been divided. One side holds that secondary education is essentially similar to elementary education, and hence all secondary students should continue to follow a common curriculum. On the other side, secondary education is seen as a stage where young people should make a major transition in their learning from a common curriculum to diversified academic and vocational studies.

George Radwanski took the side of common secondary education. He saw the credit system in Ontario, correctly, as deriving from the child-centred philosophy of the Hall-Dennis report, introduced in the early 1970s to individualize secondary education by letting students design their own learning programs. Even with the retreat from unrestricted individual course selection in the late 1970s and early 1980s, the credit system remained seriously deficient, leaving serious gaps in what students were required to learn, producing disparities among students in what they actually studied, fragmenting and trivializing learning, and creating alienation and isolation among students. Radwanski concluded, 'If a coherence of purpose is to be restored to our high schools, the belief that maximization of educational choice necessarily is a good in itself urgently needs to be rethought.'[27] Radwanski accordingly recommended that the credit system be abolished or phased out of Ontario high schools and replaced with a common program in the twelve 'essential content areas.' In grades nine and ten there would be no optional courses, and only a limited number of optional courses 'to a degree consistent with successful learning outcomes in the essential content areas' in grades eleven and twelve. To reduce student isolation and strengthen teacher-student contact, he further recommended that students remain together in the same class for most of their common subjects each year and that class teachers provide instruction in at least two subjects.[28]

An essentially common secondary education for all students was also the model supported by the Landry-Downey commission for New Brunswick and the Williams commission in Newfoundland. Landry and Downey proposed that high school be extended downward to include grade nine in order to permit more time for concentration on studies leading to post-secondary education for entry into the labour force. The strictly common curriculum would be limited to the first nine years of school, taught in either unified schools covering kindergarten to grade eight or separate primary (kindergarten to grade five) and middle (grades six to eight) schools. On their curriculum for high school, the commissioners' recommendation for a broad common core with only limited options, their criticism of differentiating between advanced and general courses, and their insistence on the need for all students to acquire a strong foundation of skills and knowledge, regardless of whether they are bound for post-secondary education or the labour force, put them closer to Radwanski than Sullivan. Similarly, the Williams commission concluded that optional courses are desirable at junior and senior high levels of education, but the commission was strongly critical of the introduction of non-academic courses and stressed the continuing centrality of language, mathematics, and science as core subjects.

Instead of a common curriculum throughout secondary education, the Sullivan report proposed an alternative model of diversified educational programs in upper secondary school. All students would follow a provincial common curriculum from kindergarten through grade ten. Everyone who completed grade ten would be entitled to two further years of state-supported education. A common core program for grades eleven and twelve should be 'designed to respond, not merely to the minority of university-bound students, but to the needs of all future citizens in a changing society.'[29] In this core program all students would take two years of English language and literature; social studies; science, technology, and the environment; and physical education. Beyond this core students would choose a program to fit their academic and vocational interests and aptitudes. The majority would probably choose a general academic program, but they also could choose to combine the core curriculum with career-oriented programs at community colleges, vocational institutes, or authorized private vocational training institutions where their fees would be paid as part of their two-year educational entitlement.

Other advocates of diversified programs in upper secondary education have been the Premier's Council in Ontario and the Economic Council of Canada. In its 1990 report, the Premier's Council proposed that a common curriculum without streaming be put in place by the year 2000 for grades seven to ten, but programs in the senior years of secondary school should be differentiated among areas of concentration, offering students a wide choice of both career-oriented and broader interest courses and allowing for much closer connections among industry, labour, post-secondary institutions, and schools. In *A Lot to Learn*, a principal conclusion of the Economic Council of Canada was the serious damage caused by the neglect of options for non-academic students and the general disrepute of vocational programs in Canadian secondary education. As a remedy the council urged closer integration of school, training, and work by promoting partnerships between business and schools, developing cooperative programs, linking formal schooling and apprenticeship training, and upgrading the status of secondary vocational education.

Educational Performance and Accountability

Educational performance is the bottom line in content-oriented education. Have young people actually acquired the basic knowledge and skills they should possess at different stages of their education? Accountability refers to those who have been given, or must take, responsibility for ensuring that young people have acquired the requisite knowledge and skills during their elementary and secondary education. In recent official policy studies, educational performance is portrayed as a problem of testing the knowledge and skills of students and thus holding accountable those who have responsibility for achieving educational outcomes.

Ultimately, accountability raises the question of whether the educational performance of students in the system meets expected standards of achievement, but the measurement of educational performance is seen to have three distinct levels of meaning for accountability. First, educational performance means measuring the extent to which students have succeeded in mastering the basic knowledge and skills set out for successive stages of the common or core curriculum. Those who have not met established standards must be helped to reach them. Here testing is diagnostic; teaching and learning become remedial. Accountability is shared by teachers, students, and parents, whose joint efforts are needed for each student to meet expected levels of accomplishment. Second, teachers and administrators have a professional and public responsibility to evaluate students at the end of their secondary education and effectively communicate to the students, their parents, prospective employers, and post-secondary institutions meaningful information about the level of attainment and quality of credentials obtained by each student. Here accountability requires teachers and administrators, both local and provincial, to develop systems of testing and accreditation that permit broad public understanding of the levels of achievement reached by individual students. Third, provincial and local educational administrators have a professional and public responsibility to aggregate measures of individual performance into measures of performance of the system as a whole. Here accountability rests with teachers, administrators, and politicians, who must evaluate the evidence of system performance and then seek ways to improve aggregate educational outcomes. Standardized testing and external examinations are advocated as useful instruments for purposes of individual diagnosis and essential for determining educational credentials and evaluating system performance.

On 'the vital issue of accountability,' George Radwanski held, 'There can be no effective pursuit of excellence in educational outcomes without meaningful accountability, and there can be no meaningful accountability without measurable standards of accomplishment.'[30] Since knowledge and skills are demonstrable, testing is the way to establish what each student knows and is able to do. For the results of testing to provide meaningful indicators of educational attainments, there must not be wide differences in testing programs and practices among teachers, schools, and districts in the province. Hence, accountability requires standardized provincial tests. Radwanski emphasized, however, that the purpose of testing was not ranking academically successful and unsuccessful individual students.

> Rather, the purpose throughout the years of schooling should be diagnostic and remedial: to establish whether a student's knowledge and skills in the essential content areas at least meet an established standard of accomplishment for that particular stage of the education process, or whether he or she needs additional help to attain that standard. And at the conclusion of high school, the purpose of testing should be credentialization: the provision of reliable assurance to the student and to the community that he or she possesses at least the minimum requisite knowledge and skills.[31]

Radwanski recommended standardized tests every two years in elementary school in reading comprehension; writing, including grammar, spelling, and punctuation; mathematics; reasoning and problem-solving; and learning skills. In high school all students should continue to be tested in these same content areas, and preferably in the other subjects of the core curriculum as well.

On accountability, the report of the New Brunswick Commission on Excellence in Education cited with approval Radwanski's dictum that effective pursuit of excellence in educational outcomes required accountability based on measurable standards of accomplishment.[32] Consistent with the aims of education and 'based on our best knowledge and judgment of what is worth knowing and knowing how to do,' the New Brunswick Department of Education should set benchmarks or standards of achievement for the major stages of educational development and establish reliable instruments for measuring student achievement. External examinations provide a more objective and consistent standard by which to assess student performance than do individual teacher evaluations and, in addition, help teachers by providing a check on their classroom assessments of students' work. Hence, evaluation of student performance should combine teachers' assessments with the results of external examinations. As a first step, the existing provincial achievement tests in English and mathematics – currently compulsory for francophone students and worth 40 per cent of their final marks, but voluntary for anglophone students – should be made mandatory for all students; examinations should be set in at least the core subjects of mathematics, sciences, language arts, and the second language; and examination results should count at least 30 per cent of the student's final mark in each subject.

Radwanski conceived educational accountability at the levels of remedial education and secondary credentials. In its 1990 report the Ontario Premier's Council gave priority to the evaluation of system performance. Provincial benchmarks should be established at all levels in the basic skills of reading, writing, speaking and listening, abstract problem-solving, mathematics, science, and technological literacy. In order to monitor how effectively the educational system is fulfilling its mission, the performance of a representative sample of students should be tested each year, and comparison of test results against provincial benchmarks should be the basis for an annual 'report card' to the Ontario public.[33]

According to the Williams commission in Newfoundland, 'All accountability must ultimately assure all sectors of the public that the resources being put into education represent a sound and cost-effective investment in the future, and that the educational experiences provided to our children are of the highest quality. This is true whether one views education as an economic investment, a means of cultural transmission, an instrument of social change or an end in itself.'[34] The commission concluded that the current system of accountability needed to be strengthened, but, as with the Premier's Council in Ontario, its primary concern was evaluating system performance rather than individual achievement. The commission proposed that system performance be measured in terms of 'input indicators' of enrolments and resources; 'process indicators,' such as class sizes, instructional resources, school organization, instructional time, and instructional methods; and 'output indicators' of student achievement, participation, levels of attainment, attitudes, and values. A central element of the department's mandate would be development and maintenance of a comprehensive set of provincial educational performance indicators, and school districts should be encouraged to develop additional local educational indicators. The department should set achievement standards to be met by all students at the end of primary, elementary, junior high, and senior high school; curriculum-specific, criterion-referenced tests, including items from national and international tests for which performance characteristics are known, should be developed and administered annually to standardized samples of students in grades three, six, nine, and twelve.[35]

GOVERNING EDUCATION IN A TECHNOLOGICAL SOCIETY

Two problems of educational governance recur in official policy studies of the late 1980s and early 1990s. Both derive from changes in educational governance associated with the development of person-regarding education in the 1960s. The theory of person-regarding education legitimized decentralization and interdependence among different levels of educational decision-making.

In practice provincial educational policy communities tended to be dominated by senior officials in departments of education and representatives of school trustees and teachers who had direct interests in educational policy and administration. Official policy studies in the late 1980s and early 1990s challenged both of these conditions. First, it was argued, policies determining overall resource allocation to public education, content of the common or core curriculum, provincial standards of educational achievement, and mechanisms of accountability must be made by provincial educational authorities. Management should be decentralized to school boards, school councils, and teaching staffs, while ensuring that accountability to the policy-determining centre is preserved. Second, the relatively narrow constitution of provincial and local educational policy communities should be extended beyond professional educational interests to incorporate important societal interests, especially organized business and labour, in designing and delivering elementary and secondary education for technological society.

Policy-Making Authority and Provincial Common Curriculum

In theory, recommendation of a common provincial curriculum might be expected to be accompanied by support for constituting the relationship of central and local educational authorities as a form of policy tutelage. The provincial educational authority would establish the policy framework by deciding the content of the common curriculum, setting standards of proficiency in basic knowledge and skills, and ensuring by formal testing and other methods of evaluation that standards were being met. School boards and teaching staffs would implement the provincial common curriculum, taking into account variations in local and individual needs and interests. In practice, recent official policy studies of education accept that no simple separation can be effected between policy and administration. Moreover, with the possible exception of the Radwanski report, 'tutelage' would be too strong a term to describe the policy relationship projected between central and local authorities. Nonetheless, provincial departments are envisaged as providing crucial and decisive 'leadership' of policy while at the same time they are admonished to leave the details of management to school boards, school councils, and teaching staffs.

In making the case for restoring common education in Ontario, George Radwanski distinguished the requirements of policy and administration in terms that fit neatly into a model of policy tutelage. Decentralization of curriculum planning was designed to permit the content of education to be adapted to the differing needs of various communities across Ontario, but students' needs for basic knowledge and skills do not vary among communities.

'Would a young person in Thunder Bay need to acquire less proficiency in mathematics, say, than one in Peterborough? Is a knowledge of history more or less important in Hamilton than in Kingston? Could reading great works of English literature be less important for students in Ottawa than for those in Parry Sound?'[36] In contrast with the content of education, which must be common, different approaches to teaching the common curriculum may be appropriate in different types of communities. Accordingly, given the central importance of education not only for the well-being of individuals but also for the economic competitiveness and future prosperity of Ontario, the Ministry of Education should prescribe educational content and standards, while leaving to local educational authorities the determination of appropriate pedagogical techniques.

Strong departmental policy leadership was also the model recommended in the Sullivan report, but, perhaps because the issue of centralization versus devolution has been much more divisive in British Columbia than in Ontario, Sullivan directed more concern towards preserving and strengthening a tri-level system of educational governance in British Columbia. Overall commitment of public resources to education must be centrally determined, Sullivan argued, because only the provincial government had access to the broad tax base essential for ensuring equalization, and the Ministry of Education ought to determine basic curricula and monitor general standards of achievement. Beyond resource allocation and curriculum, the provincial government should delegate its administrative authority over education to school boards and school councils. Provincial controls produce administrative uniformity and standardization, but the educational system must be sensitive to local interests, accommodate needs for individualized services, and give individuals greater choice and responsibility. 'To such ends, governance and administrative authority should be delegated from provincial to local levels, where further delegation may occur to individual schools.'[37] Sullivan was especially critical of excessive provincial authority in the past, citing the ministry's introduction of policy changes without adequately consulting its partners. To remedy this neglect, he proposed a provincial education advisory council and a provincial curriculum committee, which would include representatives of the trustees' association, teachers' federation, parents, business, and labour.

For commissioners Landry and Downey in New Brunswick, educational policy-making should remain strongly centralized, but the provincial educational policy community ought to be more diversified. The aims of education, standards of achievement, and provincial instruments for student evaluation should be established by the Department of Education after consultation with students, teachers, trustees, parents, and other interested parties. One of the guiding principles of educational reform was the need for wider involvement in educational governance: 'Given the way authority, responsibility and resources are distributed in our society, it will require the active support of all educational stakeholders, including business and labour, to effect significant and lasting improvements to education and training.'[38] At the same time the commission advocated 'the devolution of authority from the centre to the circumference: from the Department of Education to the school boards; from the school boards to the schools; from the schools to the teachers; and from teachers to the students.'[39] In particular, the commission thought that the role and responsibility of school boards should be strengthened and every school should have an advisory parent-community committee. In short, the model of governance recommended by Landry and Downey would preserve centralized executive policy-making while widening its participants and replace the existing relationship of administrative agency in central-local relations with one closer to policy tutelage.

The model of educational governance advocated by the Williams commission was described as 'integrated decentralization.'[40] According to the commission the Department of Education should establish and maintain the legal framework of public education, set provincial educational goals and standards, establish the means to assess the effectiveness of the system, ensure the provision of adequate public resources for the development and delivery of educational programs and services, and address the issues of public interest that transcend the responsibility of school boards and schools: 'It must ensure that the education system meets the educational needs of all individuals to the extent permitted by its resources, and that the school system addresses the larger public interests in creating a healthy individual, society and economy.'[41] The existing thirty-two denominational school districts should be replaced by nine elected interdenominational school boards, which would be responsible for regional policy and administration. As with Sullivan and Landry-Downey, the Williams commission recommended a shift in decision-making so that teachers, students, and parents made more of the important educational choices. School councils composed of school staff, parents, community leaders, and (where possible) students should be established 'with the power to make decisions on matters that directly affect the school and to advise other levels on issues which concern them.'[42] The restructuring of educational decision-making envisaged by the commission would not produce a simple separation between policy and administration. Rather it would be 'a multi-tiered response' to challenges of educational change, but leadership would still come from the Department of Education, which would remain at the centre of the educational policy community.

Educational Policy Communities as Stakeholder Partnerships

In the late nineteenth and early twentieth centuries business interests were a crucial influence on the development of occupational selection and vocational training as basic elements of public education in Canada. Business interests had little sympathy with child-centred education, however, especially its influence on secondary education, and in the years after the Second World War organized business became increasingly isolated from the formation of elementary and secondary educational policies. In the late 1980s and early 1990s, organized business renewed its claim to participate in educational policy-making, citing the necessity of business involvement in educational planning to meet the dual challenge of a technological society and a global economy. To a degree unprecedented since the years before the First World War major business associations acted to formulate their policy position and establish their presence as 'stakeholders' in educational policy communities.

An instructive example of the involvement of organized business in elementary and secondary education was the report issued in March 1992 by the Conference Board of Canada on the costs to Canada of young people dropping out without finishing high school. As with recent official policy studies, the Conference Board's study started with the assumption that individual and collective economic well-being increasingly depend on the quantity and quality of public education ('It is no longer news that Canada's educational system has a vital role to play in our industrial competitiveness or that a growing gap between skilled and unskilled labour threatens to deepen the gulf between haves and have-nots').[43] In such an economic environment the costs of dropping out are discernible and significant for both individual students and society. Because stakeholders may underestimate the true magnitude of the problem, the Conference Board report took as its objective to raise awareness of the heavy costs currently carried by society and individual students. Based on an approach to educational expenditure as an investment in human capital, researcher Brenda Lafleur estimated total private and social costs over the working lives of nearly 137,000 young people who dropped out instead of graduating with the class of 1989 at a present value of four billion dollars. These results confirmed that all stakeholders have an interest in working towards reducing the number of young people who drop out of secondary school. 'Given the kind of future that is anticipated for Canada, one in which education will play an increasingly important role in emerging technologies, international competitiveness and economic productivity, action on the secondary school dropout problem is imperative.'[44]

Another good example was the study sponsored by the Alberta Chamber of

Resources in partnership with the Alberta Department of Education. Here the empirical research involved a comparison of mathematics, physics, and chemistry curricula for grades seven to twelve in Alberta, Germany, Hungary, and Japan. The study found that physics and chemistry were introduced later as discrete subjects in Alberta, there was excessive repetition of mathematics concepts, probably a result of Alberta's reliance on a 'spiral curriculum' in which concepts are treated and materials covered by repetition at progressively more advanced levels. Alberta textbooks tended to be bulkier, heavier, more expensive, and wordier, and contained more distracting material. The comparison countries were considered to be much more concerned with mastery of curriculum content and outcomes than Alberta, and class time was more efficiently used. In comparison with Asian and European countries, education in Canada is fragmented and lacks national perspective. In particular, there is no national consensus on core curriculum, standards, or achievement. By far the major concern reported with education in Alberta was the quality of schooling for the two-thirds of students who do not proceed to post-secondary education: 'Most of these students are inadequately prepared for a job market that is demanding ever-increasing formal education and the ability to participate in life-long learning.'[45] In other countries much more attention is paid to facilitating and guiding transitions from school to work, more encouragement is given for students to enter technical careers and skilled trades, and closer relationships exist between schools and employers than is the case in Alberta. The report concluded that from the perspective of industry, 'the quality of the education system product is not good enough.'[46] Partnerships of stakeholders in education, including business, should be formed at all levels to promote public understanding of the linkage between education and economic prosperity, foster the values of the work ethic in education, promote science and technology studies, focus more attention on the quality of education for students not proceeding to post-secondary education, and develop effective transitions from school to work.

Perhaps the strongest case to reconstitute educational policy communities was made by the Economic Council of Canada. Corporatist relationships were seen by the council as a key factor in the achievement of effective national educational policies in Germany and Japan. In comparison with the 'institutional models' of Japan or Germany, which are characterized by organized interaction among firms, schools, unions, and governments, Canada and the United States rely on 'market models,' which are characterized by unclear signals about labour market trends, confused and indirect pathways connecting school to work, and inadequate involvement of employers in educational design and delivery.

To change this situation we need, first of all, a broad consensus among Canadians on the role and value of learning. Next, stakeholders must commit themselves to improving the coherence of the system. Employers in all sectors must articulate their needs and expectations clearly; school boards, counsellors, and teachers must find it to their advantage to interpret and respond to employers' needs; the numerous programs and levels within the education system must fit together so that they offer predictable pathways to students. This entails a wide spectrum of groups working together to diffuse information, design and implement programs, and adjust incentives.[47]

Realistically, the council recognized, educational reform in Canada would not be achieved by any grand design imposed by the state. The education and training systems were too large and their needs too diverse for their problems to be solved simply by creating a federal department of education, strengthening the authority of provincial departments, or convening conferences to draw up national educational goals and targets. 'Rather, Canadians must establish mechanisms to engage the stakeholders – departments of education, teachers, employers from all sectors, unions, parents and students, and social and voluntary agencies – in the pursuit of coherence on an on-going basis.' Such mechanisms of national coordination have long escaped Canadians, but the council saw welcome signs of change in the progress of the Council of Ministers of Education, Canada, towards broad consensus on objectives, indicators, and student testing; the work of the Canadian Labour Force Development Board in bringing together representatives of employers, labour unions, and educational and social agencies to link learning systems and labour markets; and the establishment of the Ontario Training and Adjustment Board and the Société québécoise de développement de la main-oeuvre as institutions for joint involvement of business, labour, and government at the level of provincial training.

REVISIONIST IDEOLOGICAL CONSENSUS AND EDUCATIONAL POLICY PRINCIPLES

Official policy studies of public education in Canada in the late 1980s and early 1990s were by no means identical in their ideological commitments. On one side, the report of Barry Sullivan in British Columbia departed least from the ethical liberal position espoused in the Parent, Hall-Dennis, and Worth reports. Indeed, in its recommendations for early and childhood education, the Sullivan report was essentially indistinguishable from the earlier advocates of person-regarding education. On the other side, George Radwanski's report in Ontario, while essentially liberal in its orientations to education for technological society and global economy, displayed strong affinities to conservative educational ideology in its concerns for a morally substantive curriculum derived from the Anglo-European cultural tradition. The reports of the Williams commission in Newfoundland and the Landry-Downey commission in New Brunswick, which evidently drew on both Sullivan and Radwanski in their analyses and recommendations, overall fell somewhere between the revisionist ethical liberalism of the Sullivan report and the conservative liberalism of the Radwanski report. The reports of the Ontario Premier's Council and the Economic Council of Canada, with their focus on acquisition of economically productive skills, presented a much more restricted liberal vision of education as predominantly instrumental and utilitarian.

Despite these ideological differences, recent official policy studies have been substantially agreed on six basic principles of educational purpose, policy, and governance. First, educational policy must be redesigned to take account of the emergence of a global economy driven by technological change and international competition. Because of this economic transformation, individual and collective economic well-being are now determined to an unprecedented degree by the type and quality of education provided at all levels. Second, the purpose of elementary and secondary education is acquisition of basic knowledge and skills. Official policy studies have differed in their definitions of basic knowledge and skills, but they all agree on the need for a common or core curriculum that would occupy persons in elementary and secondary education for most of their time in school. Third, because there must be a substantially common curriculum, reforming elementary and secondary education to be relevant to a technological society necessarily means putting limits on the accommodation of individual differences. Restricting cultural pluralism in public education does require consideration of legitimate expectations about the protection and promotion of social diversity in educational institutions and curricula, but the cultural pluralism that characterized the policies of person-regarding education cannot be sustained against the imperatives of technological society and global economy. Fourth, the public problems of education are best described and measured by the results of educational policies rather than allocations of public resources to educational activities or intrinsic properties of educational processes. Directly measuring and comparing the levels of knowledge and skills attained by young people during their schooling is the only way to get the information necessary to evaluate how well those in school are being served by their education. Fifth, public accountability must be restored to educational governance and the functions of policy and administration clearly divided between provincial and local educational authorities. The policy framework of public education involving decisions about overall resource allocation to public education, content of the common or core curriculum, provincial standards of educational achievement, and mechanisms of accountability should be determined by provincial educational authorities. The function of management should be devolved onto school boards, school councils, and teaching staffs while ensuring that accountability to the policy-determining centre is preserved. Sixth, the relatively narrow constitution of provincial and local educational policy communities, which was typical of the era of person-regarding education and policy interdependence, should be extended beyond professional educational interests to incorporate important societal interests, especially organized business and labour. In particular, institutionalized educational partnerships between government and business are essential to refit public education for the new era of global economic competition.

Despite some overlapping and inconsistencies, the set of common policy principles articulated in official policy studies of the late 1980s and early 1990s represents a significant shift away from the ethical liberal ideology that guided official policy studies of the late 1960s and early 1970s. This agreement on common policy principles has generated in turn a range of policy recommendations in recent official policy studies that, taken together, set a powerful agenda for educational reform.

13

Educational Reform in the 1990s: Policy Development and Political Prospects

Official educational policy studies in the late 1980s and early 1990s reached remarkably similar conclusions in their assessments of contemporary educational effectiveness and efficiency, explanations of institutional and educational failure, conceptions of justice and legitimacy in the design and operation of Canadian public elementary and secondary education, and recommendations for reform. Their reports set the agenda for educational politics and policy-making in the 1990s, but their conclusions have not been uncontested. The implementation of educational reforms based on these official policy studies is too recent to make a fair evaluation of their educational and political successes and failures. Nonetheless, from the emerging public debate about the need for educational reform, it is possible to identify several problems of policy theory and public philosophy that have not been adequately addressed in recent liberal thinking about refitting Canadian public education for a technological society and a global economy.

OFFICIAL POLICY STUDIES AND EDUCATIONAL REFORM IN THE 1990S

As educational policy studies multiplied in the early 1990s, a revisionist liberal consensus on educational ideology and the need for policy reform continued to grow. Nonetheless, the translation of policy studies into institutional and policy reform proved to be an uncertain business. In the five years following his report, George Radwanski's analysis and recommendations failed to gain official support in Ontario. In British Columbia the fortunes of the Sullivan report fell as the Social Credit government got closer to the provincial election held in the fall of 1991, then rose again with the election of the New Democratic party. Between the throne speech of May 1991 and the constitutional agreement of August 1992, the Conservative federal government first boldly asserted its responsibility to become actively involved in national education and training, then quietly retreated to its customary low profile. In the Council of Ministers of Education, Canada, a vigorous debate over the development of a national testing program ended with a compromise between standardized national and curriculum-based provincial test items. Only in Alberta and New Brunswick, it seemed, did governments make commitments and move decisively to implement the agenda of content-oriented education.

Putting Radwanski on the Shelf in Ontario

In the legislative committee hearings that followed the publication of the Radwanski report in Ontario, revisionist economic liberals, who wanted schools to produce graduates trained for the new global economy, were opposed by die-hard ethical liberals, who wanted schools to stress the growth of students as individuals. As one astute observer put it: 'One side invoked nightmarish visions of schools as assembly lines, producing human widgets for the economy; the other foresaw armies of pseudo-philosophers attempting to discuss the state of humanity but unable to read or write.'[1] In his appearance before the committee, Lloyd Dennis said Radwanski's approach graded children 'like eggs.' Radwanski replied that Dennis's approach left students 'floundering around in intellectual mush.' The alignment of opposing interests was clear: on one side, representatives of the Ontario Chamber of Commerce, the Retail Council of Canada, and the Canadian Federation of Independent Business advocated a return to provincial standardized testing; on the other side, representatives of teachers' unions and trustees' associations criticized Radwanski's proposal to end streaming.

In its report the legislative committee endorsed the existing goals of education in Ontario with 'their underlying theme of "helping each student" towards individual self-actualization and development' and recommended only incremental adjustments to the existing organization. The first four elementary grades should be replaced by a single division, in order to avoid the traumatic effects of early failures. Grades nine and ten should have a stronger core program with fewer optional courses and more stress on language and mathematics skills in order to preserve a continuum in the development of basic skills from elementary into secondary school. In the strongest of its recommendations, the select committee urged that high schools should delay streaming students into different levels of ability until at least grade ten.[2] The 'action plan' issued by the Ministry of Education in 1989 proposed to refocus the curriculum of grades one to six on literacy, communication, and analytical skills; set benchmarks to define learning expectations in reading, writing, mathematics, and sciences; eliminate streaming in grade nine; implement a core curriculum in grades seven to nine; and rejuvenate technological education in senior high school, now redefined as the 'years of specialization.'[3]

In September 1992 the minister of education in the NDP government (Tony Silipo) confirmed that beginning in September 1993 grade-nine students would no longer be streamed into basic, general, and advanced courses. In addition, the grade-nine curriculum would be converted from credit courses in conventional subjects to integrated studies in four areas: language, the arts, self and society; and mathematics, science, and technology. These reforms (dubbed the 'three D's,' for delabelling, destreaming, and decoursing) encountered stiff criticism from parents' groups and business interests, and an emergency meeting of the Ontario Secondary School Teachers' Federation called for the minister to resign. In November 1992 the embattled minister announced that destreaming would proceed as scheduled, but rather than starting in September 1993, 'decoursing' would be implemented over a three-year period.[4]

Delabelling, destreaming, and decoursing were evidently motivated by the NDP government's commitment to improve racial and ethnic equity in education, but the forthcoming educational reforms also promised approaches more oriented to results. A 'common curriculum' would specify desired learning outcomes for students in mathematics, reading, and writing at the end of grades three, six, and nine. Under the new provincial benchmarks program, teachers and school boards would be expected to use a variety of assessment methods – including tests, written work by students, teacher's observations, and student self-assessment – to determine whether students were achieving expected standards. A new form of student evaluation in terms of 'comprehensive achievement profiles' would include information from all these sources.[5]

When the 'common curriculum' was formally unveiled in April 1993, it was accompanied by the establishment of the Royal Commission on Learning, the first comprehensive official policy study of education in Ontario since the Hall-Dennis committee. Commenting on his government's move, Premier Rae observed that public education had become an ideological battleground and as a result public debate about education had gone awry: 'We've been bedevilled by the notion ... that it is unprogressive to talk about standards in the sense of literacy, numeracy and basic skills, and on the other hand that somehow those arguments are elitist and right wing.'[6] The four areas of the royal commission's mandate signalled the NDP government's revisionist tendency: accountability, to meet public demands for the evaluation of student progress in terms of recognized standards of achievement; organization of the educational system, including the role of school boards and increased parental and public involvement; curriculum design and implementation, to ensure that students have the knowledge and skills they will need in technological society; and development of a 'shared vision' of public education in Ontario.[7] Thus, as the common curriculum policy finally reached the stage of implementation in the summer of 1993, the report of the Premier's Council more so than the Radwanski report could be seen to have had an important influence on shifting the focus of educational concerns and creating an agenda for educational reform. As public debate from the 1988 hearings of the select committee on education to the clash over destreaming and decrediting made evident, there also was a lingering commitment to the goals of person-regarding education and an inclination towards incrementalism and compromise.

Year 2000: *Implementing the Sullivan Report in British Columbia*

With unusual alacrity the Social Credit government accepted the recommendations of the Sullivan report and proceeded to implement them. Upon receiving the report in August 1988, the government immediately established a provincial educational policy advisory committee, with representation based on Sullivan's recommendation, and this was succeeded by a permanent Education Advisory Committee with the proclamation of a new school act in September 1989. In January 1989 the minister of education, Anthony Brummet, announced the government's acceptance of the vast majority of the Sullivan report's recommendations, and, following a year of consultation with teachers, parents, and other interested groups, the Ministry of Education released its planning document *Year 2000: A Framework for Learning* and three working plans with schedules of proposed changes that 'read like a battle plan.'[8]

Year 2000 adopted the Sullivan commission's proposal for a provincial core curriculum based on four 'strand areas' of humanities, fine arts, sciences, and practical arts. From kindergarten to grade twelve learning would be continuous, with 'differentiated programming' rather than streaming to provide learning resources and teaching methods appropriate to the needs of students, who would learn in different ways at different rates. In the first four years of the primary division, subjects would be integrated in areas. During the seven intermediate years teaching might be organized by traditional subjects, subjects and areas might be integrated as in the primary division, or subject and integrated organization might be combined. As suggested by the Sullivan report, the provincial common curriculum would constitute 80 per cent of primary and intermediate education, with the remainder allotted to locally developed courses such as French immersion, Japanese, Mandarin, Native studies, and heritage languages. The graduation program in grades eleven and twelve would consist of general studies in the core areas, with optional programs that would be career oriented, general liberal arts, or designed for admission to post-secondary education. Again following Sullivan's recommendation, grade-twelve examinations were expanded to cover the general studies area of the graduation program and all advanced courses in humanities and sciences; the weighting of provincial examinations in final standing was reduced from 50 to 40 per cent.

Opposition to the implementation of the plan was directed primarily at the graduation program and the implications of changes in the intermediate division for the graduation program.[9] University officials complained that extension of integration from the primary into the intermediate division would have a deleterious impact on students' preparation for post-secondary studies organized by disciplines. The report on *Year 2000* by a University of British Columbia committee, for example, was unstinting in its criticism of subject integration and concluded, 'The philosophy of the program erodes attempts to achieve academic excellence.'[10] Many secondary teachers who were specialists in disciplines also voiced strong criticisms of extending integration to higher grades.

In September 1991, on the verge of a provincial electoral campaign and without consulting the trustees' association or the teachers' federation, the new minister of education Stanley Hagen announced that the revised intermediate curriculum, scheduled to be introduced in September 1992, would be delayed to permit a review by a citizens' advisory committee headed by prominent industrialist Edgar Kaiser. The ministry also would establish a provincial educational standards board. Local school boards would be required to publish information on the performance of their students, and comparisons would be made based on the established provincial standards.[11]

The retreat from *Year 2000* was short-lived. The New Democratic party, which won the provincial election in October 1991, supported the child-centred elements of the reform, which would give teachers more freedom to respond to children with different needs and different learning styles, and the Ministry of Education was directed to resume implementation of the reform program. By 1993 the *Year 2000* program had been introduced in all primary schools, implementation of the intermediate program was scheduled to begin in 1994, and implementation of the graduate program would start in 1995. Nonetheless, controversy continued to dog the reform measures. Members of the British Columbia Association of Mathematics Teachers, for example, protested that the strong performance of British Columbia students on national and international mathematics tests was a direct result of the traditional detailed curriculum and results-oriented teaching. The provincial director of school programs acknowledged that *Year 2000* had become the lightning rod for a litany of parental and public concerns about the state of elementary and secondary education in the province. For *Year 2000* Premier Harcourt conceded in September 1993, 'The report card is in and it has failed.' Two months later the new minister of education (Arthur Charbonneau) announced that the plan to replace letter grades with anecdotal reports in the intermediate grades (four to ten) was being cancelled, standard grade designations would be restored from kindergarten to grade twelve, and there would be a renewed focus on basic skills of reading, writing, and mathematics.[12]

Federal Government Involvement in Education

The 1990s marked the return of the federal government to policy analysis and political debate about national education. The throne speech of the Mulroney government delivered in May 1991 focused on the issue of educational outcomes. Citing the paradox of high per capita expenditures on education and training alongside statistics indicating that three of ten students drop out of high school before graduating and four of ten adults cannot read or do mathematics at the level required for routine tasks, the Conservative government concluded, 'The time has come to reach a national consensus on performance, goals, partnerships and priorities for learning.' In the fall of 1991 the federal ministers of industry, science, and technology and employment and immigration jointly issued a 'consultative paper' that had the professed aim of working, with provincial endorsement and cooperation, towards agreement on national educational goals. *Living Well ... Learning Well* disclaimed any intention to intrude on the jurisdiction of the provinces in the field of education, aiming only 'to stimulate a national discussion on the factors that determine our future prosperity.'[13] The government proposed as general targets 'to increase the level of basic skills that allow people to learn and adapt throughout their lives'; 'to increase excellence in more specialized and advanced skills, particularly those related to the application of S & T'; 'to develop a learning culture at home, at school and at work'; and 'to build a system of lifelong learning that is among the best in the world.'[14] A list of more specific targets to be met by the end of the decade included doubling the time Canadians spend in 'structured learning,' cutting adult illiteracy by half, and reducing the drop-out rate to 10 per cent. On programs that would realize these targets, however, the discussion paper offered only vague suggestions, and this lack of substance together with its quick rejection by the government of Quebec raised doubts about the prospects for any federal initiative in education.

By the summer of 1992 any extensive future involvement of the federal government in national policy development for education and training appeared to be very doubtful. Even before the Economic Council of Canada had released its study *A Lot to Learn*, the Mulroney government announced that the council was among twenty-three federal agencies being abolished for reasons of budgetary economy. Also among the agencies abolished was the Science Council of Canada, which had been a long-time advocate for reforming elementary and secondary education in mathematics, sciences, and technology. Moreover, in the constitutional agreement reached between the federal and provincial governments in August 1992, provincial governments gained exclusive jurisdiction over 'cultural matters within the provinces' and 'labour market training and development.' In particular, provincial legislatures would have constitutional authority to restrict federal spending directly related to labour market development and training. Although the constitutional agreement did not pass in the national referendum of October 1992, its provisions on culture and labour market development and training seemed to confirm the federal government's lack of political will to undertake a coherent, activist policy initiative in the area of education and training.

CMEC: The School Achievement Indicators Project

The School Achievement Indicators Project (SAIP) was approved by the Council of Ministers of Education, Canada, in September 1989. The objective was an annual report on levels of educational achievement in Canada using indicators such as rates of participation, retention, and graduation, and scores from tests of literacy and numeracy.[15] SAIP presented a considerable challenge to the capacity of the CMEC to coordinate, develop, and implement a national policy on indicators of educational achievement. As the director general of CMEC observed, 'In its 24-year existence, the Council has never attempted to carry out a project of this importance and complexity ... The entire process has enhanced the Council's resourcefulness and affirmed its role in bringing the provinces and territories together to address national issues in education.'[16] As SAIP became a focus for professional and public debate about content-oriented education and national testing, however, the CMEC also became a forum for interprovincial ministerial politics and national policy development.

Proponents of national testing emphasized the need to focus on educational outcomes, the acquisition of basic knowledge and skills, judged against established national standards. According to the president of the Business Council on National Issues, the business community in Canada strongly supported standardized testing because it would improve the quality of high school graduates: 'A considerable number of students arriving in the work force are unable to read, write and do their numbers. Standardized tests are one way to introduce excellence into our education systems. The tests set goals for people to shoot at.'[17]

Opponents of the proposed national tests argued that assessment of even basic knowledge and skills should be based on what is taught in schools, how it is taught, and who the learners are. The project was strongly criticized by provincial teachers' unions and the Canadian Teachers' Federation, on the grounds that the projected tests were not based on provincial curricula, a new level of testing not based on curricula would inevitably have the effect of narrowing and homogenizing the curriculum in each province, and teachers would be evaluated on the basis of test results rather than on the kind of students in their classes.

In May 1991 the minister of education in the Ontario NDP government announced that Ontario was withdrawing from participation in the project. The minister agreed with teachers' criticisms that tests were not being directly based on provincial curricula, and further objected that samples would not be large enough to analyse test results in terms of the demographic composition of students within each province. Hence they would fail to take account of Ontario's ethnic diversity. George Radwanski in turn criticized the Ontario government for its insistence that basic knowledge and skills could not be tested without reference to the Ontario curriculum ('Surely we can test whether students can perform a given math problem and whether or not they can read and comprehend a particular piece of writing') and for its implication that differences in social and ethnic background must be taken into account in testing students ('The role of the educational system is to overcome initial differences and enable a child to have the skills needed to function in our society. Differences are a challenge, not an excuse').[18]

In December 1991, based on guidelines negotiated by a committee of five deputy ministers including the deputy minister for Ontario, the CMEC agreed that material on the national test should reflect variations in provincial curricula, the test samples should be large enough to reflect variations in provincial demographic composition, the tests should be free of cultural and gender bias and stereotyping, the reported results should include a sampling of each student's best term work, and Ontario would join Alberta and Quebec on the team developing the test.[19] This agreement to revised guidelines and Ontario's subsequent return to the fold of national testing both followed the election of NDP governments in British Columbia and Saskatchewan, which may have strengthened the perception of ideological balancing over approaches to national testing. No sooner had the NDP government in Ontario rejoined the national testing program, however, than the Saskatchewan NDP government announced its withdrawal. 'It's not appropriate for us to be dissipating our efforts in a national test at this moment,' the minister said. 'We just think there are some other issues in education that are much more important than standardized testing.'[20]

Educational Reform in Alberta, New Brunswick, and Newfoundland

Beginning with the reforms to the secondary educational curriculum in 1985, the Alberta government has steadily strengthened its commitment to content-oriented education. The current priorities of the Alberta Department of Education for policy development and implementation were set out in *Vision for the Nineties ... A Plan for Action.*[21] First, educational standards in Alberta must be the highest in Canada and among the highest in the world. The Alberta public must be informed about what the standards at each level of education are and what results are being achieved. The department is developing indicators to assess both individual progress and system performance, participating in international testing projects that compare the achievement of Alberta students against students in other countries, and promoting national standards and national testing. Second, a results-based provincial curriculum will clearly specify levels and expectations for learning: 'Curriculum sets out what our students need to know and be able to do in a changing world. Our curriculum must reflect high standards, the needs of students, and the needs of Alberta's society and economy.'[22] Third, the acquisition of basic skills will be emphasized in all areas of the curriculum. 'Students need strong basic skills in reading, writing, computing and spelling as a foundation for understanding and applying their knowledge.' Fourth, the drop-out rate will be reduced by enhancing programs that will improve the basic skills, attendance, motivation, and self-esteem of the students most at risk. Fifth, the norm for students with special needs will be integration into regular classrooms. Sixth, science programs must be improved to foster higher achievement, better skills, and stronger interest; students must be encouraged to pursue careers in science-related fields. The action plan envisaged, in partnership with business and industry, the establishment of specialized science and technology schools, either public or private, for students who have exceptional abilities in sciences.[23]

Even before the New Brunswick Commission on Excellence in Education submitted its final report on elementary and secondary education, the Liberal government of Frank McKenna had announced that the number of school districts in the province would be reduced from forty-two to eighteen. Commissioners Landry and Downey acknowledged that reducing operating costs had been the most compelling reason for district reorganization, but they also urged that 'the chance this provides to strengthen the role of school boards in decision making and in providing leadership for the improvement of the province's schools is an equally important – and urgent – objective.'[24] In June 1992 the premier announced increased funding for learning-disabled children, preschool programs for disadvantaged children, and computer technology – all recommendations made by Landry and Downey. That was followed in September by a package of programs costing $61.1 million over four years. These included province-wide testing based on the core curriculum in order to monitor student achievement, to be administered in grades three, six, and nine and in senior high school; reorganization of high school to include grades nine to twelve; one more mathematics and one more science course required for graduation from high school; and compulsory provincial examinations for English-speaking graduating students in language, mathematics, and sciences, worth 40 per cent of their final mark.[25]

When the report of the Williams commission was released, the minister of education for Newfoundland and Labrador – Phillip Warren, who had chaired the Royal Commission on Education and Youth in the 1960s – admitted that the proposals for a non-denominational system were controversial and would require considerable consultation. On other recommendations, such as the common curriculum, the minister hoped to move quickly. He praised the tone and direction of the Williams commission's recommendations and expressed especial enthusiasm for its focus on excellence and accountability. 'We have a crisis of low expectations in this country,' the minister said. 'If we're going to compete in the world, we've got to do better. We have to raise expectations on the part of students and at all levels.'[26]

RECONSTRUCTING LIBERAL EDUCATIONAL IDEOLOGY: PROSPECTIVE PROBLEMS OF POLICY THEORY AND PUBLIC PHILOSOPHY

In assessing the educational projects of political, economic, and ethical liberalism, the historical record of their policy failures and unanticipated outcomes can be compared with their original ideals and claims. No such historical perspective is possible in the case of recent policy studies. As yet there is no track record to judge. Nonetheless, at least four major problems of policy theory and public philosophy can be identified in recent official policy studies of public education in Canada: their concepts of a technological society and the global economy, their theory of learning as mastery learning, their espoused models of educational governance, and their treatment of cultural pluralism in public education.

Concepts of a Technological Society and Global Economy

The first problematic aspect of recent official policy studies of public education is their theorizing of a technological society and global economy. Liberal theorists of technological society have an essentially optimistic view of the contemporary revolution in information technology and its consequences for human welfare. They believe that there is a collective choice to be made, either to embrace the technological society, with its economy in which jobs with high skills and high wages are preponderant, or to accept decline, with an economy in which most jobs have low skills and low wages. To reap the immense benefits of technological society people individually and collectively simply must act constructively to reform political, economic, and cultural institutions and practices to match the competitive demands of advanced technology, interactive organizations, and global competition. Reform of educational institutions and programs has a high priority on the policy agenda in liberal thinking about technological society.

A much more pessimistic view about the impact of technological society on human welfare, advanced by many social democrats and democratic socialists, argues that liberals misrepresent the technical division of labour in a technological society. The revolution in information technology does create high-skill, high-pay jobs, but a technological society is not characterized by a preponderance of such jobs. On the contrary, technological society is characterized by expansion of low-skill, low-pay jobs, and the disappearance of low-skill, high-pay jobs. Contrary to liberal theorists, the vast majority of workers in technological society will not require higher levels of knowledge in mathematics and science, nor will they need to meet much higher performance standards in technical and communication skills. The central problem of technological society is not achieving mass technical literacy and numeracy, as liberals contend, but creating a framework of political and economic institutions in which distributive justice is secured for people on both sides of the new technical division of labour.

Social democrats and democratic socialists share with liberal theorists of technological society a belief in the importance of developing 'collective intelligence,' but they differ in their conception of its meaning and application.[27]

Liberals give more emphasis to the application of collective intelligence in the workplace as the condition for efficient production in technological society. Social democrats and democratic socialists, by contrast, stress the development and application of collective intelligence as the condition to achieve democracy in the workplace and make progress towards a fully democratic society.

Such a conception of collective intelligence has important implications for the organization and content of elementary and secondary education. Social democrats and democratic socialists agree with liberals, for example, that streaming in schools should be abandoned in favour of mixed ability classes, but their primary purpose is the creation of a democratic educational culture by breaking down the hierarchies of class, ethnicity, race, and sex that are inherent in selective regimes of education and training. Through a critical approach to technology and work in their education, socialists believe, young people can come to understand the implications of advanced technology for human welfare, the way technology can perpetuate or enhance inequalities in the distribution of resources and power, and the material interests that underlie the technical division of labour in technological society. 'Through such an educative process people will come to discover that education is not instrumental to a prescribed, predetermined technological necessity but rather technology is subject to human critique, human choice and human agency.'[28]

From an alternative ideological perspective, the liberal educational theory of technological society fails because its curriculum is predominantly instrumental not morally substantive. Democratic conservatives concede the liberating effects of technological society in alleviating human 'suffering from hunger, disease, overwork and conflict from scarcity,' but they also urge 'the threat to liberty and plurality posed by technique, the technical control of human nature, the danger of ecological or nuclear disaster, the decline of nurturing traditions, the banality of education, the deprivation of purpose and meaning to an increasing number of modern men and women.'[29] In the moral wasteland of a technological society, formal education must give moral direction, provoke serious thought about good and evil, and enable young people to discover what is true and good in human experience. The pursuit of truth, however, cannot begin without belief because, as Allan Bloom maintained, 'The mind that has no prejudices at the outset is empty.'[30] Hence, formal education must begin by the teaching of 'strong prejudices,' which will through their visions of the good impart historically established principles of human action and by their errors point the road to knowledge of the whole by the love of truth and test of reason.[31]

In recent official policy studies, reference to this conservative educational tradition has varied, from fairly prominent in the Radwanski report to missing entirely from the reports of the Ontario Premiers' Council and the Economic Council of Canada. In general, however, recent official policy studies have treated the academic tradition of liberal arts and science as a means of creating productive skills rather than as the way to know good and evil, learn human virtues, and find moral direction.

Theory of Learning as Mastery Learning

'Mastery learning' as a pedagogical method involves identification of basic units of knowledge and skills, determination of the correct sequences of learning basic knowledge and skills as well as learning how to combine them in dealing with progressively more complex problems, and a cycle of teaching and testing until one basic unit is mastered and the learner is ready to continue to the next unit.

The theory of mastery learning, on which the project of content-oriented education and a common curriculum depends, presents two difficult problems when theory is applied in practice.[32] First, differences among learners are simply too great to be overcome by minor adjustments in the time alloted to certain topics. Hence, in practice the cycle of teaching and testing, usually has to stop after the second round of testing because otherwise faster learners are held back too long. Second, under mastery learning subjects must be broken down into units of work that can be taught and learned sequentially. For some topics such an approach is possible, but many topics across all subject areas are not sequentially definable. As Margaret McNay has said in her penetrating critique of the Radwanski report, 'Learning and making sense is complex, messy, idiosyncratic, unpredictable, and not amenable to a regular, preset timetable.'[33]

These practical problems in applying the theory of mastery learning serve again as a reminder that, in the application of scientific theories to public problems, social-scientific theories do not have the same status as natural-scientific theories. Mastery learning theory, like all theories of human learning, is interpretive theorizing from the premises of a philosophical anthropology. In this case the policy theory of mastery learning is embedded in a classical theory of liberalism. Mastery learning works as a policy theory in constructing an agenda for educational policy reform because mastery learning and liberal ideology share the same ontological premises or philosophical anthropology, the same assumptions about human learning and problem-solving as rational decision-making.

Models for Governing Public Education

Another problem of policy theory in recent policy studies of Canadian education can be seen in the common theme of national reform led by the federal government.[34] The underlying assumption appears to be that the problem of competing in the global economy affects all regions of Canada more or less the same, and, therefore, the implications for educational reform are essentially the same in all regions of Canada. The pressures of globalization of economic production and trade do not necessarily undermine regional economic differences, however, nor the need for regional differences in developing educational and other policy responses to deal with them.

Even if economic and educational problems are national ones, the necessity for involvement of the federal government as leader of educational reconstruction, which is an article of faith in some policy studies, is not thereby established. Both economic and ethical liberal educational projects became 'national' projects with only minimal participation by the federal government through conditional grants for vocational and technical training and official languages education. So far, the development of the new liberal educational ideology has been remarkably successful in following the same course as its economic and ethical predecessors. That requires the achievement of ideological hegemony, shifting the core questions of contemporary education in its favour, and winning control of the terms of political discourse. There exists a demonstrated potential in Canada for the development of national educational policies without policy intervention and harmonization by the federal government. In any case, the policy intelligence, organizational capacity, and political will of the federal government for carrying out educational reform are highly suspect, and federal policy intrusion on education is politically unacceptable in more provinces than simply Quebec. The trends of social policy-making that once created a place for federal leadership in such areas as health and welfare seem unlikely to be repeated in education, or any other important area of provincial policy-making.

Recent educational policy studies have been unanimous in their desire to widen effective participation in educational policy communities to include business interest associations. The utility of greater involvement by organized business in educational policy-making seems an obvious response to the pressures of adapting public education to competitive demands of the global economy. Greater involvement by organized labour in the process of educational policy-making can be advocated on similar grounds. The problem with advocating a stronger partnership of business and labour with educational policy-making authorities is the questionable ability of organized business or organized labour to uphold their side of the partnership. Recent studies of the political organization of Canadian business conclude that business interest associations are fragmented and weak.[35] Certainly at the national level they appear to lack the organizational capacity necessary for either concertation (business and state) or corporatism (business, labour, and state) to work as forms of state-society partnership in educational reconstruction.

Educational Implications of Cultural Pluralism

The liberal ideology that underlies official policy studies of the late 1980s and early 1990s encounters a fundamental problem of public philosophy in dealing with educational reform and cultural pluralism in contemporary Canada. Cultural pluralism is variously portrayed as a limiting condition or situation with which educational policy-making must contend. Formally acknowledged in passing, it has been largely ignored in policy analysis and prescription. As with political liberalism in the nineteenth century and economic liberalism in the early twentieth century, liberal thinking about educational policy in the early 1990s simply fails to grasp the meaning of cultural pluralism in Canada. For many, if not most, Canadians their personal identities are rooted in diverse cultural communities. Their world-views and life-worlds are grounded in cultural communities that are separated from each other by differences of language, religion, ethnicity, and racial origin. For many, if not most, Canadians these cultural differences are not to be surrendered through assimilation; they are traditions, practices, and identities to be protected and passed intact to the next generation.

Commitment to cultural pluralism as a basic principle of the Canadian public philosophy serves as a reminder of the dangers of using foreign models of public education as standards for educational reform in Canada. In recent educational policy studies, the two countries consistently cited as worthy of emulation in striving for educational excellence are Germany and Japan, presumably because of the correspondence (not theoretically or empirically established) between their economic leadership in the global political economy and the high standing of their students on international tests of mathematics and science. Educational policy analysts invariably make some formal acknowledgment of the impossibility and undesirability of importing foreign models of public education, but their conclusions for educational reform are much less circumspect.

The problem is not simply that Germany and Japan are less culturally pluralistic than Canada and hence dubious as examples to be followed; it is rather that cultural pluralism is not a primary principle in their philosophies of public education. Schools are places where cultural world-views and life-worlds are taught. If public schools fail to incorporate broadly the diverse cultural communities that comprise contemporary Canada as a political community, public education will be condemned as unjust. If public schools force a common curriculum on all persons in school, without reference to their diverse cultural communities, public education will be rejected as illegitimate. In a multidenominational, multilingual, multi-ethnic, and multiracial society in which cultural pluralism has become the hegemonic principle of justice and legitimacy, the new liberal project for reforming public education appears likely to suffer deep and enduring problems of justice and legitimacy.

LIBERAL IDEOLOGY AND OFFICIAL POLICY STUDIES: RETHINKING THE FUTURE OF PUBLIC EDUCATION IN A TECHNOLOGICAL SOCIETY

By the early 1990s the Radwanski report had evidently failed to gain acceptance in Ontario. The implementation of *Year 2000* had risen again from the ashes of the Social Credit government's electoral loss to the NDP, only to be subjected in turn by the NDP government to a critical review and modest retreat. The Economic Council and the Science Council of Canada, the federal government's main advocates of educational reform, were abolished, and the constitutional agreement reached in August 1992, despite its loss in the October referendum, seemed to imply a return to limbo for federal educational policy initiatives. A compromise was reached in the CMEC on the design of national school achievement indicators tests, Ontario rejoined the project, and Saskatchewan withdrew. This compromise and caution, even confusion, in policy-making practice was not reflected in educational policy analysis, however, where political thinking found growing consensus about the importance of national educational policy as a determinant of the well-being of Canada and Canadians in the global economy and the need for a more content-oriented education focused on basic knowledge and skills.

Despite this growing official consensus, which advocates educational reform based on a revisionist liberal theory of public education in technological society, there are major theoretical and philosophical problems in recent official policy studies with respect to their concept of a technological society and global economy, theory of learning as mastery learning, models for governing public education, and treatment of cultural pluralism in public education. So far at least, these problems have not been adequately addressed in policy studies or public debate about the future of education in a technological society. They are serious problems, however, sufficient to raise doubts about whether content-oriented education can, or even should, be realized in the form recommended by recent official policy studies. To serve the future, it seems, the new liberal educational project should not only rethink the problematic features of its policy theory; it should also learn the lessons of the liberal educational projects that constitute its genealogy.

Conclusion: Liberal Educational Projects and Canadian Public Philosophy

From its foundation in the middle of the nineteenth century, public education in Canada has been shaped by liberal political ideology. Notwithstanding the prolonged exceptions of Quebec and Newfoundland, nor substantial compromises with religious conservatism, the political principles of public education in Canada have been dominated by liberal conceptions of the purpose of public education, liberal understandings of the proper criteria of political evaluation, and liberal principles of state organization and public policy.

Yet liberal thinking about public education in Canada has changed profoundly over the past 150 years, and divided into distinctive and even opposing doctrines, as the purposes of public education have evolved and expanded from basic, practical civic education at the founding of public education in the middle of the nineteenth century, through occupational selection and educational accessibility promoted as a corollary of industrial expansion in the first half of the twentieth century, and individual development, which became the pre-eminent official aim of public education beginning in the 1960s.

In the late twentieth century, liberal thinking about public education appears to be changing, and dividing, again. Certainly, education has again become a high priority of public policy-making in Canada. A spate of official reports from royal commissions, federal agencies, and policy institutes has analysed the current problems of public education, assessed potential courses of public action, and made recommendations for educational reform. Even a cursory review of recent official educational policy studies suggests their convergence on a distinctive understanding of the purposes and problems of public education in the late twentieth century, widespread consensus about desirable reforms of school organization and curricula, and even extensive agreement on principles of state organization and structures of educational decision-making. In short, in official reports on public education in the late twentieth century there has emerged a tentative and incomplete, but nonetheless unmistakable, reconstruction of liberal educational ideology.

In order to put contemporary educational policy analysis and reform in historical perspective, the historical development of liberal thinking about public education can be typified as three successive liberal educational projects. A 'political,' 'economic,' and 'ethical' liberal educational project can each be seen to have distinctive conceptions of the purpose of public education, espouse different principles of state organization, and ascribe different meanings, or at least different degrees of importance, to the main criteria of political evaluation. Each liberal educational project has given priority to different educational problems and worked towards distinctive policy resolutions. Each has confronted strong political opposition, enjoyed important policy achievements, suffered failures, and experienced unexpected outcomes. Each liberal educational project also constitutes a vital part of the historical legacy that forms the ideological and institutional context for contemporary educational policy-making.

POLITICAL LIBERALISM AND THE FOUNDATION OF PUBLIC EDUCATION

The foundation of public education in the middle of the nineteenth century was led by the ideas of political liberalism. For political liberals public education was an essential public institution in the formation of a new political nationality. Public schools would be the instrument for providing a basic, practical civic education, which would teach the political liberties of democratic citizens and the political obligations of democratic subjects. For political liberals the primary criteria for evaluating educational institutions and policies were effectiveness and efficiency; the educational programs for civic education should be simple and their costs low.

To achieve the purpose of civic education public schools should be uniform in organization and curriculum. A common program would be followed by all pupils, progressing from lower grades to higher grades, in accordance with externally determined standards of achievement. The language of instruction in school should be the language of the majority, for reasons of both democratic principle (majorities rule) and economic efficiency (maximize utility, minimize costs).

The place of religion in public education was the central problem of educational foundation. Political liberals agreed that teaching sectarian religious doctrines should be strictly excluded from public schools. Responsibility for denominational instruction belonged to family and church, the private life of children, not to their public life in school. Political liberals disagreed about the place of non-denominational (but Christian) religious education in public schools. For many political liberals in the middle of the nineteenth century, religious principles and public institutions were inseparable. Public education should teach the common principles of Christianity as the foundation for public life in a liberal democratic state. Other political liberals, understanding that non-denominational religious instruction would never be acceptable to Roman Catholics and Anglicans who believed in the church's ultimate authority over education, advocated strict separation of church and state in education. Nonetheless, these differences among political liberals on the place of religion in public education were less concerned about principle and more concerned to ensure that public schools encompassed the mass of children. Otherwise, they feared, denominational divisions would fragment enrolments and make public schools unacceptably expensive and inefficient.

Principles on which to base the governance of public education were not at first clearly agreed in the political liberal educational project. From the outset there were differences about the proper balance between local autonomy and central superintendence, and differences, too, about the separation of politics and educational policy. Conservative liberals (such as Egerton Ryerson) who wanted to separate educational policy from partisan politics by creating relatively autonomous policy-making councils of civic notables and tutelary chief superintendents prevailed initially, but in the last third of the nineteenth century the classical liberal theory of ministerial responsibility became the standard convention of provincial educational authority and public accountability. At the same time, debates about the local autonomy of school boards were resolved in favour of central political authorities. School trustees might be elected to office by local taxpayers, but they were essentially administrative agents subject to detailed direction and regulation by provincial departments of education.

The educational ideas of political liberalism thus presented a reasonably coherent public philosophy about the aims and objectives, content, organization, governance, and criteria for political assessment of public education. None of these ideas went uncontested. Religious conservatives rejected the political liberal conception of the problem of public education as the formation of political nationality through civic education. Religious conservatives also rejected the erection of the state as the ultimate authority over the education of children; they insisted on the priority of church, not public, control and accountability. Religious conservatives rejected liberal ideas of teaching non-denominational religion or separating religious education from public education; both were abhorrent to conservatives who refused to distinguish between sectarian doctrine and public education. Communitarians who were minority-language protectionists, especially francophones who were also Roman Catholics, rejected the political liberal assumption that a political community must have one standard language of public communication, the official language should be the language of the majority, and, hence, the language of the majority had to be the language of instruction in public schools.

The institutional outcomes of the clash of liberal and communitarian ideas about the proper foundation of public education varied among the provinces depending on constellations of political forces, skills of political leadership, historical conjunctures, and chance events. Nonetheless, in eight of nine provinces the educational ideology of political liberalism set the framework of educational institutions and policies, while religious and linguistic conservatives scrambled to secure concessions. In British Columbia, without much public debate, and in Manitoba, with wrenching political conflict, the educational program of political liberalism was installed essentially intact. In the Maritime provinces, the educational program of political liberalism was also formally entrenched in provincial statutes governing public education, but important concessions were made in practice by reserving schools for Roman Catholic children in city school districts and granting linguistic (and religious) autonomy to school boards operating in Acadian communities. In Ontario, Saskatchewan, and Alberta, legal protection and state aid were granted to separate schools for Roman Catholic or Protestant minorities, although these were limited to elementary education in Ontario and Saskatchewan. After an initial period of communal autonomy in Ontario and official bilingualism in the North-West Territories, English was established as the official language of instruction in public schools. Again, however, compromises with French-speaking minorities were made, which required the teaching of English while permitting the use of French as a transitional language of instruction in elementary schools.

Looking back at the political liberal educational project as it was formulated in the middle of the nineteenth century, the unexpected outcome for the founders would no doubt be the persistence, even the expansion, of opposition by Roman Catholics to non-denominational schools and by francophones to English as the exclusive language of instruction. Contrary to political liberal expectations, Roman Catholic denominational and francophone linguistic minorities did not become reconciled over time to the form or content of public schooling envisaged in the political liberal educational project. On the contrary, they expanded their resistance to becoming assimilated to it, withheld legitimacy from public education, and persisted in protesting its injustice.

The exception to the hegemony of political liberalism in the design of provincial education was Quebec. Liberal ideas were certainly evident in the original design of Quebec education, the commitments of the first superintendents, the campaign for compulsory local taxation, and the introduction of ministerial responsibility in 1867. The liberal project soon foundered, however, as the Council of Public Instruction divided between Roman Catholic and Protestant committees took control of central policy-making and superintendence, and the office of minister of education was dropped from provincial cabinet. Similarly, in Newfoundland prior to Confederation, political liberal educational ideas were marginalized by an official policy of concurrent endowment, under which denominational schools were supported by the state but controlled by the churches.

ECONOMIC LIBERALISM AND ACCESSIBILITY OF PUBLIC EDUCATION

In the early twentieth century an economic liberal educational project began to be articulated. For economic liberals, public education should be designed primarily to serve the requirements of industrial expansion. Schools should provide general knowledge and skills as a base from which young people could acquire specific knowledge and skills; as the need for specific scientific and technical knowledge grows with advancing technology, schools should teach both general and specific knowledge and skills. In their debate about the nineteenth-century foundation of public education, political liberals and religious conservatives had divided bitterly about the place of religion in public education, but they had not disagreed about the uniform organization of schools and content of curriculum. Economic liberals directed their attack at the effectiveness and efficiency of uniform education in an industrial society.

In its initial formulation, the economic liberal educational project emphasized the importance of providing general and vocational (agricultural, commercial, domestic science, industrial, and technical) education in addition to academic education. It proposed to differentiate these types of education in partite systems, in which there would be separate schools for academic and vocational programs. For economic liberals, then, public education should culminate in secondary educational programs and schools that were occupationally class-specific and class-divided. Partite systems were only feasible in city school districts, however, which raised basic issues of efficiency and equality for economic liberals even within the terms of their own ideological commitments. Outside cities, young people were deprived of choice between academic and vocational education. Such a situation was inefficient, because many young people either enrolled in an academic program rather than a vocational program for which they were better suited or they dropped out of school. In either case the economy was being deprived of better-trained workers. Such a situation was also unjust, because young people living outside cities were being deprived, through no fault of their own but simply because of their place of residence, of the educational opportunities available to young people living in cities.

Between the wars the economic liberal educational project began to be reformulated to advocate multilateral or 'composite' secondary schools rather than partite systems. Thus, economic liberals pursued educational accessibility while continuing to defend educational programs that were occupationally class-specific. The economic liberal educational project was committed to achieving equality of opportunity, but it was a segmental equality by which schools replicated in their curricula and organization the occupational class structure of the industrial economy.

In the economic liberal educational project accessibility of education was defined in terms of occupational selection; it did not extend to religious education and linguistic protection. Economic liberals attacked the uniform education advocated by political liberals, but they simply perpetuated the political liberal commitment to non-denominational, if not secular, instruction in the language of the majority. Indeed, the economic liberal commitment to accessibility of education evidently worsened the position of religious and linguistic minorities. Vocational education was more costly to provide than academic education, both in terms of capital equipment and operating costs and because of the fragmentation of secondary enrolments among several educational programs. School district reorganization to support larger regional secondary schools resulted in the closure of many small schools in homogeneous communities where educational practices could be informally fitted to local denominational and linguistic circumstances. As with political liberalism, the economic liberal educational project gave little recognition to religious, ethnic, and linguistic pluralism in Canadian public education. Their prescriptions for fitting public education to an industrial economy only served to worsen the pressures on minority education.

The primary concern for educational governance in the educational project of economic liberals was the reorganization of small school districts into large regional or county divisions that could support the consolidated schools necessary to implement multilateral secondary education. Economic liberal advocates of district reorganization recognized that such a reform implied a change in the relationship between provincial departments and school boards. Central regulation and control of school boards as the administrative agents for departments of education, which had been required during the foundation of public education, became unnecessary and even inefficient when exercised over large school districts that potentially had effective local political leadership and cadres of professional administrators to provide effective local supervision. Faced with this prospect, economic liberals followed John Stuart Mill's theory of a distinction between central policies that required uniform local administration and hence close central superintendence and central policies that required adaptive local management. The relationship between provincial departments and school boards thus changed in the economic liberal educational project, from administrative agency to policy tutelage in which the provincial department was conceived as superior in knowledge and hence supreme over principles, but school boards should have administrative discretion to implement general policies in the light of local knowledge and experience.

Economic liberal thinking about educational governance also inspired two important changes to the constitutional conventions and political customs of political liberalism. First, the convention of individual ministerial responsibility in parliamentary government, under which the public functions of politics and policy had been combined in the political office of minister, was modified to separate politics and policy. Thus, policy was recognized as a public function shared jointly by the political heads and top administrative officials of departments of education. As provincial cabinets became decentralized into departmentalized policy-making, recognition of a legitimate contribution to central policy-making was extended to the representatives of provincial organizations of school trustees and teachers. Executive policy-making by the minister and top departmental officials was then redefined to provide formally, first, for advice from representatives of trustees and teachers and, eventually, for their participation in many important areas of provincial educational policy-making.

In contrast to the resistance by religious conservatives and linguistic nationalists to the educational project of political liberalism, the resistance against the educational project of economic liberalism was dispersed and disorganized. Perhaps that accounts for its powerful success. Certainly, the economic liberal educational project came to dominate educational politics and policy-making in Canada during the first half of the twentieth century much more effectively than political liberalism had dominated the foundation of public education in the nineteenth century. In eight provinces in the Maritimes, Ontario, and the West the educational project of economic liberalism was unreservedly accepted as the official public philosophy of public education. The implementation of the economic liberal project was admittedly very uneven, but in contrast with the foundation of public education under the hegemony of political liberalism, variations in implementation were as great within provinces as they were between provinces. By the 1950s the economic liberal educational project had come close to being the national educational policy, a development reached by interprovincial convergence rather than any national leadership by the federal government.

To be fair, of course, the contribution of the federal government should not be dismissed out of hand. The initial articulation of the economic liberal educational project in the work of the Royal Commission on Industrial Training and Technical Education was important, and the federal conditional grants for vocational education were helpful. There is no sense, however, in which the federal government provided national leadership of public education for occupational selection in the way that it picked up the work of provincial pioneers in health and welfare. The contribution was marginal and the most influential contribution, the Technical and Vocational Training Assistance Act, came when the economic liberal project was essentially at its end.

As with political liberalism, the economic liberal educational project experienced unexpected outcomes. Perhaps most important, the project's aspiration to differentiate mass secondary education among academic, general, and vocational programs never won popular acceptance. Academic secondary programs that gave admission to higher education continued to dominate both general and vocational options. The economic liberal shift from uniform to multilateral education was made on the basis of an argument for developing educational programs appropriate to needs of different types of individual students. That led easily into the ethical liberal proposal to design education appropriate to the needs of each individual, not simply the prospective members of occupational classes. Organized business helped initially to articulate the project, and to promote it. Business did not become a partner in the educational policy communities that later developed, however, and the absence of business as an active participant probably facilitated the acceptance of ethical liberal educational ideas in provincial educational policy communities.

As was the case with political liberalism, in Quebec and Newfoundland the impact of the economic liberal educational project was muted. The Quebec Protestant sector embraced the policy principles of economic liberalism, and within the constraints of its confessional organization endeavoured to implement them. The Quebec Roman Catholic sector made only tentative and belated gestures to differentiate educational programs in the state sector, and it remained essentially divided between mass public schools and elite classical colleges, with public provision for technical and vocational training severed from both state and private secondary education. In Newfoundland the principles of economic liberalism were widely espoused after Confederation, but the drastic consequences of school consolidation and district reorganization for denominational education continued to impede any major steps in practice towards educational reform.

ETHICAL LIBERALISM AND THE IDEAL OF AN EDUCATIVE SOCIETY

For ethical liberals the ultimate purpose of education is individual development. Education should be person-regarding. Schools should be child- or student-centred. Their educational programs and methods should be designed to fit the progression of human physical, intellectual, and emotional development, which can vary greatly among individual learners. Hence programs and methods must be highly flexible in order to allow teachers to structure learning experiences to meet the particular needs of each person in school. Like political liberals, ethical liberals recognize that individuals live in political communities; in contrast with political liberals, ethical liberals recognize that individuals as part of their public life also belong to cultural communities. Ethical liberal commitment to person-regarding education accordingly means that education must take account of the dual relationship between individual and community, both political and cultural.

The ethical liberal educational project rests on a theory of human learning and problem-solving as discursive, holistic, and individualistic. Learners are individuals with different needs and objectives. Even where their needs and objectives are relatively similar, they will learn in different ways. Hence, educational curricula must contain many different sequences of learning experiences, for no single sequence can be effective for all learners. Because complex problems cannot often or easily be broken down into subsets of simpler problems, topics in educational curricula must be presented holistically and repeatedly with different levels of sophistication, in a 'spiral curriculum.' The central problem of curricular design is determining relevant topics for learning, appropriate levels of sophistication, and effective spacing in learning spirals. Ethical liberal learning theory also emphasizes the discursive aspects of human learning. People learn in dialogue, through interaction with other people. Learners cannot be simply passive objects of instruction; they must be active participants in their own learning. In schools this requires a democratization of relationships in the classroom between teachers and learners (no longer 'pupils'), as learners work with each other and their teachers in the cause of their individual educations.

The ethical liberal commitment to person-regarding education that takes adequate account of the individual's membership in cultural communities determines the basic educational policies contained in the ethical liberal educational project. Ethical liberals reject the segmental equality of partite systems or multilateral schools that select students for educational programs or 'tracks' based on the occupational classes of an industrial economy. In their place, ethical liberals advocate comprehensive schools in which courses of learning experiences are differentiated in order to permit persons in school to choose, with the guidance of teachers and parents, an individual program fitted to each one's needs and potential.

On the place of religion in public education, ethical liberals recognize that membership in a religious community is the defining feature of social identity for many students and has at least some meaning for all students. In a multidenominational society, public schools cannot be maintained on the nondenominational Christianity of nineteenth-century political liberals. Neither can they ignore the importance of religion in human experience, nor the deep commitment of many believers to sectarian education. Accordingly, as with secular education in comprehensive schools, the ethical liberal project is committed to providing a place for religion in the education of each person in school that will be appropriate to that person's needs and beliefs. Public schools must be broadly, if not universally, non-denominational in teaching religion and in religious practices and observances. For those persons who are committed to grounding education in sectarian instruction, as much public support as possible should be provided through a state system of reserved schools or concurrent endowment of private schools.

Similarly, because language is a basic element of individual identity, public education in a multilingual society ought to respect as much as possible the linguistic heritage of each person in school, without ignoring the need to teach the languages that are the media of communication for political participation and economic transactions. Hence for ethical liberals the ideal linguistic regime is one of linguistic choice, in which there are majority-language, minority-language, and bilingual schools providing for individual choice as extensively as numbers warrant.

For ethical liberals the most important decisions about education are made by young people in school with the advice and guidance of adults, particularly teachers and parents. Hence, the ethical liberal project requires a massive decentralization of educational decision-making. The learning experiences needed by persons in school cannot be determined without direct reference to who they are and how they are growing. Nonetheless, there are critical policy choices about the financing of public education, the relationship between public and private schools, and the necessary limits of individual choice where numbers warrant that can only be made by more inclusive institutions of educational governance in elected school boards or provincial legislatures. Consequently, in the ethical liberal project, educational governance must be able to integrate separate levels of educational politics, policy, and administration in community schools, local boards, and provincial departments in a seamless relationship of policy interdependence.

For ethical liberals the overriding criterion in evaluating educational policies should be justice. Distributive justice means person-regarding equality. In the ethical liberal educational project all persons in school should have equal opportunity to acquire an education of equal value, but what constitutes value will vary among persons depending on their individual needs. The legitimacy of public education must be defined in terms of its capacity to provide for the universal development of individuals who live in a multidenominational, multilingual, and multicultural society; that entails educational pluralism. Effectiveness of education cannot be judged by externally determined standards set by central educational policy-makers and tested by central inspection or provincial examinations; it must be evaluated by reference to the satisfaction of the needs of each person in school. Rather than minimizing the costs of standardized educational programs, which is the criterion of both political and economic liberals, efficiency for ethical liberals means maximizing the provision of learning experiences relevant for persons in school within cost constraints that have been established by a process of open, public deliberation.

In contrast with the greatly uneven implementation of the educational project of political liberalism at the foundation of public education, the educational project of ethical liberalism became the hegemonic paradigm for educational policy-making in all provinces. In this regard, ethical liberal ideology was even more successful as a national educational policy paradigm than economic liberalism. When the educational reforms of provincial financing, school consolidation, district reorganization, and curricular reorganization came in the provinces of Quebec and Newfoundland in the 1960s, they were enveloped by ethical liberal ideas of person-regarding education. By its commitment to educational pluralism the ethical liberal educational project also achieved greater consensus about the legitimacy and justice of public education than did either political or economic liberalism. Fundamental problems of legitimacy and justice of public education with respect to the place of religion and language in schools were no longer outside the boundaries of public deliberation, political compromise, and educational policy-making. Since the 1960s substantial progress has been achieved in all provinces in alleviating, although admittedly not yet resolving, longstanding minority grievances about religion and language in public education.

The ethical liberal educational project achieved ideological ascendancy in Canadian public education in the 1960s and continues to be a powerful paradigm of educational policy-making, but ethical liberal ideas about comprehensive education, ungraded schools, and individual timetables never won the virtually uncontested status achieved earlier by multilateral school organization, educational tracking, and occupational class selection that were the central policy assumptions of economic liberalism. Ethical liberal ideas have been most influential in all provinces in shaping early childhood and primary education. Their impact has been markedly less penetrating or sustained on secondary education, where interdisciplinary studies, individual timetables, and differentiated courses have not succeeded in displacing traditional practices of grade organization, subject specialization, and differentiated tracks. Moreover, external assessment through provincial examinations and provincial requirements for standard academic core subjects for diploma requirements have been steadily reinstated since the early 1970s. Again, the degree of revisionism varies among the provinces, but its effects are evident throughout the country.

When the implementation of ethical liberal ideas is considered more broadly, beyond policies for secondary school organization and curriculum, their impact is more impressive. In spite of the depressing drag caused by declining enrolments and fiscal crisis, provincial politicians and ministry officials, educational and community interest associations, and local school boards have worked steadily towards pluralizing public education in Canada. Contemporary policies on state aid for Roman Catholic separate schools, public funding for private schools, and education in minority official languages and heritage languages affirm the legitimacy of educational pluralism and seek to institutionalize in Canadian public life the diversity of beliefs and cultures that nurture individual development in a multidenominational, multilingual, and multicultural society.

TECHNOLOGICAL LIBERALISM AND THE QUEST FOR EDUCATIONAL EXCELLENCE

As with ethical liberalism, technological liberalism has its roots in the historical ideologies of political and (for technological liberalism, especially) economic liberalism. The technological liberal educational project, however, is not simply a revisionist version of the historical projects of political and economic liberal political thought designed to combat the perceived failures of the ethical liberal educational project. Technological liberal educational policy analyses not only advance a powerful critique of ethical liberal thinking about education, but taken collectively they also present a distinctive educational project as their own policy alternative.

For technological liberals the overriding determinant of political, economic, and social life in the late twentieth century is the emergence of a global economy. The new global economy is ruthlessly competitive, not just among individuals and firms but also among nations. Material well-being, political freedom, and cultural development are already strongly determined by, and in future will be overwhelmingly dependent on, superior capacity for scientific creativity, technological innovation, and economic productivity. Public education must be redesigned and reorganized to teach basic knowledge and skills, require a high standard of educational achievement for all persons in school, and thus establish the foundation for life-long learning and retraining that will move people from technologically obsolescent occupations to technological frontiers. Public education must also reflect the high scientific, mathematical, and technical knowledge of advanced technological societies. The basic knowledge and skills of literacy and numeracy are known. The international standards of mathematics, sciences, and engineering are also known. These necessarily set the external standards against which the educational achievements of students in Canadian schools can, and must, be evaluated.

In short, for technological liberals public education should recognize the requirements for citizenship in a modern political democracy, but it must be even more concerned for the requirements for efficient production and exchange in a global economy. Education must strive for 'excellence' in the context of a global economy in which the standards are determined, not by personal needs for self-fulfilment, however desirable these may be as private pursuits, but by the educational policies and outcomes of Canada's major national competitors – the advanced technological economies of the United States, Japan and Europe (especially Germany), and also the newly industrialized Asian countries.

The technological liberal educational project generally rejects the multilateral secondary schools and differentiated educational programs that formed the core of school organization and curriculum in the economic liberal project.[1] In their place technological liberals advocate essentially uniform education. A core curriculum with strictly limited choices in the last years should be followed by everyone throughout elementary and secondary school. 'Mastery learning' as a pedagogical method involves identification of basic units of knowledge and skills, determination of the correct sequences of learning basic knowledge and skills, as well as learning how to combine them in dealing with progressively more complex problems, and a cycle of teaching and testing until one basic unit is mastered and the learner is ready to continue to the next unit. Thus, not unlike the way in which political liberalism in the nineteenth century saw (and still sees) a common civic education that all young people must have in order to participate effectively in a liberal democratic polity, technological liberalism now sees a new requirement for a common technologically oriented education that all young people must have in order to compete successfully in the global economy.

Uniform schools, core curriculum, mastery learning, and standardized testing imply an educational melting pot. As with political and economic liberalism, the educational project of technological liberalism neglects, or even resists, the pluralizing pressures on public education of a multicultural society. Reconciling the demands of cultural pluralism and economic productivity remains a major and legitimate issue of educational politics and policy for most technological liberals, but education relevant for a technological society inevitably means putting tough limits on accommodation of individual differences. Thus arises a basic ideological division in contemporary public education – between technological liberals who give priority to economic productivity and ethical liberals who defend cultural pluralism.

In the educational project of technological liberalism, educational governance reverts from a model of policy interdependence to policy tutelage or even administrative agency. Knowledge of the educational requirements of competition in the global political economy is assumed to be located at the centre, not only in provincial governments, which have constitutional jurisdiction over public education, but also in the federal government, which has constitutional jurisdiction over international relations. Most technological liberals recognize that federal policy tutelage over public education, while desirable in principle, is unacceptable in political practice. They urge instead a federal presence and commitment to public education that will assert national priorities for educational excellence. Technological liberals thus accept policy interdependence as the norm for federal-provincial intergovernmental relations in public education, but they reject it as a model of the relationship between provincial governments and school boards in favour of centralized policy-making and decentralized management.

The technological liberal educational project also aims to change the existing balance of power in educational policy communities. Technological liberal analysis of contemporary educational policy-making tends to portray ministry or department of education officials, educational administrators employed by local school boards, and school principals as overwhelmingly committed to the objectives and policies of the ethical liberal educational project. Similarly, leaders of provincial associations of school trustees and teachers' unions are seen for the most part as ideological supporters of person-regarding education and above all as selfish advocates of their organized interests. Hence, provincial (and local) educational policy communities are attacked as closed networks for protecting the interests of educational bureaucracies. Technological liberals propose to broaden the 'stakeholders,' in particular to open educational policy-making to the influence of business interest associations. Rather than ministries, school boards, and teachers, the hegemonic 'partnership in education' should be organized business with provincial governments.

On the criteria for political evaluation of educational policies, technological liberalism returns to the doctrines of political liberalism. Effectiveness and efficiency are defined by the objective of giving all persons in school a common technologically oriented education. Desired outcomes can be defined and their achievement measured by standardized testing. Legitimacy is ascribed accordingly to the enforcement of a common curriculum in elementary and secondary schools that severely restricts accommodation of cultural pluralism. The technological liberal conception of justice is equal educational lots. The educational attainments of individuals will vary above the level of basic standards that must be achieved by all, but everyone will pursue the same educational program and strive for the same set of outcomes. Thus, given individual differences in effort and ability, the education obtained by each person will be interchangeable with the education obtained by all others.

HISTORICAL LEGACIES AND CONTEMPORARY CHOICES

Public philosophies are collectively and historically constructed. They are formed out of political thinking and practice in collective conceptions of public problems, principles of state organization, designs of public policies, and criteria of political evaluation. Each of the successive liberal educational projects – political, economic, ethical, and technological – constitutes a collective ideological paradigm advocated by its partisans as a public philosophy for public education in Canada. Taken together through a prolonged and continuing process of historical construction and reconstruction, they constitute a polyphonic liberal discourse that precariously balances the public purposes, principles, and policies of political, economic, ethical, and now technological liberalism in a complex whole. Contemporary political thinking and educational policy-making must be rooted in understanding the implications of this historical legacy.

The doctrines of political liberalism provided the foundations for the formation of responsible, self-governing political communities in British North America in the middle of the nineteenth century, and in the political liberal educational project public education was presented as an essential instrument for that political achievement. Beyond the institution of federal government, however, political liberalism in the nineteenth century lacked sensitivity to the relationship between individual identity and cultural community. In particular, liberal doctrines of non-denominational (or secular) schools and majority language of instruction simply failed the crucial test of legitimacy until rights of denominations and linguistic minorities were grudgingly recognized by informal practices (the Maritimes), communally segregated in a sympathetic cultural community (Quebec), or formally protected by legal rights (Ontario, Saskatchewan, and Alberta). Even when the test of legitimacy was met, injustice in the form of inequalities in educational resources and opportunities between majorities and minorities remained a persistent failing in theory and practice of the political liberal educational project.

The economic liberal educational project articulated a new challenge for public education in Canada. An essential condition for industrial expansion was held to be the reorientation of public elementary and (especially) secondary education towards vocational, as well as academic, education and diversification of educational programs for the purposes of occupational selection. The challenge was met at first by advocacy of partite systems, but unacceptable inequalities and inefficiencies arising from disparities between urban and rural educational opportunities turned economic liberal thinking towards multilateral or composite schools to achieve its purposes of occupational selection and educational accessibility. In this process a new meaning of distributive justice was developed, as the simple lot-regarding equality of political liberalism was replaced by a concept of segmental equality. Conceiving persons in school as types of students bound for different occupational classes provided the basis for segregating them into educational programs appropriate to their economic futures. Students enrolled would have equal lots within each educational program, but differences in future occupational class and hence educational preparation justified differential treatments for those enrolled in different programs. The economic liberal educational project thus met the challenge, which it had articulated, of reforming public education to serve individual and collective needs and opportunities of industrial expansion, but economic liberal thinking failed to overcome the historical alienation of denominational and linguistic minorities. On the contrary, the administrative conditions for establishing multilateral schools and educational accessibility required school consolidation and district reorganization, which obtained equality between urban and rural education at the expense of deepening perceptions of injustice on the part of minority cultural communities.

In the ethical liberal educational project, civic education and occupational selection became subordinated to the overriding purpose of individual self-development. Ethical liberal thinking about public education articulated a different conception of distributive justice as person-regarding equality: by giving all persons in school an education suited to their individual needs, each person received an education different in content but equal in value to that person when compared with the value to others of the educations provided to them. As the policy implications of ethical liberal thinking about public education were developed from the 1960s to the 1980s, the policy principles of comprehensive education, denominational neutrality, and linguistic choice provided the basis for a growing consensus on the legitimacy of educational pluralism and justice of person-regarding education that had proved impossible to approach under the policy principles advocated by the political and economic liberal educational projects. Nonetheless, the educational ideas and political values of ethical liberalism have been fiercely contested by remnants of political liberals who have defended non-denominational Christian public education and the majority official language as the exclusive language of instruction in public schools. Much more damaging, the ethical liberal project has also been attacked for its failure to take the economic importance of public education seriously. According to the thinking of both unrepentant economic liberals and revisionist technological liberals, the ethical liberal educational project has failed miserably on the crucial tests of educational and economic effectiveness and efficiency.

In the late 1980s and early 1990s the persistent but fragmented resistance to person-regarding education that took the form of simplistic demands to get public education 'back to basics' became reformulated as a technological liberal educational project that presented individual and collective competition in the global political economy as the essential challenge confronting contemporary public education. Technological liberal thinking gives perfunctory acknowledgment to the purposes of civic education, societal integration, and cultural identity, but effectiveness and efficiency in economic production are taken to be the ultimate tests of public accountability in public education. Technological liberal thinking also proposes to replace the person-regarding concept of equality advocated within the ethical liberal project by a lot-regarding equality, similar to the concept of equality held by political liberals, or for students in senior high school perhaps a segmental equality, similar to the concept of equality held by economic liberals. Thus, technological liberal thinking has backed away from the educational pluralism embraced by ethical liberal principles and practices. Critics may well query the set of policy theories on which the technological liberal educational project has been constructed – the assumption of apparently unrestricted international economic expansion, as opposed to sustainable development, inherent in its concept of a global economy; dependence of its argument on international rankings of economic productivity; validity of the causal relationship posited between forms of public education and national economic productivity; validity of disaggregation as a universal strategy of human learning and problem-solving; and reliability of objective measurements of educational outcomes. In the Canadian context, however, the technological liberal challenge to ethical liberal principles of educational pluralism and person-regarding education raises in many ways much more difficult issues of educational politics and policy-making.

At the beginning of the century André Siegfried observed both accurately and presciently, 'In a country like Canada the schools must sooner or later become to a greater degree than elsewhere the principal stake to be struggled for by opposing forces, national and religious.'[2] At the end of the century schools in Canada are still 'the principal stake' in power struggles among religious, racial, ethnic, and linguistic cultural groups that seek to organize public education to embody their visions of individual and collective good. Schools also have become the principal stake in power struggles among political and economic elites who seek to organize public education to achieve collective, and individual, economic wealth and political power.

Yet with all that conflict there has been slowly and painfully achieved a public dialogue, which in the past two decades has begun to show its potential to reach a national consensus on the principles of public education. The present danger of the technological liberal educational project is the prospect of its uncompromised and undeliberated hegemony. Expressing this fear should not be misconstrued as an attempt to discredit the technological liberal educational project. There may be doubtful analysis and wishful thinking in the technological liberal educational project, but it does serve to refocus public attention on the undeniable economic importance of public education, for both individuals and the collectivity, in a way that was lost or diverted by the subordination of economic to ethical liberalism in the 1960s. Having taken 150 years to approach national convergence on a public philosophy of public education, however, it is imperative now to preserve educational pluralism and thus avoid a relapse into communal political conflict; to institutionalize nascent principles and processes of public deliberation, not to rest content with faint hopes for felicitous political compromises of organized interests; and above all to stimulate and enhance the space for public deliberation and rational choice that must necessarily begin from a polyphonic discourse about public education.

Evidently, there is a public interest in preserving the dialogue among these liberal educational projects, even enlarge the public space for advocates of humanist and religious conservatism, and perhaps open new space for the articulation of more radical communitarian (democratic socialist and social democratic) educational projects. Political pluralists who are inclined to see politics as analogous to competition in the marketplace may be less concerned about protecting and enhancing the space for public discourse and deliberation, content that educational interests will organize and press their alternative projects and confident that out of conflict and bargaining a widely acceptable compromise eventually will result. The historical legacy of political and economic liberal educational projects shows, however, that ideological hegemony can be achieved without legitimacy or justice being well served.

Political history can be changed by force; public philosophies are changed by historical experience, public discourse, and political rethinking. People must be able to speak and listen to each other about their experience of living together. They must attempt to understand their personal and group experiences and relate their experiences to other members of the political community. From such public discourse and deliberation comes achievement of consensus, but also acceptance of difference. Public philosophies express widespread acceptance in a political community of a set of political ideas and beliefs that serve as principles to guide and justify the making of public policies, the choosing of courses of collective action, but public philosophies also recognize the limits of political consensus. Public philosophies thus express agreements, including agreements to disagree.

The public dialogue and principled consensus that have potential to constitute a public philosophy of education in Canada also reveal an important way towards the realization of a national public philosophy. In the 1990s Canada has confronted a major constitutional crisis that is in reality a crisis of national public philosophy. In order to preserve the political union, a substantial decentralization and devolution of authority over a wide range of public policies appears to be imperative. In educational policy, however, decentralization of policy-making is the norm. Historically, educational policy-making in Canada has been, and continues to be, essentially a form of 'sovereignty-association' among provinces. Within provinces there has been a progressive, although not uncontested, pluralization of decision-making. Decentralization of authority and pluralization of decision-making have not prevented the convergence of policies for public education, however, nor the achievement of consensus on principles of public education. Indeed, not only historically, but still very much currently, they are the prerequisites for achieving public education that will meet the collective tests of effectiveness, efficiency, legitimacy, and justice.

As Canadians struggle to understand the current manifestations of their enduring problems of international economic competitiveness, fiscal integrity of the public economy, preservation of political union, protection of cultural communities, and realization of individual authenticity, and then try to devise courses of public action to deal with them, the example of educational policy perhaps offers some grounds for hope that the necessary road of Canadian political development is also the way to a more effectively democratic public life.

Abbreviations

AHSBO	Associated High School Boards of Ontario
ASSTF	Alberta Secondary School Teachers' Assocation
ASTA	Alberta School Trustees' Association
ATA	Alberta Teachers' Association
B and B commission	Royal Commission on Bilingualism and Biculturalism
BOE	Board of Education
CCF	Co-operative Commonwealth Federation
CEGEP	Collège d'enseignement général et professionel
CMEC	Council of Ministers of Education, Canada
DOE	Department of Education
MOE	Minister/Ministry of Education
NDP	New Democratic Party
RCE	Royal Commission on Education
RCEY	Royal Commission on Education and Youth
RRCE	Report of the Royal Commission on Education
RRCEY	Report of the Royal Commission on Education and Youth
TF	Teachers' Federation (preceded by initial(s) of province)

Notes

INTRODUCTION

1 See Ronald Manzer, 'Public Policy-Making as Practical Reasoning,' *Canadian Journal of Political Science* 17 (Sept. 1984), 577–94.

2 The analogy of the state with the church as ordaining authority was suggested to me by my colleague Carolyn Tuohy.

3 Margaret S. Archer, *Culture and Agency: The Place of Culture in Social Theory* (Cambridge: Cambridge University Press, 1988), 285–6.

4 Charles Taylor, *Hegel and Modern Society* (Cambridge: Cambridge University Press, 1979), 88–9.

5 For a discussion of the relationship between human needs and political goods see Ronald Manzer, *Canada: A Socio-Political Report* (Toronto: McGraw-Hill Ryerson, 1974), chap. 1, and also Ronald Manzer, *Public Policies and Political Development in Canada* (Toronto: University of Toronto Press, 1985), chap. 1.

6 Each of these three levels of policy analysis can be seen to correspond to one of the three basic elements in the paradigm of rational action. In the paradigm of rational action the policy-maker as agent believes that given the ends the action being chosen is better than any of the available alternatives, the beliefs on which the policy-maker acts are rational in the sense that there are good reasons to hold these beliefs, and the ends for which the policy-maker acts are ones that it is rational (again in the sense that there are good reasons) to pursue. In the three-fold distinction of levels of policy analysis, program analysis corresponds to the rationality of means, policy theory to the rationality of beliefs, and public philosophy to the rationality of ends.

7 See Charles Anderson, 'The Place of Principles in Policy Analysis,' *American Political Science Review* 73 (Sept. 1979), 716–21. Anderson discusses 'justice,' 'authority,' and 'efficiency' as logically necessary categories of political evaluation. His use

of the term 'authority' seems to me to be more consistent with the meaning of 'legitimacy,' which is also more generally recognized as an evaluative term in political argument.

8 For an insightful theoretical assessment of Piaget's impact on thinking about child development, see Katherine Covell and James Robert Brown, 'The Nature and Rationality of Piaget's Revolution,' *Methodology and Science* 20 (1987), 97–119.

9 C.B. Macpherson, *The Life and Times of Liberal Democracy* (Oxford: Oxford University Press, 1977), 48.

CHAPTER 1

1 See J. Stefan Dupré, 'Reflections on the Workability of Executive Federalism,' in Richard Simeon (ed.), *Intergovernmental Relations*, Research Studies of the Royal Commission on the Economic Union and Development Prospects for Canada, vol. 63 (Toronto: University of Toronto Press for Minister of Supply and Services Canada, 1985), 2–5.

2 See J.S. Mill's address on 4 April 1870 to a meeting of the National Association for the Promotion of Social Science, in John M. Robson and Bruce L. Kinzer (eds.), *Collected Works of John Stuart Mill*, vol. 29, *Public and Parliamentary Speeches* (Toronto: University of Toronto Press, 1988), 395.

3 Exceptions to the generalization that public schools are local institutions tend to be found in the provision of special education or the treatment of juvenile deviance. In such circumstances provincial institutions that are directly accountable to central political authorities have been commonly established.

4 Jeremy Bentham, 'The Constitutional Code,' in John Bowering (ed.), *The Collected Works of Jeremy Bentham*, vol. 9 (New York: Russell and Russell, 1962), book 2.

5 As a principle for organizing intergovernmental relations communal autonomy in a decentralized state has both radical and conservative versions. Communal autonomy is the theory that seems to underlie Jean-Jacques Rousseau's proposed constitution for Poland (see Stanley Hoffmann, 'The Areal Division of Powers in the Writings of French Political Thinkers,' in Arthur Maass [ed.], *Area and Power: A Theory of Local Government* [Glencoe, Ill.: Free Press, 1959], 122–3). Communal autonomy is also the theory advanced in nineteenth-century England by Joshua Toulmin Smith, who argued that the original political authorities were vestry meetings and that county courts and the House of Commons should be understood as comprising the delegates of parishes (see W.H. Greenleaf, 'Toulmin Smith and the British Political Tradition,' *Public Administration* 53 [Spring 1975], 35–9). For an excellent survey see Warren Magnusson, 'The New Neighbourhood Democracy: Anglo-American Experience in Historical Perspective,' in L.J. Sharpe (ed.), *Decentralist Trends in Western Democracies* (London: Sage, 1979), 119–56.

6 John Stuart Mill, 'Considerations on Representative Government,' in John Stuart Mill, *On Liberty, Representative Government, The Subjection of Women: Three Essays* (London: Oxford University Press, 1912), 375. In his chapter on local representative bodies in 'Considerations on Representative Government,' Mill does not specifically say that public education belongs to the category of public business which affects the national interest but requires local administration. However, that was the position put forward in his address to the meeting of the National Association for the Promotion of Social Science on 4 April 1870.

7 Ibid., 377.

8 Ibid., 364–5.

9 The term 'fiscal equivalence' has been taken from Mancur Olson, 'The Principle of "Fiscal Equivalence": The Division of Responsibility among Different Levels of Government,' *American Economic Review* 59 (May 1969), 483. As a type of intergovernmental relationship it derives from a long and distinguished tradition of Anglo-American and French political theorizing about the areal division of powers. In effect, fiscal equivalence between central and local governments may be conceived as dividing sovereignty according to the classic formula of the federal principle.

10 The metaphors of 'layer cake' and 'marble cake' have been suggested by Morton Grodzins ('Centralization and Decentralization in the American Federal System,' in Robert A. Goldwin [ed.], *A Nation of States: Essays on the American Federal System* [Chicago: Rand McNally, 1961], 3–4).

11 Jean Hamelin, *First Years of Confederation*, Centennial Historical Booklet 3 (Ottawa: Centennial Commission, 1967), 3–4; cited in Dupré, 'Executive Federalism,' 3.

12 On the concept of 'policy community' and the related concepts of 'policy network' and 'sub-government,' see William D. Coleman and Grace Skogstad 'Policy Communities and Policy Networks: A Structural Approach,' in William, D. Coleman and Grace Skogstad (eds.), *Policy Communities and Public Policy in Canada: A Structural Approach* (Mississauga, Ont.: Copp Clark Pitman, 1990), 14–33; A. Paul Pross, *Group Politics and Public Policy* (Toronto: Oxford University Press, 1992, 2nd ed.), 118–30; and Michael M. Atkinson and William D. Coleman, *The State, Business, and Industrial Change in Canada* (Toronto: University of Toronto Press, 1989), chap. 4.

CHAPTER 2

1 Joseph Lecler, *The Two Sovereignties: A Study of the Relationship between Church and State* (New York: Philosophical Library, 1952), 25, 37, 41.

2 For a particularly influential but typical statement of such criticisms see the argu-

ment by James Mill in his 1812 essay, 'Schools for All, in Preference to Schools for Churchmen Only,' in W.H. Burston (ed.), *James Mill on Education* (Cambridge: Cambridge University Press, 1969), 120–93.

3 John Locke, *A Letter Concerning Toleration*, ed. by Mario Montuori (The Hague: Martinus Nijhoff, 1963), 23. By contrast, Locke defined a commonwealth as 'a society of men constituted only for the procuring, preserving, and advancing of their own civil interests,' that is, 'life, liberty, health, and indolency of body; and the possession of outward things, such as money, lands, houses, furniture, and the like' (ibid., 15).

4 See Jeremy Bentham, *Chrestomathia* (Oxford: Clarendon Press, 1983), 89–95.

5 See John Stuart Mill, *Autobiography* (London: Oxford University Press, 1924), 327–8.

6 Ronald Manzer, *Public Policies and Political Development in Canada* (Toronto: University of Toronto Press, 1985), 118–19.

7 Ibid., 127–8.

8 If courses, programs, and schools can each be differentiated, or not, eight ideal types of systems are possible.

9 My discussion concerning the variation in concepts of equality according to types of secondary school organization and curricula draws upon the theorizing by Douglas Rae with Douglas Yates, Jennifer Hochschild, Joseph Morone, and Carol Fessler of alternative conceptions of the subject of equality, the domain of equality, equalities of opportunity, and the value of equality (*Equalities* [Cambridge, Mass.: Harvard University Press, 1981], 43, 62–3, 81, 103). The political issues raised by disagreements over equality are taken from Deborah Stone, *Policy Paradox and Political Reason* (Glenview, Ill.: Scott, Foresman / Little, Brown, 1988), 40.

10 According to Harold Entwistle, 'Education may be conceived as *classless* or as *class specific, class confirming* even *class divisive*' (*Class, Culture, and Education* [London: Methuen, 1978], 64, emphasis in the original). Here I assume that these terms refer to different features of class-based education. 'Class-specific' education involves the provision of different, distinctive programs or tracks that lead to economic careers in different occupational classes. 'Class-divisive' education refers to class-specific education in which contact between students in different educational tracks is minimized. Students in different educational tracks are socially isolated from one another and also probably physically isolated from one another by their attending different schools. 'Class-confirming' education refers to class-specific and (usually) class-divisive education that selects and educates students according to the occupational class membership of their families; as a result, there will be little or no circulation between classes from generation to generation.

11 On the concept of person-regarding equality, see Rae, *Equalities*, 92–101.

12 On the concept of lot-regarding equality, see *Ibid.*, 85–91.

13 William D. Coleman, *The Independence Movement in Quebec, 1945–1980* (Toronto: University of Toronto Press, 1984), 189.
14 Edward Andrew, 'Pierre Trudeau on the Language of Values and the Value of Languages,' *Canadian Journal of Political and Social Theory* 6 (Winter/Spring 1982), 153.
15 Charles Taylor, *Human Agency and Language: Philosophical Papers,* vol. 1 (Cambridge: Cambridge University Press, 1985), 234, emphasis in the original.
16 Andrew, 'Pierre Trudeau on Language,' 153.
17 For a discussion of linguistic regimes based on the principles of territoriality and personality as solutions for the problems of multilingual states see J.A. Laponce, *Languages and Their Territories,* translated by Anthony Martin-Sperry (Toronto: University of Toronto Press, 1987), 165–87. Territoriality and personality as alternative principles in establishing public regimes of linguistic equality are discussed by the B and B commision, (*Report of the Royal Commission on Bilingualism and Biculturalism, Book I: The Official Languages* [Ottawa: Queen's Printer, 1967], 75–87).
18 As Janet Ajzenstat has observed, classical liberalism also held that deep cultural, including linguistic, cleavages were incompatible with full realization of liberal rights ('Liberalism and Assimilation: Lord Durham Reconsidered,' in Stephen Brooks [ed.], *Political Thought in Canada: Contemporary Perspectives* [Toronto: Irwin Publishing, 1984], 243–44).
19 See Will Kymlicka, *Liberalism, Community, and Culture* (Oxford: Clarendon Press, 1989), 194–5.

CHAPTER 3

1 C.B. Sissons, *Church and State in Canadian Education: An Historical Study* (Toronto: Ryerson, 1959), 13, 223.
2 When Newfoundland entered Confederation in 1949, Term 17 of the Terms of Union provided constitutional protection for denominational rights in education ('the Legislature will not have any authority to make laws prejudicially affecting any right or privilege with respect to denominational schools, common (amalgamated) schools, or denominational colleges, that any class or classes of persons have by law in Newfoundland at the date of Union,' and all public funds for such schools must be distributed 'on a non-discriminatory basis.' In December 1987 an amendment to Term 17 was proclaimed giving constitutional protection to the denominational education rights of the Pentecostal Assemblies.
3 See Susan E. Houston and Alison Prentice, *Schooling and Scholars in Nineteenth-Century Ontario* (Toronto: University of Toronto Press, 1988), 112.

4 On Ryerson's political liberalism see Colin D. Pearce, 'Egerton Ryerson's Canadian Liberalism,' *Canadian Journal of Political Science* 21 (Dec. 1988), 771–93.

5 Section 93 of the British North America Act, 1867, assigned the provincial legislatures exclusive jurisdiction to make laws in relation to education, subject to the provision that 'nothing in any such law shall prejudicially affect any Right or Privilege with respect to Denominational Schools which any Class of Persons have by Law in the Province at the Union.' Where a minority denominational right, whether recognized at Confederation or established subsequently by provincial statute, is infringed by provincial law, a right of appeal to the federal cabinet exists. The cabinet may request provincial authorities to make appropriate remedies, and, if that fails, the cabinet may ask the Parliament of Canada to make remedial laws to protect the constitutional right of minority denominational education.

6 Sissons, *Church and State*, 237.

7 When the first man tried was found guilty of murder, the others changed their pleas to guilty of manslaughter. These convictions were later set aside on points of law following their appeal to the Supreme Court of Canada.

8 Elizabeth Dunn, 'Prince Edward Island,' in Carl J. Matthews (ed.), *Catholic Schools in Canada* (Toronto: Canadian Catholic School Trustees Association, 1977), 6.

9 D.A. Schmeiser, *Civil Liberties in Canada* (London: Oxford University Press, 1964), 160, 162. In another action, *Brophy et al.* v. *The Attorney-General of Manitoba*, in 1895 the Judicial Committee ruled that Roman Catholics of Manitoba had been affected in their minority rights and privileges by the 1890 act, but their appeal for redress should be directed to the federal government rather than to the courts.

10 Eric Waddell, 'State, Language, and Society: The Vicissitudes of French in Quebec and Canada,' in Alan C. Cairns and Cynthia Williams (eds.), *The Politics of Gender, Ethnicity, and Language in Canada*, Research Studies of the Royal Commission on the Economic Union and Development Prospects for Canada, vol. 34 (Toronto: University of Toronto Press for Minister of Supply and Services Canada, 1986), 72.

11 Roger Magnuson, *A Brief History of Quebec Education: From New France to Parti Québécois* (Montreal: Harvest House, 1980), 81.

12 C.-J. Magnan, *L'Instruction publique dans la province de Québec*; cited in *Report of the Royal Commission on Bilingualism and Biculturalism Book II: Education* (Ottawa: Queen's Printer, 1968), 34.

13 The key provision of Regulation 17 required 'That instruction in English shall commence at once upon a child entering school, the use of French as the language of instruction and communication to vary according to local conditions upon the report of the supervising inspector, but in no case to continue beyond the end of the first form.'

14 Robert M. Stamp, *The Schools of Ontario, 1876–1976* (Toronto: University of Toronto Press, 1982), 133.

15 In bilingual schools French was the language of instruction to the end of grade two, English was introduced in grade three, and time was equally divided between English and French from grades five to eight. This recommendation from the departmental committee headed by the chief director, Francis W. Merchant, was essentially what Merchant had also recommended and the Conservative government rejected in 1912. Regulation 17 was not formally rescinded until 1944.

16 By 1915 there were 126 French bilingual school districts with total enrolments of 7,393 pupils, 61 German school districts enrolling 2,814, and 111 Polish and Ruthenian districts with 6,513 total enrolments. Bilingual schools therefore accounted for one-sixth of both school districts and total enrolments in Manitoba (see C.B. Sissons, *Bi-Lingual Schools in Canada* [Toronto: Dent, 1917], 141).

17 During the debate in the Manitoba legislative assembly in March 1916 the MOE in the Norris government, R.S. Thornton, put the argument for English unilingualism as follows: 'The first essential of individual progress in any land is to know the language of the country. In an English-speaking country, as this is, a knowledge of English is more necessary than a knowledge of arithmetic. No matter what a man's attainments may be, the doors of opportunity are closed to him if he has not a knowledge of English, the common tongue' (quoted in ibid., 93).

18 John W. Chalmers, *Schools of the Foothills Province: The Story of Public Education in Alberta* (Toronto: University of Toronto Press, 1967), 17. As a result of a law passed by the Liberal government of J.M. Martin in December 1918, the use of French as a language of instruction was restricted to the first year of elementary school. Beyond the first grade French could be taught only as a subject for not more than one hour a day, and instruction was restricted to French reading, grammar, and composition (see David E. Smith, *Prairie Liberalism: The Liberal Party in Saskatchewan 1905–71* [Toronto: University of Toronto Press, 1975], 115–18).

19 Katherine F.C. MacNaughton, *The Development of the Theory and Practice of Education in New Brunswick, 1784–1900* (Fredericton: University of New Brunswick, 1946), 231–2.

20 Remi J. Chiasson, *Bilingualism in the Schools of Eastern Nova Scotia* (Quebec: Les Éditions Ferland, 1962), 228–32.

CHAPTER 4

1 J.G. Hodgins, *Documentary History of Education in Upper Canada, 1792–1876*, vol. 23 (Toronto: King's Printer, 1908), 109; cited by Robert M. Stamp, *The Schools of Ontario, 1876–1976* (Toronto: University of Toronto Press, 1982), 7.

2 Committee of Presidents of Provincially Assisted Universities and Colleges of

Ontario, *The Structure of Post-Secondary Education in Ontario*, Supplementary Report 1 (1963), 6–7; cited in W.G. Fleming, *Ontario's Educative Society*, vol. 3: *Schools, Pupils, and Teachers* (Toronto: University of Toronto Press, 1971), 45.

3 James D. Denny, 'The Organization of Public Education in Saskatchewan,' DPaed thesis, University of Toronto, 1929, 45.

4 One study of the seven collegiate institutes and 13 high schools in 1916–17 (omitting two high schools for which no data were available) found that 95 per cent of students were enrolled in the teachers' and matriculation courses (Harold W. Foght, *A Survey of Education in the Province of Saskatchewan* [Regina: King's Printer, 1918], 97).

5 D.S. Woods, *Education in Manitoba, Part 1: Preliminary Report* (Winnipeg: Manitoba Economic Survey Board, 1938), 111.

6 This distinction was officially recognized in 1953 by the sub-committee on education coordination in its report to the Catholic committee of the Council of Public Instruction (La Fédération des collèges classiques, *L'Organization et les besoins de l'enseignement classique dans le Québec* [Ottawa: La Fédération des collèges classiques, 1954], 24).

7 Secondary education for English-speaking Roman Catholics was available in the nineteenth century within the 'exclusive sector' of classical colleges. English Catholics who were aiming to enrol at McGill or other English-speaking universities pursued their pre-university studies at a bilingual classical college, Collège Sainte-Marie. Because English-language universities based their entrance requirements on high school rather than classical college, however, there were strong pressures for English Catholic secondary education in Quebec to adopt the English-Canadian model of high school. With the establishment of Loyola College and Loyola High School by the Jesuits in 1896, English Catholics acquired their own secondary school. In 1899 a second private high school, Catholic High School of Montreal, was opened, then closed from 1903 to 1907, and in 1911 came under the direction of the Presentation Brothers. After the First World War, as secondary education expanded in the Protestant system of Quebec and elsewhere in English Canada, English Catholics continued to press for public high schools. Their goal was realized in the 1930s with the opening of D'Arcy McGee High School in Montreal and St Patrick's High School in Quebec City (Roger Magnuson, *A Brief History of Quebec Education: From New France to Parti Québécois* [Montreal: Harvest House, 1980], 81–2).

8 In 1923 the basic elementary course was established as six years and provision was made for a two-year continuation (complémentaire) course which was divided into agricultural, industrial, commercial, and domestic science. In 1929 the cours primaire supérieur was introduced as a three-year course beyond the cours complémentaire. Subsequently, in 1939, the courses were reorganized into seven years

elementary and five years higher elementary. Thus the cours primaire supérieur corresponded in the age of its pupils to grades eight to eleven in English-Canadian high schools.

9 Frederick W. Rowe, *The Development of Education in Newfoundland* (Toronto: Ryerson, 1964), 82, 107.

10 S.J.R. Noel, *Politics in Newfoundland* (Toronto: University of Toronto Press, 1971), 268.

11 Quoted in Alison Prentice, *The School Promoters: Education and Social Class in Mid-Nineteenth Century Upper Canada* (Toronto: McClelland and Stewart, 1977), 132.

CHAPTER 5

1 R.D. Gidney, 'Centralization and Education: The Origins of an Ontario Tradition,' *Journal of Canadian Studies* 7 (Nov. 1972), 34.

2 This was the reaction of the *Brockville Recorder* (20 Dec. 1832) to a bill, proposed by Mahlon Burwell but conceived by John Strachan, to extend and consolidate the authority of the General Board (ibid., 37). The *St. Thomas Liberal* (21 Feb. 1833) went even further with its charge that Burwell was plotting 'under the spurious and deceitful pretence of advancing the interest of the rising generation ... to rivet chains, designed to bind them down in the condition of the basest and most detestable slavery.'

3 R.D. Gidney and D.A. Lawr, 'The Development of an Administrative System for the Public Schools: The First Stage, 1841–50,' in Neil McDonald and Alf Chaiton (eds.), *Egerton Ryerson and His Times* (Toronto: Macmillan, 1978), 175–6.

4 Gidney, 'Centralization and Education,' 45.

5 Gidney and Lawr, 'Development of an Administrative System,' 175.

6 Ross was a graduate of the provincial normal school and a former teacher and inspector before entering politics. 'He was also a strong and powerful personality, a man who, like Egerton Ryerson, tended to dominate any organization with which he was connected' (Robin S. Harris, *Quiet Evolution: A Study of the Educational System of Ontario* [Toronto: University of Toronto Press, 1967], 107).

7 Ibid., 108. Hodgins's immediate successor was Alexander Marling, who had been the chief clerk and accountant in 1867, but he died within the year. At the time of his appointment as deputy minister, John Millar had been principal of St Thomas Collegiate Institute for 15 years.

8 In New Brunswick, when the political membership of the BOE was criticized during debate on the 1871 education bill, the attorney-general pointed out that New Brunswick preferred to follow the examples of England, where members of the privy council comprised the central board, and Nova Scotia, rather than the non-

political boards of the American states or the colonies of Canada East and West. 'The attorney-general did not think it was necessary that the Board should be composed of men of profound scholastic attainments. A Superintendent competent in that respect was all that was required. What was needed was a body of men of fairly sound judgment and good business talent ... The duties of the Board, he said, were largely administrative, therefore politics could not play a part, unless in the case of the appointment of the inspectors' (Katherine F.C. MacNaughton, *The Development of the Theory and Practice of Education in New Brunswick, 1784–1900* [Fredericton: University of New Brunswick, 1946], 190). The attorney-general also questioned, on the basis of experience with the board of the University of New Brunswick, the regularity of attendance of non-political board members and the cost of grants for their travel, whereas the executive council was often in Fredericton and available to meet.

9 Under the Tupper government (1864–7), according to Laidlaw, the Council of Public Instruction left the details of implementing the school acts to the superintendent: 'The Council was satisfied to leave the execution of the Act in his hands, approved regulations which he drew up and recommended, and generally gave him a free hand except in matters having political implications' (Alexander F. Laidlaw, 'Theodore Harding Rand,' in Nova Scotia, DOE, *Journal of Education*, 4th series, 15 [Mar. 1944], 211). Prior to Rand's dismissal, however, the Annand government had met on occasion as the Council of Public Instruction, conducting business and reaching decisions without notifying the superintendent or asking his advice (ibid. [April–May 1944], 326).

10 Katherine MacNaughton found that the agenda of New Brunswick's BOE from 1872 to 1900 comprised matters of routine administration such as 'enquiries from inspectors and teachers on minor points of law, requests from boards of school trustees for permission to levy taxes for school purposes and to borrow money for the building of new schools, the laying off of new districts, the settlements of local disputes involving the location of school buildings and the division of districts, the removal of delinquent trustees, the selection of school texts, and the framing of regulations regarding the time, place, and scope of examinations for Normal School entrance and for school licences' (MacNaughton, *Education in New Brunswick, 1784–1900*, 237). Presumably the premier and cabinet ministers who comprised the BOE reviewed the recommendations of the superintendent with a view to their potential political implications in various constituencies of the province and left the superintendent and inspectors to carry out the details. Elsewhere, MacNaughton's accounts of the political conflicts over religion and language in education make clear that on these major issues of educational politics the premier and cabinet constituted the political and policy executive.

11 Manoly R. Lupul, *The Roman Catholic Church and the North-West School Ques-*

tion: A Study in Church-State Relations in Western Canada, 1875–1905* (Toronto: University of Toronto Press, 1974), 43.

12 Ibid., 81.

13 When Charles-Eugène Boucher de Boucherville, the last minister of public instruction (and also premier), introduced the bill to replace the ministry with a superintendent responsible to the Council of Public Instruction, he made clear his government's intention that the superintendent should be a distinguished educator able to stand above parties and political considerations. In his words, disbanding the ministry had the purpose of 'protecting primary education from more or less harmful influences by placing it in an elevated and serene position where it would not be affected by class distinctions or political pressures' (quoted by Louis-Philippe Audet, 'Education in Canada East and Quebec: 1840–1875,' in J. Donald Wilson, Robert M. Stamp, and Louis-Philippe Audet [eds.], *Canadian Education: A History* [Scarborough, Ont.: Prentice-Hall Canada, 1970], 186).

14 See Mark W. Graesser, 'Church, State, and Public Policy in Newfoundland: The Question of Denominational Education,' paper presented to the annual meeting of the Canadian Political Science Association, University of Victoria, Victoria, BC, 1990, 4; and Phillip McCann, 'Denominational Education in the Twentieth Century in Newfoundland,' in William A. McKim (ed.), *The Vexed Question: Denominational Education in a Secular Age* (St John's: Breakwater Books, 1988), 66–7.

15 Ibid., 67.

16 Ronald G. Penney, 'The Constitutional Status of Denominational Education in Newfoundland,' in McKim, *Vexed Question*, 82–3.

17 New Brunswick, *Report of the Royal Commission on the Financing of Schools in New Brunswick* (Fredericton: Queen's Printer, 1955), 14.

18 British Columbia, *Report of the Commission of Inquiry into Educational Finance* (Victoria: King's Printer, 1946), 9.

19 Departmental regulations in Ontario in 1918 required each board of trustees to provide their school with a flag, a clock for each classroom, a Fahrenheit thermometer, a 12-inch globe, a given list of maps, a numeral frame, a set of mensuration and geometrical models, a blackboard set with compasses and pointers for each classroom, a pair of scales to weigh from half an ounce to four pounds, a set of capacity measures, a set for linear measurement, a set for square and cubic measurement, and a school library containing a number of specified books (Peter Sandiford, 'Education in Canada,' in Peter Sandiford [ed.], *Comparative Education: Studies of the Educational Systems of Six Modern Nations* [London: Dent, 1918], 368–9).

20 British Columbia set its requirement at six months for children aged seven to 12 in 1876 and gradually extended it to a full school year for children aged seven to 14, first in municipal districts in 1912 and in all school districts after 1921. By 1921

Saskatchewan and Manitoba also required children aged seven to 14 to attend for a full school year, and Alberta had compulsory attendance for those aged seven to 15. In the Maritime provinces, the laws were less stringent. Prince Edward Island required 20 or 30 weeks for children aged seven to 13, Nova Scotia covered children aged seven to 12 at the option of local boards, and New Brunswick provided for 80 days of schooling for children aged seven to twelve. Neither Quebec nor Newfoundland had compulsory attendance laws until 1942.

21 Sandiford, 'Education in Canada,' 364–5.

22 According to one assessment of the historical impact of Ontario on educational legislation and practice, 'The similarities between the West and Ontario were so great that one is tempted to conclude that Ryerson was as much the architect of the western school systems as he was of the Ontario system' (Alan H. Child, 'The Ryerson Tradition in Western Canada, 1871–1906,' in McDonald and Chaiton, *Egerton Ryerson*, 297).

23 Bruce Curtis, *Building the Educational State: Canada West, 1836–1871* (London, Ont.: Althouse Press, 1988), 131–2.

24 Alison Prentice, 'The Public Instructor: Ryerson and the Role of Public School Administrator,' in McDonald and Chaiton, *Egerton Ryerson*, 139–41.

25 See Charles E. Phillips, *The Development of Education in Canada* (Toronto: Gage, 1957), 286; and Audet, 'Education in Canada East and Quebec,' 175. The option of voluntary assessment remained on the statute books until the turn of the century, but only seven municipalities still held out against compulsory assessment in 1855 and one, Saint-Michel d'Yamaska, until 1876.

26 See Norman Henchey and Donald Burgess, *Between Past and Future: Quebec Education in Transition* (Calgary: Detselig Enterprises, 1987), 51–2.

27 Ibid., 192.

28 See Frederick W. Rowe, *The Development of Education in Newfoundland* (Toronto: Ryerson, 1964), 137–8.

29 Ibid., 143–4.

30 In 1949 the Council of Higher Education was abolished, and its function was absorbed by the DOE.

CHAPTER 6

1 Seath's approach to understanding the public problem of education in 1910 bears a striking resemblance to official policy studies of Canadian education in the late 1980s and early 1990s. He began his report by observing that the problem of 'Education for Industrial Purposes' had three main causes: rivalry among the nations for commercial supremacy, imperfect provision for training skilled workers, and widening the scope of state education to include vocational as well as cultural train-

ing. 'Of the foregoing causes the most potent is the keen rivalry amongst the nations for the control or at best a due share of the markets of the world – a rivalry which is continually being intensified by increasing facilities for communication and transportation' (Ontario, DOE, *Education for Industrial Purposes: A Report by John Seath* [Toronto: King's Printer, 1911], 1).

2 Ibid., 340. Seath's comments were directed at the organization of industrial schools, but the same principles applied to the organization of technical schools, even though it might be some years before conditions in Ontario would justify their establishment: 'To be efficient, they will require different courses of study, separate staffs, and, to a large extent, separate equipment, class rooms, work shops, and laboratories' (ibid., 341).

3 For the royal commission's summary of the relationship of technical education and national economic problems, see Canada, Royal Commission on Industrial Training and Technical Education, *Report* (Ottawa: King's Printer, 1913), vol. 1, 159–66.

4 Ibid., 136.

5 Ibid., 22, see also, 227–8.

6 Ibid., 181. Accordingly, the objective of educational policy was to ensure 'that all might become qualified, to the full extent of their capacities, to fill their places as individuals, as contributing earners, as citizens and as members of the race' (ibid., 170).

7 The commission noted that in Germany academic and technical high schools usually had separate staff and buildings. In the United States, however, opinion was divided between those who advocated 'union' high schools and whose who wanted to establish special high schools for commerce, technical, and housekeeping courses (see ibid., 245). The commission concluded that decisions whether to establish commercial, technical, and housekeeping classes as departments of a union high school or locate them in separate premises with separate teaching staffs should be made by local authorities based on local conditions and needs.

8 I use 'vocational' as a generic term to cover technical, industrial, commercial, domestic science, and agricultural education in secondary schools.

9 J.M. McCutcheon, *Public Education in Ontario* (Toronto: T.H. Best, 1941), 187–8.

10 Ontario, RCE, *RRCE in Ontario, 1950* (Toronto: King's Printer, 1950), 20.

11 See the memories of Kelvin and St John's, especially about their graduates, in J.W. Chafe, *An Apple for the Teacher* (Winnipeg: Winnipeg School District 1, 1967), 94, 105–6.

12 An investigation in 1917 into the allegedly poor record of passes at King Edward High School concluded that one of the problems was the attempt to combine the work of a commercial and a technical school with an academic school. It recommended separating the academic course from the commercial and technical courses

(John Henry Wormsbecker, Jr, 'The Development of Secondary Education in Vancouver,' PhD thesis, University of Toronto, 1961, 80–1).

13 Canada and Newfoundland Education Association, *Report of the Survey Committee to Ascertain the Chief Educational Needs in the Dominion of Canada* (Toronto: Canada and Newfoundland Education Association, 1943), 46

14 Robert M. Stamp, *The Schools of Ontario, 1876–1976* (Toronto: University of Toronto Press, 1982), 80.

15 J.H. Putman and G.M. Weir, *Survey of the School System* (Victoria: King's Printer, 1925), 85.

16 Groups represented on the revision committees included the Alberta Teachers' Alliance, Alberta Education Association, Roman Catholic separate schools, Alberta School Trustees' Association, University of Alberta, city school superintendents, high school inspectors, the United Farmers of Alberta, United Farm Women of Alberta, Women's Institute, University Women's Club, Alberta Federation of Labour, and the Associated Boards of Trade. As T.C. Byrne has explained, 'Despite increasing enrolments the public generally refused to accept the solutions developed by the Committee. Local authorities, outside the major cities, not being able to provide the facilities for technical and vocational training, chose to stress the university and normal entrance courses. Experience with the technical curriculum in the cities indicated that students thus trained had not been able to step into positions more readily than their academically educated colleagues and that many, ill-adjusted to bookish subjects, were equally misfitted in the vocational areas' ('Alberta,' in John H.M. Andrews and Alan F. Brown [eds.], *Composite High Schools in Canada*, University of Alberta Monographs in Education 1 [Edmonton: University of Alberta Committee on Educational Research, 1958], 69).

17 John W. Chalmers, *Schools of the Foothills Province* (Toronto: University of Toronto Press, 1967), 212.

18 Alexander Gregor and Keith Wilson, *The Development of Education in Manitoba* (Dubuque, Iowa: Kendall/Hunt, 1984), 130.

19 Manitoba, Legislative Assembly, *Report of the Special Select Committee on Education* (Winnipeg: King's Printer, 1945), 38–9.

20 Ontario, *RRCE*, 117.

21 Ibid., 104.

22 According to the Hope commission in Ontario, for example, 'One fact is clear: children differ so widely in accomplishment, needs, interests and abilities that they cannot pursue a common course in secondary schools. We can see no alternative to a classification of students into at least three groups or streams for teaching and administrative purposes: below average, average, and above average' (ibid., 83).

23 Canada and Newfoundland Education Association, Educational Policy Committee,

Trends in Education, 1944 (Toronto: Canada and Newfoundland Education Association, 1944), 30.

24 Canada and Newfoundland Education Association, *Report of the Survey Committee*, 46.

25 Manitoba, Legislative Assembly, *Report of the Special Select Committee on Education*, 41.

26 Manitoba, RCE, *RRCE* (Winnipeg: Queen's Printer, 1959), 140–1.

27 Alberta, *RRCE in Alberta, 1959* (Edmonton: Queen's Printer, 1959), 45, 92.

28 British Columbia, *RRCE* (Victoria: Queen's Printer, 1960), 253, 245.

29 The earliest initiatives were taken by city school boards. The superintendent of Vancouver schools introduced a plan for the development of composite schools in 1934, and by 1948 all but two Vancouver high schools had become multilateral schools. The first composite high school in Alberta (Western Canada Composite High School) was opened by the Calgary school board in 1935, offering matriculation, normal school entrance, commercial, and technical programs.

30 H. Janzen, 'Saskatchewan,' in Andrews and Brown (eds.), *Composite High Schools*, 56.

31 Saskatchewan, Royal Commission on Agriculture and Rural Life, *Report No. 6: Rural Education* (Saskatoon: Queen's Printer, 1956), 44. The 39 schools included the three vocational high schools and six collegiate institutes in the three major cities, ten collegiate institutes in smaller urban centres, and 20 composite high schools operating under the Public Schools Act.

32 J.M. Brown, 'Manitoba,' in Andrews and Brown, *Composite High Schools*, 49. Of the 28 schools 17 were located in Winnipeg and its suburbs.

33 Alberta, *RRCE*, 95.

34 On the choice between the matriculation and general programs, the commission estimated that 60 to 70 per cent of students in most high schools were electing to follow the university program and concluded that the policy of separating secondary students into two streams of junior matriculation and general course had failed (BC, *RRCE*, 244).

35 In New Brunswick, in addition to the Carleton County and Saint John vocational schools, composite schools had been established in the 1920s in Campbellton, Edmundston, Fredericton, McAdam, and Newcastle under the 1918 Vocational Education Act. Following the 1935 electoral victory of the Liberals led by Allison Dysart, Fletcher Peacock was appointed to the new position of director of educational services (deputy minister). Peacock had been local director of vocational education in Saint John. In his 1941–2 annual report Peacock set out a detailed plan to improve rural education based on 50 composite high schools, each with at least three departments: college preparatory, homemaking, and agricultural or fishing and navigation (see New Brunswick, *Annual Report of the Department of Educa-*

tion of the Province of New Brunswick for the School Year Ended June 30th., 1942 [Fredericton: King's Printer, 1942], 5–40). Note also that Peacock was a member of the Canada and Newfoundland Education Association survey committee which in 1943 recommended adoption of the composite school model.

36 The increase in the number of composite schools occurred during the 1950s. In 1950–1 there were 19 composite and 19 vocational high schools. Note that overall enrolment in vocational programs declined from 30 per cent of secondary enrolments before the war to 23–4 per cent in the 1950s. The numbers of schools for 1939–40 and 1950–1 and the estimated number for 1960–1 are based on reports on enrolments in vocational courses by type of school given in the annual reports of the Ontario DOE.

37 According to Morrison, the division of vocational education in the Nova Scotia DOE held the view that efficient and effective vocational education could not be carried out as an adjunct to an academic high school (see A.B. Morrison, 'Nova Scotia with Brief Reference to the Other Atlantic Provinces,' in Andrews and Brown, *Composite High Schools*, 9). Vocational high schools in Halifax and Yarmouth were established in the late 1940s; four more vocational high schools were opened in Sydney, Springhill, Kentville, and Stellarton in the early 1960s.

38 Arthur Tremblay, 'Quebec Catholic School System,' in Andrews and Brown, *Composite High Schools*, 21.

39 Prince of Wales College in Charlottetown did offer a commercial course in the 1950s which accounted for about 15 per cent of the college enrolment.

40 The delay of over a decade between the Hope commission's recommendation in favour of multilateral schools and the announcement of the Ontario government's policy commitment is no doubt explained by the opposition of the MOE in the 1950s, John Dunlop. He was an advocate of traditional academic education and aimed at getting the curriculum 'back to fundamental education, getting it back to stress the subjects that are really essential, in order to equip young people for the work they have to do' (Ontario, Legislative Assembly, *Debates*, 12 Mar. 1958, 777). W.G. Fleming reports that 'a departmental official with a responsible position at the end of the 1960s recalls that the 1950s were a grim time for vocational education. In his opinion Dunlop saw no educational value in the program' (*Ontario's Educative Society*, vol. 3, *Schools, Pupils, and Teachers* [Toronto: University of Toronto Press, 1971], 141).

41 Ontario, Legislative Assembly, *Debates*, 30 Nov. 1961, 128. The 'Robarts plan' proved to be far more rigid in practice than had been projected in its design (Stamp, *The Schools of Ontario*, 206). Students tended to be streamed into a branch and program by the end of grade nine (or even sometimes grade eight) and found themselves unable to transfer later. Streaming was based more on academic achievement

than on the occupational goals of students. The four-year arts and science program was the major hope to provide a basic general education for students not continuing to university, but because of its perceived inferior status very few students elected to take it.

42 L.H. Bergstrom, 'School Reorganization in Saskatchewan,' *Canadian Education and Research Digest* 5 (Sept. 1965), 253–5.

43 In PEI a partite system was created with the opening of Prince County Vocational School in 1963, and the addition of a high school division to the Provincial Vocational Institute in 1964. The Newfoundland and Labrador RCEY recommended against incorporating vocational education into the high school curriculum, except for a terminal practical program for those students unable to complete the matriculation or general program. Instead, six regional community colleges should be built to provide an educational level between secondary education and university (*RRCE*, vol. 2 (St John's: Queen's Printer, 1968), 98–9.

CHAPTER 7

1 In 1932 township councils in Ontario were authorized to form all or any part of their municipality into a township school area and abolish the constituent school districts. There was little response until 1938, when the DOE began a campaign for township school areas. Between 1938 and 1950 the number of township school areas increased from 30, replacing 154 rural school districts, to 534 which comprised 3,465 former school districts. The DOE's advocacy was stopped in the 1950s by an unsympathetic minister (John Dunlop). Eventually the township was made the basic unit of local administration of elementary education in 1964, only to be replaced by the county in the reorganization of 1968.

2 Four provinces reorganized school districts along both elementary-secondary and urban-rural dimensions simultaneously. In BC the Commission of Inquiry into Educational Finance in 1945 recommended complete reorganization of the province into 74 districts covering both elementary and secondary education. The New Brunswick school system was reorganized into 33 school districts, subject to a high degree of provincial control, beginning in 1967, and PEI consolidated 217 school districts into five regional units in 1972. Reorganization in Newfoundland in 1968 continued the historical system of denominational districts. In each of these four provinces the problems of rural secondary education were central considerations in motivating reorganization.

3 The following four paragraphs describing modern provincial grant policies in Canada are taken from Ronald Manzer, *Public Policies and Political Development in Canada* (Toronto: University of Toronto Press, 1985), 130–1.

4 For Vincent J. Pottier's recommendations as royal commissioner on educational finance, see Nova Scotia, *Report of the Royal Commission on Public School Finance in Nova Scotia* (Halifax: Department of Education, 1954).

5 For the details of M.A. Cameron's recommendations regarding educational finance and school reorganization in BC, see British Columbia, *Report of the Commission of Inquiry into Educational Finance* (Victoria: King's Printer, 1945).

6 Fees were abolished for all public secondary schools in 1961. Enrolments then fell sharply in francophone private secondary schools, from 40,000 in 1965–6 to 16,000 in 1968–9. The decline of private schools was reversed by the Private Education Act of 1968 which provided provincial funding for private schools (Roger Magnuson, *A Brief History of Quebec Education: From New France to Parti Québécois* [Montreal: Harvest Home, 1980], 110).

7 Because provincial means for expenditures per pupil and pupil/teacher ratios vary widely over time, I have used the coefficient of variability to make diachronic comparisons. The coefficients of variability are calculated by dividing the standard deviation for each fiscal/school year by the mean (Hubert M. Blalock, *Social Statistics* [New York: McGraw-Hill, 1960], 73–4).

CHAPTER 8

1 In Ontario, e.g., the DOE created seven new divisional heads in the first two decades of the twentieth century: inspector of manual training and household science (1901); chief public and separate school inspector (1909); director of industrial and technical education (1912); inspector of elementary agricultural education (1911); and director of professional (teacher) training, inspector of auxiliary classes, and provincial attendance officer (1919) (Robin S. Harris, *Quiet Evolution: A Study of the Educational System of Ontario* [Toronto: University of Toronto Press, 1967], 110). In BC the DOE appointed an inspector of manual training (1907), a supervisor of the summer school of education (1914), a supervisor of industrial and technical education (1914), and a director of elementary agricultural instruction (1915); the department also established a textbook branch (1908) and took over operation of the school for the blind from the Vancouver school board (F. Henry Johnson, *A History of Public Education in British Columbia* [Vancouver: University of British Columbia Press, 1964], 92).

2 One exception was the Alberta DOE where only nine officials reported directly to the deputy minister. This narrower span of control resulted primarily from the appointment of a chief superintendent of schools in 1939 who was given charge of curriculum, provincial supervisors of instruction, and the office of the registrar. In addition, teacher training was under the jurisdiction of the University of Alberta rather than a provincial normal school. Another exception in the 1940s was PEI

where eight or nine officials reported to the deputy minister and director, but by 1967–8 just prior to reorganization the deputy minister had 15 departmental officials reporting to him as well as seven elementary school superintendents and one high school superintendent.

3 In Ontario under Conservative governments (1905–19, 1923–34, 1943–56) there was an attempt to divide responsibility for educational policy and administration between a superintendent (1905–19) or chief director and a deputy minister who had responsibility to manage the DOE. During the era of John Seath as superintendent (1905–19) and Francis W. Merchant (1923–30) and J.G. Althouse (1944–56) as chief director, however, there was no doubt about who was the senior administrative official. Under the government of the United Farmers of Ontario (1919–23) no chief director was appointed, and under Liberal governments (1934–43) the two offices were combined. An attempt to divide educational policy and administration between a superintendent and a deputy minister was also made in Saskatchewan from 1912 to 1932. In this case the former deputy minister assumed the office of provincial superintendent, so again there was no doubt about the seniority of the superintendent.

4 Ontario, RCE, *RRCE in Ontario, 1950* (Toronto: King's Printer, 1950), 350.

5 The RCE proposed divisions of elementary education, secondary education, further education, professional education, curriculum, business administration, and registrar. All would be headed by a superintendent except for the office of registrar who would have the rank of superintendent. The RCE clearly envisaged an important policy function for these seven officials. They would constitute a committee of superintendents, chaired by one of them, to devise ways and means to implement policies determined by the minister, collate and integrate recommendations to the associate deputy minister, and coordinate divisional relations (see ibid., 351).

6 Manitoba, RCE, *RRCE* (Winnipeg: Queen's Printer, 1959), 194.

7 Robert M. Stamp, *The Schools of Ontario, 1876–1976* (Toronto: University of Toronto Press, 1982), 75.

8 The only exception seems to have occurred in Manitoba when Robert Fletcher retired in 1939. Fletcher had been appointed first as secretary of the provincial educational advisory board in 1903 and then became deputy MOE when the office was established in 1908. The minister (Ivan Schultz), apparently frustrated by his inability to control the department under Fletcher, opted not to replace his deputy minister and instead had the chief inspector and chief administrative officer report directly to him. This arrangement lasted until 1945 when a new minister found himself overwhelmed by the work, a deputy minister (R.O. MacFarlane) was again appointed, and the department was reorganized. I am grateful to my colleague Wilbur Grasham for bringing this case to my attention.

9 J.T.M. Anderson, who was premier as well as MOE, was a former teacher, inspector

of schools from 1911 to 1918, and director of education for new Canadians in Saskatchewan from 1918 to 1924. His doctoral dissertation at the University of Toronto was published as *The Education of the New-Canadian: A Treatise on Canada's Greatest Educational Problem* (Toronto: Dent, 1918). George Weir had been principal of Saskatoon normal school, director of teacher training at UBC, and joint author with J.H. Putman of the seminal survey of education in BC (1925). Woodrow Lloyd was a teacher, vice-president, and president of the STF from 1939 to 1944, and member of the executive of the CTF. William Aberhart, premier and MOE in Alberta from 1935 to 1943, was a school principal in Calgary from 1915 to 1935 but, in contrast with Anderson, Weir, and Lloyd, was not actively involved in educational politics before he became premier. Since the 1940s there have been two cases of professional educators becoming MOE, both in Newfoundland. Frederick W. Rowe, who served as MOE 1956–9 and 1967–71, was a school principal, school inspector, and president of the St John's branch of the Newfoundland Teachers' Association before entering politics; he authored two books on the history of education in Newfoundland. Phillip Warren, MOE in the Clyde Wells government which was elected in 1989, was formerly a high school principal in Joe Batt's Arm, professor of education at Memorial University of Newfoundland, and chair of the RCEY 1964–7.

10 As premier and MOE J.T.M. Anderson worked first with A.H. Ball, who was deputy minister from 1912 to 1931, and then J.S. Huff, former chief superintendent of education and principal of the normal school. During his first term as minister George Weir's deputy minister was S.J. Willis, superintendent from 1919 to 1946; and for his second term, F.T. Fairey, who was formerly provincial director of technical and vocational education (1938–46) and deputy minister and superintendent from 1945 to 1953. At the time Woodrow Lloyd became MOE in 1944, J.H. McKechnie retired after ten years as deputy minister because of ill health. The new deputy minister, A.B. Ross, had been a superintendent of schools, director of correspondence instruction, and director of curricula. When Ross reached retirement age in 1947, he was replaced by the superintendent of high schools, Allan McCallum, who continued as deputy minister until 1960.

11 Walter D. Young and J. Terence Morley, 'The Premier and the Cabinet,' in J. Terence Morley, Norman D. Ruff, Neil A. Swainson, R. Jeremy Wilson, and Walter D. Young, *The Reins of Power: Governing British Columbia* (Vancouver: Douglas and McIntyre, 1983), 54.

12 Ronald Manzer, 'Selective Inducements and the Development of Pressure Groups: The Case of Canadian Teachers' Associations,' *Canadian Journal of Political Science* 2 (Mar. 1969), 105–6.

13 The first provincial educational association seems to have been the Teachers' Association of Canada West which was organized in 1861 with the president of the Uni-

versity of Toronto as its president. In 1892 it merged with the Provincial Association of Public and High School Trustees, started in 1887, to form the Ontario Educational Association. The Provincial Association of Protestant Teachers of Quebec was founded in 1864 with its leadership provided by the principals of McGill and Bishop's universities, Protestant clergy, and departmental inspectors. Other early examples were the Educational Association of Nova Scotia (1863) and the Teachers' Federation of Prince Edward Island (1880).

14 J.M. Paton, *The Role of Teachers' Organizations in Canadian Education* (Toronto: Gage, 1962), 34.

15 Teachers' salaries failed to match increases in the cost of living caused by wartime inflation. Compulsory attendance legislation increased enrolments in elementary schools and created a shortage of teachers which increased their potential power to bargain for better working conditions. As schools became larger and teachers became better qualified because of the expansion of secondary education, the professional and political organization of teachers was also facilitated. The nine associations newly established were the Saskatchewan Union of Teachers (later the Saskatchewan Teachers' Alliance) in 1914; the BCTF in 1916; the Alberta Teachers' Alliance in 1917; the Manitoba Teachers' Society, New Brunswick Teachers' Association, and Federation of Women Teachers' Associations of Ontario in 1918; the Ontario Secondary School Teachers' Association in 1919; and the Ontario Public School Men Teachers' Federation and the Nova Scotia Teachers' Union in 1920. In addition, Quebec's Provincial Association of Protestant Teachers (1916) and the PEITF (1920) were reorganized to assert more strongly the collective interests of their teacher members. In Newfoundland, a provincial teachers' association was first formed in 1890 but had little success until it was reconstituted in 1924.

16 Eric W. Ricker, 'Teachers, Trustees, and Policy: The Politics of Education in Ontario, 1945–1975,' PhD thesis, University of Toronto, 1981, 246.

17 Other provincial teachers associations gained statutory membership as follows: Manitoba and New Brunswick, 1942; PEI and the Provincial Association of Protestant Teachers in Quebec, 1945; Newfoundland, 1951; and Nova Scotia, partially automatic membership in 1951 and fully automatic membership in 1953.

18 See John W. Chalmers, *Schools of the Foothills Province: The Story of Public Education in Alberta* (Toronto: University of Toronto Press, 1967), 379–82, 441. The United Farmers' government which was elected in 1921 was much more sympathetic to the ATA, but continued to attempt to preserve a balance between it and the ASTA.

19 Stamp, *Schools of Ontario*, 145. According to Stamp, 'The AHSBO immediately declared war on an unpractical high school curriculum, exorbitant teachers' salaries, the power of the OSSTF, and the alleged collusion between the department of education and the teachers' movements ... Yet politics made strange bedfellows, for

before long the AHSBO and the OSSTF had joined forces to counter a challenge from municipal councils for control of school financing.'

20 Of the first seven teachers' unions to gain statutory membership, only the New Brunswick Teachers' Association and the Provincial Association of Protestant Teachers in Quebec did not have their counterpart trustees' association given comparable statutory recognition.

21 Ricker, 'Teachers, Trustees, and Policy,' 265–8

22 Following the election of the CCF government in 1944, a three-person committee representing the DOE, the STF, and the Saskatchewan School Trustees' Association negotiated a provincial salary schedule to serve as a guide within which local teachers' unions and school boards would negotiate. By 1948 most local salary schedules were established after negotiations with teachers, but opposition to the provincial salary schedule at the 1948 trustees' convention and refusal to bargain led the provincial government to give statutory protection to the teachers' right to bargain.

23 The BC Public Schools Act first authorized school boards to enter into collective agreements with teachers following a strike in 1919 by the Victoria Teachers' Association. In 1937, after lobbying by the BCTF, the provision for voluntary arbitration was amended to compulsory arbitration. Compulsory arbitration was retained in 1958.

24 A report to teachers on the STF executive's meeting with the CCF government on 9 Sept. 1944 included the comment: 'The reception accorded by the Cabinet was most cordial and encouraging. In fact there were occasions when even the Premier seemed to be in some doubt as to just who were Cabinet members and who were S.T.F. executive members' (quoted in Clarence Stirling McDowell, 'The Dynamics of the Saskatchewan Teachers' Federation,' PhD thesis, University of Alberta, 1965, 123).

CHAPTER 9

1 Ontario, Provincial Committee on Aims and Objectives in the Schools of Ontario, *Living and Learning* (Toronto: Newton Publishing, 1968), 55.

2 Quebec, Royal Commission of Inquiry on Education in the Province of Quebec, *Report of the Royal Commission of Inquiry on Education in the Province of Quebec*, vol. 4 (Quebec: Government Printer, 1966), 3.

3 Ibid., 8.

4 Ibid., vol. 2 (1965), 4–5.

5 Ibid., 17.

6 Ibid., 126.

7 Ibid., 138–9.

8 The Parent commission argued that multilateral institutes were essential to the realization of a democratic system of state education. 'It is not enough to make the top-level administration of the system more democratic through a Department of Education inviting participation by the public. It is far more important to eliminate from the system that aristocratic bias which still permeates it in large measure. Of course the most gifted students must be given opportunity fully to develop their talents. Yet it would be profoundly unjust to build the entire system for their benefit as is almost everywhere the case. What must be avoided is favouring, by the very nature of the system, a small group of children and dispensing only second-rate instruction to the remaining mass. It is our firm belief that composite education will allow the best pupils to make better and quicker progress than does the present rigid system. At the same time it will place at the disposal of all a varied, broad, elastic education, able to arouse and maintain the widest range of interests and to prepare for all fields of activity or production' (ibid., vol. 4 [1966], 5).

9 Ibid., 167–8. Passed by the Quebec National Assembly in Jan. 1967, Bill 21 created the CEGEPs as public, secular, and tuition-free post-secondary institutions which would offer a two-year general academic program for university preparation and a three-year technical-vocational program leading directly to employment; 21 of the proposed CEGEPs opened during 1968–9, enrolling about 35,000 students.

10 Ontario, *Living and Learning*, 55.

11 Ibid., 21.

12 Ibid., 67.

13 Ibid., 82.

14 Alberta, Commission on Educational Planning, *A Choice of Futures / A Future of Choices* (Edmonton: Queen's Printer for Alberta, 1972), 28

15 Ibid., 45.

16 Ibid., 31.

17 Ibid., 45–6.

18 Ibid., 170.

19 Ibid., 198.

20 W.G. Fleming, *Ontario's Educative Society*, vol. 3, *Schools, Pupils, and Teachers* (Toronto: University of Toronto Press, 1971), 108.

21 CMEC, *Review of Educational Policies in Canada: Western Region*, Submission of the Ministers of Education for the Provinces of British Columbia, Alberta, Saskatchewan, and Manitoba to the OECD Review of Educational Policies in Canada (Toronto: CMEC, 1975), 43.

22 In the early 1970s about 60 per cent of final marks in grade 12 subjects were awarded by accredited teachers (ibid., 47).

23 *The Organization of Instruction for New Brunswick Schools* (Elementary Educa-

tion), 1972 revision, 3; cited in CMEC, *Review of Educational Policies in Canada: Atlantic Region,* Submission of the Ministers of Education for New Brunswick, Newfoundland, Nova Scotia, and Prince Edward Island to the OECD Review of Educational Policies in Canada (Toronto: CMEC, 1975), 15.

24 Verner Smitheram has summarized the impact of person-regarding ideals on PEI schools: 'If formerly schools seemed bent on producing conformity through a standardized curriculum, a rigid grading and testing system, and a strict disciplinary code, the new methods seemed diametrically opposite. Continuous progress offered a pupil-centered curriculum, which would vary widely depending on the needs, interests, and abilities of the learners: individuals were to progress through a subject (not a grade level) at their own rate; learning activities were tailored to the individual or to the small group; testing was related to individual norms rather than group standards; and discipline was relaxed to allow for movement, discussion, and group projects. In short, instead of teaching to the mythical average student, schools would adapt to individual differences' ('Development and Debate over School Consolidation,' in Verner Smitheram, David Milne, and Satada Dasgupta [eds.], *The Garden Transformed: Prince Edward Island, 1945–1980* [Charlottetown: Ragweed Press, 1982], 189).

25 CMEC, *Atlantic Region,* 25.

26 Newfoundland and Labrador, RCEY, *RRCEY,* vol. 1 (St John's: Queen's Printer, 1967), 162

27 Ibid., vol. 2 (1968), 98–9.

28 The new curriculum removed the distinction between the former Secondary School Graduation Diploma (27 credits) and the Secondary School Higher Graduation Diploma (33 credits) which was granted after any six honour credits in grade 13. The new Ontario Secondary School Diploma would be granted on the basis of 30 credits, 16 of them compulsory, including five English (or French) with at least two at the senior level, two mathematics, two science, one French (or English), one Canadian geography, one Canadian history, one senior social science, one physical and health education, one arts, and one business or technological studies.

29 See Rajinder S. Panna and Anne-Marie Decore, 'Alberta Political Economy in Crisis: Whither Education?' in Terry Wotherspoon (ed.), *Hitting the Books: The Politics of Educational Retrenchment* (Toronto: Garamond Press, 1991), 81.

30 The Alberta DOE began standardized tests on a voluntary basis in 1983; but only 20 per cent of graduating students, about half what the department had anticipated, volunteered to take them. As a result the minister of education announced that the tests would be made compulsory.

31 According to the minister of education, David King, the goal was not a return to public education as it stood before the experimental 1970s, but to develop a sophis-

ticated system that would enable students to deal with 'Japanese traders and European moneylenders.' Premier Peter Lougheed added that the current curriculum was not sufficiently challenging for students, and it was time to recapture the goals of the system from 'the experts.' See *Globe and Mail*, 14 June 1984.

32 Norman Henchey and Donald Burgess, *Between Past and Future: Quebec Education in Transition* (Calgary: Detselig Enterprises, 1987), 75.

33 Quebec, MOE, *Primary and Secondary Education in Québec: Green Paper* (Quebec: MOE, 1978), 147; cited by Henchey and Burgess, *Between Past and Future*, 76.

34 To qualify for the Diploma of Secondary Studies students were required to pass at least 130 of the possible 176 credits, including 40 compulsory credits at the levels of secondary III, IV, and V as follows: mother tongue (French/English), 12 credits at secondary IV and V; second language (French/English), 8 credits at secondary IV and V; mathematics, 4 credits at secondary IV; moral or religious instruction, 2 credits at secondary IV or V; physical education or personal and social training or career guidance, 2 credits at secondary IV or V; chemistry or physics, 4 credits at secondary IV; and geography of Quebec and Canada, history of Quebec and Canada, or economics, 4 credits at secondary III, IV, or V.

35 Henchey and Burgess, *Between Past and Future*, 93.

CHAPTER 10

1 Will Kymlicka, *Liberalism, Community, and Culture* (Oxford: Clarendon Press, 1989), 135

2 Ibid., 209.

3 See Quebec, Royal Commission of Inquiry on Education, *Report of the Royal Commission of Inquiry on Education in the Province of Quebec*, vol. 1 (Quebec: Government Printer, 1963), chs. 6, 7; and ibid., vol. 4 (Quebec: Government Printer, 1966), chs. 5, 6.

4 Norman Henchey and Donald Burgess, *Between Past and Future: Quebec Education in Transition* (Calgary: Detselig Enterprises, 1987), 47. The council's voting membership of sixteen Catholics, four Protestants, and usually one Jewish member includes the presidents of the Catholic and Protestant denominational committees. The deputy minister and two associate deputy ministers of education are ex officio members.

5 In addition to the four school boards of Montreal and Quebec city, there are five small school boards which were active in 1867 and therefore protected under section 93. Where all school councils opt for religious status, Bill 107 provides for parents in the religious minority to set up a 'dissident' board.

6 As their political campaign makes clear, the opposition of the Montreal Catholic School Commission to both Bill 3 and Bill 107 was motivated by a concern to pro-

tect Catholic schools through Catholic school boards; but the interest of the Quebec Association of Protestant School Boards and its allies was primarily linguistic rather than denominational, a defence of English-language educational institutions against the press of Québécois nationalism. Bill 107 was supported by a major pressure group for anglophone rights, Alliance Quebec. Alliance Quebec argued that the 1990 decision of the Supreme Court of Canada in *Mahé* had established constitutional protection for minority-language rights in educational governance under section 23 of the Charter. By contrast, English-language boards were not guaranteed under section 93 of the Constitution Act, 1867 because francophones might gain control of a Protestant school board. See also the editorial endorsement of Bill 107 by *Gazette* (Montreal), 23 Sept. 1990.

7 See Mark W. Graesser, 'Church, State, and Public Policy in Newfoundland: The Question of Denominational Education,' paper presented to the annual meeting of the Canadian Political Science Association, University of Victoria, Victoria, BC, 1990, 7–8.

8 See John A. Scott, 'A Council Examined,' in William A. McKim (ed.), *The Vexed Question: Denominational Education in a Secular Age* (St John's: Breakwater Books, 1988), 159–66.

9 The Pentecostal Assemblies and Seventh Day Adventists each have one school district. The Pentecostal Assemblies operated 43 schools with 5.0 per cent of total provincial enrolment in 1989–90, and the Seventh Day Adventists had seven schools with just 0.2 per cent of total enrolment (Newfoundland and Labrador, Royal Commission of Inquiry into the Delivery of Programs and Services in Primary, Elementary, Secondary Education, *Our Children Our Future* [St John's: Queen's Printer, 1992], 136). In its Mar. 1992 report the royal commission recommended that the existing 32 denominational school boards be replaced by nine publicly elected, non-denominational school boards. Under its plan the denominational educational councils would be dissolved; and the Denominational Policy Commission would become responsible for advising government on educational policy which affects the rights of denominations, overseeing the development of religious education and family life programs, facilitating pastoral care, and advising the new school councils on educational policy which affects the rights of denominations (ibid., 217–50).

10 According to Sister Genevieve Hennessey in 1977 there were approximately 7,250 pupils in 27 Catholic schools. More than 4,500 (including 450 non-Catholics) were in 11 Catholic schools in the city of Saint John ('New Brunswick,' in Carl J. Matthews (ed.), *Catholic Schools in Canada* [Toronto: Canadian Catholic School Trustees Association, 1977], 12). On the situation in the other two Maritime provinces see Elizabeth Dunn, 'Prince Edward Island,' and Haidee Patricia MacLellan, 'Nova Scotia,' in ibid., 5–6 and 15–16.

11 See Pierre Michaud and Lionel Desjarlais, 'L'école de langue française du Nouveau-Brunswick,' *Canadian Journal of Education* 11 (Fall 1986), 526–7.

12 Ontario, Legislative Assembly, Standing Committee on Social Development, *Hansard: Official Report of Debates*, 20 Sept. 1985, S1351–2.

13 In 1959 the Manitoba RCE recommended that parochial schools receive 80 per cent of per pupil grants going to public schools. The Conservative government did not adopt this recommendation; but in 1965 legislation was passed under which independent schools were supplied with textbooks 'in regular use in public schools,' transportation of independent school students was authorized 'from points on a regular public school bus route to other points on the same route,' and public school boards were permitted to provide other services in their schools requested by independent schools. An attempt by Edward Schreyer's NDP government to pass legislation providing for direct financial assistance to independent schools failed in 1972 because of a split on the issue within the governing party, and an attempt to salvage the situation by appointing a commission to study the problem was rejected in the legislative assembly.

14 Ontario, Commission on Private Schools in Ontario, *Report* (Toronto: Queen's Printer, 1985).

15 In May 1992 five Jewish families and four Christian families, with support from the Canadian Jewish Congress, Ontario Alliance for Christian Schools, and Ontario Federation of Independent Schools, launched a legal action claiming state aid for denominational schools. Based on the Canadian Charter of Rights and Freedoms, they claimed a right to equal funding under the charter's guarantees of freedom of worship and, given existing state aid to Catholic education, equal protection under the law. In August 1992 Mr Justice William Anderson in the Ontario Court of Justice (General Division) found that 'those whose religious and conscientious beliefs do not permit them to attend the public schools do not receive equal benefit of the law' as guaranteed under section 15 of the charter and that their right to freedom of religion also was being infringed. He dismissed the claim for funding denominational schools, however, on the grounds that existing legislation fell within the 'reasonable limits' acceptable in a democratic society, as provided under section 1 of the charter. See *Toronto Star*, 5 Aug. 1992.

16 See Robert M. Stamp, *The Schools of Ontario, 1876–1976* (Toronto: University of Toronto Press, 1982), 177–8.

17 Ibid., 223. Mackay argued that the presentation of Bible stories and Christian morals 'does not provide for the objective examination of evidence, nor stimulate the inquiring mind; it does not teach children to think for themselves.' Hence, it had no place in the curriculum.

18 In issuing this regulation the MOE rejected recommendations of a task force on religious education that education about religion be compulsory and that at least

one-third and possibly as much as two-thirds of related class time be devoted to Christian religions. MOE lawyers concluded that the latter recommendation could be construed as giving primacy to the Christian faith and would contravene the charter as interpreted by the Court of Appeal. The ministry also announced that new curricular guidelines for religious education would be developed over the next 18 months. See *Globe and Mail*, 7 Dec. 1990, and *Toronto Star*, 7 Dec. 1990.

19 See Judith C. Anderson, 'Students and the Law: Curriculum Implications,' *Education Canada* 30 (Spring 1990), 26–8.

20 In Toronto, school opening exercises consist of singing the national anthem; reading one or more selections from a book of readings and prayers drawn from a number of sources including Bahaism, Buddhism, Christianity, Confucianism, Hinduism, Islam, Jainism, Judaism, Native peoples, secular humanism, Sikhism, and Zoroastrianism; and a moment of silent meditation.

21 The BC requirement for Scripture reading and reciting the Lord's Prayer resulted from a 1944 amendment to the Public Schools Act. The 1876 act had required that state education be conducted on 'strictly secular and non-sectarian principles.' In 1936 an amendment was passed to permit, but not require, recitation of the Lord's Prayer.

22 *Globe and Mail*, 14 Aug. 1992

23 See Eric Waddell, 'State, Language, and Society: The Vicissitudes of French in Quebec and Canada,' in Alan C. Cairns and Cynthia Williams (eds.), *The Politics of Gender, Ethnicity, and Language*, Research Studies for the Royal Commission on Economic Union and Development Prospects for Canada, vol. 34 (Toronto: University of Toronto Press for Minister of Supply and Services Canada, 1986), 86.

24 Canada, B and B Commission, *Report of the Royal Commission on Bilingualism and Biculturalism Book I: The Official Languages* (Ottawa: Queen's Printer, 1967), 145

25 Ibid., *Book IV: The Cultural Contribution of the Other Ethnic Groups* (1969), 14.

26 Ibid., 138. According to the B and B commission, educational policy for languages other than the official languages should be guided by three general principles: first, members of non-British, non-French cultural groups should have opportunities to maintain their own languages and cultures within the system of state education; second, state support for bilingualism and biculturalism should take precedence over non-British, non-French cultural development, in particular, provision for learning of third languages should not be made at the expense of public support for learning the second official language; and, third, policies for linguistic diversity should concentrate on elementary education as the vital stage for maintenance of languages.

27 Canada, B and B Commission, *Book II: Education* (1968), 7.

28 Canada, B and B Commission, *Book I*, xlvi.

29 The 1969 Official Languages Act did not explicitly authorize the federal government to take measures for the advancement of English and French, but from the outset such authorization was assumed to be implied by the act. Under the 1988 Official Languages Act the secretary of state of Canada is authorized to 'take such measures as he considers appropriate to advance the equality of status and use of English and French in Canadian society.' In particular, this includes measures to 'encourage and support the learning of English and French in Canada' and to 'encourage and assist provincial governments to provide opportunities for everyone in Canada to learn both English and French.' See section 42(1)(b) and (e) of the 1988 act.

30 Under the previous protocol (1985–8) Quebec received a total of $238 million, 40.2 per cent of total federal contributions for minority-language and second-language education. This compared with $164 million (27.6%) for Ontario and $77 million (12.9%) for New Brunswick. On a per capita basis, however, New Brunswick received the greatest support – $110.17 per capita – compared to $37 in Quebec which was the second highest among the provinces. Both the Northwest Territories ($56.14) and the Yukon ($45.03) also received more on a per capita basis than did the Province of Quebec. See Tables 1 and 4 in the newsletter published by CMEC, *Dialogue*, 6 (June 1991), 5.

31 *L'Express* (Toronto), 1–7 Sept. 1992, 8–14 June 1993. This legislation was based on the work of the Coordinating Committee for the Governance of Francophone Schools by Francophones, *A Fransaskois Component for the Saskatchewan School System: A Report to the Minister of Saskatchewan Education* (Saskatoon: Saskatchewan Education, 1989). The committee proposed that each francophone school be governed by a council elected by parents. At the provincial level a general council would have one or two representatives from each school council. Legal right to attend a francophone school should be based on section 23 of the charter. Rights of access should not be legislated for other children, but school councils should have discretion to admit children not eligible under section 23.

32 *Western Report*, 18 Oct. 1993.

33 *L'Express* 9–15 Mar. 1993. The first French-language school board to be established in Manitoba covered 3,000 students in the Winnipeg metropolitan region.

34 Canada, B and B Commission, *Book I*, 122–3. See also the commissioners' discussion of education in Book II of their report.

35 In 1983 the Ontario MOE announced the removal of the restriction 'where numbers warrant' (in practice, 25 francophone elementary students or 20 high school students), thus giving all French-speaking children an absolute right to primary and secondary school instruction in French.

36 With enrolments declining French immersion has been accused by some parents and trustees of undermining English-language schools by taking children away

from their neighbourhood schools. Others attack it as elitist. Advocates of English unilingualism reject French immersion as a costly educational frill; public money and effort would be better invested in improving English-language instruction. The proponents of territorial bilingualism dismiss it as perhaps educationally rewarding for individual students, but essentially irrelevant to finding a workable language policy in Canada. All of these criticisms fail to appreciate the force of the principle of person-regarding education in justifying claims for educational programs based on linguistic choice.

37 'Linguistic equality will exist in Canada only if Francophones are treated in other provinces as Anglophones now are in Quebec' (B and B Commission, *Book I*, 145).

38 In 1973–4 over 75,000 francophone children were attending English schools (Roger Magnuson, *A Brief History of Quebec Education: From New France to the Parti Québécois* [Montreal: Harvest Home, 1980], 127).

39 Henchey and Burgess, *Between Past and Future*, 29.

40 Other exceptions to the general requirement that instruction be received in French include persons temporarily residing in Quebec, children with learning disabilities, and the use of indigenous languages in providing instruction to children of Native peoples. Bill 86, introduced in May 1993, extended these exceptions to cover the brothers and sisters of children with learning disabilities and also the children of parents who went to a French school but had the legal right to attend an English school.

41 Bill 86 introduced by the Bourassa government in May 1993 authorizes English immersion classes in French schools. As a result francophone students have the prospect of a measure of linguistic choice with respect to the official languages which previously was available only to anglophone students.

42 A fourth type of instruction in heritage languages, not considered here, is provided through part-time programs operated outside regular school hours by voluntary ethnocultural organizations which derive some financial support from the federal and provincial governments.

43 Jim Cummins and Marcel Danesi, *Heritage Languages: The Development and Denial of Canada's Linguistic Resources* (Toronto: Our Schools / Our Selves Education Foundation and Garamond Press, 1990), 45.

44 Ibid., 114.

CHAPTER 11

1 Quebec, Royal Commission of Inquiry on Education in the Province of Quebec, *Report of the Royal Commission of Inquiry on Education in the Province of Quebec*, vol. 4 (Quebec: Government Printer, 1966), 157.

2 Ibid., 157.

3 Ibid., 149.
4 Ibid., 160.
5 Ontario, Provincial Committee on Aims and Objectives in the Schools of Ontario, *Living and Learning* (Toronto: Newton Publishing, 1968), 158.
6 Ibid., 153.
7 See ibid., 149. This suggestion was not nearly so developed in the Hall-Dennis report, nor so central to its recommendations, as the proposal for school committees by the Parent commission. Nonetheless, their ideas were very close.
8 Alberta, Commission on Educational Planning, *A Choice of Futures / A Future of Choices* (Edmonton: Queen's Printer for the Province of Alberta, 1972), 225
9 Ibid., 39.
10 Ibid., 137. Worth recommended that provincial authority for public education be shared between a DOE with separate divisions of early and basic education and a department of advanced education comprising divisions of higher and further education. These four divisions would provide coordination and 'leadership-service' for the four stages of 'recurrent education.' In addition to the joint planning unit the commissioner proposed joint units for support services and field services and observed, 'This common service unit approach typifies the flexible non-linear organizational structure of tomorrow, rather than the more familiar hierarchical one of today.'
11 Ibid., 232.
12 Ibid., 123.
13 Ibid., 126.
14 Quebec, *Report of the Royal Commission of Inquiry on Education in the Province of Quebec*, vol. 1 (1963), 96.
15 Ibid., 98.
16 See David M. Cameron, *Schools for Ontario: Policy-Making, Administration, and Finance in the 1960s* (Toronto: University of Toronto Press, 1972), 215–17.
17 Ibid., 220.
18 Ontario, Legislative Assembly, *Debates*, 4 June 1968, 3881–2; quoted in Cameron, *Schools for Ontario*, 224–5. Consistent with its commitment to local autonomy, the Hall-Dennis committee in 1968 also proposed that the department's activities should be focused on three areas of legislation and planning, educational research and development, and systems evaluation (Ontario, *Living and Learning*, 156–7).
19 The Ontario MOE experimented briefly in the early 1980s with a two-fold division between education programs under one assistant deputy minister and administration and planning headed by a second assistant deputy minister. In 1983 a third division was again established, education technology development, with the former director of planning and policy analysis as its assistant deputy minister.
20 Planning, budgeting, and finance became finance and budgeting in 1979, with pub-

lic school operations left as the third division. When vocational, technical, and continuing education were transferred to the new department of vocational and technical training in 1985, the activities of the public school operations division were redistributed between education programs (inspection, curriculum) and finance and budgeting (school planning and conveyance).

21 A major reorganization of the DOE in September 1968 had established four divisions for administration, elementary and secondary education, vocational and continuing education, and youth and educational services. By the time of the 1973 reorganization the DOE had acquired two more divisions: planning and provincial libraries.

22 The PEI DOE was further simplified in 1981 to form two branches, one for programs and services and the other for administration and finance, when the director of planning became chief director of the programs and services branch and provincial libraries were placed under programs and services.

23 The royal commission had recommended a functional organization based on four divisions of instruction, administration, further education, and special education. See Newfoundland and Labrador, RCEY, *RRCEY*, vol. 1 (St John's: Queen's Printer, 1967), 61–8.

24 The two divisions of technical and vocational education and adult and continuing education were subsequently merged with instruction, school services, and special services, but in 1983 they were reorganized as a separate branch under their own assistant deputy minister of advanced and continuing education. Thus the three divisions of the Newfoundland department became primary, elementary, and secondary education; advanced and continuing education; and finance and administration.

25 A third associate deputy minister for post-secondary educational programs was appointed in 1976, but this division was subsequently transferred to the new ministry of higher education.

26 The delay in establishing an office of educational planning in the BC MOE may be attributed to the rather late introduction of an institutionalized cabinet in that province. The Social Credit governments of W.A.C. Bennett from 1952 to 1972 operated on the model of decentralized cabinets dominated by the premier. The NDP government from 1972 to 1975 also operated very much in the old-fashioned style of decentralized cabinets. A cabinet committee on planning and priorities and two policy committees for economic development and social services were not established until early 1976 by the Social Credit government of William R. Bennett (Walter D. Young and J. Terence Morley, 'The Premier and the Cabinet,' in J. Terence Morley, Norman J. Ruff, Neil A. Swainson, R. Jeremy Wilson, and Walter D. Young, *The Reins of Power: Governing British Columbia* [Vancouver: Douglas and McIntyre, 1983], 77–81).

27 As noted above, the Quebec MOE was reorganized into four divisions in 1985. The main exception to the persistence of departmental organization from the early 1970s to the early 1990s was the Saskatchewan DOE. Under the Conservative government of Grant Devine a major reorganization in April 1987 brought the departments of education, advanced education and manpower, and Saskatchewan Library together in one department. The three basic units of the former DOE (curriculum, instruction, and program development; financial services and professional administration; and planning and evaluation) were preserved in Saskatchewan Education, although planning was merged with university affairs; but the addition of divisions for skill training and apprenticeship, northern Saskatchewan, human resources, and Saskatchewan Library with no associate or assistant deputy ministers gave the deputy minister of education the widest span of control since the reorganization of 1962.

28 Hugh A. Stevenson, 'The Federal Presence in Canadian Education 1939–1980,' in J.W. George Ivany and Michael E. Manley-Casimir (eds.), *Federal-Provincial Relations: Education Canada* (Toronto: Ontario Institute for Studies in Education Press, 1981), 9.

29 The executive committee of the CMEC is composed of the chairman, the vice-chairman, and three other ministers of education chosen to ensure adequate regional representation.

30 CMEC, *Review of Educational Policies in Canada: Foreword and Introduction* (Toronto: CMEC, Canada, 1975), 36.

31 Quebec, *Report of the Royal Commission of Inquiry on Education in the Province of Quebec*, vol. 1, 75; cited in CMEC, *Foreword and Introduction*, 8. On the convergence of provincial educational philosophies compare the four regional background reports published by the CMEC: *Atlantic Region*, 15–16; *Quebec*, 14–24; *Ontario*, 15–20; and *Western Region*, 12–16.

32 The four types bear a resemblance to the four types of policy networks – pressure pluralism, corporatism, concertation, and state-directed – proposed by Michael M. Atkinson and William D. Coleman in *The State, Business, and Industrial Change in Canada* (Toronto: University of Toronto Press, 1989), 82–7.

33 In theory, a percentage equalizing grant plan results in greater local autonomy and restricts the use of fiscal measures to control and direct the kind and levels of services offered by local school boards. In practice, however, governments set ceilings on the level of expenditures they will share; and, as school boards reach those ceilings, the percentage equalizing grant plan operates as a foundation grant plan. In Ontario virtually all school boards were spending below the governmental ceilings in the early 1970s; but by the 1980s most boards had reached the grant ceilings, thus making the Ontario grant plan a foundation plan for the vast majority of school boards (Stephen B. Lawton, *The Price of Quality: The Public Finance of Ele-*

mentary and Secondary Education in Canada [Toronto: Canadian Education Association, 1987], 46, 55). In Manitoba the foundation plan was replaced in the early 1980s by a combination of block funding based on student enrolments, categorical grants, and an equalization support grant equal to the weighted difference between 'supportable expenditures' and the total of the block and categorical grants (ibid., 54). This change in Manitoba's grant plan did not significantly affect the structuring of relationships in the educational finance policy network.

34 The report of the Royal Commission on Finance and Municipal Taxation, on which the reforms in New Brunswick were based, had observed that because of improvements in transportation and communication, public education could be administered 'centrally rather than locally without any significant loss of contact of the citizens with the government doing the administering, especially if the provincial administration is accompanied by the division of the province into a number of administrative regions under superintendents who are attuned to the peculiar characteristics and needs of the regions, and if local school boards continue to play the vital role of helping to gear the programme to local circumstances, in hiring teachers, providing supplements to the standard educational programme, and providing the essential liaison between the members of the community and the government' (New Brunswick, *Report of the Royal Commission on Finance and Municipal Taxation in New Brunswick* [Fredericton: Queen's Printer, 1963], 131). Under the New Brunswick educational reform legislation of 1966, 422 small school districts were reorganized into 33 large districts (subsequently increased to 41). The five regional administrative units in PEI which began operation in 1972 replaced 217 small school districts.

35 Gerald Hopkirk, 'Public Education in Prince Edward Island: Focus on School Boards,' in Edward H. Humphreys, Stephen B. Lawton, Richard G. Townsend, Victoria E. Grabb, and Daina M. Watson, *Alternative Approaches to Determining Distribution of School Board Trustee Representation*, vol. 1, *Trustee Representation: Theory and Practice in Canada* (Toronto: Queen's Printer for Ontario, 1986), 271; Robin J. Enns and Valerie M. O'Hara, 'School Trustee Election Bases: The Case of New Brunswick,' in ibid., 209.

36 Lawrence M. Bezeau, *Educational Administration for Canadian Teachers* (Toronto: Copp Clark Pitman, 1989), 392.

37 A 1984 decision by the Supreme Court of Canada resulted in exemption (under section 93 of the Constitution Act, 1867) of the denominational school boards in the cities of Montreal and Quebec from these taxation limits, but not other boards.

38 Lawton, *The Price of Quality*, 61.

39 In BC provincial-municipal relations have long been characterized by a partisan conflict between 'centralists' and 'devolutionists.' (Norman Robinson, 'To Have or Not to Have: The Persisting Ambivalence towards Autonomous School Boards in

British Columbia,' in Humphreys et al., *Trustee Representation*, 339).

40 The NDP government restored the spending ceiling on school boards to 110 per cent of provincial approved expenditures and removed the requirement for a local referendum to approve spending above the ceiling as long as two-thirds of the members of the school board had voted for spending above the ceiling.

41 The regime for educational finance that came into effect in BC in 1984–5 was based on a 'resource cost model.' In a resource cost model funding levels for particular programs are determined by the prices of various educational inputs at the local level and the amount of these inputs needed to provide specified levels of service. A resource cost model can be used to determine total programs offered in each school district, basic levels of services with options left to local discretion, or simply the funding prices of eligible inputs with programs left to be designed locally. Usually a resource cost model is introduced to increase accountability, however; and hence it ties school boards to offering approved programs and thus reduces local autonomy. See Lawton, *Price of Quality*, 46–8. Under the BC resource cost model elementary and secondary education continued formally to be jointly funded by the provincial government and school boards. The province paid 60 per cent of the costs of education directly, shared the next 35 per cent according to the relative wealth of school districts as measured by assessment per pupil, and school boards were required to raise the remaining 5 per cent.

42 Norman Henchey and Donald Burgess, *Between Past and Future: Quebec Education in Transition* (Calgary: Detselig Enterprises, 1987), 150. After teachers returned to work and attempts at further negotiation failed, the government issued a series of decrees which set new working conditions for teachers, including new salary schedules incorporating temporary reductions of 17 per cent, increased working hours (subsequently modified by negotiations), and changes in procedures for identifying surplus teachers.

43 See Crawford Kilian, *School Wars: The Assault on B.C. Education* (Vancouver: New Star Books, 1985), 86, 97.

44 Henchey and Burgess, *Between Past and Future*, 196

CHAPTER 12

1 George Radwanski, *Ontario Study of the Relevance of Education, and the Issue of Dropouts* (Toronto: Ministry of Education, 1987); BC, RCE, *A Legacy for Learners: The Report of the Royal Commission on Education 1988* (Victoria: Queen's Printer for British Columbia, 1988).

2 In addition to the Radwanski report and the report of the BC RCE (the Sullivan report), my interpretation of official policy analyses of state education in the early 1990s depends on the following reports: Ontario, Premier's Council, *People and*

Skills in the New Global Economy (Toronto: Queen's Printer for Ontario, 1990); Canada, Economic Council of Canada, *A Lot to Learn: Education and Training in Canada* (Ottawa: Minister of Supply and Services Canada, 1992); Newfoundland and Labrador, Royal Commission of Inquiry into the Delivery of Programs and Services in Primary, Elementary, Secondary Education, *Our Children Our Future* (St John's: Queen's Printer, 1992); and New Brunswick, Commission on Excellence in Education, *Schools for a New Century* (Fredericton: Commission on Excellence in Education, 1992).

3 Radwanski, *Ontario Study*, 2, 11.

4 Ontario, *People and Skills in the New Global Economy*, 13, 14.

5 Ibid., 3.

6 Economic Council of Canada, *A Lot to Learn*, 1.

7 Radwanski, *Ontario Study*, 22.

8 New Brunswick, *Schools for a New Century*, 14.

9 Ibid., 39, 36.

10 Radwanski, *Ontario Study*, 24.

11 Stacy Churchill and Isabel Kaprielian-Churchill, 'Ethnicity, Language, and School Retention in Ontario: The Unfinished Agenda,' in Derek J. Allison and Jerry Paquette (eds.), *Reform and Relevance in Schooling: Dropouts, De-Streaming, and the Common Curriculum*, Research in Education Series 18 (Toronto: Ontario Institute for Studies in Education Press, 1991), 42.

12 New Brunswick, Commission on Excellence in Education, *Excellence in Education, Issues Paper I: Schools for a New Century* (Fredericton: Commission on Excellence in Education, 1991). 8.

13 See New Brunswick, *Schools for a New Century*, 19-20. The commission also devoted a special section to the problems of aboriginal education, but in its analysis and recommendations the commission did not attempt to consider any adaptation or reformulation of the common curriculum to meet the cultural needs of aboriginal students (ibid., 45).

14 Ibid., 44.

15 Ibid., 44, emphasis in the original.

16 Radwanski, *Ontario Study*, 39. Radwanski sets out the 12 essential content areas of the common curriculum in ibid., 40-53.

17 BC, *A Legacy for Learners*, 95. Sullivan proposed that the prescribed common curriculum should leave 20 per cent of instructional time for locally developed courses consistent with the principles of the common curriculum, such as French immersion, Mandarin, Native studies, heritage languages, and regional career explorations.

18 In its discussion of curriculum the New Brunswick Commission on Excellence in Education recommended that at all levels of education the curriculum should be

based on a common core of studies in humanities (French/English, social studies, French/English as a second language), mathematics and sciences, fine arts (music, visual arts), and practical arts (physical education, technology, cooperative education) – the same core areas of provincial common curriculum as were proposed for BC in the Sullivan report.

19 Ontario, *People and Skills in the New Global Economy*, 14. See also the council's further elaboration of this principle: 'Schools must provide a solid foundation for the unending development of the skills and knowledge needed to meet the demands of a changing society and a changing economy' (ibid., 17); 'The Council believes that the ideological and practical mission of the school must be to provide all students with a platform for lifelong learning' (ibid., 27).

20 Newfoundland, *Our Children Our Future*, 301

21 Radwanski, *Ontario Study*, 2.

22 Ibid., 36.

23 BC, *A Legacy for Learners*, 79.

24 The commission set out seven principles to guide reform: equity, quality, freedom of choice, integration, responsiveness, accountability, and autonomy (*Our Children, Our Future*, 205–8).

25 The commission defined equity as fairness for all individuals without discrimination. To achieve equity might require unequal distribution of resources in order to achieve a high standard of education.

26 New Brunswick, *Schools for a New Century*, 38.

27 Radwanski, *Ontario Study*, 166.

28 Ibid., 173–4.

29 BC, *A Legacy for Learners*, 105.

30 Radwanski, *Ontario Study*, 56.

31 Ibid., 57.

32 New Brunswick, *Schools for a New Century*, 64

33 See Ontario, *People and Skills in the New Global Economy*, 41–3. In addition to setting benchmarks and monitoring performance, the Premier's Council proposed the compilation of 'comprehensive profile assessments' to provide guidance to individual students about their educational careers. The council recognized that monitoring, benchmarking, and assessment are distinctive methods to define, measure, compare, and improve achievement. The methods serve different ends, but the most important is setting goals and determining accountability for progress towards goals. The primary meaning of accountability is thus system performance rather than individual diagnosis or educational credentials.

34 Newfoundland, *Our Children Our Future*, 380.

35 A criterion-referenced test measures the degree of a student's acquisition of a body of knowledge or set of skills against some established standard or criterion of what

would constitute mastery of the knowledge or skills for a given level or stage of education. It may be contrasted with a norm-referenced test which measures a student's performance relative to the performance of other students belonging to the same comparison group.

36 Radwanski, *Ontario Study,* 53.
37 Ibid., 192.
38 This is one of the ten guiding principles set out in New Brunswick, *Issues Paper I: Schools for a New Century,* 7–8, and repeated in an appendix to the commission's final report (*Schools for a New Century,* 71–2).
39 Ibid., 63.
40 Newfoundland, *Our Children Our Future,* 223.
41 Ibid., 245.
42 Ibid., 231.
43 Brenda Lafleur, *Dropping Out: The Cost to Canada* (Ottawa: Conference Board of Canada, 1992), 1.
44 Ibid., 18.
45 Alberta Chamber of Resources, *International Comparisons in Education – Curriculum, Values, and Lessons* (Edmonton: Alberta Chamber of Resources and Alberta Education, 1992), 4.
46 Ibid., 4.
47 Ibid., 48.

CHAPTER 13

1 The reporter was Sandro Contenta (*Toronto Star,* 30 July 1988).
2 Ontario, Legislative Assembly, Select Committee on Education, *First Report of the Select Committee on Education* (Toronto: Queen's Printer, 1988), 2. The committee argued that public concern about stereotyping suggested an additional goal, that 'education develop an awareness of those stereotypes and assumptions that contribute to the unequal position of women in contemporary society.'
3 Mark Holmes, 'The Future of the Public School in Canada,' in Derek J. Allison and Jerry Paquette (eds.), *Reform and Relevance in Schooling: Dropouts, De-Streaming, and the Common Curriculum,* Research in Education Series 18 (Toronto: Ontario Institute for Studies in Education Press, 1991), 117–8.
4 In a cabinet shuffle in February 1993 Premier Rae replaced Tony Silipo with David Cooke who became minister of education and training with responsibility for the former ministries of education, colleges and universities, and skills development. The new minister confirmed that destreaming would proceed but a few school boards would be excused from implementation in September 1993. Subsequently,

four school boards were given a one-year delay before being required to destream their grade-nine classes (*Toronto Star*, 4 Sept. 1993).

5 Other policy changes under consideration included elimination of grade 13, offering heritage language programs during the school day rather than after school, full integration of special education students into regular classrooms, an end to streaming of grade-ten students as well as grade-nine students, and establishment of parent advisory councils in every school. See *Globe and Mail*, 4 Sept. 1992; *Toronto Star*, 6 Nov. 1992.

6 *Globe and Mail*, 29 Apr. 1993.

7 *Globe and Mail*, 5 May 1993.

8 Philip Gammage, 'Changing Ideologies and Provision in Western Canadian Primary Education,' paper presented at the annual meeting of the British Association of Canadian Studies, University of Nottingham, Nottingham, England, 1991, 21.

9 The main criticism directed at the primary division concerned the adoption of Sullivan's recommendation for dual entry to kindergarten in September and January. Many local boards resisted introducing this policy, and in January 1992 the NDP government announced that it was terminating this innovation (*Vancouver Sun*, 3 Jan. 1992).

10 *Globe and Mail*, 7 May 1991.

11 In making this announcement the minister also expressed his support for letter grades, extensive testing in schools, and evaluation of the school system by graduating students, employers, and post-secondary institutions (*Globe and Mail*, 7 Sept. 1991).

12 *Globe and Mail*, 3 July 1992, 14 May 1993, 10 Sept. 1993; *Maclean's*, 6 Dec. 1993.

13 Canada, Prosperity Secretariat, *Living Well ... Learning Well* (Ottawa: Minister of Supply and Services Canada, 1991), i.

14 Ibid., 30.

15 CMEC, *Annual Report, 1989–90* (Toronto: CMEC, 1991), 10.

16 CMEC, *Annual Report, 1990–91* (Toronto: CMEC, 1992), 4, 6

17 Thomas d'Aquino, quoted in *Toronto Star*, 21 Sept. 1991.

18 *Toronto Star*, 2 May 1991.

19 *Toronto Star*, 7 Dec. 1991.

20 *Globe and Mail*, 21 May 1992. In April 1993 the first national test of mathematics achievement was administered to 65,000 students aged 13 and 16 in 1,400 schools across the country. The first national test of reading and writing was postponed until 1994 in order to spread rising costs and allow time to prepare more complex assessments. See *Globe and Mail*, 8 Feb. 1993, 26 Apr 1993.

21 See Alberta Education, *Vision for the Nineties ... A Plan of Action* (Edmonton: Alberta Education, 1991), 30–3.

22 Ibid., 31.

23 Other priorities included training and professional development of teachers to improve their ability to assess student learning needs and achievement and adapt their teaching to be more specific to the needs of each student; develop and implement effective solutions to the problem of inequities across school jurisdictions so that all school boards have adequate fiscal resources; making sure parents are well informed about educational standards and results and have opportunities to be more involved in schools and in decisions about the education of their children; and encouraging active partnerships between business and schools to provide opportunities for students to learn about the workplace and opportunities for business to be more actively involved in education.

24 New Brunswick, Commission on Excellence in Education, *Schools for a New Century* (Fredericton: Commission on Excellence in Education, 1992), 61. Elections for the new school boards were held in May 1992, and the new boards assumed office at the beginning of the 1992–3 school year.

25 *Daily Gleaner* (Fredericton), 14 Sept. 1992; *New Brunswick Telegraph Journal* (Saint John), 15 Sept. 1992. Compulsory provincial examinations already exist for French-speaking graduating students. All of these actions were recommended by the Commission on Excellence in Education. In a speech to an IODE meeting in St Stephen, NB, James Downey said that most of the recommendations of the commission had been addressed and he was pleased by the government's announcement.

26 *Globe and Mail*, 20 May 1992. The Wells government's proposal to reform school boards in Newfoundland, issued in November 1993, closely followed the recommendations of the Williams commission. Under this plan the 27 denominational boards would be reorganized into ten interdenominational boards, each having ten elected members plus up to five members appointed by the churches where numbers warrant, and a school council would be established for each school to increase parental influence (*Globe and Mail*, 1 Dec. 1993).

27 The term 'collective intelligence' is taken from Phillip Brown and Hugh Lauder, 'Education, Economy, and Society: An Introduction to a New Agenda,' in Phillip Brown and Hugh Lauder (eds.), *Education for Economic Survival: From Fordism to Post-Fordism?* (London: Routledge, 1992), 27–34.

28 Peter Watkins, 'High Technology, Work, and Education,' in David Dawkins (ed.), *Power and Politics in Education* (London: Falmer Press, 1991), 226.

29 Edward Andrew, 'George Grant on Technological Imperatives,' in Richard B. Day, Ronald Beiner, and Joseph Masciulli (eds.), *Democratic Theory and Technological Society* (London: Sharpe, 1988), 301. Andrew is referring here specifically to the political thought of George Grant; but Grant's position on the benefits of technol-

ogy would be shared by many, if not most, conservatives while his worries about the human costs of technological society would be shared by all conservatives.

30 Allan Bloom, *The Closing of the American Mind* (New York: Simon and Schuster, 1987), 43.

31 Conservatives assume that there is an academic tradition that has been lost and must be recovered as the foundation for education. That tradition comprises, not only the great texts of Western literature, philosophy, and science, but also the national heritage of language, literature, and history of the community in which young people live. The vocation of teachers in elementary and secondary schools is instruction of young people in the content of this academic tradition first and foremost; but in later years, when students have begun to acquire the rudiments of knowledge, teachers should be expected to initiate more open forms of inquiry.

32 See Margaret McNay, 'The Radwanski Report: Elementary Misunderstandings about Elementary School Education,' in Allison and Paquette, *Reform and Relevance in Schooling*, 75–9.

33 Ibid., 78.

34 In addition to the federal government's own initiatives, both the Williams commission and the Landry-Downey commission make recommendations supporting a role for the federal government in developing a national educational strategy. See New Brunswick, *Schools for a New Century*, 56–7, 72; and Newfoundland and Labrador, Royal Commission of Inquiry into the Delivery of Programs and Services in Primary, Elementary, Secondary Education, *Our Children Our Future* (St John's: Queen's Printer, 1992), 417–19. Organized business has been strongly supportive of federal involvement in the design of a national educational policy. An important exception among recent studies, however, was the Economic Council of Canada (see *A Lot to Learn: Education and Training in Canada* [Ottawa: Minister of Supply and Services Canada, 1992], 48).

35 See especially Michael M. Atkinson and William D. Coleman, *The State, Business, and Industrial Change in Canada* (Toronto: University of Toronto Press, 1989), 32–52; and also William D. Coleman, 'Canadian Business and the State,' in Keith G. Banting (ed.), *The State and Economic Interests*, Research Studies for the Royal Commission on Economic Union and Development Prospects for Canada, vol. 32 (Toronto: University of Toronto Press for Minister of Supply and Services Canada, 1985), 245–90. Carolyn Tuohy has found tripartite structures to be more developed in the area of occupational health and safety at the provincial level of government in Canada (see 'Institutions and Interests in the Occupational Health Arena: The Case of Quebec,' in William D. Coleman and Grace Skogstad [eds.], *Policy Communities and Public Policy in Canada: A Structural Approach* [Mississauga, Ont.: Copp Clark Pitman, 1990], 238–65).

CONCLUSION

1 An important exception to this generalization is the Economic Council of Canada which expressed a strong interest in the partite system found in Germany (see *A Lot to Learn: Education and Training in Canada* [Ottawa: Minister of Supply and Services Canada, 1992], 42, 44).

2 André Siegfried, *The Race Question in Canada*, ed. Frank H. Underhill (Toronto: McClelland and Stewart, 1966), 59.

Bibliographical Notes

Compared with industrial, stabilization, regulatory, health, welfare, or foreign policy, elementary and secondary educational policy in Canada has not received much attention from political scientists in their scholarly research and writing. Three exceptions are the overviews by Marsha A. Chandler and William M. Chandler, *Public Policy and Provincial Politics* (Toronto: McGraw-Hill Ryerson, 1979), 216–37; Ronald Manzer, *Public Policies and Political Development in Canada* (Toronto: University of Toronto Press, 1985), chap. 6; and Leslie A. Pal, 'Canada,' in Fredric N. Bolotin (ed.), *International Public Policy Source Book*, vol. 2, *Education and Environment* (Westport, Conn.: Greenwood Press, 1989), 11–29.

Among books on the politics of education Frank MacKinnon, *The Politics of Education: A Study of the Political Administration of the Public Schools* (Toronto: University of Toronto Press, 1960) is a polemic against bureaucratic organization of public education rather than a scholarly study. The collection of essays in *The Politics of the Canadian Public School* (Toronto: James Lewis and Samuel, 1974) edited by George Martell presents a lively critique of Canadian educational institutions and practices from a radical democratic perspective. The Canadian Society for the Study of Education, *1977 Yearbook: The Politics of Canadian Education* 4 (June 1977) edited by J.H.A. Wallin includes several cases of educational policy-making which are still interesting as well as a variety of suggestions for developing the study of educational politics in Canada.

Three political studies of educational policies in Ontario are essential sources. David M. Cameron, *Schools for Ontario: Policy-Making, Administration, and Finance in the 1960s* (Toronto: University of Toronto Press, 1972) provides a careful and perceptive analysis of provincial-local relations in public education. Although somewhat peripheral to my concern with elementary and secondary educational policies, J. Stefan Dupré, David M. Cameron, Graeme H. McKechnie, and Theodore B. Rotenberg, *Federalism and Policy Development: The Case of Adult Occupational Training in Ontario* (Toronto: University of Toronto Press, 1973) describe the end of the federal Technical and Vocational Training Assistance Act and the design and implementation of its successor in what is rightly counted among the classic studies of federal-provincial relations in Canada. Eric W. Ricker's 1982 PhD thesis at the University of Toronto, entitled 'Teachers, Trustees and Policy: The Politics of Education in Ontario, 1945–1975,' examines the cases of setting educational objectives, religious instruction, French-language schools, elementary teacher training, and teachers' salary determination using alternative conceptual frameworks of pluralism, corporatism, and consociationalism to assess interest-group influences on political and bureaucratic authorities.

On Quebec educational politics and policy Henry Milner in *The Long Road to Reform: Restructuring Public Education in Quebec* (Kingston: McGill-Queen's University Press, 1986) has written a superb account of the efforts by the Parti québécois government to reform school boards from a religious to a linguistic basis in the late 1970s and early 1980s. Mark W. Graesser has provided a concise summary of Newfoundland's policy of denominational education, as well as a perceptive analysis of the potential for reform, in 'Church, State, and Public Policy in Newfoundland: The Question of Denominational Education,' a paper presented at the annual meeting of the Canadian Political Science Association, University of Victoria, Victoria, BC, 1990.

Richard G. Townsend, *They Politick for Schools* (Toronto: Ontario Institute for Studies in Education Press, 1988) shares my concern to understand the ideologies of educational politics in Canada; but Townsend's approach is behavioural rather than historical/institutional. Between 1979 and 1983 he interviewed 47 members of provincial legislative assemblies and 133 members of local school boards. Based on these interviews Townsend explores the ideological stances of educational politicians, their styles of political thinking, and their standards of political evaluation. Two other ventures into analysing the ideological structure of educational politics in Canada are Vincent di Norcia, 'Ideological Conflict in Canadian Education,' in Richard G. Townsend and Stephen B. Lawton (eds.), *What's So Canadian about Canadian Educational Administration?* (Toronto: Ontario Institute for Studies in Education Press, 1981), 65–79, and Stephen Schecter, 'Capitalism, Class, and Educational Reform in Canada,' in Leo Panitch (ed.), *The Canadian State: Political Economy and Political Power* (Toronto: University of Toronto Press, 1977), 373–416.

Policy studies rely on good historical research in order to reconstruct the narratives of public policies. The pre-eminent general history of Canadian education continues to be *Canadian Education: A History* (Scarborough, Ont.: Prentice-Hall, 1970) edited by J. Donald Wilson, Robert M. Stamp, and Louis-Philippe Audet. The essays in this book are uniformly excellent including Audet on the history of education in New France and Quebec, Wilson on Upper Canada, and Stamp on the evolution of English-Canadian education from 1870 to 1914 and the role of government in education from 1945 to 1970. The editors are supported by contributions from William B. Hamilton on education in the Atlantic provinces; Manoly R. Lupul on education in the West before 1873, as well as a superb treatment of educational crises from 1867 to 1917; Robert S. Patterson on society and education from 1914 to 1945; Hugh A. Stevenson on educational development in post-war Canada; and Edward W. Sheffield on post-secondary educational development after 1945. Unfortunately, this text is now somewhat dated. More recent collections such as *Canadian Education in the 1980s* (Calgary: Detselig Enterprises, 1981) edited by J. Donald Wilson; E. Brian Titley and Peter J. Miller (eds.), *Education in Canada: An Interpretation* (Calgary: Detselig Enterprises, 1982); and *Canadian Education: Historical Themes and Contemporary Issues* (Calgary: Detselig Enterprises, 1990) edited by E. Brian Titley each make useful contributions; but they have not succeeded in providing a comparably systematic treatment of the changes that occurred in Canadian education during the 1970s and 1980s.

Prior to the publication of *Canadian Education: A History* the leading history of Canadian education was Charles E. Phillips, *The Development of Education in Canada* (Toronto: Gage, 1957). Phillips's work is less well focused on the evolution of public policies towards education and less structured in depicting the historical phases of educational development than Wilson, Stamp, Audet, and their colleagues; but Phillips is still a helpful source on historical details of educational policies and practices. Among earlier surveys of Canadian education I have found helpful are Pierre-Joseph-Olivier Chauveau, *L'Instruction publique au Canada: précis historique et statistique* (Quebec: Imprimerie Augustin Coté, 1876) and Peter Sandiford, 'Education in Canada,' in Peter Sandiford (ed.), *Comparative Education: Studies of the Educational Systems of Six Modern Nations* (London: Dent, 1918), 343–437.

Provincial histories of education are dominated by studies of Ontario and Quebec. Robert M. Stamp, *The Schools of Ontario, 1876–1976* (Toronto: University of Toronto Press, 1982) is distinguished by its strong focus on educational politics and policies. A brief but still useful survey is Robin S. Harris, *Quiet Evolution: A Study of the Educational System of Ontario* (Toronto: University of Toronto Press, 1967). W.G. Fleming's *Ontario's Educative Soci-*

ety is also an essential source on the history of educational policies in Ontario. I have found especially useful vol. 1, *The Expansion of the Educational System*; vol. 2, *The Administrative Structure*; and vol. 3, *Schools, Pupils, and Teachers* all published by University of Toronto Press (1971).

Among the various works of Louis-Philippe Audet on the history of education in Quebec, I have relied mainly on his book with Armand Gauthier, *Le Système scolaire du Québec: organisation et fonctionnement*, 2nd ed. (Montreal: Librairie Beauchemin, 1969) and also *Histoire de l'enseignement au Québec: 1608–1971*, 2 vols. (Montreal: Holt, Rinehart, and Winston, 1971). Two excellent histories in English are Roger Magnuson, *A Brief History of Quebec Education: From New France to Parti Québécois* (Montreal: Harvest House, 1980) and Norman Henchey and Donald Burgess, *Between Past and Future: Quebec Education in Transition* (Calgary: Detselig Enterprises, 1987). Roger Magnuson has also advanced an intriguing analysis of a major shift in the world-view of the Quebec state since the 1960s from localism to centralism in 'Gallicism, Anglo-Saxonism, and Quebec Education,' *Canadian Journal of Education* 9 (1984), 1–13.

Outside Ontario and Quebec there is a fairly recent history by Alexander Gregor and Keith Wilson, *The Development of Education in Manitoba* (Dubuque, Iowa: Kendall/Hunt, 1984), and there are three good collections of essays: *Shaping the Schools of the Canadian West* (Calgary: Detselig Enterprises, 1970) edited by David C. Jones, Nancy M. Sheehan, and Robert M. Stamp; *Schooling and Society in Twentieth Century British Columbia* (Calgary: Detselig Enterprises, 1980) edited by J. Donald Wilson, and David C. Jones; and *Schools in the West: Essays in Canadian Educational History* (Calgary: Detselig Enterprises, 1986) edited by Nancy M. Sheehan, J. Donald Wilson and David C. Jones. Among older histories Frederick W. Rowe, *The Development of Education in Newfoundland* (Toronto: Ryerson Press, 1964); John W. Chalmers, *Schools of the Foothills Province: The Story of Public Education in Alberta* (Toronto: University of Toronto Press, 1967); and F. Henry Johnson, *A History of Public Education in British Columbia* (Vancouver: University of British Columbia Press, 1964) are all useful as sources on specific provincial policies or educational practices, but for a coherent view of the development of educational politics and policies they are disappointing. Perhaps the best of earlier provincial studies is Katherine F.C. MacNaughton, *The Development of the Theory and Practice of Education in New Brunswick, 1784–1900* (Fredericton: University of New Brunswick, 1946), but it is limited by its failure to give any account of New Brunswick education in the twentieth century.

Historical studies of the politics of religious instruction and observance in public schools begin with the classic work of C.B. Sissons, *Church and State in Canada: An Historical Study* (Toronto: Ryerson Press, 1959). A detailed account of the campaign for fully state-provided Roman Catholic schools in Ontario is provided by Franklin A. Walker's three volumes: *Catholic Education and Politics in Upper Canada* (Toronto: J.M. Dent, 1955); *Catholic Education and Politics in Ontario: A Documentary Study* (Toronto: Nelson, 1964); and *Catholic Education and Politics in Ontario*, vol. 3, *From the Hope Commission to the Promise of Completion (1945–1985)* (Toronto: Catholic Education Foundation of Ontario, 1986). The definitive historical study of religion in the public schools of Western Canada is Manoly R. Lupul, *The Roman Catholic Church and the North-West School Question: A Study in Church-State Relations in Western Canada, 1875–1905* (Toronto: University of Toronto Press, 1974). On the Manitoba school crisis see also Paul Crunican, *Priests and Politicians: Manitoba Schools and the Election of 1896* (Toronto: University of Toronto Press, 1974). On Newfoundland, in addition to Mark W. Graesser's paper at the 1990 Canadian Political Science Association meeting, William A. McKim has edited an excellent volume entitled *The Vexed Question: Denominational Education in a Secular Age* (St John's: Breakwater Books, 1988) in which the essays by Ronald G. Penney on the constitutional status of denominational education in Newfoundland, Phillip McCann on the history of denominational education, and Mark W. Graesser on public opinion and the politics of denominational education are especially good for educational policy studies. A helpful general reference on recent policies is Andrew G. Blair, *The Policy and Practice of Religious Education in Publicly-Funded Elementary and Secondary Schools in Canada and Elsewhere: A Search of the Literature* (Toronto: Queen's Printer for Ontario, 1986).

On secondary education a helpful account of the rise of multilateral secondary schools and their status in the mid-1950s is provided by the contributors to *Composite High Schools in Canada*, University of Alberta Monographs in Education 1 (Edmonton: University of Alberta Committee on Educational Research, 1958) edited by John H.M. Andrews and Alan F. Brown. Otherwise the best histories of secondary education are focused on the province of Ontario. They are led by the work of Susan E. Houston and Alison Prentice, *Schooling and Scholars in Nineteenth-Century Ontario* (Toronto: University of Toronto Press, 1988) and R.D. Gidney and W.P.J. Millar, *Inventing Secondary Education: The Rise of the High School in Nineteenth-Century Ontario* (Montreal: McGill-Queen's University Press, 1990). Essential reading on the class structure of nineteenth-century Ontario education includes Alison Prentice, *The School Promoters: Education and Social Class in Mid-Nineteenth Century Upper Canada* (Toronto: McClelland and Stewart, 1977) and the volume of essays edited by Michael B. Katz and Paul H. Mattingly, *Education and Social Change: Themes from Ontario's Past* (New York: New York University Press, 1975). On the Canadian experience with progressive education, and also the impact of multiculturalism on educational ideologies, see Nick Kach, Kas Mazurek, Robert S. Patterson, and Ivan DeFaveri (eds.), *Essays on Canadian Education* (Calgary: Detselig Enterprises, 1986).

Among historical studies of the politics of language in Canadian education, C.B. Sissons, *Bi-lingual Schools in Canada* (Toronto: Dent, 1917) is still useful on specific details of issues and events. An outstanding study which is marked by its juxtaposition of provincial policies and local realities is found in Chad Gadfield, *Language, Schooling, and Cultural Conflict: The Origins of the French Language Controversy in Ontario* (Kingston: McGill-Queen's University Press, 1987). On bilingual schools in the Maritime provinces there is *Bilingualism in the Schools of Eastern Nova Scotia* (Quebec: Les Éditions Ferland, 1962) by Remi J. Chiasson. A good summary of provincial policies on minority-language education prior to the proclamation of the Canadian Charter of Rights and Freedoms can be found in CMEC, *The State of Minority Language Education in the Ten Provinces of Canada* (Toronto: CMEC, 1978). On heritage languages an excellent descriptive analysis, which includes a compelling defence of linguistic choice as the best regime, is that of Jim Cummins and Marcel Danesi, *Heritage Languages: The Development and Denial of Canada's Linguistic Resources* (Toronto: Our Schools / Our Selves Education Foundation and Garamond Press, 1990).

There is no comprehensive study on the governance of public education in Canada. The best provincial studies are found in works cited above by David M. Cameron and Eric W. Ricker on Ontario for the 1950s to 1970s and Henry Milner on Quebec in the 1970s and early 1980s. The historical foundation of educational governance in Ontario has been the object of superb analysis in two books by Bruce Curtis – *Building the Educational State: Canada West, 1836–1871* (London, Ontario: Althouse Press, 1988) and *True Government by Choice Men?: Inspection, Education, and State Formation in Canada West* (Toronto: University of Toronto Press, 1992) – and in three essays by R.D. Gidney, 'Centralization and Education: The Origins of an Ontario Tradition,' *Journal of Canadian Studies* 7 (Nov. 1972), 33–48; R.D. Gidney and D.A. Lawr, 'The Development of an Administrative System for the Public Schools: The First Stage, 1841–1850,' in Neil McDonald and Alf Chaiton (eds.), *Egerton Ryerson and His Times* (Toronto: Macmillan, 1978), 160–83; and R.D. Gidney and D.A. Lawr, 'Bureaucracy vs. Community? The Origins of Bureaucratic Procedure in the Upper Canadian School System,' *Journal of Social History* 13 (Spring 1980), 438–57. Essential reading on Ryerson's philosophy of educational governance is Alison Prentice's essay, 'The Public Instructor: Ryerson and the Role of the Public School Administrator,' also in the volume of essays edited by McDonald and Chaiton (129–59). On the organization of local educational authorities Edward H. Humphreys, Stephen B. Lawton, Richard G. Townsend, Victoria E. Grabb, and Daina M. Watson in the published results of their research project conducted for the Ontario Ministry of Education, *Alternative Approaches to Determining Distribution of School Board Trustee Representation*, vol. 1, *Trustee Representation: Theory and Practice in Canada* (Toronto: Queen's Printer for Ontario, 1986) have assembled a collection of essays which is the best source of basic information, including much useful historical material, on these amazingly complex and varied institutional arrangements. There are a number of general surveys of educational administration, intended as textbooks for graduate courses in faculties of education. Among these I have found Lawrence M. Bezeau, *Educational Administration for Canadian Teachers* (Toronto: Copp Clark Pitman, 1989) to be helpful, and also recommended is T.E. Giles and A.J. Proudfoot, *Educational Administration in Canada*, 4th ed. (Calgary: Detselig Enterprises, 1990).

To understand the structuring of provincial educational policy communities I have emphasized the importance of provincial policies on educational finance and collective bargaining. The leading student of educational finance in Canada is Stephen B. Lawton and his brief survey *The Price of Quality: The Public Finance of Elementary and Secondary Education in Canada* (Toronto: Canadian Education Association, 1987) is an excellent and accessible introduction to this abstruse subject. On the history of collective bargaining in education I have relied on J. Douglas Muir, *Collective Bargaining by Canadian Public School Teachers*, Privy Council Office, Task Force on Labour Relations, Study 21 (Ottawa: Information Canada, 1971). An excellent summary of provincial legislation on collective bargaining in the late 1970s is given by William A. Marcotte in his EdD thesis at the University of Toronto, 'An Examination of Collective Bargaining between Canadian Public School Teachers and Their Employers' (1980), and also helpful is William A. Marcotte, *Teachers' Collective Agreements: A Study of Certain Aspects of Employment Concerning Canadian Public School Teachers* (Toronto: CMEC, 1984).

Official policy studies of public education have been crucial sources of information about the development of Canadian educational policies, as well as key objects of analysis about changing commitments to policy theories and public philosophies. Among official policy studies prior to the Second World War, four stand out as deserving special attention: Egerton Ryerson's 1846 'Report on a System of Public Elementary Instruction for Upper Canada,' in J.

George Hodgins (ed.), *Documentary History of Education in Upper Canada (Ontario)*, vol. 6 (Toronto: DOE, 1899); Ontario, DOE, *Education for Industrial Purposes: A Report by John Seath* (Toronto: King's Printer, 1911); Canada, Royal Commission on Industrial Training and Technical Education, *Report* (Ottawa: King's Printer, 1913); and J.H. Putman and G.M. Weir, *Survey of the School System* (Victoria: King's Printer, 1925). On official thinking during the war see the *Report of the Survey Committee to Ascertain the Chief Educational Needs in the Dominion of Canada* (Toronto: Canada and Newfoundland Education Association, 1943), which was done at the suggestion of Cyril James, chair of the federal government's Advisory Committee on Reconstruction.

From the 1940s to the early 1960s there were four provincial royal commissions on education which are important sources for assessing the state of official thinking about educational governance and policy design in the immediate post-war period. By far the largest report in size, if not in policy impact, was the royal commission chaired by Mr Justice John Andrew Hope, *Report of the Royal Commission on Education in Ontario, 1950* (Toronto: King's Printer, 1950). Three reports of provincial royal commissions at the end of the 1950s provide useful information for assessing the tenuous balance of economic and ethical liberalism in official thinking about public education at that time: Alberta, *Report of the Royal Commission on Education in Alberta* (Edmonton: Queen's Printer, 1959); Manitoba, *Report of the Royal Commission on Education* (Winnipeg: Queen's Printer, 1959); and British Columbia, *Report of the Royal Commission on Education* (Victoria: Queen's Printer, 1960). Among various commissions on educational finance during this period perhaps the most interesting, because of the way it sets out the case for a foundation program and district reorganization, is the report by Milton Ezra LaZerte for Prince Edward Island, *Report of the Commissioner on Educational Finance and Related Problems in Administration* (Charlottetown: DOE, 1960).

Undoubtedly the single most important royal commission on education in Canadian history was the Royal Commission of Inquiry into Education in the Province of Quebec chaired by the Right Reverend Alphonse Marie Parent. The five volumes of the Parent commission beginning with volume 1, *The Structure of the Educational System at the Provincial Level* (Quebec: Government Printer, 1963) and concluding with volumes 4 and 5 on *Educational Administration* (1966) articulated a coherent philosophy of education, carried out an impressively comprehensive policy analysis, and had an unprecedented impact on educational policy in Quebec.

In Newfoundland a comparable task of developing an agenda for educational reform was given to a royal commission chaired by Phillip Warren, and the *Report of the Royal Commission on Education and Youth*, volume 1 (St John's, Queen's Printer, 1967) and volume 2 (1968) are important sources of information about the development of education in Newfoundland and orientations to policy development in the late 1960s and early 1970s.

Compared with the Parent commission or the Warren commission, the Provincial Committee on Aims and Objectives in the Schools of Ontario had a much more narrow mandate, but its report *Living and Learning* (Toronto: Newton Publishing, 1968) is still seen as the archetype of progressive thinking about educational policy and practice.

The report of the Alberta Commission on Educational Planning, *A Choice of Futures / A Future of Choices* (Edmonton: Queen's Printer for the Province of Alberta, 1972) is also interesting, first, because of its explicit commitment to Abraham Maslow's radical humanist psychology of basic human needs and, second, because of its attempt to join an ethical liberal concept of participatory democracy with an economic liberal concept of educational planning as systems analysis.

At the federal level of government the Royal Commission on Bilingualism and Biculturalism had a strong and sustained impact on language policies in Canada. In particular the commission's first book, *The Official Languages* (Ottawa: Queen's Printer, 1967), and second book, *Education* (1968), of its final *Report of the Royal Commission on Bilingualism and Biculturalism* articulated an approach to the official languages in public education that came to dominate trends towards minority-language rights in education and sustained the official languages in education programs of the federal government.

An interesting and influential external assessment of Canadian education was made by Michel Crozier, Kjell Eide, Hildegarde Hamm-Brucher, Harold Noah, and Pierre Vanbergen as examiners for the Organization for Economic Cooperation and Development, *Reviews of National Policies for Education: Canada* (Paris: OECD, 1976). The six reports prepared under the aegis of the Council of Ministers of Education, Canada, as background for the OECD commission are an important source of information on policy development in the mid-1970s and include *Review of Educational Policies in Canada: Foreword and Introduction* (Toronto: CMEC, 1975) and separate volumes on the Atlantic provinces, Quebec, Ontario, the West, and the federal government. Provincial reviews during this period that merit attention are John Graham's *Report of the Royal Commission on Education, Public Services, and Provincial-Municipal Relations*, vol. 3: *Education* (Halifax: Queen's Printer, 1974) and the Parti Québécois government's policy statements on education in the late 1970s and early 1980s, issued by the Quebec Ministry of Education, *Primary and Secondary Education in Québec: Green Paper* (1978), *The Schools of Québec: Policy Statement and Plan of Action* (1979), and *The Québec School: A Responsible Force in the Community* (1982).

In the burgeon of contemporary official policy studies, six stand out because of the clarity with which they recommend their ideological perspectives, policy theories, curricular designs, and institutional reforms: George Radwanski, *Ontario Study of the Relevance of Education, and the Issue of Dropouts* (Toronto: Ontario Ministry of Education, 1987); British Columbia, Royal Commission on Education, *A Legacy for Learners: The Report of the Royal Commission on Education 1988* (Victoria: Queen's Printer for British Columbia, 1988); Ontario, Premier's Council, *People and Skills in the New Global Economy* (Toronto: Queen's Printer for Ontario, 1990); Canada, Economic Council of Canada, *A Lot to Learn: Education and Training in Canada* (Ottawa: Minister of Supply and Services Canada, 1992); Newfoundland and Labrador, Royal Commission of Inquiry into the Delivery of Programs and Services in Primary, Elementary, Secondary Education, *Our Children Our Future* (St John's: Queen's Printer, 1992); and New Brunswick, Commission on Excellence in Education, *Schools for a New Century* (Fredericton: Commission on Excellence in Education, 1992). In due course the report of the Ontario Royal Commission on Learning, chaired by Monique Begin and Gerald Caplan, no doubt will be added to this list.

Two volumes of essays on recent educational reform should be noted. The essays in Terry Wotherspon (ed.), *Hitting the Books: The Politics of Educational Retrenchment* (Toronto: Garamond Press, 1991) provide a stimulating radical democratic critique of contemporary policy developments in Alberta. More mixed in ideological outlook but consistently insightful throughout is the volume of essays on the Radwanski report in Ontario edited by Derek J. Allison and Jerry Paquette, *Reform and Relevance in Schooling: Dropouts, De-Streaming and the Common Curriculum*, Research in Education Series 18 (Toronto: Ontario Institute for Studies in Education Press, 1991).

Notes on Statistical Sources

GROSS DOMESTIC PRODUCT

See Statistics Canada, *National Income and Expenditure Accounts, Annual Estimates, 1926–1986* (catalogue 13–531), Table 1, and *National Income and Expenditure Accounts* (catalogue 13-001). GDP statistics for two calender years have been averaged to make comparisons with expenditure data referring to fiscal or school years. For 1913–14 the estimates of GNP are those of O.J. Firestone as given by Robert E. Ankli, 'A Note on Canadian GNP Estimates 1900–1925,' *Canadian Historical Review* 62 (March 1981), 61.

LABOUR FORCE

Statistics on the total labour force are taken from F.H. Leacy (ed.), *Historical Statistics of Canada*, 2nd ed. (Ottawa: Minister of Supply and Services Canada, 1983), series D127 for 1921 to 1938 and D137 for 1950 to 1971. After 1971 the source is Statistics Canada, *Historical Labour Force Statistics* (catalogue 71-201). Estimates of the labour force for 1913 (2,791,000) and 1914 (2,838,000) are derived by interpolation from the census labour force aged 14 and over reported for 1911 and 1921. Labour force statistics for two calender years have been averaged to make comparisons with data on public sector employment that refer to fiscal or school years.

GOVERNMENT EXPENDITURES

For fiscal years 1913–14, 1926–7 and 1937–8, see Canada, *Report of the Royal Commission on Dominion-Provincial Relations, Book III: Documentation* (Ottawa: King's Printer, 1940), Tables 9 and 19. The functional distribution in Table 7.2 assumes that capital expenditures (which are not broken down by function in the commission's report) are distributed in the same proportions as current expenditures (minus debt charges). For fiscal years 1937–8 to 1965–6 see Leacy (ed.), *Historical Statistics of Canada*, 2nd ed., series H148-60 and H197–220. Because municipal expenditures are not available for 1950–1 by province, in Table 7.3 the total for 1950–1 ($682 million) has been distributed by province based on statistics for fiscal year 1951–2. For fiscal years from 1965–6 to 1990–1 the source is Statistics Canada, *Public Finance Historical Data 1965/66 – 1991/92: Financial Management System* (catalogue 68-512), but defence expenditures are taken from Statistics Canada, *Consolidated Government Finance* (catalogue 68-202) for fiscal years 1965–6 to 1980–1 and the public accounts for fiscal years 1985–6 and 1990–1.

PUBLIC SECTOR EMPLOYMENT

The sources for federal and provincial governmental employment from 1960 are Statistics Canada, *Federal Government Employment* (catalogue 72-004), *Provincial Government Employment* (catalogue 72-007) and *Public Sector Employment and Remuneration 1990/91* (catalogue 72-209). Missing provincial data for British Columbia (1960 to 1975) and Quebec (1960) have been estimated from statistics on taxable and non-taxable income tax returns. Since provincial distributions of non-taxable returns are not available, in making these estimates I have assumed non-taxable returns are distributed among the provinces in the same way as taxable returns. Taxation statistics also have been used to estimate municipal governmental employment for all years and federal and provincial governmental employment in 1946, 1950, and 1955. For taxation statistics from 1946 to 1975 see David K. Foot, *Public Employment in Canada: Statistical Series* (Toronto: Butterworth, 1979); after 1975, Department of National Revenue, *Taxation Statistics* (annual). The source of statistics on employment in federal and public hospitals from 1946 is Statistics Canada, *Hospital Annual Statistics* (catalogue 83-232). Estimates of civilian governmental employment in 1913–14, 1926–7 and 1937–8 were derived by interpolation from census returns for 1911, 1921, 1931, and 1941 (see Richard M. Bird, 'The Growth of the Public Service in Canada,' in David K. Foot [ed.], *Public Employment and Compensation in Canada: Myths and Realities* [Toronto: Butterworth, 1978], 41) and combined with statistics for teachers and armed forces.

GOVERNMENT EXPENDITURES ON EDUCATION

Total government expenditures on elementary and secondary education

(Table 7.1) include provincial government expenditures on public schools, provincial schools for blind and deaf children, Department of National Defence expenditures for public schools in Canada, and federal expenditures on Indian and Inuit schools. Breakdowns of government expenditures on education by province (Table 7.3) exclude expenditures on federal Indian and Inuit schools; and comparisons of provincial expenditures per pupil (Tables 7.8 and 7.9) are based on expenditures for public schools only. The sources from 1950–1 are Statistics Canada, *Historical Compendium of Education Statistics from Confederation to 1975* (Ottawa: Minister of Industry, Trade, and Commerce, 1978), Table 20, and Statistics Canada, *Financial Statistics of Education* (catalogue 81-208). Statistics for 1900–1 to 1945–6 are variously compiled from provincial DOE annual reports; provincial public accounts; expenditures of boards of publicly controlled elementary and secondary schools as given in M.C. Urquhart and K.A.H. Buckley (eds.), *Historical Statistics of Canada*, 1st ed. (Toronto: Macmillan, 1965), series V171–83 and Leacy (ed.), *Historical Statistics of Canada*, 2nd ed., series W275–300; Dominion Bureau of Statistics, *Historical Statistical Survey of Education in Canada* (Ottawa: King's Printer, 1921); Dominion Bureau of Statistics, *Annual Survey of Education in Canada, 1935* (Ottawa: King's Printer, 1937), Table 3; and Dominion Bureau of Statistics, *Annual Survey of Education in Canada, 1936* (Ottawa: King's Printer, 1938), Table 3. Revenues of public school boards are taken from Urquhart and Buckley (eds.), *Historical Statistics of Canada*, 1st ed., series V158–70; and Statistics Canada, *Financial Statistics of Education* (catalogue 81-208).

PUBLIC SCHOOL TEACHERS

Statistics for full-time teachers in public, provincial, and federal elementary and secondary schools for Canada and the provinces for 1890–1 to 1970–1 are taken from Statistics Canada, *Historical Compendium of Education Statistics from Confederation to 1975*, Tables 13 and 14. From 1975–6 the source is Statistics Canada, *Education in Canada: A Statistical Review* (catalogue 81-229). Teachers in provincial schools for blind and deaf children and teachers in federal schools for Indian and Inuit children are not included in comparisons of provincial pupil/teacher ratios.

ENROLMENTS IN PUBLIC ELEMENTARY AND SECONDARY SCHOOLS

Total enrolments in public elementary and secondary schools by province to 1975–6 are taken from Statistics Canada, *Historical Compendium of Educa-*

tion Statistics from Confederation to 1975. The sources since 1975–6 are Statistics Canada, *Elementary-Secondary School Enrolment* (catalogue 81-210), *Advance Statistics of Education 1990–91* (catalogue 81-220), and *Education in Canada: A Statistical Review for 1991–92* (catalogue 81-229). Enrolments in provincial schools for blind and deaf children, federal schools for Indian and Inuit children, and overseas schools of the Department of National Defence are not included. Enrolments in second-language, minority-language, and French-immersion programs are taken from Statistics Canada, *Minority and Second Language Education, Elementary and Secondary Levels* (catalogue 81-257). Enrolments and schools for calculating average size of schools for 1925–6 are taken from Dominion Bureau of Statistics, *Annual Survey of Education in Canada 1925* (Ottawa: King's Printer, 1926), Tables 1, 2.

CONSUMER PRICE INDEX

An index of consumer prices has been used to estimate real expenditures per pupil in Table 7.9. See Urquhart and Buckley (eds.), *Historical Statistics of Canada,* 1st ed., series J128; Leacy (ed.) *Historical Statistics of Canada,* 2nd ed., series K8; and Statistics Canada, *Consumer Prices and Price Indexes* (catalogue 62-010).

Index